LEGAL EVIDENCE AND PROOF

Legal Evidence and Proof

Statistics, Stories, Logic

Edited by

HENDRIK KAPTEIN
Leiden University

HENRY PRAKKEN
University of Groningen and Utrecht University

BART VERHEIJ
University of Groningen

Routledge
Taylor & Francis Group
LONDON AND NEW YORK

First published 2009 by Ashgate Publishing Limited

Published 2018 by Routledge
2 Park Square, Milton Park, Abingdon, Oxon, OX14 4RN
52 Vanderbilt Avenue, New York, NY 10017

First issued in paperback 2018

Routledge is an imprint of the Taylor & Francis Group, an informa business

British Library Cataloguing in Publication Data
Legal evidence and proof : statistics, stories, logic. -
(Applied legal philosophy)
1. Evidence (Law)
I. Kaptein, Hendrik II. Prakken, Henry III. Verheij, Bart
347'.06

Library of Congress Cataloging-in-Publication Data
Kaptein, Hendrik.
Legal evidence and proof : statistics, stories, logic / by Hendrik Kaptein, Henry Prakken, and Bart Verheij.
p. cm. -- (Applied legal philosophy)
Includes index.
ISBN 978-0-7546-7620-1
1. Evidence (Law) 2. Evidence, Criminal. I. Prakken, Henry. II. Verheij, Bart. III. Title.

K2261.K37 2008
347'.06--dc22

2008033518

ISBN 13: 978-1-138-25196-0 (pbk)
ISBN 13: 978-0-7546-7620-1 (hbk)

Contents

Series Editor's Preface

The objective of the Applied Legal Philosophy series is to publish work which adopts a theoretical approach to the study of particular areas or aspects of law or deals with general theories of law in a way which focused on issues of practical moral and political concern in specific legal contexts.

In recent years there has been an encouraging tendency for legal philosophers to utilize detailed knowledge of the substance and practicalities of law and a noteworthy development in the theoretical sophistication of much legal research. The series seeks to encourage these trends and to make available studies in law which are both genuinely philosophical in approach and at the same time based on appropriate legal knowledge and directed towards issues in the criticism and reform of actual laws and legal systems.

The series will include studies of all the main areas of law, presented in a manner which relates to the concerns of specialist legal academics and practitioners. Each book makes an original contribution to an area of legal study while being comprehensible to those engaged in a wide variety of disciplines. Their legal content is principally Anglo-American, but a wide-ranging comparative approach is encouraged and authors are drawn from a variety of jurisdictions.

Tom Campbell
Centre for Applied Philosophy and Public Ethics
Charles Sturt University, Canberra

List of Figures

List of Tables

Preface

Studies in the theory of legal reasoning increasingly turn to issues of evidence and proof. This may be welcomed, if only because adjudication and legal conflict resolution in general are related to contested facts rather than contested law. Indeed, this development may further the cause of the facts, against legal scholars' and lawyers' tendency to identify legal scholarship with knowledge of the law.

This collection of contributions originated in a research project on conflict resolution organized by the University of Amsterdam. Next, an important impetus for this book came from a workshop on Reasoning about Legal Evidence in Cracow organized by Floris Bex, Henry Prakken and Bart Verheij (as part of the IVR Conference, August 2007). Most contributors to this book were present. Lively debate led to a good part of the results presented here.

It is to be hoped that these chapters contribute to further improvement of theories or even the theory of legal evidence and proof, and thus to humanly important qualities of legal practice.

The Editors[1]

1 The editors would like to thank Khadija Kadrouch for indexing this book.

Preface

General Introduction

Legal Evidence and Proof: Past, Present, Future

Legal evidence has to do with facts (though even this basic stance has been questioned, in the already extensive literature on the subject). In fact, the law has to do with facts in so many more ways. Law itself consists of institutional facts. Facts determine the content of law: think of Hart's minimum content of natural law, based on elementary facts of human and social life. Law sets factual limits to human conduct, through threats of punishment and so much more, just as it creates possibilities for important kinds of conduct and its factual consequences, such as legislating and contracting. Lawful (and unlawful) conduct changes the facts of the world. So many more relationships of law and fact remain to be investigated.

Most important, of course, are facts determining the application of legal rules to parts of the living (and sometimes dead) world, or: the problem of legal evidence and proof. Establishment of such facts, needed in order to realize the law (and hopefully justice and right) may go without much further saying, in any case if all parties and others concerned reasonably agree on them. But more than a few legal and other conflicts on the application of rules are fought over disputed facts, rather than disputed law, in courts of law and in the real world. So methods and standards have to be devised to settle conflicts over facts in some or other authoritative or even rational manner. A rather ancient but still probably well-known example of this is to be found in the Code of Hammurabi:

> If a man charge a man with sorcery, but cannot convict him, he who is charged with sorcery shall go to the sacred river, and he shall throw himself in the sacred river; if the river overcome him, his prosecutor shall take to himself his house. If the river show the man to be innocent and he come forth unharmed, he that charged him with sorcery shall be put to death. He who threw himself into the river shall take to himself the house of his accuser.

A rather unconventional way to establish strange facts, one might say with the benefit of hindsight, though a later and probably still better-known issue of evidence and proof offers a comparable semblance of the complete disparity of methods of discovery and facts to be established. Here is the story of fact-finding by King Solomon, once again (1 Kings 3, verse 16, New King James translation):

> Now two women who were harlots came to the king, and stood before him. And one woman said, 'O my lord, this woman and I dwell in the same house; and I

> gave birth while she was in the house. Then it happened, the third day after I had given birth, that this woman also gave birth. And we were together; no one was with us in the house, except the two of us in the house. And this woman's son died in the night, because she lay on him. So she arose in the middle of the night and took my son from my side, while your maidservant slept, and laid him in her bosom, and laid her dead child in my bosom. And when I rose in the morning to nurse my son, there he was, dead. But when I had examined him in the morning, indeed, he was not my son whom I had borne.'
>
> Then the other woman said, 'No! But the living one is my son, and the dead one is your son.' And the first woman said, 'No! But the dead one is your son, and the living one is my son.' Thus they spoke before the king. And the king said, 'The one says, "This is my son, who lives, and your son is the dead one"; and the other says, "No! But your son is the dead one, and my son is the living one."' Then the king said, 'Bring me a sword.' So they brought a sword before the king. And the king said, 'Divide the living child in two, and give half to one, and half to the other.'
>
> Then the woman whose son was living spoke to the king, for she yearned with compassion for her son; and she said, 'O my lord, give her the living child, and by no means kill him!' But the other said, 'Let him be neither mine nor yours, but divide him.' So the king answered and said, 'Give the first woman the living child, and by no means kill him; she is his mother.' And all Israel heard of the judgment which the king had rendered; and they feared the king, for they saw that the wisdom of God was in him to administer justice.

However, some progress seems to have been made. Reconstruction of King Solomon's argumentation, or better still, justification in terms of implicit premises brings to light a reasonably strong connection between testimonies cunningly elicited and the fact to be proven. Arguments referring to riverside experiments in order to determine sorcery seem all too enthymemetic to pass muster in terms of more modern standards of evidence and proof. King Solomon applied a method of investigation brilliantly devised to solve a seemingly intractable problem. That is, intractable in those days: today, a simple (or sometimes not so simple) DNA test would do the job just as well, according to the same high standards, albeit at the cost of rather reduced drama.

Progress in forensic sciences and technologies has been formidable indeed. But human wisdom did not always keep up with it, as is probably conclusively proven by recent and not so recent scandals involving sentencing or even killing the innocent in the name of criminal law. This (and more evidential mishaps in application of the law) still happens in the most civilized of jurisdictions. Why?

One major reason may be the deep-seated tendency of the judiciary to regard the handling of matters of evidence and proof as presupposing no special knowledge and skills, and acting on it. Of course things go wrong at times, it will be added, but then there is no perfect human practice anyway. Strange as this may sound, at least to evidence scholars, it is a deep-seated conviction, repeatedly expressed by prominent court members who are probably not conversant with a rather extensive literature in the field of evidence and proof. Thus a prominent district court vice-president in The Netherlands, W.M. Van den Bergh, expressed his conviction on 'the simplicity of basic facts' as follows (as recently as 2008):

> In order to decide whether the criminal defendant did commit the crime no special professional judges' expertise is needed. No special knowledge or skills are needed in order to become convinced of a criminal defendant's guilt, or to have doubts about it.

Probably not much special knowledge nor many skills are needed to comprehend that this kind of conviction behind convictions may be rather dangerous for the innocent. This is amply demonstrated by so many death row inmates in the United States owing their lives and liberty to non-legal people applying special knowledge, skills and zeal to their wrongly decided cases. Just as more than a few victims of misadministration of criminal justice in Great Britain, The Netherlands and elsewhere were freed as a consequence of 'laypeople's' unrelenting zeal on behalf of their cases. (Derksen's scathing and, in the end, effective public criticism of courts' misuse of basic statistics in a nurse's conviction for infant killing is a case in point: see also his contribution to this book.)

In line with this is legal people's tendency to incorporate issues of fact into the law. Indeed one important feature of legal evidence and proof is the regulation of legal fact-finding. Rules of procedure govern police authorities in search and seizure, admissibility of evidence and of witnesses, distribution of burdens of proof, legal standards of proof, determination of proof by authoritative bodies and so much more of course. This may indeed lead to legalizing or better still, legally formalizing issues of evidence and proof. Or: as long as the rules are faithfully adhered to, the outcome of legal processing of evidence is taken to be equivalent to legally relevant certainty as to the facts of the case. A notorious expression of this legal attitude towards facts (or 'facts') is United States Supreme Court member Scalia's well-known dictum in *Herrera* v. *Collins* (506 US 390, 1993):

> Mere factual innocence is no reason not to carry out a death sentence properly reached.

Thus doubts about the redundancy of special expertise and skill in the determination of legal evidence and proof (is it really true that malice, negligence or innocence are plain to see?!) seem to be done away with by reference to the authority of legal procedure. (Scalia even seems to be in postmodern company, doubting the very concept of a fact independent from 'authoritative establishment'.)

Still this is not a generally accepted standpoint, outside or even inside judiciaries. To limit the discussion to criminal procedure: it may be true that the great majority of criminal cases relate to certainty (according to whatever standards) of offender identification. Even then, issues of malice and negligence may not always be simple. Next, more than a few hard cases remain. There may be circumstantial evidence only, witnesses may appear not to be completely trustworthy, expert witnesses may contradict each other, and so on. It does not seem plausible or even viable to do away with such kinds of uncertainties by simply referring to standards of legal procedure, let alone by appealing to commonly available knowledge and skills as sufficient to solve such riddles.

Thus questions about rational standards of evidence and proof crop up, as distinct from rules of procedure determining issues such as the division of burdens of proof and admissibility of evidence. Obviously, availability of direct evidence in the sense of exhaustive demonstration of the facts of the case before adjudicators' eyes and ears is rather exceptional. It would be hard even to think of a convincing example of this. In a grimly captivating story of a lawyer, herself caught in the machinery or machinations of criminal justice, Janet Malcolm comments on this with the following fundamental remark (1999, 19):

> Historical reconstruction in all cases gives rise to structures that are more like ruins than proper buildings: there is never enough solid building material and always too much dust.

How to clear this dust away, to a sufficient extent? What counts as dust, what is a sufficient extent? (Scalia probably would not mind.) Probability considerations plaguing so many criminal and other issues of fact set in here already. Next, there is the different and more practical distinction between direct and circumstantial evidence. Such evidence may be available to adjudicators with or without the intervention of witnesses.

In any case, the absence of 'the facts of the case themselves' (if this is a sensible concept at all) raises questions on standards of evidence and rules (in a wide sense) governing relationships between 'available evidence' and 'the facts of the case'. This is related to the long-standing and recently revived discussion of the 'logic' of evidence and proof, dominated for so long by the towering figures of Bentham and Wigmore. To further introduce this discussion it seems apposite to quote Bentham at some length (1827, Book I, Part 1):

> By the term evidence, considered according to the most extended application that is ever given to it, may be, and seems in general to be, understood, any matter of fact, the effect, tendency, or design of which, when presented to the mind, is to produce a persuasion concerning the existence of some other matter of fact—a persuasion either affirmative or disaffirmative of its existence.
>
> Of the two facts thus connected with each other, the latter may, for the purpose of expressing the place it bears in its relation to the other, be distinguished by the appellation of the *principal* fact, or matter of fact: the other, by that of the *evidentiary* fact, or matter of fact.

> Taking the word in this sense, questions of evidence are continually presenting themselves to every human being, every day, and almost every waking hour, of his life.
>
> ...
>
> The impression, or something like an impression, I see in the grass—the marks of twisting, bending, breakage. I think I see in the leaves and branches of the shrubs—the smell that seems to present itself to my nostrils—do they afford sufficient evidence that the deer, that the enemy, I am in chase of, have passed this way? Not polished only, but even the most savage men—not human kind only, but even the brute creation, have their *rules*—I will not say, as Montesquieu would have said, their *laws*—of Evidence.

Just as so many issues of evidence and proof remain the same in human life, at least some issues of legal evidence and proof have, of course, changed since the days of Bentham. Still, miscarriages of justice continue to the present day. We may have come a long way since Hammurabi, but King Solomon seems less easily surpassed. One driving force, apart from intellectual zeal, behind the recent revival of research into evidence and proof is the hope that (still) more rational rules or even principles of fact-finding, evidence and proof may be discovered and/or devised. Two more introductory cautionary remarks are in order then.

First, and even if the issue is limited to facts relevant for application of the law, many different kinds of evidence may be relevant. This ranges from specific facts determining 'who did what, and why' or specific forensic facts like collar bone x-rays determining the legally relevant age of refugees, or specific facts determining damage to be established by comparing two complete future courses of events (with and without tort), to general facts like: what are customs in specific parts of society determining 'what may be reasonably expected in commercial dealings'. Studies in the logic of evidence and proof tend to concentrate on offender identification, probably the most important issue in this field indeed.

Second, this book does not aim to represent more than a small part of the current state of the art in studies of legal evidence and proof. Thus issues of witness reliability, and issues of psychology in general, however important, are generally left out of account. The focus is on reasoning, logic, in a very broad sense. This may be further detailed as follows.

Three Current Approaches to the Study of Logic and Argumentation in Legal Evidence and Proof

Studies of argumentation and logic in factual legal inference have broadly speaking been of three kinds: statistical, story-based, and argument-based. First, statistical approaches acknowledge that evidence cannot provide watertight support for a factual claim but almost always leaves some uncertainty. They then apply the 'standard' theories for reasoning under uncertainty: statistics and probability theory. Much work in the statistical approach is not focused on general statistical models of legal fact-finding but instead criticizes particular uses of statistics in court cases (e.g. Dawid 2005). Those who do focus on general models sometimes advocate a Bayesian approach, according to which domain experts provide conditional probabilities on hypotheses given the available evidence, while the fact-finder estimates the prior probabilities on the hypotheses. The mathematics of Bayesian probability theory then allows the computation of the posterior probability of the hypotheses, given the evidence. If, for a certain hypothesis, this probability exceeds the proof standard, the hypothesis can be accepted. Probabilistic theories of evidential reasoning have been thoroughly studied by David Schum (e.g. 1994).

Statistical methods can be very useful for investigating the relevance of evidence, for instance, by performing so-called sensitivity analysis, i.e., testing how a change in the likelihood of a statement affects that of other statements (see, e.g., Kadane and Schum 1996). However, the statistical approach is by no means uncontroversial (a useful critical overview of the debate is Lempert 1986). One objection is that in legal cases the required numbers are usually not available, either because there are no reliable statistics, or because experts are unable or reluctant to provide reliable estimates of probabilities. Another objection is that statistics and probability theory impose a standard of rationality that cannot be attained in practice, so that their application would lead to more instead of fewer errors. To overcome these and other limitations of statistical models, other models have been proposed.

Second, the story-based approach was initially proposed by the psychologists Bennett and Feldman (1981). Their main claim was not normative but empirical, being that the way lawyers make factual judgements is not by statistical reasoning but by constructing and comparing stories about what might have happened. Wagenaar et al. (1993) go a step further, arguing that this is in fact the only way for fact-finders to reason about the facts of the case, given the cognitive limitations of humans. Their research then takes a normative twist, studying how story-based factual judgement may be more rational. An important point here is that specific stories must be 'anchored' in factual generalizations which may, however, be less than certain, so that their applicability to a case must be critically examined. The story-based approach has also been embraced by some artificial intelligence (AI) researchers, based on the idea that story-based reasoning is not unlike abductive reasoning and inference to the best explanation, for which elaborate AI models exist (Josephson 2001; Poole 2001; Keppens et al. 2005; Thagard 2005).

A third approach takes not stories, but arguments, as the main concept. Bentham looms large here as well. In contemporary theory, however, Wigmore's charting method of legal evidence is prominent. With this method alternative arguments from evidence to hypotheses can be graphically displayed and sources of doubt in these arguments can be revealed (e.g. Wigmore 1931). Generalizations are important here as well, since they are the 'glue' that connects the evidence with the hypotheses, and since their general plausibility and possible exceptions are important sources of doubt. Wigmore's charting method has been extended and refined by the 'New Evidence Scholars' (e.g. Anderson et al. 2005). One study of legal evidential reasoning from the perspective of dialogical argumentation theory is Walton's (2002). In AI and Law the argument-based approach has been founded on so-called non-monotonic, or defeasible logics, which were developed in AI to formalize reasoning with uncertain and incomplete information in cases where uncertainty cannot be quantified. In AI and Law one type of non-monotonic logic is particularly popular: argument-based logic, modelling defeasible reasoning as the construction and comparison of arguments and counter-arguments (e.g. Verheij 2000; Bex et al. 2003; Prakken 2004).

Finally, some have studied combinations of approaches. For example, Keppens (e.g. Keppens et al. 2005) has studied combinations of probability theory and abduction in the context of investigation. Kadane and Schum (1996) and Schum (2001) have reinterpreted Wigmore charts as so-called Bayesian networks. Such networks, developed in AI, combine probability distributions with graphical models of probabilistic dependencies (which may be based on commonsense generalizations).

Although the three approaches are different in important respects, they also share an important feature. In all three approaches, defeasibility is prominent. For example, in probabilistic models new evidence may reduce the posterior probability of hypotheses, in story-based approaches new evidence may reduce the credibility of a story, and in argument-based logics new evidence may give rise to arguments that defeat a previously undefeated argument. In all these cases the deeper reason for this phenomenon is that evidence almost always leaves room for doubt: sources of evidence (such as witnesses) are fallible, and general world knowledge is uncertain and leaves room for exceptions.

Defeasibility of legal evidential reasoning is related to both investigative and procedural aspects of legal evidence and proof. Legal reasoning about the facts takes place in a variety of contexts, which may be broadly divided into contexts of investigation and contexts of judgment. This distinction is, of course, related to the well-known epistemological and methodological distinction between contexts of discovery and contexts of justification. It was long held that these contexts are completely separated: how a scientist came to a certain theory was regarded as irrelevant for the truth of the theory. Legal logicians have long had a similar attitude to the justification of legal judgments: the process by which a certain judgment was reached was regarded as irrelevant for the quality of the judgment. However, developments in philosophy and AI have softened the sharp distinction between the two contexts. For these reasons, this book takes a broad perspective, studying both the investigative and the judgment phase.

Relationships between phases of investigation and judgment raise interesting issues, such as whether both phases are governed by the same or by different models of inference. For instance, looking for hypotheses about the facts of a case, as in the investigative phase, may require abductive models of reasoning with a relatively low proof standard, while deciding whether a hypothesis can be accepted as true involves critical adjudication with a high standard of proof. Another issue is to what extent the soundness of an inference in the judgment phase depends on the quality of the preceding investigation.

A further theme relevant for reasoning about the facts of a case is the relation between rationality requirements and legal constraints. At first sight, since this book's focus is on rational models of factual legal reasoning, it would seem that specific features of legal systems may be ignored. However, it will turn out that one stumbles quite quickly on the tension between a rational ideal and legal reality. The simplest example of this tension is the necessity to decide about a case even though perfect knowledge about what has happened is unattainable. Human imperfection in deciding cases necessarily implies that some offenders go free, while some innocent people are punished. Also, evidence on which a case is decided is not simply given but established by rules of procedure and admissibility of evidence. Moreover, the inferences that can be drawn from the admissible evidence are not only determined by rules of rational inference but also by legal procedural rules on, for instance, burdens of proof and presumption.

In conclusion, studies of legal evidence and logic should not just focus on models of inference but should embed such models in accounts of investigation and different kinds of procedure.

An Overview of the Book

This book aims to cover these different issues as follows. Chapter 1 offers brief discussion of why legal evidence and proof seems desirable at all, or even imperative. Chapters 2 and 3 represent statistical approaches in a broad sense. Story-based discussion is to be found in Chapters 4 to 6; Chapters 7 and 8 compare story-based with argument-based accounts. The remaining three chapters are firmly on argumentative grounds. Summaries of the chapters may clarify this:

1. *Hendrik Kaptein* (Leiden University) discusses the basic question why legal evidence and proof are needed at all. Reasons against singling out offenders are expounded. Also, practical obstacles to the reliable establishment of evidence and proof pass muster. This leads to questions concerning the very concept of proof, presumably linking present evidence with past (or future) events. Brief discussion of (Benthamite) ideals seems to lead inexorably to the conclusion that proof of past events is impossible in principle. Lawyers' standard answer to such theoretical scepticism refers to proceduralism: there need be no such thing as historical truth in adjudication and conflict resolution in general, as 'legal truth on the facts of the matter' is exhaustively determined by the outcome of reasonable legal procedures. This 'practical solution' is argued to be deeply implausible in principle, not just because it may lead to legal establishment of fact at odds with historical reality.

One suggestion would be to limit troublesome issues of evidence and proof to determination of harm done (in a wide sense), leaving issues of authorship alone. Thus problems of evidence and proof may be 'halved'. Against this is put forward that individual liability is a basic presupposition of personal identity and thus of meaningful human relationships. Or: it is argued that there can be no humanly feasible society without ascription of individual liability and its consequences. So it is contended that there still is an issue of evidence and proof concerning offenders, not just concerning harm done. Legal forms and limits of this are discussed, including implications for standards of evidence and proof.

2. *Ton Derksen* (University of Nijmegen) and *Monica Meijsing* (University of Tilburg) discuss a notorious criminal case from The Netherlands. Nurse Lucia de B. was convicted of seven murders and three attempted murders with the penalty of life imprisonment. Yet there was little evidence apart from the fact that at the hospital where it all started, quite a number of resuscitations happened during the nurse's shifts. Then, after one more resuscitation, it was felt that that all this could not be just a coincidence. Very early in the process a quantification was given to the uneasy feeling that proportionally there were too many resuscitations during the nurse's shifts. The probability that such a coincidence could have happened by mere accident was calculated by one expert as 1 in 342,000,000. With that number out in the open, the general notion was that what had happened could not be just an accident. The nurse definitely had to be a serial killer, even in the absence of any further evidence. It is argued that this idea was in fact the driving force in the whole judicial process. It coloured everybody's perception, including that of the prosecution and the courts. And it fabricated a whole series of incriminating facts which inexorably led to the completely unwarranted conclusion against Lucia de B. Important general lessons may be learned from this. Throughout the process three dangerous reasoning instincts may be seen at work: (1) the Small Chance Instinct (2) the No Smoke without Fire Instinct, and (3) human inclination to pay little attention to base rates (in non-everyday situations).

3. *Ton Broeders* (University of Maastricht and Leiden University) discusses rational and probabilistic models of forensic decision-making in individuation problems. In such problems a forensic scientist is confronted with a trace (for example, a fingerprint, some handwriting, a DNA sample, or a bullet) and has to determine its source (a specific person, a specific firearm). Traditional forensic approaches are criticized for requiring that identification and elimination should be categorical and that therefore the reasoning involved should be deductive. Against this it is claimed that this kind of reasoning has to be inductive, since, when determining the source of a trace, it is practically impossible to compare the source with the entire population of all potential sources. Therefore probabilistic assessments are inevitable. Accordingly, a Bayesian model of factual judgement is proposed: forensic experts should provide conditional probabilities on the relevance of evidence to certain hypotheses, while the fact-finder should estimate

the prior probabilities of these hypotheses and combine them with the expert's conditional ones to calculate the impact of new evidence on the hypotheses' posterior probability. It is also argued that in order to avoid misunderstandings it is essential that the expert report his findings to the adjudicator in a rationally correct format. Traditional conclusion formats are argued to be logically flawed and misleading. A more plausible conclusion format is suggested.

4. *Floris Bex* (University of Groningen) focuses on the story-based approach to reasoning about the facts of a case. After a discussion of previous work on the role of stories in legal evidential reasoning, the notion of story schemes as a tool to assess story plausibility is developed. Stories are argued to be plausible if their facts fit story schemes. A story scheme is a description of typical event structures, such as the typical facts of a robbery or, more generally, an intentional crime. It is noted that story schemes can be more or less abstract and he emphasizes that it is important to match a story with the most specific available story scheme. For instance, a robbery story's plausibility is best established using a story scheme for robberies, and less so by using a story scheme for intentional crimes. This account of story schemes is also used to explicate the role of causal generalizations that connect causally related facts in a story, and it is noted how story schemes have different uses, e.g., for story analysis (in decision-making), hypothesis generation (in investigation) and for building persuasive stories (in pleading).

5. *Marijke Malsch* (Netherlands Institute for the Study of Crime and Law Enforcement, NSCR) and *Ian Freckelton* (Monash University, Melbourne) discuss two broad types of evidence evaluation within criminal cases. One of them concerns a 'holistic' way of looking at the various items of evidence and coming to conclusions about how convincing they are in terms of their probative value. The use of stories, comparing different accounts of what happened, and looking at events as a whole, are central to this model. The other way in which evidence is evaluated is atomistic, whereby each item of evidence is weighed and scrutinized independently from the other evidence. It represents, in principle, a bottom-up way of coming to conclusions regarding what happened in a case. Advantages and disadvantages of each approach are discussed. Attention is paid to two archetypes of legal systems: the adversarial and the inquisitorial. Taking The Netherlands and Australia as examples of the two types of legal systems, this chapter examines those characteristics that can be expected to contribute to a preference for either a holistic way or an atomistic way of evaluating evidence. An answer is sought to the question, which type of legal system would prefer to use one of the modes of evidence evaluation over the other. Some legal systems may be more inclined to a holistic approach than others, and vice versa. Some cautious recommendations are made.

6. *Amalia Amaya* (formerly Harvard University, now National Autonomous University of Mexico) discusses the combination of story-based approaches

with AI and cognitive science models of inference to the best explanation. It is argued that most arguments about facts in law are instances of 'inference to the best explanation', that is, patterns of inference whereby explanatory hypotheses are formed and evaluated. A coherentist interpretation of inference to the best explanation is offered, according to which reasoning about facts in law involves first the generation of several plausible explanations of the evidence at trial and then the selection, from among them, of the one that is best according to a test of explanatory coherence. It is shown how the explanationist model of legal proof proposed would deal with the O.J. Simpson case. Next, there is discussion of a major criticism against a model of inference to the best explanation in law, namely, the objection from the bad lot, which says that the best available explanation might still be a bad one. Against this it is noted that the investigation phase in which the explanations are constructed is governed by principles of epistemic responsibility and that respecting these principles increases the chance that the best explanation available is rationally acceptable.

7. *Bart Verheij* and *Floris Bex* (University of Groningen) contribute one more piece of the puzzle as to how the story-based and argument-based approaches are related. The main result of this chapter is a set of argumentation schemes, reconstructing anchored narratives theory. Such schemes are kinds of semi-formal analogues of the rules of inference of logic. An argumentation scheme specifies conditions that can support a conclusion and possibly also exceptions that can apply and conditions of use for the scheme. The central argumentation scheme of the set makes explicit how a story can be accepted as true according to the anchored narratives theory: the story must be good and the story must be well anchored. An important exception to the rule that good, well anchored stories can be accepted as true is the availability of another good story, with equally good or perhaps even better anchoring. Thus the argumentation schemes developed in the chapter lead to some refinements and clarifications of the anchored narratives theory. In particular, it is explained how accepting a story about the facts of a crime can depend recursively on stories about pieces of evidence. It is proposed that the acceptance of the truth of a story about a piece of evidence should be treated in the same way as the acceptance of the truth of a story about the crime facts, but using different measures of the plausibility of such stories (in the form of different story structures).

8. *Hendrik Kaptein* discusses the often belittled but in fact fundamental conflict between anomism (evidence and proof are to be established by any means, as long as they conform to relevant facts) and proceduralism (legally relevant facts are to be established by authoritative procedure). Anomism is shown to be related to strict distinctions between contexts of discovery and contexts of justification, related in their turn to ideals of monotonic reasoning. Proceduralism, on the other hand, implies the dependence of justification on procedure, with the attendant relevance of defeasible reasoning. Several objections against anomism are discussed, ranging

from the problem of the *argumentum ad ignorantiam* and doubtful objectivist ontological and epistemological presuppositions to its practical impossibility. At first sight this would seem to reinstate proceduralism and its basic idea of constructed 'reality'. Still, such 'pure' proceduralism is shown to come down to giving up the idea of reasonable conflict resolution as such. What is left to be done, then, is the devising of rational procedures for unearthing the truth of the matter, or: proceduralism is one important (heuristic) tool in reconstructing reality.

9. *Henry Prakken* (University of Groningen and Utrecht University) and *Giovanni Sartor* (CIRSFID, University of Bologna and European University Institute, Florence) continue with the argumentation approach. The starting point is the claim that logics for defeasible argumentation provide the means to logically characterize the difference between several kinds of proof burdens, but only if they are embedded in a dynamic setting that captures the various stages of a legal proceeding. It is also argued that 'standard' argumentation logics for AI must be adapted in order to model shifts in burdens of proof. Thus this analysis illustrates in two ways that logics cannot be simply imposed on the law but that features of legal systems must be taken into account. First there is the claim that the burden of persuasion, which legally is the burden to prove a statement to a specified degree (the standard of proof), with the penalty of losing on the issue, can be verified by applying an argumentation logic to the evidence available at the final stage of a proceeding. Then a precise distinction is made between two burdens that are sometimes confused, namely the burden of production and the tactical burden. In this analysis, the tactical burden of proof is automatically induced by the defeasible nature of the reasoning. The burden of production, by contrast, concerns the legal question of whether an issue can be submitted to trial or must be decided as a matter of law against the one who fails to produce any evidence. Finally the issue is raised as to what extent this account can be generalized to statistical and story-based approaches.

10. *Burkhard Schafer* (University of Edinburgh School of Law, Joseph Bell Centre) aims at a tentative exploration of a legal theory of rational argumentation, that is a theory that takes the rules of legal procedure as a starting point and aims to describe the way in which they function in a legal argument. The relationship between rational and legal procedural principles of evidentiary reasoning is addressed, taking Kaptein's distinction between anomism and proceduralism (see Chapter 8) as a starting point. It is claimed that when these clash, it is not always the law that is at fault. Indeed it is argued that rational inquiry in the natural sciences may not be the paradigm of fact-finding in the law. Typically, legal rational values may be at least as important. Legal-procedural rules should not be seen as contingent extra-rational add-ons to rational models, merely meant to promote extra-rational legal values such as fairness and due process. Instead it is argued that several such constraints enhance rational truth seeking, since they restore the epistemic asymmetry that sets legal trial apart from scientific debate. The difference shows

itself most clearly in criminal trials, where the defendant has privileged access to the truth, while the prosecution has privileged access to the means of proof. Legal procedure aims at restoring the epistemic symmetry between the parties by, for instance, rules on burdens of proof and pre-trial disclosure rules. Because of the epistemic asymmetry of legal procedure, it is also argued that legal evidential reasoning is not about what is true but about what can be proven to be true. Against Prakken and Sartor, in this book and elsewhere, it is put forward that this can be modelled as deductive instead of defeasible inference since the question 'what has been proven' is not addressed until the end of a proceeding, at which point no new evidence can be introduced, which excludes any further defeat.

References

Anderson, T.J., Schum, D.A. and Twining, W.L. (2005), *Analysis of Evidence*, 2nd Edition (Cambridge: Cambridge University Press).

Bennett, W.L. and Feldman, M.S. (1981), *Reconstructing Reality in the Courtroom: Justice and Judgment in American Culture* (London: Methuen-Tavistock).

Bentham, J. (1827), *Rationale of Judicial Evidence, Specially Applied to English Practice*, in Bowring and Mill (eds).

Bergh, W.M. van den (2008), 'Het oordeel is aan de rechter én jury' ('Both judge and jury are to judge'), *NRC.NEXT*, 19.

Bex, F.J., Prakken, H., Reed, C. and Walton, D.N. (2003), 'Towards a formal account of reasoning about evidence: Argumentation schemes and generalisations', *Artificial Intelligence and Law* 11, 125–65.

Bowring, J. and Mill, J. (eds) (1843), *The Works of Jeremy Bentham*, vol. 6 onwards (Edinburgh: William Tait).

Dawid, A.P. (2005), 'Probability and Statistics in the Law', in Ghahramani and Cowell (eds).

Ghahramani, Z. and Cowell, R.G. (eds) (2005), *Proceedings of the Tenth International Workshop on Artificial Intelligence and Statistics* (Barbados: AISTATS).

Josephson, J.R. (2001), 'On the proof dynamics of inference to the best explanation', *Cardozo Law Review* 22, 1621–43.

Kadane, J.B. and Schum, D.A. (1996), *A Probabilistic Analysis of the Sacco and Vanzetti Evidence* (New York: John Wiley and Sons, Inc.).

Keppens, J., Shen, Q. and Schafer, B. (2005), 'Probabilistic Abductive Computation of Evidence Collection Strategies in Crime Investigation', *Proceedings of the Tenth International Conference on Artificial Intelligence and Law* (New York: ACM Press), pp. 215–24.

Koppen, P.J. van and Roos, N.H.M. (eds) (2000), *Rationality, Information and Progress in Law and Psychology: Liber Amoricum Hans F. Crombag* (Maastricht: Metajuridica Publications).

Lempert, R. (1986), 'The new evidence scholarship: Analyzing the process of proof', *Boston University Law Review* 66, 439–77.

Malcolm, J. (1999), *The Crime of Sheila McCough* (New York: Borzoi Books, Alfred A. Knopf, Inc.).

Poole, D.L. (2001), 'Logical argumentation, abduction and Bayesian decision theory: A Bayesian approach to logical arguments and its application to legal evidential reasoning', *Cardozo Law Review* 22, 1733–45.

Prakken, H. (2004), 'Analysing reasoning about evidence with formal models of argumentation', *Law, Probability and Risk* 3, 33–50.

Schum, D.A. (1994), *The Evidential Foundations of Probabilistic Reasoning* (New York: John Wiley and Sons).

——(2001), 'Alternative views of argument construction from a mass of evidence', *Cardozo Law Review* 22, 1461–1502.

Thagard, P. (2005), 'Testimony, credibility and explanatory coherence', *Erkenntnis*, 63, 295–316.

Verheij, B. (2000), 'Dialectical Argumentation as a Heuristic for Courtroom Decision-making', in Van Koppen and Roos (eds).

Wagenaar, W.A., Koppen, P.J. van and Crombag, H. (1993), *Anchored Narratives: The Psychology of Criminal Evidence* (New York: St. Martin's Press).

Walton, D.N. (2002), *Legal Argumentation and Evidence* (University Park, PA: Pennsylvania State University Press).

Wigmore, J.H. (1931), *The Principles of Judicial Proof*, 2nd Edition (Boston: Little, Brown & Company).

Chapter 1

Burdens of Evidence and Proof: Why Bear Them? A Plea for Principled Opportunism in (Leaving) Legal Fact-finding (Alone)

Hendrik Kaptein

1. Introduction

Sometimes some things are done the wrong way, and then next it is time, high time at times, to single out offenders, give them a sermon (shout, or even shriek at them) and sentence them, with or without some or other kind of punishment. With offenders caught in the act (leading to ostensive proof of misdemeanour), there may be no big problems of evidence and proof. But given circumstantial evidence only, evasive answers may be expected. Broken crockery may point to a certain family member more or less renowned for unwittingly destroying things. But this potential offender may well deny that he did it, fearful as he may be of the shameful consequences (and worse) of admitting his 'tort' and unwilling to experience feelings of guilt and associated sentiments of inferiority and shame. This is (probably rather an unwelcome) part and parcel of daily and not so daily (legal) life. Actors' willing cooperation in establishment of evidence and proof is to be expected only if such actors are to gain by it. Normal people are not shameful of doing good, only of doing wrong (apart from that rather unwelcome category of people lacking any kind of guilt and shame).

Thus there seem to be at least two problems with actor identification in cases of wrongdoing (in any human sense, legal or otherwise). First, ostensive proof against offenders is not the rule, if only because offenders may think they have good reason to hide their misdemeanour from the outside world. So 'proof' against possible offenders is not that often self-evident (unless they confess, though such confessions may not always be completely reliable). Second, even if there is full agreement (or even certainty) as to who did it, offenders are generally unwilling to pay the price: experiencing feelings of guilt, being shamed and made to suffer, to say the least. So, after harm is done (or even just happens), new harm crops up, as a seemingly unavoidable consequence of trying to deal with the original harm.

This of course is one main reason why such conflicts tend to be formalized. Legal procedure and the strong arm of the law may solve such problems, at times.

Most legal conflicts relate to disputed facts, not to disputed law. Legal procedure may lead to finding out the facts of the case, but of course not necessarily so. Criminal defendants are well-known exceptions here, as most of them confess, in terms to be reliably tested in the light of other evidence available (which of course does not at all imply that every confession is trustworthy by itself).

Even if the facts of the case are successfully established, legally or otherwise, and related to norms violated, the solution of the original problem may not yet be in sight. Here is a third problem: in more than a few cases of harm done, it would seem that it cannot be undone. Certainly offenders may be forced to offer apologies (though some may even take their own initiative in this), and be made to suffer as 'retribution' (whatever that may be) for their sins. Payment of damages may be in order, but not even all material harm may be simply compensated for. A crumpled bike may be straightened, but an old family painting repeatedly punctured by young nephew's new air gun may be gone for ever. A wound may be healed, but the dead will not be resurrected.

So why not leave things, and leave offenders alone? Why pay the dear price of proof, that is, if reliable proof against offenders can be furnished at all? Is not this really the preliminary question, before any issues of logic and argumentation in evidence and proof are to be discussed at all? Of course there are very many kinds of legally relevant facts, the establishment of which does not lead to any kind of problem in itself, ranging from parties' identification in contracting to determination of chemical substances (wrongly) sold as expensive perfumes. Problems set in as soon as things go wrong, and as soon as interests or even rights in the case are at odds. From then on, the burden (and burdens) of evidence and proof need to be balanced some or other way. What is gained or lost by burdening parties and/or official bodies like the police and the public prosecution with the tasks of finding reliable evidence and proof? And can really trustworthy evidence and proof be established at all?

No doubt much of what will be discussed here is rather self-evident. Still it may be worthwhile to inquire why, and when, legal evidence and proof are needed, by way of introduction to the so much more important discussion of real issues of evidence and proof.

Discussion of this preliminary issue will proceed as follows. In section 2, assorted standard and not so standard reasons for establishment and proof of individual (and corporate) liability will be briefly discussed: both ubiquitous reference to human conduct in (moral and) legal norms and deep-seated resentment against wrongdoing by others are apposite here. Next, section 3 expounds a plethora of reasons against singling out offenders, ranging from the (huge) human and financial costs involved to Stoic *amor fati* and Christian forgiveness or even determinism in its most recent guises, depicting legal principles and practice as obsolete remnants of pre-scientific pasts. In section 4, a few of so many more well-known practical obstacles to reliable establishment of evidence and proof pass muster. This leads to questions concerning the very concept of proof, presumably linking present evidence with past (or future) events. Brief discussion of (Benthamite) ideals seems to lead inexorably to the conclusion that proof of events past or future is impossible in principle (section 5). Lawyers' standard answer to such theoretical scepticism refers to proceduralism: there need be no such thing as historical truth in adjudication and conflict resolution in general, as 'legal truth on the facts of the matter' is exhaustively determined by the outcome of reasonable procedures, including division of burdens of proof, and so on. This 'practical solution' is shown to be deeply implausible in principle, not just because it may lead to legal establishment of fact at odds with historical reality (section 6). Section 7 offers a possible solution to these problems. Though troublesome issues of evidence and proof cannot be circumvented completely, they may well be limited to determination of harm done (in a wide sense), leaving all possible issues of authorship alone. A startling suggestion maybe, at odds with deep-seated intuition and senses of justice, but rather more plausible than it seems at first sight. Still, a fundamentally convincing argument against this 'general abolitionism' will be unfolded in section 8. Individual liability is a basic presupposition of personal identity and thus of meaningful human relationships. Thus there can be no humanly feasible society without ascription of individual liability and its consequences. So there is an issue of evidence and proof concerning offenders, not just concerning harm done. Some more good reasons for establishment of evidence and proof pass muster as well. Legal forms and limits of this will be discussed in section 9, including material law implications for standards of evidence and proof. Also, balancing costs of obtaining evidence and proof, and related risks of uncertainty, against gains in terms of material results of allocating liability remains an all-important issue. But still: *in dubio abstine* (section 10).

Anyway, observations and remarks to be made here are to be interpreted predominantly as a kind of earthly (and probably slightly moralizing) prelude, in order to prepare the mind for the real thing, i.e. the high science of logic and argumentation in matters of legal evidence and proof.

2. Standard Reasons for Establishment of Evidence and Proof Against Offenders

Reasons for singling out perpetrators (with all attendant problems of evidence and proof) in order to establish their criminal, civil and/or administrative liabilities and legal positions in general seem all too obvious to require any further mention. First, both material and procedural law are of course shot through with references to human conduct, both past and future. It could not be otherwise, as the law is meant to regulate human conduct in some or other way, even in the most sceptical conceptions of law. Second, it seems self-evident that offenders (again in a wide sense) ought still to do what they promised, to pay for the harm they did themselves, to be punished for their own misdeeds. Why should others bear the brunt of costs completely outside their legal or even moral liabilities and/or competences?

In most cases, identification of actors and their legally relevant qualities and circumstances is of course no problem at all. Most people and most (other) bodies freely identify themselves and their legally relevant conduct, willingly and generally obey the law and acknowledge doing this, that is, in more or less civilized jurisdictions. In very many cases, this is in their own best interest, even without threats against disobedience in the background. Problems arise as soon as actors are unwilling to do what they ought to do, as a consequence of their disregard of the law, and/or of contract, and/or of others' legally relevant interests and rights. Problems of evidence and proof follow naturally, then. Still, misconduct may go completely unnoticed of course, or come to light in terms of harmful consequences only.

Next, even if malefactors may be apprehended some or other way, they may still go free. It may be considered too expensive to take these offenders and their likes to task. Leaving some offenders alone is considered to be more expedient in several respects. Not just problems of evidence and proof are obviated in such a way. Other costs, including those of further procedure and execution against unwilling and/or well-armed malefactors, do not need to be paid for either. Thus any conception of the rule of law as implying effective establishment of individual liability through evidence and proof is naive.

But then leaving offenders alone is unacceptable in principle, one would say. Even if it may not be worthwhile, for economic and other reasons, to even try to single out offenders (individuals, corporations, public bodies and so on), the end result is that the innocent are made to pay. Payers may be victims themselves, being left alone with 'their' harm, and/or third parties paying insurance money and/or taxes to cover the costs of public funds. What would be more natural, moral, and so on than making offenders pay themselves? Even if not everybody may be caught and confronted with conclusive evidence and proof, ought not there to be a reasonably serious chance of being caught and identified, if there is to be anything like a civilized jurisdiction, and civilized society, for that matter?

Giving up matters of identification and its attendant issues of evidence and proof seems tantamount to licence. (Though it is to be noted again of course that any legal order is more than just a collection of orders backed by threats and that prescriptions and prohibitions are logically distinct from legal consequences of breaches of them. Many legal rules are adhered to and/or made use of without any effective or even formal threat against disobedience, without any noticeable chaos ensuing.) In addition: if individuals and all kinds of bodies derive rights from a legal order, what then would be more natural than to ascribe responsibilities to them as well?

Costs of harm are to be borne by their creators, not by victims. This seems to be not just a legal principle. Thus nothing seems more natural than the idea of individual (or corporate, or public body) liability, however high attendant costs in terms of obtaining evidence and proof may be.

3. The Price of Proof: Too High?

There may be more prices to pay however, not just by victims and others trying to obtain adequate evidence and proof, and not just in terms of costs and convenience. A compact catalogue of costs concerned, human and otherwise, may lead to at least the semblance of conclusive evidence and proof against evidence and proof.

Collecting reliable evidence and proof may indeed be (very) expensive. Such costs in terms of time and money are to be balanced against other interests. A purely economic approach may sensibly dictate abolition of any (further) inquiries. Adding to this are the costs of ever-expanding industries of lawyers and other legal people, living by making factual disputes as complex as possible, greatly assisted in this by a sometimes incomprehensibly technical system of legal procedure regulating matters of evidence and proof. For this and other reasons, total costs of the practice of tort law greatly exceed the sum total of damages paid in most civilized jurisdictions. To mention just one of so many different kinds of examples here: the huge collateral economical and other damage caused by blocking roads in order to find out 'who caused the accident' (if this is a sensible question at all) is paid for by completely innocent victims of such road blocks themselves. Even if perpetrators are singled out in the end, insurance companies pay. So why bother? What more is it than legal folklore, irrational remnants of ideas of individual liability completely out of place in the complexities of contemporary society?

Added to this is the difficulty, if not impossibility, of balancing all interests concerned against each other. Not all interests and rights may be measured in terms of money. Also, and often overlooked in legal practice, the human costs of pursuing evidence and proof are to be taken into account. For most people, unaccustomed to legal procedure as they are, getting involved or even being forced into any kind of formality is deeply disagreeable, fearful and worse. Feelings of shame, fear of stigmatization or even wrongly felt guilt may be caused by 'official' attempts to uncover 'the truth' (or not even the truth). More often than not, ordinary people experience legal dealings as nothing more than varieties of strangely formalized meta-conflict, duplicating original conflicts instead of solving them. Remember that most normal people are interested in solving material conflicts, concerning real life interests and rights, while legal people live by proceduralizing issues (away from the real problems).

All this raises the question whether all the time, money, effort and emotion dedicated to the collection and establishment of evidence and proof may not be better spent on more sensible enterprises. Just as more than a bit of human suffering may be avoided by leaving issues of evidence and proof alone. Still, such issues of balancing may be regarded as practical quibbles in the end, to be dealt with in some or other orderly fashion and thus not excluding the establishment of evidence and proof beforehand.

Balancing all interests concerned may involve some powers of imagination, however, in terms of human equality. Most people shun inquiries possibly leading to establishment of offences committed by them, as this is felt to be against their own 'best interests', at least in terms of social standing (however wrong they may be in this: see section 8). Searching for incriminating facts is something to be effected against others, not against ourselves. Few people are ready to be branded as guilty, however much many people may suffer from inner feelings of neurotic guilt. (In relationship to our fellow human beings, we would rather be a vengeful God, however unconsciously, than just one more sinful human being ourselves.) So elementary equality and honesty seem to require leaving all others alone as well, or, maybe better still: freely cooperating in fact-finding against ourselves, just as we expect in relation to others. However, and strangely in line with this, leaving issues of evidence and proof alone surely has the immensely moral advantage of dramatically reducing amounts of human mendacity (protected by the doubtful practice of lawyers' client confidentiality: no evidence and proof needed? No client confidentiality either). Or: trying to redress moral and legal wrongs by fact-finding leads to other wrongs in its turn.

Leaving such (sometimes seemingly slightly otherworldly) problems of balancing alone, it is high time for real, or even theoretical, doubts about legal dealings with evidence and proof, and the (witch) hunt after suspects and related facts in the past in order to take some body to task. First, there is the uneasy relationship between revenge and mercy. In many world religions, the value of forgiveness and mercy is ranked higher than any desire for revenge (in a broad sense). Even if forgiving misdeeds seems to presuppose identification of wrongdoers, problems of evidence and proof become much less pressing. If offenders cannot be found, so be it, with attended mercy directed to some anonymous body. How can one sit down in church and pray for mercy, as a supreme expression of love for another, and go after evidence and proof in order to take (presumed) offenders to task? What exalts legal values above the highest religious and moral values? A rhetorical question maybe, but still an uneasy one. And there are also the well-known advantages of mercy in terms of subjective well-being and flourishing. Forgiving attitudes lead to happier lives than ever-frustrating and frustrated vengefulness (but see section 8 on retribution as a precondition for mercy). Summarizing such considerations:

> Then the scribes and Pharisees brought to Him a woman caught in adultery. And when they had set her in the midst, they said to Him, 'Teacher, this woman was caught in adultery, in the very act. Now Moses, in the law, commanded us that such should be stoned. But what do You say?' This they said, testing Him, that they might have something of which to accuse Him. But Jesus stooped down and wrote on the ground with His finger, as though He did not hear. So when they continued asking Him, He raised Himself up and said to them, 'He who is without sin among you, let him throw a stone at her first.' And again He stooped down and wrote on the ground. Then those who heard it, being convicted by their conscience, went out one by one, beginning with the oldest even to the last. And Jesus was left alone, and the woman standing in the midst. When Jesus had raised Himself up and saw no one but the woman, He said to her, 'Woman,

> where are those accusers of yours? Has no one condemned you?' She said, 'No one, Lord.' And Jesus said to her, 'Neither do I condemn you; go and sin no more.' (From *The Gospel According to St. John*, 8, New King James Version.)

Not much Christian belief is needed to see the moving (and manifold) wisdom in this. There seemed to be no problem of evidence and proof, the question was what to do with it. Though adultery is no longer a legal crime in most civilized jurisdictions, lots of other facts constituting legal 'crime' according to the books of today are best left alone as well.

Second, there is the no less fundamental human value of being *aequo animo*, as famously advocated by many scholars, theologians and philosophers, like Epictetus, the great Stoic. Outstanding in a manifold of reasons to remain unmoved is the well-argued idea that there can be no really meaningful distinction between actions and events. Somebody hitting me over the head is not different in principle from any natural force befalling me, like a stone falling down from the mountain. Bear it, and do not waste any time in fruitless resentment. (Apart from any relevance for issues of evidence and proof and notwithstanding Nietzschean and other answers to such stoicism, wisdom as expounded by Epictetus remains highly important for daily and not so daily life. Reading the *Enchiridion* may do anybody good.)

In line with this is the idea that the world cannot be changed anyway. It is as it is, it will be what it will be. This leads to varieties of ('hard') determinism, implying that there is no such thing as freedom of choice. In more modern varieties, such determinism is often based on a causalist, scientific view of the whole of reality, including the neuro-physiological mechanisms behind human action, however complex. And however complex the determinism issue may be itself, predetermination does seem to be incompatible with freedom of choice as a presupposition for any liability, legal or moral. No liability? Then no issues of evidence and proof of liability either. Thus regarded, legal liability and its presuppositions of evidence and proof seem irrational remnants of a past long overtaken by the enlightenment of modern science and its incomparable successes in explaining reality.

Returning to the concept of guilt, as a presupposition for criminal liability at least: what is it anyway? Apart from its incompatibility with determinism, it may well be thought that 'guilt' is excluded by a 'free' world as well. Is all guilt neurotic guilt? Nietzsche famously remarked (in 1887, p. 870):

> Although the most acute judges of the witches and even the witches themselves, were convinced of the guilt of witchery, the guilt nevertheless was non-existent. It is thus with all guilt.

Or: the witch-hunt after guilt, and thus after varieties of legal liability. In line with this, and related to purely physical/physiological world views behind varieties of determinism, is the still more radical reductionism of the 'I' as ideology (echoes of postmodernism here as well). No 'I' in even the minimal sense of personality as distinct from others and the rest of the world? Then no liability either, of course.

All that may be said about anything raising any issue of liability, then, is that an infinitely small part of the world, resembling a possible offender (if this still is a sensible concept at all) seemed to be more directly linked to some or other mishap than an enormous complex of other states of affairs and events in the world. But what is 'more directly linked'? What notions of causality are presupposed here? Causation in the law is a notoriously vexing issue anyway (see Kaptein 1999 for a brief overview).

Apart from theoretical issues of determinism there are the inescapable human realities of fate. Honest introspection has it that few if any pieces of human behaviour may really be said to be the result of totally detached ratiocination, in terms of the objectively determined interests and possibilities concerned. This seems to hold good all the more for all these poor people erring from right paths (not defined by themselves at that). So (again): who is to throw the first stone?

If all these probably all-too-theoretical if not even moral and religious doubts may be swept aside, and offenders may still be taken to task, at least one more uneasy question remains to be answered. Even if determinism may be proven to be wrong, implying that there is (some) freedom of choice and thus a (more or less) 'open' future after all, it seems indubitable that the past is, in principle, as it is (however difficult it may be to really ascertain what 'really happened'). So any harm done in the past, however quickly or slowly it may disappear out of the minds and bodies of people hit by it, remains the same harm, just as everything in the past remains what it was and is. How could any harm be undone, then, by inflicting new harm to offenders? Modderman (outstanding legal scholar and cabinet minister in The Netherlands) expressed the problem as follows (in 1864, translated by the author):

> Moral theories of retribution pose the following question: how much factual suffering is needed in order to redeem a moral debt? Would it really be an exaggeration to maintain that this question is as unanswerable as the question how much iron would be needed in order to make a first class dress-coat?

Or: the whole idea of redressing wrongful harm by making offenders pay (in a wide sense), or even by inflicting pain through punishment seems a category error. The past cannot be changed by definition, or it would not be the past (but see section 8).

But then all kinds of preventive purposes are surely served by making offenders pay, it will be retorted. Maybe in certain cases (see again section 8), but then it has been observed many times before that it is at least highly doubtful whether the sum total of costs caused by evidence and proof against offenders, and its consequences in terms of punishment and other measures against them, may ever be made good by gains in terms of fewer offences of whatever kind (see Kaptein 2004 for further discussion of this).

If this all may seem a bit theoretical, a real life problem may be rather more pressing. Evidence and proof of facts past and future are subject to many different kinds of error of course, or at least to margins of probability, quite apart from bad faith and worse in officials and others concerned with adducing 'conclusive' proof against their innocent victims. If making offenders pay for their wrongs is a good thing at all, given all these objections, it still presupposes the rather imperfect practice of collecting evidence and constructing proof. If one more price to be paid for this is sentencing the innocent as well, then there is at least one real balancing issue. What may outweigh the capital wrong of punishing the innocent? 'Niemals empört etwas mehr als Ungerechtigkeit' (nothing is so repulsive as injustice) (as Kant famously put it) is apposite in the administration of justice in the very first place (as pointedly expressed by Peter Ustinov, as quoted by Woffinden, in 1988, p. 7):

> I regard injustice, or even the risk of injustice, perpetrated in the august precincts of a court of law, with calm consideration and time for reflection, as utterly repellent.

4. Practical Problems of Proof

Not just the problem of wrongly punishing the criminally innocent, or even executing them, refers to imperfections in evidence and proof. Or: there is more than marginal evidence of at least practical impossibilities in relating reliable evidence to conclusive proof. To put things in some perspective: of course there is the semblance of proof beyond reasonable doubt, even in everyday practice. Thus alibis linking completely reliable evidence to conclusions explicitly excluding facts of charges may be regarded as paradigms of proof. Confessions fitting in with other evidence and further tested by defendants' knowledge of crime details (before informing them of such facts) may be clear cases as well, probably making out the majority of criminal court cases. Maybe so, but even then things may go wildly wrong, as is amply displayed by the history of wrongful confessions and convictions.

Compounding the problem is ignorance in principle on the nature and number of cases in which evidence and proof led to factually wrong conclusions, with all their consequences. Some cases come to light, sometimes thanks to persevering public attention, while other cases and their attendant injustice may remain hidden forever. This is inherent to the problem itself of course. If there were reliable proof of the contrary, or even if there were conclusive proof that the original 'proof' was wanting, corresponding verdicts would be reversed of course. (Or so one would think, as it appears that some judiciaries are willing to deploy every legal means against drawing the right consequences from clearly mistaken cases of criminal evidence and proof.)

A very brief, incomplete and probably self-evident summary of so many things which may go wrong may further reduce any remaining faith in evidence and proof. Witnesses may be (intentionally) mistaken for so many well-documented reasons. Too often it is simply forgotten that reference to witnesses' statements really is the last ditch in evidence and proof. Witnesses ought to be called to the stand only if no more solid evidence is available (like physical traces of criminal activities). Witnesses and (other) professionals may suffer from various kinds of preconceptions, starting with the selection of evidence 'on the spot' to misinterpreting various data in terms of foregone conclusions to be 'derived' from 'available evidence'.

Next there is an endless variety of mala fide motives for witnesses and others, including public prosecution officials and court members, to lie and cheat. It appears that at least some members of the judiciary willingly shun respecting the truth if it means contradicting their original standpoints, or those of their colleagues. This is the problem of mistaken professional and personal pride against principles of justice for the innocent.

Next there is the ever-increasing importance of forensic sciences. No doubt legal application of recent progress in DNA testing has solved several hard cases, and mitigated the problem of reliance on witnesses. On the other hand, different experts' interpretation of DNA results led to completely contrary results in more than a few cases. Forensic psychiatry is another case in point. Thus Szasz (1977), in one more attempt to demystify such expertise, suggested that psychiatrists' assessments of liability in terms of inner freedom of choice are linked to the moral quality of the crime in the first place: the more horrendous the crime, the less freedom of choice will be imputed: 'Nobody in his right mind would do such a thing.' (See also Dershowitz 1995.) But then nobody in his right mind would accept this as proof of an unsound mind in the sense of criminal irresponsibility. Unless determinism is true after all, of course, denying any responsibility whatsoever.

Apart from problems ranging from partial observation to neglect of relevant evidence and outright lying, there are problems of linking evidence to some or other conclusion of the case at hand. For example, explanations of available evidence in terms of facts of charges may be abductive in nature, with all the attendant problems. Even if such explanations may seem reasonably plausible, there may be more plausible explanations whose only problem is that they are not available or may not be convincingly brought out by defendants. Next, abductive argumentation is related to probabilistic reasoning, be it interpreted in (fashionable) Bayesian style or otherwise. This again raises vexing queries about the applicability of any probabilistic reasoning to unique historical events like crimes (though statistics may play fruitful roles in fact-finding related to the future, in establishing damages to be paid or otherwise).

Attempts to approach such linking problems are found in the (once again fashionable) 'storytelling' approaches to problems of evidence and proof.

Originally, the story telling approach was critically labelled 'the psychology of evidence and proof' (which is evident even in the subtitle of a major book dedicated to it by Crombag et al., from 1991, see Wagenaar et al. 1993). Since then, several contributions to the debate on evidence and proof tried to constructively 'reform' the approach of storytelling. This may be on the right track, as long as the original problems with storytelling are kept in mind. Briefly summarized: in issues of evidence and proof storytelling is unavoidable, but stories create their own 'logic' and preconceptions of historical reality. Also, stories are necessarily anchored in doubtful common sense generalizations (think of principles like: 'Policemen do not lie'). But then if proof is to come down to something like necessarily linking evidence as premises to a conclusion stating the facts to be proven, then storytelling as proof is wanting in principle anyway, however unavoidable it may be in practice.

5. Ideals of Proof and their Attendant Impossibility in Principle: Certainty on Specific Facts as a Will-o'-the-Wisp

May such practical problems be solved in principle? That is, given unlimited amounts of time, money, expertise and good will? Before even trying to answer this probably slightly rhetorical question some more attention to the concept of proof itself is in order.

As Bentham famously stated (in 1812, Chapter 1, Part 1): 'The field of evidence is no other than the field of knowledge.' Already in Bentham's times, some kinds of general knowledge, like Newtonian mechanics, could reasonably be taken to represent paradigmatically scientific certainty. But though legal evidence and proof may have to do with generic or even general facts of varying certainty at times (think here of issues of life expectancy as relevant in certain tort cases, or of proof of the nature of a chemical substance), paradigmatic legal evidence and proof have to do with historically unique facts, such as: did person x really commit act y? Or: did person z intentionally do a, or did it just happen to him? Or: what are the costs of this case of wrongful harm? And so on. So proof in the most immediate sense possible would be direct and indubitable observation of some or other basic human conduct, like one man hitting another over the head. (Note that problems of interpretation of physical movement in terms of human conduct and their relationships with motivational notions like malice and negligence are passed over here.)

Such proof is both factually and legally extremely rare of course. First, and as noted before, observation itself may be flawed in several respects. It may even be questioned whether any notion of 'objective observation' makes sense at all. Second, most evidence is circumstantial, in the minimal sense of requiring something or other 'in between' in order to connect what is seen with what is to be proven. So witnesses are needed, and/or causal and/or motivational links between different facts (or possible facts). Thus leftovers from a crime scene may be related to somebody's authorship, according to general knowledge.

Indeed, witnesses may not just be no good in specific cases (section 4), they seem to be unreliable in principle. For what kind of objective knowledge could be produced from any subject's own specific standpoint? Next, the ideal link between indubitable evidence at hand and facts to be proven would be a completely closed causal sequence. Thus descriptions of some or other present evidence, conjoined with proven laws of causation, would logically lead to description of facts to be proven. This is just an ideal of course. Also, rather more doubtful motivational laws, or better, rules of subjective probability, are needed for part of the linking as well, in most if not all legally relevant cases. In addition to this, there ought to be reasoned exclusion of any other explanation of evidence available in terms different from the facts to be proven. (And so on, see further Chapter 8.)

So both direct observation and links from such direct observation to facts to be proven seem to be uncertain in principle. If proof is to be tantamount to certainty in the sense of 'it could not have been otherwise', the whole idea of proof may be better given up in principle. More or less educated guesswork of badly defined probabilities is all there is, then, not really offering rational and reasonable bases for any kind of conviction of some body to certainly suffer under it.

In addition to this are intractable problems of causation (as already mentioned in section 3). Even if some or other actor may be causally linked with some or other legally significant state of affairs, this will not suffice as a precondition of liability in terms of causation. A bare minimum is causation as *conditio sine qua non*. This may suffice in some civil law contexts, but certainly not in the administration of criminal justice. So for this reason alone, causally adequate linking of human conduct with states of affairs (if it can be established by itself at all) will not suffice in terms of legally adequate proof.

These doubts, serious enough by themselves, all relate to evidence and proof relating to 'hard facts', to be established in some or other empirical way in principle. But that is only part of the story. 'Soft' facts may be as important. Think of problems in determination of immaterial harm, or of establishing the facts of 'normal mutual expectations'. Still more important are issues of (criminal) malice and/or negligence. But then malice and negligence may not be reduced to purely physical terms in any, however remotely plausible, concepts, let alone conceptions, of them. (Of course, psychological reductionism does imply such definition, but then remains largely programmatic and also implies the moral and legal irrelevance of malice and negligence just because of their reduction to physiology and so on). Whatever malice and negligence may be, in practical contexts such concepts seem to be implicitly and operationally defined in terms of acceptability of excuses. Malice, negligence and related concepts are determined by dialogue, for example: convincing excuses in terms of force majeure may exclude malice or negligence (see Hart 1948 for a well-known and authoritative explanation of this).

Thus the whole idea of legal proof of the facts of the case, if coherent at all, seems nothing much more than a will-o'-the-wisp. Go after it and get lost, it seems.

Thus the expensive (section 3) and difficult (section 4) pursuit of legal evidence and proof seems misguided in principle. Which of course should not imply (to briefly return to common sense and daily reality) that conclusive evidence and proof of at least some legally relevant 'hard facts' are nowhere to be found. Sure enough, but where are the lines between such simple cases and so many other cases, complex in so many different dimensions, given so many problems of proof in principle?

6. Legal Proceduralism (the Practical Solution?) Refuted

Such issues of proof, in a strict historical (or futurological) sense, and their problems are all very interesting, but legally rather irrelevant, legal scholars and practitioners would answer. Legal evidence and proof are said to be procedural in the first place. Different parties contribute their version of 'what really happened', may contradict each other and then the court (and/or the jury) decides whether 'the rules of the game' have been observed and who succeeded in offering the most plausible story.

In such fashion, difficult problems of 'reconstructing the past (or even the future) in terms of the present' are simply circumvented. Facts are established by trial, and decided upon by courts judging each party's contribution. Indeed, it is parties' own responsibility to convince the court of the plausibility of their factual standpoints. Thus regarded, the whole idea of an objective historical reality on which 'real' proof is to be based becomes irrelevant. Or: legal proof is different from historical proof in principle. This is of course highly visible in the detailed formalities of Anglo-Saxon litigation.

Or there could be no proof at all, more than a few legal scholars and practitioners would add to this. Procedural proof is just a part of procedural law in general, offering both just and pragmatic solutions to legal conflicts. Also, such proceduralism seems to offer a reasonably acceptable solution to otherwise intractable problems of malice and negligence, criminal and otherwise. Remember that varieties and degrees of intention are not things to be found or lost in reality, but end results of dialogues between parties concerning possible excuses for some or other piece of human conduct (see again Hart 1948). Such a dialogical definition and determination of malice and negligence fits in well with proceduralism of course.

Plausible, or at least workable, as such proceduralism may seem (even in much simplified form as presented here), it may still be fatally flawed. Taken to its logical extreme, proceduralism implies that the plausibility of evidence and proof depends on the impact of parties' 'version of the story' upon the adjudicator. A responsible court will of course try to check parties' stories in terms of historical reality. But then any evidence of historical reality depends on parties' contributions in principle. This is an essential part of proceduralism. Thus there is no role for any historical reality per se at all.

For this reason alone proceduralism implies 'locking up' the process of finding evidence and proof in legal procedure. Courts are to take for granted whatever makes the best impression at the moment. Such best impressions may be caused by many factors, ranging from parties' abilities to plausibly tell their stories to judges' preconceptions and much more. However strict the rules of procedure, outcomes may still be completely irrational. Note that there is no appeal to any objective historical realities in this anti-proceduralism, as such an appeal would come down to no more than using one conception of evidence against another. (More on this in Chapter 8.)

7. The Lure of Abolitionism: Repair and Leave Alone

To the extent that evidence and proof seem problematic, or even problematic in principle, arguments against establishing evidence and proof seem all the more convincing. That is of course, unless a new and hitherto untested conception of legal evidence and proof comes to the fore, but no such thing seems to be reasonably expected in the near future.

So why not leave issues of evidence and proof alone and try to repair harm done (in a wide sense) in more sensible ways? Or even: why not leave burdens of harm to victims themselves, thus avoiding any burden of evidence and proof against offenders? Remember the long-standing legal principle that everybody is to bear his own harm, unless there are convincing reasons to burden others with it. Though rapidly disappearing in contemporary claim cultures, modern times may assuage such burdens by offering all kinds of advanced free market insurance schemes.

Alternatively, if victims are not to be left alone with their harm, one option may be to cut the original problem of evidence and proof in half. Harm is to be duly established, and paid for by some or other third party fund, and offenders may be left alone. Or: forget about the past (which cannot be changed anyway) and start working on a better future. Thus a parked bicycle may have been damaged in some way. Instead of embarking upon expensive searches for possible offenders, establishment of the harm done may be sufficient to make an insurance company pay. Thus the more difficult and problematic part of evidence and proof is done away with. Apart from determination of harm done, all that is further needed is exclusion of claimants' liabilities. Thus a bike owner might have parked his vehicle in an irresponsible fashion, thus losing part or even all of his right to compensation.

Indeed, problems of evidence and proof are worsened by ever more extravagant claims of supposedly injured individuals and (other) bodies not really heeding their own responsibilities. The rise of claim cultures created not just more and more issues of evidence and proof, it also widened concepts of legally acceptable evidence and proof. Thus the Supreme Court of The Netherlands decided in 2006 that a 0.*n* probability of having caused harm implies paying 0.*n* of the damages.

(Seemingly merciful courts may still be rather bad fact-finders and statisticians!) Some more stoicism (see section 3) may do the legal order (and the quality of human life) more than a bit of good here.

But somebody has to pay at least some compensation (damages and other reparative costs). Insurance schemes may be less expensive and more effective if offenders do not need to be singled out first. (The well-known New Zealand Accident Compensation System, as revised in 2001, and related schemes are successful cases in point.) Also, victims will much more easily receive their dues, as payment to them no longer depends on finding the offenders first. In any case, in existing regimes, singling out offenders often serves no other purpose than determination of the insurance company which is to pay.

But what about deterrent effects? Will not leaving offenders alone lead to complete licence, and worse? Though this may be one price to pay, it should not be overestimated in the first place. The preventive effects of the administration of criminal justice may by themselves be too small to justify the whole system (section 3, but see also section 8, on preventive purposes of specific kinds of criminal law). Next, the manifold motives of civil law parties to stick to what they promised, not to cause unnecessary harm and so much more may be based on threats of being taken to task only to a very small extent. Education, habit and enlightened self-interest in not wanting to be exposed as a malefactor may be more important than any legal threats. Added to this are a few more basic facts: not all offenders get caught (to put things mildly, see earlier section 2 on this), trying to get hold of them all would be rather expensive, and anyway, if they do get caught then insurance companies often free them from paying damages, and so on. Thus regarded, cutting the problem of evidence and proof in half by leaving offenders alone may not really be any less deterrent than existing regimes.

One more basic disadvantage of the current system of individual liability is the problem of crimes and wrongs without offenders. If no offender can be identified, victims are left alone, which seems neither reasonable nor right. This problem is radically solved if harm (again in a wide sense) is to be paid for by third party funds, commercial insurance funds or even state funds.

Actually, and certainly in so far as consequences of crime are to be compensated for, state liability may be based upon the same state's failure to realize its primary responsibility for protection of citizens against crime in the first place. (It remains a strange fact that such responsibility and attendant care for and payment to crime victims is not realized anyway.) Thus the state, failing to do its primary duties, is taken to task and made to pay for what it did wrong, by not preventing crime and wrong. Against this it will no doubt be put forward that the state protects citizens by catching and punishing criminals in the first place. But remember (again) that preventive effects of the administration of criminal justice may be too small to justify the system. Other state measures may be rather more effective.

Such (probably counter-intuitive) cutting the problem of evidence in half still seems to solve theoretical and practical problems with evidence and proof (as outlined in sections 3ff.). To mention just a few of them in this connection: first, and of course simplifying things somewhat, problems of evidence and proof are limited to present and future consequences, leaving (past) causes out of account. (Which of course does not imply that clear and present causes persistently causing wrongful harm should not be done away with.) Thus the problem of reconstructing the past (or the future) on the basis of present evidence disappears, at least as far as actor identification is concerned. Second, the fundamental injustice of sentencing the innocent is obviated in principle. This gain by itself may well justify the whole scheme of cutting problems of evidence and proof in half, intolerable and thus incommensurate with any other values as sentencing the innocent is in principle. More generally, the problem of innocent parties' inability to prove their innocence, not just in criminal procedure, is done away with.

Thus such a general 'abolitionist' scheme, in its most extreme form in criminal law (widely advocated about forty years ago, and more or less conveniently forgotten since then it seems) may be much more plausible than it seemed at first sight. Still, problems have to be solved in order to make it work, at least on paper. For example: damages, whether paid by third parties or even by malefactors themselves, may not always be the right answer in cases of breach of contract. In family law and elsewhere, legally important consequences may not be relevantly determined in terms of harm at all.

Limiting problems of evidence and proof to harmful consequences may give rise to intractable problems in determination of harm as well. Remember that harm is legally relevant only if it is legally wrongful. So many kinds of rightful harm, caused by free market competition, self-inflicted accidents and much more, cannot be counted as worthy of compensation in principle. But then determination whether harm is wrongful or not seems to presuppose the determination of right- and wrongfulness of causes. This of course holds good for issues of force majeure concerning contracts and so much more as well. Then issues of evidence and proof of authorship (causation, motives, the past) are back again, presupposed as they are by the legally relevant determination of harm. Or might it still be preferable to simply pay, 'by any means' for any harm? Which raises the question of what would count as evidence and proof of harm as such, which may not be much easier to solve than the original issues of evidence and proof which inspired the 'abolitionism' propounded here.

8. The Elephant in the Room: Resentment, Responsibility and (Self-)Respect as Cements of Society

By now, the predominant attitude towards all of this may be something like: this can't be true, come on. First suggesting doing away with issues of evidence and proof altogether (section 3), next explaining that evidence and proof are deeply problematic and cannot be saved by proceduralism (sections 4 to 6), then trying to cut the problem in half by reducing problems of evidence and proof to determination of legally relevant harm (section 7). Strange, otherworldly and incompatible with gut feelings such as: offenders should do what they ought to do, ought to receive their dues and make up for the harm they did. But then gut feelings may be as pressing as they are irrational, seemingly stalling the whole issue.

This is not just a gut feeling however, as it may be explained in terms of rather fundamental principles of human conduct. This may resolve at least part of the problem, and return pride of place to individual liability and its attendant problems of evidence and proof. Or: it will be shown that individual liability (in a wide sense) is a precondition for respect and self-respect, and thus of sociability and solidarity. The argument runs as follows (coming down, in fact, to a version of Strawson's famous anti-determinist argument, as developed from 1962, put on its head).

What would a world without any resentment against wrongdoing look like? People would bear whatever happened to them, and in fact make no distinction at all between what befalls them as consequences of internal and/or external forces of nature (like illnesses and earthquakes) on the one hand and human wrongdoing on the other. It would be a world without human boundaries, in the sense of anybody explicitly stating what may be or may not be done to him.

For example: somebody seriously hurts somebody else by running him down, as a consequence of being in a hurry and not really taking care of other people present. A stoic like Epictetus would probably remain completely silent, while acting internally to master his pain (good hard work, as he himself admitted). The offender may be as puzzled about this as any possible bystanders. Somebody is clearly wronged, yet behaves as if nothing has happened. Such a 'philosophical' stance may befit saints, but may not really be a part of what normal human life and communication amount to.

Remaining silent in the face of wrongdoing seems at odds with elementary human reactions. In fact, resentment in a general sense may be loosely defined as a combination of sentiment and judgement, of disapprobation, and the expression of it: 'You did wrong, I did not deserve this!' Somebody who never feels and expresses such sentiments and judgements cannot be regarded as a human being in any full sense. Such a 'person' would not set any limits to what may be done to him, as a consequence of elementary fear of other human beings or some mental disorder (or even philosophical persuasion, though it remains doubtful whether Epictetus really meant to be simply silent about any wrongdoing).

In fact, the concept of a person, and of personality, seems to be inextricably bound up with setting limits to what others may do to him. This is an important part of taking oneself seriously, in personal, anonymous or even merely legal relationships. At the same time, it is an essential part of taking other people seriously, in the sense of treating them as responsible actors instead of as mere parts of complex nature. Also, self-respect presupposes being respected by others. One important part of this is recognition of and in moral resentment: the feeling, judgement and expression of disapprobation of wrong done to others. Such moral resentment is an essential part of human solidarity and thus of sociability. Not reacting at all to harm done to others in some or other sympathetic fashion, or not taking sides with victims and turning against offenders, would lead to collective loneliness.

But personal (victims') and moral (others') resentment by themselves cannot be anything like adequate reactions to wrongful harm. Offenders ought to be taken to task. If they do not offer apologies by themselves, they ought to be forced to it, by social pressure or even by the law. Apologies can be taken seriously only if they are accompanied by some or other form of material reparation effected by offenders themselves. Retribution in a literal and strict sense is compensation and reparation by offenders themselves of harm done by them. If this is done successfully, forgiveness and reconciliation are the natural consequences, leading to restoration of the original positions of everyone concerned. This is retributive justice in a strict sense indeed, relating to other indispensable values of individual and social life.

So stoic ideals of leaving offenders alone and simply (or not so simply) bearing one's own harm seem not just to be rather lofty, but otherworldly in a lonely sense as well. Human communication really presupposes the 'fundamental language' of reaction to wrong done, and its respectful reparation. Thus remaining silent in the face of wrong done by others leads to the additional harm of being (left) alone. 'Leave the past alone, start working on a better future' was a related argument against liability and attendant problems of evidence and proof (section 3). Retributive justice would seem to be a thing of the past, referring to what went wrong in the first place, instead of leaving things alone. But reparative retributive justice is essentially future oriented: 'undo wrongs, so as to be able to start again with clean slates.' Or: free the future of burdens from the past.

Of course just a few prototypical main lines of a rather more complex picture can be sketched here (for more extensive treatment, albeit in a different context, see Kaptein 2004). But if there is truth in these fundamental relationships of wrongdoing, resentment, reparation and reconciliation, problems of evidence and proof related to actor identification are back again, this time to stay. Or: the fundamental human, social and thus legal values of respect and self-respect do presuppose identification of wrongdoers as fundamentally different from natural causes of suffering.

Note that the whole argument started with anti-determinism. Resentment in some or other form is an indispensable part of human life. Such resentment presupposes freedom of action in a minimal sense, in that somebody could have acted otherwise. This is incompatible with 'hard' determinism. (Whether freedom of action in any relevant sense is compatible with 'soft' determinism may be left out of account here.) Thus determinism no longer counts against ideas and practices of evidence and proof of liability. Stoic arguments against collecting evidence and proof of wrongdoing seem to have lost at least part of their force as well. However attractive such 'quietism' may seem, it seems all too incompatible with resentment as an essential part of individual and social life.

This indispensability of liability and its concomitant issues of evidence and proof are of course rather like the elephant in the room. Indeed it relates not just to tort, but also to the law dealing with wrongful harm in a wider sense, thus of course including important parts of criminal law. Contract law is also covered by principles of restorative justice, as wrongful breach of contract is to be repaired or compensated for as well.

Once the elephant is in full view, other reasons not to give up actors' liability follow naturally. For example: wrongfulness of harm in terms of wrongful offenders' conduct is now more easily determined, as such offenders are now to be taken to task. Remember that wrongful harm only is to be compensated for (section 7). Also, reasons for liability easily transcend spheres of wrongful harm. Thus in family law, contract law and related fields not all issues of individual liability can be done away with without giving up seemingly essential parts of the law. What would a contract be worth without proper identification of parties? Or: how are the consequences of non-performance to be determined without appeal to possible force majeure? This presupposes identification and qualification of contract parties (see again section 7). Or: what should be done with last wills without identifiable beneficiaries? Still, not many vexing problems of evidence and proof may arise in these areas.

This may be different in other spheres, wherein actor identification may serve broadly preventive and directive purposes, such as in traffic law and tax law. Reasonably safe and orderly road traffic seems scarcely imaginable without violators being fined or even punished from time to time, even if there were no direct harm at all. This inevitably saddles society with still more problems of evidence and proof.

It still remains an interesting question whether such additional reasons for actors' liability may be reduced to requirements of retribution as reparation. Traffic law may serve as an example. The preventive effect presupposes offender identification. But then, in principle, traffic rules serve road safety. So violating such rules implies potential or actual harm, to be repaired by offenders according to retributive justice. Sure enough this may be far-fetched, but not irrational for this reason alone. Anyway, the need for retribution as reparation by offenders is the main reason why actors' liability and concomitant issues of evidence and proof cannot be abolished in principle.

Lastly, and probably going without much further saying, no objection against collecting evidence and proof may ever hold good against directly preventive measures as well. That is, if properly identified actors are reasonably expected to do wrong, ranging from the threat of a spontaneous punch to posing seriously psychopathic dangers, reasonable measures may of course be taken against them.

9. Restorative Consequences for (Standards of) Evidence and Proof

So issues of evidence and proof are back again in full, to stay this time. Not just restorative justice in a wide sense, but also specific fields ranging from family law to traffic law are inconceivable without actor identification and concomitant issues of evidence and proof. Seemingly convincing objections against (reliable) establishment of evidence and proof (sections 3–6) seem to be outclassed in their turn.

So what does restorative justice mean for (standards of) evidence and proof? What kinds of evidence and proof are indispensable and what may be done away with? First, identification of offenders is really necessary in cases of mala fide wrongful harm, implying victims' rights to compensation by offenders themselves. This of course covers only a small part of positive tort law, law of contract and other law. Thus the greater part of it, and its attendant industries of evidence and proof, may still be replaced by public insurance schemes and the like (section 7).

Second, the actual administration of criminal justice does not seem to comply with restorative standards at all, focused as it is on punishment as infliction of harm instead of victims' compensation. On the other hand, such infliction of pain, however unjustified otherwise (see section 3), may still satisfy some victims to some extent and may thus qualify as rather imperfect realization of aspects of restorative justice (at a huge price). Abolition of punishment is not to be expected in the near future anyway. Thus evidence and proof as preconditions for conviction still reign here as well.

Restoring issues of evidence and proof in the name of restorative justice implies not just actor identification, but determination of malice and negligence as well. This may not lead to serious problems in civil law adjudication, based as it is on normative standards of conduct not referring to states of mind but to outwardly visible effects only. (So if somebody subjectively, completely unwittingly and against all good intentions destroys somebody else's antique Ming period King Kong vase, actor liability follows naturally. This is based on the rule that such conduct is not normally to be expected.) In criminal law, however, more factual concepts of malice and negligence and their applications are notoriously elusive, whether determined dialogically (see sections 5 and 6) or otherwise. (Which of course is one reason why such concepts are more or less abandoned in civil law.)

Perspectives of restorative justice may still point in the right direction here. If restorative justice is to be realized for victims, then malice and negligence ought to be seen as they are from the victims' perspectives in the first place. Of course individual victims are not to judge the criminal liability of 'their' offenders. It is prototypical or counterfactual victims' or better: normal persons' judgements that really count. Forensic/scientific judgements may be rather different to 'common' judgements on malice and negligence at least in the following respect. Common judgement differentiates between doing (or abstaining from doing) something and being a victim of visibly superior forces. Given authorship, malice, negligence and liability follow naturally. Thus somebody hitting somebody else in the face presupposes some or other kind of intent, or reasoning, at least in estimating distances, and so on. This may be rather complex to establish. On the other hand it may be relatively easily distinguished from a movement of the fist induced by some or other heteronomous force, such as an attack of epilepsy or even somebody else moving the fist to hit a third party.

Malice and negligence as related to outwardly visible authorship as distinct from what befalls somebody may be less difficult to establish than forensic psychiatric notions of inner forces, movements, their determination by different kinds of inner and outer factors and so on. So if there is truth in restorative justice, such principled simplification of one major problem of evidence and proof may be relevant for positive criminal procedure as well (see also Kaptein 2004). Problems will remain of course, both in principle and in practice: think of cases of offenders' inner compulsion, not visible to any victims at all, and many more vexing issues. And what is the relationship between observers' judgements on authorship as distinct from being a victim of superior forces, and dialogical determination of liability on the other hand?

10. *In Dubio Abstine*

Problems of evidence and proof start with material law to be applied to facts. So reforming the law may lead to the solution of problems of evidence and proof. Thus parts of tort and other law may still be more effective without offender identification and its concomitant issues of evidence and proof, in as far as is compatible with restorative justice. Even apart from that, there may be good reasons to abolish the legal war on drugs, to decriminalize other kinds of conduct, to radically simplify tax law (think of the long-standing project to replace all different taxes by a single VAT system, as pleaded for by Rawls (1999) and others), and to do away with so many more material laws not really serving essential rights and interests. (Think here of family law as well. Abolishment of rights of inheritance will do away with many problems of evidence and proof, financial and otherwise, still apart from avoidance of so many more conflicts.) Less law? Fewer problems of evidence and proof. (This is not to be expected in the near future of course. In fact, bodies of law are growing, not just in the books: 'the legal pathology of autopoietic elephantiasis'.)

Still, more law in the books may lead to less law in action, in a positive sense. For law consists not just of compulsory rules, but also of legal possibilities and opportunities of so many different kinds. This ranges from buying something (or not), contracting in general and in special cases, being able to start a legally recognized company to suing a non-performer, or tortfeasor, or even prosecuting a suspect, or leaving them alone, and so on. Different kinds of reasons then, not all of them legal of course, may dictate what to do with the law. Such decisions presuppose factual evidence in their turn: given the facts of case x, and legal options y, z is to be done in terms of realizing the law. (This may lead to problems of evidence and proof on a meta-level as well.)

Citizens may be reasonably expected to make use of legal opportunities in their own bona fide best interests (though they may of course be mistaken in this). One kind of reason to be considered by them is, again: what are the costs of fact-finding, financial and otherwise (sections 3ff.)? Lawyers' roles as 'gatekeepers', discouraging clients from starting all-too-expensive procedures are not always duly realized here.

Officials on the other hand are expected to realize law and right (and general interests). So legal possibilities and opportunities ought to be made use of in terms of justice and right in the first place. Determination of this in the complex reality of positive law is to be based on the related costs of evidence and proof as well. In more than a few conflicts over disputed or disputable facts the best solution after all may well be to simply leave things alone.

However much at least some kinds of evidence and proof may be indispensable in principle (section 8), in practice, and all things considered, the costs of obtaining evidence and proof may well outweigh any other considerations. Criteria of proportionality and subsidiarity ought to be applied here. Anyway – and to be stressed one more time – the one overwhelming advantage of doing nothing is the certainty of letting the innocent (criminally or otherwise) go free. Again: protection of the innocent against any undeserved legal burden is not to be balanced against any other interests and rights.

There are indeed very many ways to forestall legal problems and thus problems of evidence and proof, some of them patently obvious but still not widely practised. First and foremost (and more or less recalling stoic wisdom as briefly sketched in section 3): harm is to be dealt with and borne without bothering others in the first place. Contemporary claim cultures have really inflated several kinds of liability for any kind of harm. The law seemed to be there to thwart or at least channel vindictiveness, but claim cultures have deformed the law into an instrument of the same vengeful vindictiveness. Such vicious circles need to be broken. Also, doing any wrongful harm is to be avoided in the first place. But if the harm is still done, sincerely offered and heartfelt apologies may even make reparation redundant. Still, voluntary retribution through reparation may forestall conflict formalization and the prices to be paid for it.

Though the administration of criminal justice may not be abolished this or any other way, it should still be remembered that punishment as the infliction of pain (as is the unhappy essence of the actual regime) ought to be *ultimum remedium* only. Crimes which are not just to be left alone may be dealt with by some or other form of mediation. Even its preventive effects, through offenders' confrontation with the consequences of their crimes, may be superior. Though there may still be discussion about degrees of malice or negligence, suspects' readiness to participate in mediation readily solves problems of evidence and proof related to the identification of the offender. (Although plea bargaining remains dangerous of course). Many more human conflicts and their attendant problems of evidence are better solved by keeping a distance from the law and its dire prospects of legal proof.

There are only so many problems of evidence and proof as there is law, material and otherwise, considered worthy of actual application to some or other historic or future human reality. Principled opportunism in these matters ought to be the rule, then. Legal evidence and proof are to be pursued only when no other good solutions of the problems at hand are in sight. If such evidence and proof are still to be established, all reasonably available means to find the truth of the matter ought to be used.

So there are always at least two questions. First, are evidence and proof to be pursued at all? Second, and only if so, what really happened (or is bound to happen)? If evidence and proof are to be established after all, never try just to win any case. Be as precise and objective as possible. These standards are mainly what the rest of the book is about.

References

Barnett, R.E. and Hagel, J. (eds) (1977), *Assessing the Criminal: Restitution, Retribution, and the Legal Process* (Cambridge, MA: Ballinger Publishing Company).

Bentham, J. (1812), *An Introductory View of the Rationale of Evidence: For the Use of Non-Lawyers as well as Lawyers*, in Bowring and Mill (eds).

Bowring, J. and Mill, J. (eds) (1843), *The Works of Jeremy Bentham*, vol. 6 onwards (Edinburgh: William Tait).

Dershowitz, A. (1995), *The Abuse Excuse* (New York: Little, Brown & Company).

Flew, A.G.N. (ed.) (1951), *Logic and Language* (Oxford: Basil Blackwell).

Gray, C.B. (ed.) (1999), *The Philosophy of Law: An Encyclopedia* (New York and London: Garland Publishing).

Hart, H.L.A. (1948), 'The Ascription of Responsibility and Rights', *Proceedings of the Aristotelian Society*, 171–194, also in Flew (ed.).

Kaptein, H.J.R. (1999), 'Causation, Criminal', in Gray (ed.).

—— (2004), 'Against the Pain of Punishment: On Penal Servitude and Procedural Justice for All', in Kaptein and Malsch (eds).

Kaptein, H.J.R. and Malsch, M. (eds) (2004), *Crime, Victims and Justice: Essays on Principles and Practice* (Aldershot: Ashgate Publishing).

Modderman, A.E.J. (1864), 'Straf, geen Kwaad' (Amsterdam: inaugural lecture).

Nietzsche, F. (1887), *Zur Genealogie der Moral*, in Slechta (ed.).

Parliament of New Zealand (2001), Injury Prevention, Rehabilitation, and Compensation Act, Public Act 2001 No. 49, Date of Assent 19 September 2001.

Rawls, J. (1999), *A Theory of Justice*, 2nd Edition (Boston, MA: Belknap Press of Harvard University Press).

Slechta, K. (ed.) (1966), *Nietzsche: Werke in drei Bänden*, vol. II (München: Carl Hanser).

Strawson, P.F. (1962), 'Freedom and Resentment', *Proceedings of the British Academy*, also in Strawson 1973.

—— (1973), *Freedom and Resentment, and Other Essays* (London: Methuen).

Supreme Court of The Netherlands, '*Karamus* v. *Nefalit*' (31 March 2006, RvdW 2006, 328).

Szasz, T.S. (1977), 'Psychiatric Diversion in the Criminal Justice System: A Critique', in Barnett and Hagel (eds).

Wagenaar, W.A., Koppen, P.J. van and Crombag, H.F.M. (1993), *Anchored Narratives: The Psychology of Criminal Evidence* (London: Harvester Wheatsheaf).

Woffinden, B. (1988), *Miscarriages of Justice* (Sevenoaks: Hodder and Stoughton).

Chapter 2

The Fabrication of Facts: The Lure of the Incredible Coincidence

Ton Derksen and Monica Meijsing

1. Introduction: The Charge, the Conviction and Three Reasoning Instincts

The nurse Lucia de B.[1] was convicted by the Court of Appeal[2] in The Hague, The Netherlands, for seven murders and three attempted murders, with the penalty of life imprisonment. This conviction is backed by the Supreme Court of The Netherlands to the present day. She had been charged by the prosecution with 13 murders and four attempted murders. The police examined a total of some 30 allegedly suspicious cases. Yet there was little evidence apart from the fact that at the hospital where it all started, quite a number of resuscitations happened during the nurse's shifts. Then, after one more resuscitation, it was felt that all this could not be just a coincidence.

Very early in the process a quantification was given to the uneasy feeling that proportionally there were too many resuscitations during the nurse's shifts. The probability that such a coincidence could have happened by mere accident was calculated as 1 in 7 billion,[3] and somewhat later as 1 in 342,000,000. With that number out in the open the general notion was that what had happened could not be just an accident. The nurse definitely had to be a serial killer, even if no one had any further evidence.

This notion was in fact the driving force in the whole judicial process. It coloured the perception of the hospital, the medical experts, the prosecution and

1 See also Van Lambalgen and Meester 2004; Meester et al. 2007; Gill et al. 2008.

2 In the Dutch legal system, courts of first instance determine both the facts and the extent of the punishment. There is no jury. After a conviction, appeal is possible at a Court of Appeal. This court has a second look at the (alleged) facts and determines the degree of punishment all over again. A further, higher appeal at the Supreme Court is – in essence – only about the proper application of the law and legal procedure. The prosecution presents a *requisitoir* (final argument) to the court and after the reaction of the defence lawyers (*pleitaantekeningen*, pleadings) they present their reply (*repliekaantekeningen*, rebuttal of the pleading) to which the lawyers reply in their turn with their *dupliek*. As expert of the defence, one of the authors had access to these documents, as well as to the PVs (*proces verbaal* – official police report) of the case.

3 This is the American billion, to wit 7,000,000,000.

both the district court and the Court of Appeal. And it fabricated a whole series of incriminating facts which inexorably led to the conclusion.

In the first part of this paper (sections 1–7) we will document the driving force of the Incredible Coincidence, the disbelief of people that the spectacular coincidence was just a coincidence. We also examine the fabrication of the facts that resulted from this disbelief. In the second part we expose the statistical elaboration of this idea as it was presented before the court. We shall detect also in the statistical elaboration that the facts were manhandled. Careful attention to the facts would have yielded a very different outcome. Actually, when all the facts are in, the coincidence shrinks drastically. Nothing particularly shocking remains. So there is every reason to think that the remaining coincidence is just that – a coincidence.

Throughout the process we see three reasoning instincts at work:[4] (1) the Small Chance Instinct which makes us pay little attention to the small chances of p occurring and automatically turn to the belief that p has not occurred; (2) the No Smoke without Fire Instinct, which caused colleagues of the nurse to get worried about those many incidents during her shifts, and which later on caused the general public to be content with the verdicts of the courts in spite of the shaky evidence (someone convicted of so many murders must be a murderer); and (3) our instinct to pay little attention to base rates (in non-everyday situations). These instincts are natural in the sense that they guide our cognitive housekeeping. They yield quick conclusions which usually are evolutionarily good enough. Unfortunately, in the case of Lucia de B. their influence was disastrous.

2. The Smoke and the Fire

The nurse Lucia de B. was indeed convicted for seven murders and three attempted murders. So what was the evidence? No one saw the nurse do anything suspicious, there were no needles or bruised skin or any other incriminating evidence, there were just incidents during the nurse's shifts. But there were lots of them, too many – or so it was felt.

In spite of the public awareness that there was little evidence, the reaction was: with so many alleged murders and so many suspicious incidents, the nurse must have committed at least some murders. The prior concern was that society should be protected. So it did not matter that in many cases proof was somewhat shaky and not beyond reasonable doubt. There was so much smoke, there must be a fire.

Here we see a human reasoning instinct in full operation: where there is smoke, there must be fire. Any careful judicial examination may contain a mistake or two but it cannot have been mistaken in all 10 (attempted) murder convictions. Moreover the court had dropped seven (attempted) murder charges. So it must

4 They are related to the heuristics of Nisbett and Ross (1980). We prefer the term 'instinct' as the term 'heuristic' suggests too much conscious awareness of the operation.

have looked carefully into the cases. Let us rejoice that a murderer is behind bars and let us not worry about some small flaws in the administration of criminal justice.

Earlier the same No Smoke without Fire Instinct had done its work in the hospital: Lucia was present at so many incidents (resuscitations) within such a short period of time (two years and especially during the last year as a qualified children's nurse) that people became suspicious. Actually, Lucia herself had become distressed by all those resuscitations during her shifts and she had talked about it with her superior and the hospital's social worker. The official reaction to her had been of a practical nature: such a concentration of incidents often happens and it happens to almost every nurse once in a while, so don't worry, it will be over and done with. The problem for Lucia was that the series of incidents did not stop in time. When on 4 September 2001, during Lucia's night shift, yet another child had to be resuscitated and died, a colleague told her superior in the morning that she was worried because 'during the two years that Lucia had worked at the Juliana Children's Hospital she had been present at nine resuscitations'[5] and she also remembered an incident in a previous hospital in which Lucia had been involved. Though there was no incriminating evidence whatsoever against Lucia – and the incident mentioned had nothing to do with Lucia – the train took off at that moment. At the end of the day the police had been informed and the next day the interrogations started. There was too much smoke; there had been too many incidents during her shifts.[6]

3. A Chance that Was Too Small

Apart from this No Smoke without Fire Instinct, there was an idea that soon became the driving force of the process, namely the idea that the chance that the concurrence of all those resuscitations during one nurse's shifts was just a coincidence was so extremely small that it was incredible that the coincidence was just that – a coincidence.

This chance-argument became explicit in the thinking of the managing director of the hospital, Mr. S. He made some statistical calculations (an amateurish

5 As reported by Tony B., head of intensive care PV 5 September 2001. B. herself told the police: 'I can tell you that speaking from my experience nine resuscitations in medium care are many for one nurse' and 'I can tell you that in our hospital it was generally known that Lucia had been present at many resuscitations.'

6 After about one year the prosecution thought it had found evidence for digoxin poisoning and chloral hydrate poisoning. It was especially the alleged digoxin poisoning which later on provided the crucial evidence next to the statistical reasoning. We refer to Derksen 2006, for both scientific and clinical reasons why there cannot have been digoxin poisoning. The alleged chloral hydrate poisoning was rather a case of overmedication. The baby recovered after several hours.

calculation of sorts, as he himself called it) and came up with an extremely small chance. After that everybody knew for sure: the coincidence is not just a coincidence, Lucia must have had a hand in the incidents.

Let us remind ourselves here that it is quite common that people die in hospitals and that, as the social worker knew and all nurses know, sometimes there will be an accumulation of deaths during somebody's shifts.[7] Should we conclude that all of them are serial killers? So what was the specific argument in Lucia's case, or rather what made the minds lean so quickly and so inexorably in one direction?

The answer is – we think – the Small Chance Instinct, a basic human intuition based on the Small Chance Principle:

> when the chance is very small that p will occur (where *p* stands for some statement), then it is reasonable to believe that p will not occur.

It is a principle that works in everyday situations. For example, when we go to the beach and we see written in the wet sand a message 'I'll be back in a moment', we do not consider the possibility that this is a freak cooperation between the sand and the forces of wind and water. The chance that such a message would be formed is so small that we may reasonably pay little attention to it.

It is not just at the normative level that this Small Chance Principle operates. It also operates in the domain of actual belief. Doubt in such a case does not occur – unless the risks involved get very high. The winner takes all. This is a basic principle of actual belief which parallels the normative Small Chance Principle.

As long as there is no specific reason for distrust, we automatically use the Small Chance Principle, and we feel justified in applying it. We shall see that the principle needs to be supplemented. The Small Chance Instinct which makes us pay little attention to the small chances (that is, makes us apply the Small Chance Principle automatically) is not, however, 'aware' of these complexities and conditions for proper use. The Small Chance Instinct may well lead us astray. We will see that the Lucia situation is one in which this instinct ran amok.

During Lucia's trial the Small Chance Instinct ran the show. The chance that all those incidents happened during one person's shifts just by accident was too small for comfort. That is what the nurses, the doctors and the managing director of the Juliana Children's Hospital in The Hague believed and this is what in the end the prosecution, the district court and the Court of Appeal took for granted.

The hospital installed its own research team that re-examined all cases of death since Lucia began working at the Juliana Children's Hospital. The team found 10 suspect incidents (resuscitations, deaths, poisonings) during one year, and the nurse was present during all of them. The extremely small chance that this would happen by accident, while the nurse worked only 142 of all 1029 shifts, made it

7 For instance, a nurse wrote in the Dutch newspaper *NRC Handelsblad* (20 March 2004) that during her two-year training period she was present at 30 cases of death, while a colleague did not see any death.

incredible that what had happened was just an accident. On 17 September, 13 days after the last incident, the media were informed by the hospital and excuses were offered to the parents, leaving no doubt in the public's eye that the hospital had spotted a monstrous murderer.

We do not know what actual number occupied the minds of the people in the hospital, but we do know that the police soon talked about a chance of 1 in 7,000,000,000. The police told Lucia's family: 'Look, the chance that Lucia has not committed these crimes is 1 in 7,000,000,000, and there are only 6,000,000,000 people in the world. So she must be the murderer.'

In the meantime three other hospitals in The Hague, where Lucia had worked previously, had been warned. They were asked to investigate whether during Lucia's shifts there had been inexplicable incidents.[8] And these hospitals soon complied. The Red Cross Hospital found that seven deaths during Lucia's shifts turned out to be suspicious once their status was reconsidered. The Leyenburg Hospital discovered two cases serious enough to be prosecuted, while 12 deaths raised enough doubt for the police to look into these cases. The Penitentiary Hospital brought in one more death.

Such a coincidence had never been shown before. The assistance of an official statistician was called for. The data of three wards were sufficiently reliable for statistical treatment (or so it was thought). Then the expert called in by the court, E., calculated the chance that Lucia would – by accident – have been present at 'her' incidents at these three wards. He found the shockingly small chance of 1 in 342,000,000. Then everybody knew for certain that Lucia must be a dangerous serial killer. The idea that the concurrence was just an accident was preposterous. Lucia herself must have caused this abundance of incidents.

The press described her as the Angel of Death. Her name was even mentioned in international newspapers. And what about the hospital that had admitted to five murders and five attempted murders, what about the parents whose wounds had been reopened, and what about the newspapers that had been notified about a serial murderer in Dutch hospitals? One had to come up with a killer and because of the incredible coincidence everybody knew before the trial even started that Lucia was the killer.

There was one problem, and a serious problem at that: there was very little evidence, if any, beyond the seemingly spectacular coincidence. So the prosecution set out to collect independent evidence, yet all the time it was the Incredible Coincidence (1 in 342,000,000) that bewitched the minds and was the driving force behind the process.

---

8 Mr T., board member of the Leyenburg Hospital, testimony 10 February 2004: 'We started our search at the request of the police and the prosecution. Questions to be asked were: notification of all patients who died during the shift of the defendant or just after her shift, resuscitations during the shifts of the defendant or just after her shift.'

4. The Two Little Engines that Could Not

The prosecution had pinned its hope on two cases that stood out: only in those two cases had the prosecution managed to specify the (alleged) toxic substance supposedly causing the (alleged) poisoning (digoxin, chloral hydrate) and only in those cases could they give some evidence for their charge of poisoning – or so it was claimed. The other cases were merely medically inexplicable incidents, which either had been classified as natural deaths at the moment of death, or as non-suspicious incidents. The prosecution called the two allegedly strong cases their two locomotives which had to pull the other cases (the wagons) to the station called 'proof beyond reasonable doubt'.

One of the authors has already argued in detail that these two little engines could not.[9] The allegation of the digoxin poisoning is fraught with problems. During the time that the nurse is supposed to have administered the poison two medical doctors were examining the baby.[10] And the charge of an *acute* digoxin poisoning is refuted or at least made severely questionable by the non-contracted state of the heart of the baby at the autopsy[11] and by the absence of any digoxin in the liver even though digoxin was found in the kidneys.[12] This is considered

9 See Derksen 2006.

10 The Court of Appeal noticed that the monitors of the baby patient, Amber, had not worked during the very 30 minutes during which – in their reconstruction – the poison (digoxin) must have been administered, and that Lucia was the nurse responsible for the baby patient. So the court concluded that Lucia must have switched off the monitors during those 30 minutes to make sure that she could safely commit her hideous crime. This coincidence (monitor inoperative during the crucial period and Lucia being in control of these monitors) could not have been an accident! But this argument is based on readings of the trend tables of the monitor. Since the trend table indicates the readings only every 15 minutes, there is an apparent time window of 30 minutes when one such reading drops out. The court uses this time window to settle the time of the examination of the baby by two medical doctors. But the continuous trend graphs tell us that the actual time opening is only six minutes (time for a diaper change), much too short for the examination, which lasted some 20 minutes. So we have to find another time frame for the medical examination. According to the trend graphs there is just one such period, but that is the very period that the alleged poison administration had taken place according to the reconstruction of the court. So we find that at the very moment of the alleged murder two medical doctors are quietly examining the baby girl, and that the charge against Lucia is based on wilfully restricting the attention to the trend tables and neglecting the trend graphs.

11 In the case of acute digoxin poisoning, the heart is contracted. At the autopsy, some nine hours after the demise, this should still be the case. But the heart was not contracted, according to the coroner.

12 In June 2004 the remaining tissue and blood were examined by the 'Institut de Médicine Légale et de Médicine Sociale' (Strasbourg). It used a highly digoxin-specific HPLC-MS method. It found a digoxin level of 10.2 ng/ml in the kidney tissue, but repeated examination did not find any digoxin in the liver. Assuming (and following the prosecution's reconstruction of the alleged poisoning) that a fatal dose had been administered 60 minutes

an impossible (extremely unlikely) distribution of digoxin after one hour. So the locomotive driven by digoxin poisoning cannot even get going, let alone pull some eight wagons.

The second engine was fuelled by the allegation of chloral hydrate poisoning. But since the hospital prescribed the maximum amount (625 mg) for the boy in question, and allowed that two extra doses of that amount might be added – in case of restlessness – and the nurses complained about the restlessness of the boy, there is a real possibility of overmedication. Actually, there is evidence that on two consecutive days, shortly before the incident, the boy received a double dose. So we need much more than Lucia's presence to convict her for attempted murder.[13]

So the two engines that should, could not. It was the Incredible Coincidence that in fact carried all the weight.

5. The Incredible Coincidence Did It

If anything is responsible for the conviction it is the Incredible Coincidence, the coincidence of all those incidents during the shifts of one nurse. The chance that this would happen by accident is extremely small. In that sense the coincidence is spectacular or incredible. How small is the Incredible Coincidence? It does not matter much, it is extremely small anyway, whether it is 1 in 7,000,000,000, as the police first conjectured, 1 in 342,000000, as E. calculated for all the incidents or 1 in 9,000,000, as he initially calculated for eight incidents in the Juliana Children's Hospital.[14]

The coincidence is incredible in another sense as well: the chance that this spectacular/incredible coincidence would happen by accident is thought to be so small that it is *incredible* that the coincidence is *just* an accident (just a coincidence).

We have already seen the underlying argument, which depends on the Small Chance Principle:

---

before the baby's death, this is an extremely unlikely distribution of digoxin in the organs. Thirty minutes after an intravenous administration 50 per cent of the digoxin is still in the blood. Gradually most of it disappears to the organs, especially the heart, the kidneys and the liver. So after an injection with digoxin, after 30 minutes, one should expect a fairly high concentration in both the blood, the kidneys and the liver. The fact that nothing was detected in the liver suggests that the digoxin found was left over from therapeutic use. (The girl had been treated with digoxin therapeutically. The digoxin concentration in the kidney tissue was also much too small.)

13 This case is especially shocking because Lucia was the only one who was worried all day long, trying to convince the doctors to come and look at the patient. During the day two assistant doctors appeared and did not do much. When in the afternoon the medical specialist appeared she was really annoyed that she was not called earlier. (However, Lucia, being just a nurse, was not allowed to call the specialist). See Derksen 2006.

14 All these ratios were mentioned and taken seriously.

> the chance that the coincidence of all those incidents (resuscitations and deaths) during Lucia's shifts is just an accident is so small that, by the Small Chance Principle, we may reasonably pay little attention to that chance and reasonably believe that the coincidence is not just an accident (just a coincidence).

According to this principle we may then reasonably believe – and due to the Small Chance Instinct we will actually believe – that the coincidence is not just a coincidence. There must be some specific cause.

The statistical expert witness reminded the courts that this does not imply that Lucia must be the cause of the incidents. There may be another cause. For instance: (1) someone who worked the same shifts as Lucia may be responsible, or (2) Lucia worked many night shifts and more deaths occur during the night. But these alternative options were excluded quickly by the court – and by almost everyone else. So the practical and actual conclusion of the Coincidence Argument is: the coincidence is too incredible, Lucia must be the murderer.

So both E. and the court (and the general public at the time as well) assumed that there must be a specific cause for the coincidence. Someone, or some circumstance, must be responsible for it – or so they thought. But notice that the chance of winning a lottery is also extremely small – it simply happens to one of the ticket buyers – and in that case no one thinks that that person (or anyone else, for that matter) *caused* his or her winning. Coincidences do happen.

6. The Incredible Coincidence and the Fabrication of Facts

This Incredible Coincidence (combined with the Small Chance Instinct) was the driving force behind the process which led to Lucia's conviction for seven murders and three attempted murders. We will illustrate this by giving a brief history of the fatal influence of the Incredible Coincidence. It led to the fabrication of many incriminating facts.

6.1. The Nurse who Complained about Lucia on 4 September 2001

We have already mentioned the nurse for whom the death that night was one too many. Her superior, to whom she confided her suspicions, summarized her worries as follows:

> She really had the feeling that this could not just be a coincidence any longer.[15/16]

15 Tony B., head of intensive care, PV 5 September 2001.

16 PV Moniek 10 September 2001: 'If I consider how many resuscitations I had during all those years during my work and if I compare this with the number of resuscitations that Lucia had, then that just does not add up.'

6.2. The List of Lucia-related Incidents Circulating in the Hospital, 4 September 2001

The baby Susan died in the early morning of 4 September 2001. Already that very morning a list with nine (suspect) resuscitations during Lucia's shifts was circulating through the wards.[17] And this influenced many of the nurses. On 6 September 2001 nurse Martine told the police that she had 'an uneasy feeling about it. It was all too accidental.'[18] On 11 September 2001 nurse Ingrid declared:

> If I am honest about it, I think it is too much of a coincidence that within a few days' time two of Lucia's patients had to be resuscitated.[19]

She also reported that she overheard other nurses saying: 'Lucia again'.[20]

So we may assume that it is the coincidence (expressed by this list of resuscitations – and already known by many) which caused the general feeling of uneasiness about Lucia. For there were no concrete facts concerning the Juliana Children's Hospital which could be referred to. Although there is indeed a coincidence between Lucia's shifts and incidents, she was present at only one death.

Another nurse claimed to remember an incident in a previous hospital. This incident was examined, and it was just a mix-up. Someone else remembered some death in yet another hospital due to an improperly working infusion. Further examination led to Lucia's conviction of murder by the district court. However, during the trial before the Court of Appeal it turned out that during the alleged incident Lucia was not in the hospital; actually she had been off sick for three days. The murder charge was dropped, and the qualification 'murder' was dropped as well. The alleged murder became a case of natural death again, as it was before Lucia was accused of murder. No Lucia, no murder.

6.3. The Coordinating Paediatrician, Van M.

By 16:00 on the same 4 September the coordinating paediatrician, Van M., notified the police about the (attempted) murders. Apart from the death of A., whose natural

---

17 Tony, PV 5 September 2001: 'I can tell you that in our hospital it was generally known that Lucia had been present at many resuscitations. I do not know whether the number nine is correct. Marianne has told me about that number and it is this number that circulated in the hospital.'

18 Martine, PV 6 September 2001.

19 Ingrid, PV 11 September 2001.

20 For instance, K.B., team leader of Medium Care Unit-1, PV 5 September 2001: 'I had already witnessed a number of other incidents with Lucia. It went through my head once or twice 'Lucia again, those incidents happen really often around her.'

death certification had been changed into a non-natural death during the day, he informed the police about 'five similar [inexplicable] deaths'.[21]

6.4. The Police

That very evening the police visited the hospital. On 5 September the interrogations of the nurses started. Soon the police calculated the 1 in 7 billion chance that Lucia had not committed the murders. There being only 6 billion people, Lucia had to be the murderer. We need not comment on the crooked reasoning, but it is intriguing to see how quickly the police caught on as well: the coincidence was too large to be just a coincidence.

6.5. The Managing Director of the Juliana Children's Hospital, Mr S., Uses Statistics

During the evening of 4 September 2001, managing director Mr S. made some calculations.

> Using a computer program I have combined the number of deaths with a specific period and the shifts of Lucia and have done a statistical calculation. The result was that Lucia was involved in an extremely unlikely high number of these incidents.[22]

To the police he stressed:

> With this calculation nothing further happened. It only contributed to my own conviction of the need to notify the police.[23]

The statistical calculation contributed to the notification to the police of five possible murders and five possible attempted murders. The Incredible Coincidence made a huge difference.[24]

21 PV 4 September 2004.

22 PV 17 September 2001.

23 PV 17 September 2001.

24 Incidentally, we do not know why this general manager incriminated Lucia in the case of Ahmad (death) by telling the police that 'The evening shift ends at 23:30 … [and that] Lucia, having the evening shift that day, was presumably present at the death, in view of the moment of the death (23:30).' (PV 17 September 2001). As all the nurses knew, the evening shift ended at 22:45 and there was a transitional period till 23:15. Her colleague told the police that on that very evening Lucia left early (around 23:00).

6.6. The Independent Research Team of the Juliana Children's Hospital

The managing director, Mr S., did do more. He set up a committee to 'separate the rumours from the facts'.[25] In this committee the Incredible Coincidence played a crucial role as well. The story is that the committee first examined each death and resuscitation since Lucia started working in the Juliana Children's Hospital (without knowing if Lucia was on duty) to see whether the death (resuscitation) was non-natural after all, in spite of the fact that immediately after the death, all deaths had been declared natural. The committee came up with 10 cases, five non-natural deaths (possible murders) and five non-natural incidents (related to resuscitations, poisonings, or attempted murders). Subsequently the committee checked which nurses were on duty. It found out that Lucia was always present. After finishing the research, the committee asked an outside expert to evaluate their findings.

There may well be some doubt about the alleged anonymity with which the deaths and resuscitations were examined. Remember that at the very start of the crisis in the hospital the paediatrician Van M. informed the police that beside baby Susan there were already five other suspect cases and that at that time a list of nine Lucia-related incidents was circulating in the hospital. So it is hardly credible that the research team consisting of doctors from the ward did not know whether Lucia was involved or not, when it examined a specific incident. And indeed there is further indirect evidence that they knew and that their judgement, however sincere, was influenced by the Incredible Coincidence.

One would think that the issue here was the possible non-natural status of the deaths and resuscitations. Yet the outside expert who was consulted,[26] Professor V., a paediatrician himself, tells us differently and very illuminatingly:

> The first question that I was asked was: is it more than a coincidence that five children died and that four children had to be resuscitated?[27]

The next worry is that, with the Incredible Coincidence apparently at the back of their minds, the committee moved more easily to a non-natural death (and resuscitation) when Lucia was involved and that, being very worried about a possible serial killer in the hospital, it thus fabricated some new facts. There is some indication that this happened.

For example, the committee claimed that the death of baby Susan must have been non-natural because her heart was in excellent shape. This is a 'fact' that continued to play a role in the discussion. But at the moment that the committee

---

25 PV 17 September 2001.

26 He was not quite such an independent expert as he knew the leader of the research team very well indeed. This questions the independence, not the integrity, of his judgement.

27 Testimony 12 February 2004.

took the excellent condition of baby Susan's heart for granted, the coroner had already written that the heart was dilated (which indicates heart weakness) and that the death could have been caused by heart problems.[28] He declared that for him 'it was hard to understand that the declaration of a natural death was changed into a declaration of non-natural death some hours later'.[29]

Another fact was inexplicably introduced when the committee decided that Lucia had shown non-professional behaviour just before the death of baby Tom. She combined two actions, namely measuring blood pressure and administering an inhaler. None of the nurses present objected to this behaviour; actually it was fairly common. So the fact that Lucia's behaviour was non-professional was manufactured by the committee itself. And because of this so-called non-professional behaviour – no other argument was ever mentioned in this case – the committee decided that the death of baby Tom was non-natural.

There is also some doubt about the consistency of the committee's judgements about incidents, the outcome depending on Lucia's presence or absence. For instance, the committee decided that the resuscitations of baby John on 20 December 2000 and on 1 March 2001 were suspect. But baby John's resuscitation on 10 October 2000, which was very similar to that of 20 December 2000 (during the resuscitation John's heart never stopped beating and John did not need any heart massage) remained a natural incident. Why? The only difference is that Lucia was not present. The resuscitation is never mentioned and it was not counted among the statistical data of incidents outside Lucia's shifts, a crucial category in the statistical test used by expert E.[30] Whether a resuscitation is suspect seems – at least in part – to depend on the presence or absence of Lucia.

Another case: why is baby Harry's comatose state on 25 January 2001 due to a suspected choral hydrate poisoning, while baby John's comatose state on 6 June 2000 due to chloral hydrate is not? The concentration of chloral hydrate was not measured in John's case but the visiting doctor expressed his worries in the medical files. Again, does Lucia's absence make the difference?

One more case: why did the committee call the alleged incident of Sadia on 18 January 2001 suspect when she only stopped breathing for less than a minute and started breathing after some physical assistance? Was it because Lucia was present? No one else saw anything suspicious here. Yet the hospital notified the police of a possible non-natural resuscitation.

Here we run into another general cause for concern: as regards each of the allegedly suspect incidents (suspect according to the hospital) there were always medical experts who declared before the court that the death (resuscitation) was natural rather than non-natural. Actually, in most cases most medical experts believed in a natural death or resuscitation. So the judgement of the committee

28 Testimony 19 February 2004, p. 11: 'My conclusion is ... that it is not wholly excluded that the serious congenital defects [of the heart] are the cause of the death.'

29 Testimony 19 February 2004, p. 11.

30 We will discuss this test, Fisher's Exact Test, in sections 7–10.

that the incidents were suspect is not undisputed and hence not obvious and far from objective. For the same reason the allegations against Lucia lack an objective base.

The research team emphasized that the examination was not suspect-driven. We do not question the good faith of the committee, but when we look at the actual situation it is hard to ignore the strong influence of the Incredible Coincidence.

6.7. Medical Experts in Court

The court's judgment was guided by the judgements of the medical experts. But at least some of the crucial medical judgements turned out to be co-determined by the Incredible Coincidence. They were not just medically motivated. Thus the Incredible Coincidence haunts even the arguments of the medical experts. We will give five examples in which the coincidence is explicitly mentioned.

6.7.1. Paediatrician Professor V. Professor V. was asked to examine the report of the Juliana Children's Hospital research committee, but he was also an expert witness for the district court and the Court of Appeal. Speaking about all of the incidents in the Juliana Children's Hospital he testified:

> The point is here that it happened so often with so many children ... Each incident viewed individually, it is possible and cannot be excluded that a child with such a medical history dies suddenly without a clear cause of death.[31]

That is to say, looked at individually the deaths and resuscitations would not have raised enough questions to notify the police. Individually each case could be understood as natural. Only in combination do the deaths and resuscitations turn suspect.

Professor V. explicitly recognizes the importance of the Incredible Coincidence:

> It is because of the medical situation of the children and the extremely unlikely statistical chance that one specific nurse was involved with every incident, that I deem it improbable that all these children have died a natural death.[32]

That is, from a purely medical viewpoint there was insufficient reason to regard the deaths as non-natural. When the court relied on Professor V.'s judgement, as it did in many cases, in fact the court was not relying on his medical expert knowledge. It relied on the Incredible Coincidence. Professor V. judged that six children in

31 Testimony 12 February 2004, p. 14.

32 It is an interesting question how V. could be so sure of the extremely unlikely statistical chance so early on in the process. Testimony 12 February 2004, p. 14. (*Requisitoir* before district court, p. 4.)

the Juliana Children's Hospital died a non-natural death. Since we have to remove the effect of the Incredible Coincidence, we have to discount six judgements of non-natural deaths.

6.7.2. Surgeon L., who Treated Mrs S. Surgeon L. also relied in his medical judgement on the Incredible Coincidence. This is of crucial importance as his allegedly medical judgement that Mrs S. died a non-natural death was used by the Court of Appeal to back *its* judgement that the death of Mrs S. was non-natural.

The court noted that on 27 August 1997 Lucia wrote in her diary: 'Today I gave in to my obsession.' That very day Mrs S. died during Lucia's shift. Surgeon L. testified that she died a non-natural death. So the court reasoned: the obsession is an obsession to kill very ill patients. Lucia denied this. She said the obsession was an obsession to lay tarot cards for patients. The psychiatrist and psychologist, who examined her for six months, concluded that her explanation was plausible. The court chose not to believe Lucia. It needed an obsession to kill as background support for all the convictions. But apart from the psychiatric report the court faced another major problem: six out of the seven medical experts in this case and two nurses stated very clearly and without any hesitation that the death of Mrs S. was a natural death. They may have been surprised at the precise timing of the death, but they did not have any qualms about the death itself.

The exception is surgeon L. At the time of her death (she was his patient) he was surprised about the exact moment of her death. He declared in court that he had expected her to live some more hours or days. Yet immediately after the death of Mrs S. he stated a natural cause of death in his letter to the family's general practitioner and told the chief nurse Van B. that he had no doubts about the case.[33] Only four years later, in 2001, did he change his opinion. He started to believe that the death was non-natural after all, when, as he clarified before the Court of Appeal in 2004,

> in the media attention was given to the inexplicable deaths in different hospitals in The Hague.[34]

This second and revised judgement is not a medically informed judgement at all of course. It crucially depends on the Incredible Coincidence.

That is, only after the incidents and inexplicable deaths had been in the newspapers did surgeon L. change his mind. His later judgement that Mrs S. died a non-natural death is determined by the force of the Incredible Coincidence. The medical facts known to him were insufficient for that judgement. So the alleged fact of Mrs S.'s non-natural death is fabricated, and it is fabricated on the basis of the Incredible Coincidence.

---

33 Pleading of the defence lawyers before the Court of Appeal. p. 92.

34 Testimony 11 May 2004.

6.7.3. Paediatrician S. at the Juliana Children's Hospital When paediatrician S. ordered an extensive blood test while Harry was in coma, she made her reliance on the Incredible Coincidence quite clear:

> You ask why I had my suspicions. It was not so much the death of Harry in itself but the piling up of crises, which occurred in the presence of the nurse Lucia.[35]
>
> I ordered this blood test because I did not understand the situation and because I had my suspicion against the nurse present, namely Lucia, who according to my knowledge had been present at many inexplicable death cases of children at Medium Care Unit 1.[36]

We do not suggest that the blood test should not have been ordered, but we note the reliance on the Incredible Coincidence in the decision-making of this medical specialist.

6.7.4. Medical director S. of the Free University Medical Centre The district court had asked medical director S. to comment on the medical condition of the elderly patients. Both the district court and the Court of Appeal judged that three of those patients were murdered by Lucia. The problem is that almost all the medical experts declared before the court that these deaths were natural. In two cases medical director S. agreed with the court that the deaths were (somewhat) suspect but in his argumentation he relied on the Incredible Coincidence:

> Although it is not generally uncommon that patients from this (elderly) group will be found dead in their beds, there is – in my judgement – an (accidental?) concentration of this kind of dying within a relatively brief period in one surgical ward.[37]

6.7.5. Paediatrician D. at the Juliana Children's Hospital Paediatrician D. was chairman of the research committee set up by the managing director Mr S. She too was struck by the coincidence between the many incidents (resuscitations) and Lucia's shifts:

> In the period that Lucia worked in our hospital, there was a striking number of resuscitations in the ward Medium Care Unit 1.[38]

And though – again – we do not cast doubt on the integrity of this medical specialist, we are surprised at the ease with which the conclusion of non-natural death is reached. In the case of patient Jaouad doctor D. complains that

35 Testimony 24 September 2004.

36 Testimony 24 September 2004.

37 Report 12 March 2002.

38 PV 7 August 2002.

> it is peculiar that the death was not entered by Lucia in the medical files.[39]

But (1) we do not know whether it was entered by Lucia as the relevant page is missing, and (2) another nurse claimed to have reported the death and complains to the police that the page has apparently been lost.[40] So, apart from the Incredible Coincidence, there is no reason whatsoever to hold Lucia responsible and imply that Lucia has something to hide. Yet it became an incriminating fact that was brought forward by the Court of Appeal in its argument for the conviction of Lucia.

6.8. The Prosecution before the District Court

The prosecution before the district court stressed the importance of the Incredible Coincidence.

> The picture painted by the witnesses was ever the same: the defendant was excessively often involved with cases of death and resuscitation.[41]

They quote the famous ratio of 1 in 342,000,000 purportedly describing the chance that the coincidence happened by accident. They add that though

> it cannot be proved [on this basis] that the defendant has in fact caused the incidents, but this calculation can show that it cannot be just an accident that the defendant was present at all these incidents.[42]

They quote with approval expert witness De M.:

> In view of the fact that the incidents occurred in four different hospitals and that no other cause can be inferred from the medical record and the testimony of the defendant, it has to be concluded that there is a causal relation between the occurrence of inexplicable cases of death and life-threatening incidents involving patients on the one side and the presence of the defendant in the four hospitals.[43]

The prosecution also fabricates a new fact. It states:

---

39 PV 7 August 2002.

40 Compare Jenny PV 27 September 2001 (Derksen 2006, p. 227).

41 *Requisitoir*, p. 2.

42 *Requisitoir*, p. 72. For the causal link between the presence of the defendant and the incidents the prosecution claims to have independent proof (*Requisitoir*, p. 73).

43 Testimony before the Court of Appeal, p. 73.

> From the declaration of the managing director Mr S. of the Juliana Children's Hospital it can be inferred that in the period from 1996 till the present day only five patients died at the ward MCU-1. At all five deaths the defendant was present. That is to say, during the last five years there have not been cases of death at which the defendant was not present. This cannot be just an accident.[44]

But the occurrence of only five deaths from 1996 till the present is not a fact! The ward changed its name on 9 November 1999 from IN-1 (Internal-1) to MCU-1. And it only changed its name. If with this knowledge we look at the period from 1996 till 2001, a very different picture emerges: in the three years 1996, 1997 and 1998, the years that Lucia did not work in MCU-1, there were seven cases of death in that ward. In the years 1999, 2000 and 2001, years that Lucia did work in MCU-1, there were six cases of death in that ward.[45]

What are we to make of the fact that in a period when a serial killer is supposed to be active in the ward, the number of deaths drops rather than increases sharply? The most plausible explanation is: there was no serial killer.

Note that technically the prosecutor did not lie. In the ward with the name MCU-1 there were just five cases of death.[46] But in the ward which was given the name MCU-1 in November 1999, there were 13 cases of death, seven deaths in the years that Lucia did not work there and six while she worked there.

6.9. The District Court

The district court is explicit about its dependence on the Incredible Coincidence and the Small Chance Instinct on which it is based:

> 11. The court judges that it follows from the probability calculation of the expert E ... that it should be deemed extremely improbable that the defendant was accidentally present at all the incidents in the Juliana Children's Hospital and the RKZ which she has been charged with. This calculation indicates therefore that it is highly likely that there is a connection between the conduct of the defendant and the occurrence of the incident mentioned.

---

44 Prosecution before the district court, *Requisitoir*, p. 73.

45 The reader may be confused about these six deaths and the five deaths mentioned by the prosecution. The answer is: there were five deaths from November 1999 till 9 September 2001.The sixth death during 1999–2001 was in March 1999, when the ward was still called Internal-1.

46 By the way, the prosecution charged Lucia with only four of those. Perhaps that should also have been mentioned, for clarity's sake.

6.10. The Prosecution before the Court of Appeal

In their case the prosecutors appeal to the big number (1 in 324,000,000) to convince the court of Lucia's guilt:

> In the meantime it is generally known that the suspicion which has led to the prosecution of Mrs de B. depends on the fact that in the last hospital she worked in, she was uncommonly often involved with suspect deaths and resuscitations. One has tried to give a better quantification to this 'uncommonly often'. For this purpose Mr E. has been approached ... From his calculations the general conclusion emerged that the fact that so many incidents occurred during the defendant's shifts is not compatible with mere accident.[47]

After the exclusion of some alternative explanations the Incredible Coincidence settles the guilt question for the prosecution.

The prosecutors also create a coincidence of their own. They do not feel embarrassed when they refer to their own 'shoddy, amateurish statistics':

> Finally [we] note that with respect to the poisonings the probability that there is an external factor in all these cases, or the need to search for a cause outside the defendant's conduct is so small that we may reasonably speak of an impossibility. Granted, this is a shoddy, amateurish statistics of sorts.[48]

Apparently, shoddy amateur statistics of sorts, even if its unreliable status is recognized publicly, is acceptable in the context of a murder charge with a possible conviction leading to lifelong imprisonment. The prosecutors do hope that the 'professional and expert statistical reports' support their claims.[49] So they recommend that the Court of Appeal take the statistical considerations 'as their starting point and guiding principle in their deliberation'.[50] The Incredible Coincidence could not have been clearer in their mind. And it apparently exculpates the use of their own shoddy and incompetent statistics, as long as this is self-acknowledged.

6.11. The Court of Appeal

The Court of Appeal claims that statistical considerations did not play any role in their considerations, but in fact they did, as the consideration in the court's verdict

---

47 *Requisitoir* by C.J.M.G. Strack and G.C. Haverkate, prosecution before the Court of Appeal, pp. 2–3.

48 Prosecution before the Court of Appeal, *repliekaantekeningen*, June 2004, p. 24.

49 Prosecution before the Court of Appeal, *repliekaantekeningen*, June 2004, p. 24.

50 Prosecution before the Court of Appeal, *repliekaantekeningen*, June 2004, p. 24.

demonstrates. For the court, the coincidence of seven incidents during the shifts of one nurse was deemed too improbable to be believed to be merely accidental.[51]

> 11.13 There is no plausible explanation for the fact that the defendant was involved in so many cases of death and life-threatening incidents.

This is not just a remark. It is part of their construction of 'proof' against Lucia de B.

7. The Incredible Coincidence Argument in its Statistical Version

We have seen that both the hospital and the judicial system shared the intuition that the coincidence of seven incidents during Lucia's shifts in the Juliana Children's Hospital could not just be a matter of chance. Lucia must have done it! But how can the reliability of this intuition be determined? The police and the prosecution asked E., a professor in psychology of law and erstwhile statistician, to work out the mathematics of the case.

E. started from the hypothesis that the coincidence of seven incidents and Lucia's shifts was a matter of chance. Call this the Chance Hypothesis. He then calculated how probable it was that such a coincidence of incidents (seven out of seven) within Lucia's shifts (142 out of 1029) would have occurred by chance. If that probability does not reach a certain limit (the significance level), then the Chance Hypothesis is rejected. In other words, the probability that the coincidence is just a matter of chance is deemed too small and it is accepted that what happened is not a matter of chance.

E. compares the situation with the drawing of balls (shifts) from a box. In the box there are 1029 balls, seven black balls (shifts with an incident) and 1022 white balls (1022 incident-free shifts). The probability that Lucia will draw a specific ball (shift) is the same for all balls (shifts), namely 1 in 1029. This is E.'s translation of the hypothesis that the seven incidents all occurred within Lucia's shift by chance. E. used Fisher's Exact Test to precisely calculate this probability.

---

51 Compare consideration 11.24 E in the construction of the proof. The Court of Appeal reminds the reader 'that seven cases of death and life-threatening incidents that occurred in the Juliana Children's Hospital happened in a relatively brief period (18 September 2000–4 September 2001)'.

Table 2.1 E.'s input data

Juliana Child Hospital, Medium Care Unit-1: 11 October 2000–9 September 2001	No incident	Incident	Total
shifts of Lucia	135	7	142
shifts without Lucia	887	0	887
total number of shifts	1022	7	1029

Fisher's Exact Test yields this result: in those circumstances the probability[52] that by pure chance someone would be present at seven out of seven incidents is 0.0000008370726, or 1 in 1,194,640.[53] This probability is way below the significance level that E. thought absolutely safe, which is 1 in 10,000. Actually he could not imagine that someone would disagree with him: 'In this case the coincidence is so improbable that I cannot imagine that someone could think that the coincidence is compatible with chance.'[54]

So the conclusion is: the Chance Hypothesis should be rejected. The coincidence is not a matter of chance. E. told the court that this conclusion does not imply that Lucia is guilty. There are some alternative explanations which have to be ruled out first. For example, it may be that Lucia had many night shifts and that during the night more people die, or someone else may have been with her at all those seven shifts. The court had no trouble in quickly getting rid of these alternatives.[55] It then concluded that the coincidence could not plausibly be explained in any other way than by assuming that Lucia was guilty of four murders and three attempted murders.

8. Problems with the Data

This statistical argument is plagued by many problems. Apart from serious problems with the data used, there are problems with the way E. used the method, and problems with the method itself.

52 Statisticians will tell you that it is a p-value and that these p-values may not be multiplied. See note 56.

53 Fisher's Exact Test calculates here the probability that by chance the person will be present at seven out of seven incidents, given that she has 135 out of 1022 shifts. Actually, it calculates the probability that she will be present at at least seven incidents. In this case there were exactly seven incidents (and no more), so 'at least seven incidents' comes to the same thing as 'seven incidents'. In the text I will not always mention the 'at least' clause.

54 E., testimony 29 January 2007, p. 11.

55 Verdict, consideration 10.13 and following considerations.

8.1. The Selection and Collection of the Data Were Biased

Three of the four hospitals involved were asked to search for incidents during Lucia's shifts. However, there was no determined search for incidents outside her shifts. And it is precisely these incidents outside her shifts which crucially determine how remarkable it is that Lucia 'drew' seven shifts-with-incidents. For example, with 40 shifts-with-incidents it is much less improbable that seven incidents occurred during Lucia's shifts.

The prosecution did not only neglect to search for incidents outside her shifts, it actually removed incidents which fell outside her shifts from the lists of incidents. This may at first sight be understandable from a lay person's point of view: the prosecution was concerned with its indictment against Lucia. What happened outside her shifts seemed to be irrelevant. Yet it is the Dutch Prosecutor's legal and explicit duty to serve the public interest, which includes the defendant's interest. Indeed prosecutors in The Netherlands are legally bound to put both incriminating and exculpatory evidence before the court. So if the prosecutor could surmise that incidents outside Lucia's shifts could be exculpatory, such incidents are relevant and should have been mentioned in court. From a statistical viewpoint these incidents are in fact very relevant indeed. Leaving them out of the calculation actually changes the chance that Lucia met with all these incidents during her shifts by accident from rather small to incredibly small. It changes neutral evidence into incriminating evidence.

We have examined the incomplete records available and found three new incidents outside Lucia's shifts, and five more in which it was not clear whether the incidents were within or outside Lucia's shifts. We also discovered from these records and from the *requisitoir* that only five of the seven incidents at the Juliana Children's Hospital fell within Lucia's shifts – one of these seven actually happened after her shift had ended and the other fell outside the relevant period as determined by the statistician. If one does statistics based on shifts, one should do it properly.

All this brings out that the data as used are quite unreliable. The least that can be done is to recalculate Fisher's Exact test on the basis of the new (less biased) data.

8.2. Data Were Restricted to Three Wards and Fifteen Months

There is another bias in the data which we cannot even begin to straighten out: the data used for the calculation concern only three of the five wards where Lucia worked, and only one year and three-and-a-half months out of the 11¾ years that she worked in those hospitals. The data of the other hospitals and other periods were not available, or so it was said. But in view of a possible life sentence one should have been worried about this limitation. There is now a risk that the alleged extremely small probability that the coincidence is a matter of chance is the result of highly specific collection of the data, namely of those data that stand out. Those periods are selected in which there are proportionally more incidents. Small wonder that we find more incidents than on average.

8.3. The Data Were Used Twice, Both in the Formulation of the Hypothesis and in the Testing of the Hypothesis

The situation is just as bad as it looks. The seven incidents in the Juliana Children's Hospital triggered the investigation. They led to the formulation of the hypothesis that Lucia might well have murdered patients in the Juliana Children's Hospital. But subsequently these data were used a second time to test that very hypothesis. This is just bad statistics. To encounter seven incidents during one's shifts is very improbable, but it may happen by chance. So we have to examine whether the coincidence is just a chance event, due to bad luck, or an indication of questionable conduct. But then we may not use the old coincidence again. We need to find other evidence.

An example may serve to clarify this. Suppose we find that Mr A. has won the lottery. Now, a priori, there is only a small probability of winning a lottery. Yet he won. It happens. But he may have cheated. To demonstrate that he cheated we cannot again point to his winning. We need other evidence, for example that he has won many other lotteries recently or that he had special contacts with the notary public who did the draw. You cannot use his winning per se as an argument that his winning was achieved with illegal means. In that case we should have to arrest all winners of lotteries.

This is ridiculous of course. But then a similar mistake is made in Lucia's case when she is first picked out as a possible murderer because of the seven incidents during her shifts and then sentenced because of these same seven incidents.[56]

9. Problems within the Method Used

Before the relevant probability using E.'s method is recalculated one adjustment is needed. E. calculated the probabilities related to three different wards, and then multiplied those probabilities. Richard Gill, professor of statistics at Leiden University, calls this a 'technical blunder', which 'biases the result against Lucia'.[57]

---

56 To compensate for the double use, E. made a *post hoc* correction. He multiplied the outcome of Fisher's Exact Test by 27, because in the period referred to by E. 27 nurses worked at Lucia's ward. We will not argue here why this is a wrong theoretical move. It should suffice that the number E. reached after this *post hoc* correction (27 x 0.0000008370726 = 0.0000226009602, or 1 in 44,246) is still way off compared to the 1 in 44 which emerges from a recalculation with the proper data.

57 See his personal website <http://www.math.leidenuniv.nl/~gill/lucia.html>, where he gives references to support his claim: 'A technical blunder further biases the

The inappropriateness of multiplying can be shown in a simple way. Suppose that the probabilities related to different hospitals were multiplied (which in fact is not the case). Now look what happens when a nurse changes hospitals. For her first hospital we calculate the probability that by chance she would encounter a certain number of incidents during her shifts. Suppose this probability is around one-third. Nothing remarkable has happened.[58] In the next hospital this history repeats itself, and so on. So far still nothing remarkable has happened. But then the prosecution starts to multiply all the probabilities of one-third. It will take some time but in the end the resulting probability will get below the significance level, and prosecutors may improve their career prospects with another brilliant catch: here is another nurse during whose shifts something so improbable happened that it cannot be a matter of chance. Bingo! Here we have a new serial killer, although her colleague, who stayed in the first hospital, may have encountered exactly as many incidents during her shifts.[59]

This is a travesty of reasoning of course, but it demonstrates that multiplying the probabilities of the different hospitals cannot be an acceptable move within the legal system: the mathematics alone makes murderers out of people. Nothing untoward needs to have happened, and yet the nurse who changes hospitals once too often will face a life sentence.

This then is a serious problem with the method as used by E.: the multiplication of the probabilities of the different hospitals and wards is both statistically and legally wrong.[60]

---

conclusion: combination of p-values by multiplication instead of by the easy "last resort" Fisher's method or the more appropriate Cochran–Mantel–Haenszel test; see the standard textbook Agresti (2002), website Categorical Data Analysis, and the accompanying manual Thompson (2006). ... Expert for the prosecution Henk Elffers, Professor at the University of Antwerp, senior-researcher at the Netherlands Institute for the Study of Crime and Law Enforcement (a friend, former colleague and co-author of mine from our Mathematical Centre days thirty years ago, before he moved to geography, economics, psychology and law) apparently does not know the meaning of p-value. He multiplies three independent p-values (from three wards where Lucia has worked) and appears to present the product as a p-value rather than using one of the well-known ways to compensate for the *number* of statistical tests being combined. This error biases the result against Lucia.

58 The nurse has eight-hour shifts.

59 Gill subscribes to this conclusion (on his previously mentioned website): 'E.'s method of combining wards by multiplying p-values is blatantly incorrect, since data from a large enough number of wards would make *any* nurse eventually guilty.'

60 The second problem is that E. assumed that the balls were all equally likely to be drawn. Richard Gill objects to this assumption: the balls were sticky. We should not assume that all nurses have the same chance to get shifts-with-incidents. He may well be right, but in a recalculation we do not need this extra complication. As we will see in a moment, the simplified version with equally sticky balls already yields a clear enough verdict: there is no statistical reason whatsoever to suspect Lucia because of the coincidence between incidents and her shifts.

10. Recalculation with Fisher's Exact Test

So both the data and the method have to be adjusted. With respect to the Juliana Children's Hospital we have to add two recently discovered incidents outside Lucia's shifts,[61] we have to remove two incidents from her shifts (incidents outside her shifts which had been wrongly treated as being incidents within her shifts), and we should not multiply the probabilities of the different hospitals.

Let us redo the calculation just for the Juliana Children's Hospital.

Table 2.2 Improved input data

Juliana Child Hospital, Medium Care Unit-1: 11 October 2000–9 September 2001	No incident	Incident	Total
shifts of Lucia	137	5	142
shifts without Lucia	883	4	887
total number of shifts	1020	9	1029

Fisher's Exact Test now yields this result: in these circumstances the probability that by accident someone would be present at (at least) five out of nine incidents is 0.003704, or 1 in 270. This probability is way above E.'s significance level of 1 in 10,000.

When the recalculation is done for all three wards, Fisher's Exact Test gives a chance of 1 in 44, and with a more sophisticated calculation (taking account of confounding factors) Richard Gill reaches an outcome of 1 in 9.

That is, in all calculations the Chance Hypothesis should not be rejected, it should be accepted. That is to say, in all calculations it should be accepted that the occurrence of the incidents during Lucia's shifts could have been a matter of chance.

11. Problems with the Method: The Wrong Question Is Being Asked

Note that on 4 September 2001, the day when the hospital and the police started investigations, there was no direct evidence of any murder. There was just a coincidence between incidents and Lucia's shifts, and the powerful intuition that this was very fishy. So a statistician was called in, and he was asked: could this coincidence just be a matter of chance?

The statistician reformulated this as:

61 The third recently discovered incident outside Lucia's shifts was in the Red Cross Hospital, not in the Juliana Children's Hospital.

> What is the probability that such a coincidence of incidents and shifts would occur by chance (given the number of Lucia's shifts and the total number of shifts)?

Or:

> Assuming the innocence of the nurse, what is the probability that there was such a coincidence of incidents and shifts by chance?

But this is the wrong question. We want to know:

> Given the coincidence, what is the chance that the nurse Lucia is innocent?

The complication is that E. answered the wrong question in such a way that it seemed to yield an answer to the right question (about Lucia's guilt or innocence). E. found that the probability that the coincidence was a matter of chance was below the significance level he set in advance. So he told the court: 'This cannot be a matter of chance.' He added that this did not prove that Lucia was the murderer. There were some alternative explanations of why the coincidence was not a matter of chance. However, the court had no trouble in getting rid of these alternative explanations. So E.'s question led to the conclusion that Lucia must be guilty. It seems the right question after all, for it gave the right conclusion – or so it seemed.

However, does E.'s conclusion 'This cannot be a matter of chance!' follow from his finding an extremely low probability that the coincidence was a chance affair?

Prima facie the implication seems to be self-evident. There is an extremely small probability (in E.'s calculation) that the coincidence occurred by chance. And it is an everyday rule of objectivity that if p is very unlikely, it is reasonable (in normal circumstances) to believe that p has not occurred. E. told the court that there was only a very small probability that the coincidence occurred by chance, so it is reasonable to believe that the coincidence was not a matter of chance. And after having rejected the alternative explanations, the court may conclude: Lucia is a serial killer.

Yet in spite of appearances the conclusion does not follow. Paid little attention are both the base rates and the probability of the opposite hypothesis, namely that a Dutch nurse is a serial killer.[62] Rather than using a theoretical argument to support this claim, we give two examples illustrating what went wrong.

The first example is that of Peter. In his parental home, during card games, he once had a number of terrific hands in a row. The chance that he would get such hands was incredibly small, say 1 in 44,000. (This is the chance E. calculates for

62 Human reasoners are notoriously prone to neglecting base rates; see e.g. Nisbett and Ross 1980; Tversky and Kahneman 1981.

the Juliana Children's Hospital alone, after correction.)[63] Given E.'s significance level of 1 in 10,000, we should reject the Chance Hypothesis (that Peter got these incredible hands by pure chance), and after having excluded alternative explanations (his mother gave him these cards intentionally), we conclude (following E.'s method) that Peter cheated.

But that is not what his family concluded. They just knew that he did not have the dexterity to cheat – he never was that handy. The probability that he cheated was therefore so small that they stuck to this conclusion: those incredible hands happened by accident. The Chance Hypothesis has a very small probability (1 in 44,000), but the probability of Peter's cheating is even smaller – or so they thought. What, after all, can be the probability that such a clumsy fellow as Peter has fiddled with the cards without anyone noticing?

Similarly in Lucia's case, even if the probability that all those incidents during Lucia's shifts occurred by chance is extremely small (which in fact is not the case), this in itself does not imply the conclusion that the coincidence is not a matter of chance. That depends on the probability of the alternative, namely that a Dutch nurse is a serial killer. So, apart from the fact that coincidences do happen, our first example brings out the following:

> E.'s conclusion 'The coincidence cannot be a matter of chance!' does not follow automatically from the extremely small probability that Lucia's coincidence happened by chance. The alternative may be even more improbable.

What is this probability of a Dutch nurse's being a serial killer? We have no idea, but we may reasonably assume that there have been very few serial killers among Dutch nurses throughout the years. As far as we know, Lucia is the only Dutch nurse who has been convicted as a serial killer, and we may assume further that serial killers would not go unnoticed too often. So let us take the ridiculously high estimate that every year there is a serial killer nurse in Dutch hospitals. There are 60,000 nurses in The Netherlands, so the probability that some nurse would be a serial killer is 1 in 60,000. (A more appropriate guess would be 1 in 600,000 – one every 10 years – or 1 in 1,200,000 – one every 20 years.)

Given these probabilities it is not so clear anymore why we should reject the Chance Hypothesis that Lucia's coincidence happened by chance. The probability that the coincidence would happen by chance (as calculated by Fisher's Exact Test) was small, but the probability of a Dutch serial killer nurse is even smaller.

This may seem very abstract but we can translate all this into a decision strategy for courts. And this is our second example. Assume that the courts follow E.'s strategy: If the probability of the coincidence (of incidents and shifts) happening by chance falls below the significance level of 1 in 10,000 and there is no other explanation for the coincidence, then convict the nurse to life imprisonment. We

63 There are two corrections: (1) seven instead of eight incidents; (2) a statistical correction applied by E. himself to mitigate the problem of double use of data.

have seen that E. calculated an extremely small probability. We have also seen that 1 in 44 or 1 in 9 are closer approximations of that probability in Lucia's case. A simple example: let us choose a probability of 1 in 44,000, the probability E. calculated for the Juliana Children's Hospital alone.

Let us now ask what this 1 in 44,000 implies for the number of nurses the court may expect to see. Remember there are 60,000 Dutch nurses. So each year – on average – there will be at least one nurse with seven incidents[64] during her shifts. Assuming that the hospitals are as vigilant as the Juliana Children's Hospital and thus do catch any nurse with a high coincidence between incidents and shifts, at least one innocent nurse will be convicted each year. With one serial killer nurse each year, the courts would also – on average – be confronted with one serial killer. This serial killer will also be caught by a coincidence between incidents and shifts – and not by chance this time.[65] This nurse will be convicted as well.

Note now that in this situation in which we loaded the dice against Lucia (1 in 44,000 rather than 1 in 44; 1 in 60,000 rather than 1 in 600,000 or 1 in 1,200,000), the courts will on average convict two nurses, one guilty and one innocent, each year. There is then no reason to rejoice when the courts convict a nurse. Verdicts will be mistaken in more than 50 per cent of the cases.

The situation becomes even more dramatic of course when the ratio is 1 in 44 or 1 in 9. With a ratio of 1 in 44 the court may expect to see 60,000 ÷ 44 = 1366 innocent nurses with Lucia's coincidence, against one serial killer nurse.

So when the court's decision strategy is 'Follow the advice of the statistical expert', we find that it will very often convict innocent nurses, simply because it neglects the general probability of a Dutch nurse's being a serial killer.[66]

Rather than following E., the court should have asked the right question: given that Lucia encountered x of the total of y incidents and had z shifts (of all r shifts), how likely is it that she has committed murders?

To answer this question the court should consider both the probability of such a coincidence occurring by chance (1 in 44,000 or 1 in 44), and the probability of a Dutch nurse's being a serial killer, and, of course, other additional evidence.

Asking the wrong question is called the prosecutor's fallacy. And E.'s approach does imply a fallacy indeed. Both when the case is perceived from everyday experience (Peter) and when it is viewed from the perspective of a rational decision strategy, we see that that E.'s approach leads to the wrong outcome: we do not

---

64 The number of incidents in the Juliana Children's Hospital Lucia was convicted for.

65 We assume a stupid serial killer who kills only during his/her shifts.

66 The court did not know more about Lucia than that she was a Dutch nurse with so many shifts and so many incidents. The court did make the claim that Lucia was a liar because she denied that she had killed people. Her alleged mendacious character was further evidence against Lucia, or so the court claimed. The court also concluded that there was independent evidence that Lucia fatally poisoned two children. If the court had had good reason for doing so (which in fact is not the case), the statistical argumentation would have been superfluous.

think that Peter cheated, nor do we appreciate sentencing so many innocent nurses. We conclude that E.'s approach is wrong, his question is wrong, his conclusion is based on a fallacy and its adoption by the courts has led to a disastrous result in the case of Lucia de B.

Summarizing, the court should not ask: 'Assuming Lucia's innocence, what is the probability she meets with such a coincidence by chance?', and then, when that probability turns out to be smaller than the significance level, conclude: 'She is the cause of the coincidence' (once the alternatives have been quickly excluded). The question should be: 'Given the coincidence, is there any good reason to convict Lucia?' The court has to take into account both the probability of the coincidence occurring by chance, and the probability of a Dutch nurse's being a serial killer – and of course other evidence as well.

12. Other Relevant Data: Total Collapse of the Case

Lucia's position is even stronger. There was no incriminating evidence against her,[67] but actually there was exculpatory evidence, as we have already seen in section 6: during the three years (1996–1998) before Lucia worked at the Juliana Children's Hospital, seven children died in the ward MCU-1, while during the three years that she was employed there (1999–2001) six (!) children died in that ward. This should cast serious doubt on the idea that a serial killer was active during the years that Lucia worked at MCU-1.[68]

Table 2.3 Additional exculpatory data

	Number of deaths in ward MCU-1 (which had the name Internal-1 before 1999)
1996–1998 (Lucia not in MCU-1)	7
1999–2001 (Lucia in MCU-1)	6

67 One of us argued for this claim, in Derksen 2006.

68 Lucia did not work all 36 months of 1999–2001 in the hospital. In Derksen 2006 a precise calculation is made in terms of months (rather than years) of employment by the hospital. The outcome is similar: during the months that Lucia worked in the Juliana Children's Hospital, there were (proportionally) fewer deaths than in the months that she did not work there. Again, this should cast serious doubt on the idea that a serial killer was active during the years that Lucia worked at MCU-1.

Nobody noticed these numbers. How was this possible? The only reason we can think of is that the prosecution before the district court gave another twist to these numbers. As mentioned above (in 6.8) the ward MCU-1 changed its name from IN-1 to MCU-1 on 9 November 1999. So the following presentation of the statistics of deaths is literally correct, but actually quite misleading:

Table 2.4 Misleading data representation

	Number of deaths in ward Internal-1	Number of deaths in ward MCU-1
1996-1998 (Lucia not in MCU-1)	7	0
1999-2001 (Lucia in MCU-1)	1*	5

Note: * The patient died in March 1999 when the ward was still called Internal-1. At that time Lucia did not yet work in the Juliana Child Hospital. The ward changed its name in November 1999.

The prosecution could now state (almost) truthfully: during the last six years only five people died in ward MCU-1 and they all died during Lucia's shifts. But this is an outrage. It turns highly exculpatory evidence into incriminating evidence. For in the ward MCU-1, which changed its name in November 1999, there were 13 deaths, five of which occurred in the time that Lucia worked at the Juliana Children's Hospital.[69] So there were actually fewer deaths in that ward when Lucia worked there than during a similar time before. One would have expected the number of deaths to rise with the arrival of a serial killer, not to decline. So the actual statistics suggest that there was no serial killer at work in the time Lucia worked there.[70]

So not only is the popular figure of 1 in 342,000,000 based on a fundamental mistake and wrong data, there is other statistical evidence as well, which was totally misinterpreted and which should have cleared Lucia.

69 To be exact there were five deaths during the months that she worked there.

70 The objection that Lucia only murdered seriously ill patients, so that their deaths would now show up as extras in any statistics is totally at odds with the prosecution's and the court's assertions that her alleged victims were doing quite well and that their deaths were rather unexpected.

13. Conclusion

In sections 1–6 we argued that it was the Incredible Coincidence which controlled the minds of all who played a crucial role in the trial of Lucia de B.

In sections 7–12 we gave a quick overview of mistakes of reasoning and other mistakes involved. Apart from a biased data set we noticed a mistaken method and mistakes even in the way the mistaken method was used. The infamous coincidence was neither incredible nor incriminating. We also found that important exculpatory statistical evidence was not taken into consideration.

Once we remove the bias and the mistakes and add the neglected statistical evidence there is no statistical reason even to suspect Lucia of any crime.

Many people who played a crucial part in the trial of Lucia were deeply impressed by the (purportedly) extremely small chance that all those incidents happened during her shifts purely by accident – the Incredible Coincidence. As we have shown in sections 7–12, the calculations of the statistical expert of the court were wrong, and the wrong question was asked. But it is remarkable that the Incredible Coincidence had been around long before the statistical expert was asked to do his calculations. And no one seemed to have noticed that the wrong question was being asked. Yet we cannot imagine that so many people were either just wicked or plain stupid.

It is evolutionarily based reasoning instincts that are the real culprits (we assume). The human cognitive system has evolved to serve us well enough in everyday situations. For the far greater part of our evolutionary history we human beings were hunter-gatherers in environments fraught with physical danger. Quick decisions were essential for survival. So our cognitive system has developed rough-and-ready methods for deciding – our reasoning instincts. These methods are, however, not sufficient for complicated situations where probabilities are involved. Human beings are notoriously bad at reasoning with probabilities.[71]

In our study of the Lucia de B. case we have identified three reasoning instincts that have led astray almost all people involved in the case: the Small Chance Instinct, the No Smoke without Fire Instinct and the instinct to pay little attention to base rate probabilities.

The Small Chance Instinct leads people to neglect small chances. In everyday life this is often all right: if something has only a (very) small chance of happening, we may safely assume that it will not happen. After all, we cannot take account of every foreseeable possibility and we must take risks if we are not to be stuck in endless deliberation. To be sure, even then we will be occasionally surprised by an event that was considered unlikely beforehand. But the quickness of our decisions makes up for their occasional faultiness. However, when large numbers and complicated probabilities are at stake, the neglect of small chances can have even more serious consequences. Moreover, it is questionable to use the Small Chance Principle *ex post facto*. Maybe the probability of something happening is

71 Again see e.g. Nisbett and Ross 1980; Tversky and Kahneman 1981.

very small beforehand, but should we attach any meaning to this small chance after the event? For instance, the chance of one specific individual winning a lottery is arguably very small, yet after the draw that very individual does win, however improbable it was beforehand. The chance of a nurse encountering many incidents during her shifts is small beforehand, but this should not lead us to any specific conclusion when such a coincidence actually does happen.

The No Smoke without Fire Instinct has less to do with probabilities than with our propensity to see causal connections. Here it is not the probability that a large number of incidents occurs, but simply the number itself that plays a role. The instinct makes us believe that where events of two types (incidents and shifts in this case) often concur, there must be a causal connection. Again, this may be true often enough in everyday life. This instinct has served us well in general. But there is no guarantee whatsoever that every coincidence or correlation is the sign of a causal connection. In an even more unsavoury form the instinct could also be termed 'mud will stick': if someone is accused often enough, some of the accusations will be believed.

Both instincts are fed in a certain way by the instinct to pay little attention to base rates. Yes, the probability that one nurse will meet with such a number of incidents during her shifts by accident is very small. But what does this imply? When we take into account the actual number of nurses we see that such coincidences are to be expected more often. And when we compare this probability with the probability of the alternative, the coincidence is suddenly not incredible at all – it is the alternative that is actually more incredible. Our instincts prompt us to say: the chance that the coincidence happened by accident is so small that it must be murder. But the chance that it was murder may be even smaller. What we know is that the coincidence occurred. So we should no longer ask the question: what is the chance that this coincidence happened by accident? What we should ask is: given this coincidence, is it more likely that it was murder or that it was an accident?

So our reasoning instincts lead us astray. We are impressed by the wrong things, we see too many causal connections and we ask the wrong questions. Empirical studies have taught us that we are bad at reasoning with probabilities. In important matters, where someone's life and liberty are at stake, we should do well to exercise the utmost care in appealing to statistics. Our study demonstrates how fatal the result can be when we are not aware of the operation of these instincts.

References

Agresti, A. (2002), *Categorical Data Analysis*, 2nd Edition (Hoboken, NJ: John Wiley & Sons).

Derksen, T. (2006), *Lucia de B.: Een Reconstructie van een Gerechtelijke Dwaling* (Lucia de B: A Reconstruction of a Judicial Error) (Diemen: Veen Magazines).

Gill, R.D., Grunwald, P., Sherps, M. and Derksen, T. (2009 forthcoming), 'The statistics applied to the Lucia de B. case', to be published in *Annals of Applied Statistics*.

Lambalgen, M. van and Meester, R. (2004), 'Wat zeggen al die getallen eigenlijk? De statistiek rond het proces tegen Lucy de B.', *Trema, Tijdschrift voor de Rechterlijke Macht* 7: September, 286–93.

Meester, R., Collins, M., Gill, R.D., Van Lambalgen, M. (2007), 'On the (ab)use of statistics in the legal case against the nurse Lucia de B.', *Law, Probability and Risk* 5, 233.

Nisbett, R.E. and Ross, L. (1980), *Human Inference: Strategies and Shortcomings of Social Judgment* (Englewood Cliffs, NJ: Prentice-Hall).

Thompson, L.A. (2008), *S-PLUS (and R) Manual to Accompany Agresti's Categorical Data Analysis (2002)*, 2nd Edition, available at <https://home.comcast.net/~lthompson221/Splusdiscrete2.pdf>.

Tversky, A. and Kahneman, D. (1981), 'The framing of decisions and the psychology of choice', *Science* 211, 453–8.

Chapter 3
Decision-making in the Forensic Arena

Ton Broeders

1. Forensic Science in the Real World

These days, forensic science is 'hot'. As TV shows like *Crime Scene Investigation* and *Forensic Detectives* are commanding top ratings and record numbers of students are enrolling in forensic science courses, interest in the subject continues unabated. In just two years, between 2002 and 2004, the number of forensic science courses at UK universities more than doubled, from 150 to close to 400, and it is still rising. However, while the casual observer of the scene might be forgiven for thinking otherwise, not everything is rosy in the forensic garden. In the real world, forensic science is increasingly criticized for its lack of a scientific basis, as much of what passes for forensic science does not on closer examination qualify as science. If anything, recent insights suggest that decision-making in the forensic arena tends to be fraught with difficulty, as the following examples illustrate.

Stephan Cowans

On 23 January 2004, Stephan Cowans was released from prison in Boston, Massachusetts, after DNA analysis had demonstrated that biological trace material on the baseball hat and the sweatshirt of an unknown perpetrator and on a drinking glass used by this same perpetrator could not be Cowans'. The three DNA profiles obtained from the cell material on these objects were identical but they did not match Cowans' profile. It subsequently appeared that a thumb print on the glass which the Boston police had attributed to Cowans did not originate from him either. This fingerprint and an identification from a photo line-up by two eye witnesses, the victim and another witness, had been the only evidence against him at the time of his conviction. Cowans' is the first case in which DNA evidence has led to the release and subsequent exoneration of a suspect whose conviction was based on flawed fingerprint evidence. Cowans, who was convicted for the nonfatal shooting of a policeman with his own gun, spent nearly seven years in prison.[1]

1 Loftus and Cole 2004.

Brandon Mayfield

On 6 May 2004, 37-year-old US born attorney and Muslim convert Brandon Mayfield was arrested as a 'material witness' in his home town of Portland, Oregon, and placed in solitary confinement in a federal jail. Under the Material Witness Statute of 1984 prosecutors may seek an arrest warrant if a potential witness's testimony is material to a criminal proceeding and it can be shown that it may become impracticable to secure the individual's presence. A judge must approve the warrant, and the witness is entitled to a court-appointed lawyer. Since 9/11 the statute is believed to be used to detain persons who are not seen as potential witnesses but as suspects against whom there is (as yet) insufficient evidence and who may thus be detained without being charged with a crime.

However that may be, soon after Mayfield's arrest it turned out that he was actually arrested on suspicion of involvement in the bombings at the Atocha train station in Madrid, on March 11, 2004, in which 191 people were killed and almost 2,000 were wounded. Following a search of the Integrated Automatic Fingerprint Identification System (IAFIS) of the FBI, containing over 440 million fingerprints of more than 44 million persons, three senior FBI fingerprint experts categorically – but wrongly – identified a fingerprint on a plastic bag containing detonators as his.[2] The bag had been found a few days after the attack in a van parked near the station from which three of the four affected trains had departed. An independent expert appointed by a federal judge at the request of Mayfield's defence lawyer reached the same conclusion. In spite of the fact that the Spanish authorities had advised the FBI that Mayfield's reference print did not match the finger mark even before he was arrested, it was only after Mayfield had been detained for two weeks and the Spanish authorities had informed the FBI that the mark in fact originated from an Algerian national that Mayfield, who as a lawyer represented a man convicted on a charge of terrorism in a family law dispute, was released.

An international committee of fingerprint experts asked by the FBI to examine the case concluded that: 'the failure was in the application of the ACE-V methodology during this particular examination' (Stacey 2004). The problem with this analysis, which tries to save the method by blaming the expert, is that the method and the expert cannot be separated because the expert plays an essential role as judge/measuring instrument in the fingerprint examination process.

Sally Clark

Sally Clark, a solicitor by profession, spent more than three years in prison after being found guilty of murdering her two baby sons in 1999. The case against her initially rested partly on erroneous statistical evidence. The probability of the two

2 On the forensic implications see Rudin and Inman 2004. For a description of the case by the defence see Wax and Schatz 2004. For a final assessment of the FBI handling of the Brandon Mayfield case by the US Department of Justice see Fine 2006.

cot deaths (by SIDS, or Sudden Infant Death Syndrome) occurring in a family like the Clarks was said to be 1 in 73,000,000, a figure arrived at by – unjustifiably – squaring the probability of a single cot death occurring in a middle-class family (1 in approximately 8,500). However, the probability of a second cot death occurring in a family was later estimated to be somewhere in the region of 1 in 100. Multiple infant deaths were viewed with considerable suspicion at the time, after Professor Sir Roy Meadow, paediatrician, in a book entitled *ABC of Child Abuse*, formulated what came to be known as 'Meadow's Law': one infant death is a tragedy, two is suspicious and three murder, unless proved otherwise. Meadow was the first to describe a condition he called 'Munchausen by Proxy', in which mothers might harm or even kill their children as a means of calling attention to themselves. Sally Clark died on March 15, 2007.[3]

The Schiedam Park Murder

On 10 December 2004, after serving four years of an 18-year sentence for the rape and murder of 10-year-old Nienke Kleiss and the assault and attempted murder of her 11-year-old friend Maikel, 35-year-old Kees Borsboom was conditionally released from prison after post-conviction DNA testing had shown that DNA profiles obtained from biological trace material found on the little girl's denim jacket matched the profile of 26-year-old Wik H., who was arrested in July 2004 on suspicion of two unrelated sexual offences, including assault, rape and homicide. In the course of the following investigation H. declared that he was the killer of Nienke, whose friend Maikel only survived the ordeal by pretending to be dead. No trace material was ever found that linked Borsboom to the murder and partial profiles obtained from nail debris and trace material from the left boot of the victim pointed to an unknown man.

The partial profiles failed to produce a hit in the Dutch national DNA database, which, at the time, only held the reference profiles of just over a thousand persons. After a reference profile became available for H. in late 2004, they proved to match his profile. In spite of the absence of DNA-evidence pointing towards Borsboom and the presence of DNA material pointing to another man, Borsboom was nevertheless convicted of the murder both by the district court in Rotterdam and the Court of Appeal in The Hague, largely on the basis of a confession he made to the police during his detention but later retracted. Following a revision of his conviction by the Dutch Supreme Court in January 2005, after two earlier confirmations, Borsboom's sentence was suspended and his case ordered to be retried by the Court of Appeal in Amsterdam.

On 27 April 2005, H. was convicted of the rape and murder of Nienke Kleiss and the assault and attempted murder of her friend Maikel, and sentenced to 20 years' imprisonment plus TBS (*terbeschikkingstelling*), a 'hospital order', i.e., a non-punitive sanction involving compulsory placement in a psychiatric hospital

3 For details visit <www.sallyclark.org.uk>.

which may be imposed on perpetrators who are deemed to be suffering from diminished responsibility. The case provides a powerful illustration of the value of a DNA reference database containing the profiles of repeated (sexual) offenders. Sadly, in its exclusive focus on the confessing suspect the investigative approach adopted by police and prosecution is somewhat reminiscent of that of the drunk looking for his car keys under a lamppost. Even though he has no idea where he dropped them, he keeps searching under the lamppost because the light is better there.

Shirley McKie

About 10 years ago, Detective Constable Shirley McKie was charged with perjury when she denied entering a crime scene where a finger trace was found which the Scottish Criminal Records Office claimed belonged to her. McKie's denial led to a charge of perjury. Although she was not found guilty of perjury, the Scottish Criminal Records Office maintained that the identification was correct and no corrective action was undertaken. Two years later some of the world's leading dactyloscopists pointed out that the latent print did not match the policewoman's reference fingerprint and could not be hers. On February 12, 2006 Ms McKie was awarded £750,000 in compensation by the Scottish Executive.[4]

In spite of the popular media image and notwithstanding the undeniable impact of DNA evidence, forensic science – especially forensic identification science or criminalistics – has come under fierce attack in recent years.[5] Some of the graver miscarriages of justice which have come to light in several countries in the last decades were seen to be at least partly associated with inadequate standards of forensic expertise or with erroneous interpretations of otherwise correct findings. What were long held to be tried and trusted forensic identification procedures like dactyloscopy (fingerprint examination) and questioned document examination are now said to lack a sound scientific basis, and the traditional claims of forensic identification science have come to be dismissed as logically untenable. Studies like those by Evett and Williams (1996) and recent cases like those of Shirley McKie in Scotland, Brandon Mayfield in the USA, Sally Clark in England and the Schiedam Park Murder and Lucia de B. (see below) in The Netherlands provide further evidence of the present crisis in the forensic arena.

At the same time, forensic science is rapidly expanding. DNA profiling in particular may fairly be said to have revolutionized forensic science. It not only constitutes a powerful investigative and evidential tool in its own right, it is, ironically perhaps, also largely as a result of the growing familiarity with the scientific paradigm associated with DNA evidence that traditional identification science is now lying so heavily under siege. More specifically, it could be argued

4 For details visit <www.shirleymckie.com>.

5 For a more detailed discussion see Broeders 2006; for a concise but authoritative assessment of the state of play in the forensic arena see Saks and Koehler 2005.

that it is primarily through post-conviction DNA testing that the limitations of many forms of evidence, more specifically eyewitness identification, have been demonstrated. A major force here is The Innocence Project, which was set up as a non-profit legal clinic by Barry C. Scheck and Peter J. Neufeld at Cardozo Law School in 1992. The project only handles cases where post-conviction DNA testing of evidence can yield conclusive proof of innocence. In the clinic, students handle the case work while supervised by a team of attorneys and clinic staff. To date (April 2008), the project has produced 215 exonerations.[6]

2. Limitations of Forensic Science

The rise of forensic DNA analysis and the accompanying increase in the prominence of the probabilistic model associated with it have sparked off a renewed interest in the interpretation of forensic evidence, more specifically with regard to the interpretation of the findings of the examination of the origin of physical traces. Discussion of these issues takes place primarily within the ranks of forensic experts but it is increasingly beginning to extend beyond this group to those who find themselves at the receiving end of forensic expertise: defence lawyers, judges and prosecutors. The various ways in which the findings of forensic identification expertise are presented reflect the different assumptions that – explicitly or otherwise – underlie the various approaches that can be distinguished within the field of forensic identification science and forensic science in general. The very existence of these different approaches increasingly raises the question of the scientific status of forensic identification evidence and in a wider sense of the scientific status of criminalistics and the forensic sciences as such. Interestingly, these questions are intimately bound up with the role forensic evidence plays in reducing uncertainty in the context of the investigation of criminal incidents and in providing a basis for decisions made throughout the investigative and evidential chain, starting with the selection of traces by the crime scene officer and extending all the way to the ultimate issue decision about the guilt of the suspect by the trier of fact.

Differences in the basic assumptions underlying criminalistics as a science are reflected in the methods used and have important implications for the interpretation and reporting of the various types of forensic (identification) evidence. In addition to the questions relating to the scientific status and to the fundamental principles underlying forensic investigations, the present state of play in the forensic arena raises important questions about the role and the responsibility of the forensic expert as opposed to that of the trier of fact, and about the expert lawyer interface. These are questions whose importance cannot easily be overstressed in view of the increasing use of technical and scientific expertise in legal contexts, and the existence of a wide gap separating lawyers and scientists.

---

6 <www.innocenceproject.org>.

3. Forensic Identification: Individualization

At this point, it may be good to pause for a moment to see what distinguishes *forensic identification science* from other forms of forensic science. Essentially, this difference can be described in terms of what Inman and Rudin (2002) have termed the various forensic processes, i.e., identification, classification, individualization, association and reconstruction.

Table 3.1 Different forensic processes

Identification:	determination of physical-chemical composition (e.g., illicit drugs)
Quantification:	determination of the quantity of a particular substance (e.g., illicit drugs; concentration of a substance in a matrix, e.g., MDMA, cocaine or digoxin in blood)*
Classification:	determination of class, type (e.g., hair, fibres, blood type, DNA)**
Individualization:	determination of unique identity of source (e.g., fingerprints, handwriting)
Association:	determination of contact between two objects (e.g., through transfer of fibres, glass, presence of gunshot residue)
Reconstruction:	determination of facts of the case: nature and place of events in time and space (e.g., murder, explosion)

Note: * Quantification is not listed as a separate process by Inman and Rudin but is added here as forensic scientists are frequently asked to determine the quantity or concentration of a particular substance. ** Although the purpose of forensic DNA analysis is individualization, the forensic process involved is technically one of classification, based as it is on the use of class characteristics, in the form of DNA markers or alleles.

It is the individualization process, *the inference of identity of source*, which is the ultimate aim of all forensic identification science.[7] The criminal investigator as well as the trier of fact are anxious to know if the incriminating trace material originates from a particular suspect or object, which would make it possible to establish a relation between that individual and a particular criminal act. In trying to answer this question, the various types of forensic identification science do not use the same scientific paradigm for source attribution and consequently do not report their conclusions in the same format. The situation may be summed up as follows:

7 Kirk (1963, 235) defined criminalistics as 'the science of individualization'.

Table 3.2 Identification (identity of source), more properly called Individualization

Discipline	Type of conclusion	Example
Dactyloscopy	categorical source attribution statement: yes or no	finger trace does (not) originate(s) from the suspect
DNA	statement of probability of evidence, in quantitative terms	probability of a random match (RMP) of the profile of the suspect with that of crime scene cell material
Other*	probabilistic source attribution statement, in verbal terms**	crime scene material (very) probably (does not) originate(s) from the suspect

Note: * Handwriting, hair, fibres, firearms, tool marks, impression marks. ** Increasingly, following the DNA model, these types of evidence may be reported using a likelihood ratio or a likelihood ratio-based scale, as proposed by Evett, Jackson, Lambert and McCrossan (2000).

Largely as a result of the growing prominence of the scientific paradigm associated with DNA evidence, traditional identification science, as exemplified by dactyloscopy and the remaining identification disciplines, is now lying heavily under siege. What is at issue here is nothing less than the scientific status of forensic identification procedures. Critics point to the lack of scientific rigour in the methodology applied, to the presence of various types of examiner bias and to the prosecutorial orientation inherent in many traditional and firmly-established forensic procedures.[8] In one such field, dactyloscopy or fingerprint identification, practitioners almost universally subscribe to the so-called 'positivity doctrine', which is premised on the notion that 'Friction ridge identifications are absolute identifications. Probable, possible, or likely identification are outside the acceptable limits of the science of friction ridge identification.'[9] As a result, within the dactyloscopist community, identifications are exclusively reported as absolute under penalty of excommunication from said community. Arguably, this practice may well have served to perpetuate fundamental misunderstandings about the nature of scientific evidence, which – contrary to widespread belief – is essentially not of a categorical or deterministic but of a probabilistic nature.[10]

8 Saks et al. 2003. An almost identical version of this article appeared earlier as Risinger et al. 2002.

9 McRoberts 2002.

10 Broeders 2003.

4. The Induction Problem

One of the central questions in forensic identification science concerns the way the findings of a comparative examination are reported. As Kwan (1977), in his seminal dissertation, and others have pointed out, any form of individualization is an essentially inductive process. While forensic identification procedures may lead to *categorical elimination*, as the example of DNA profiling demonstrates, unless the number of potential sources is limited and known, no forensic identification procedure can lead to a *categorical identification*. More than that, we will see below that even *probabilistic identification* is highly problematic.

Ultimate proof that a hypothesis is correct cannot, according to Popper, be furnished.[11] Confirmation, verification or corroboration of hypotheses are all valuable test procedures but in and of themselves none of these can deliver conclusive proof and absolute certainty. What is possible is an approach in which uncertainty is reduced by formulating promising hypotheses, testing these and rejecting them if there is insufficient support for them. But the remaining, as yet unrejected, hypotheses do not reach the status of scientific fact; they essentially retain a probabilistic status. In this view, what we accept as scientific knowledge is – at best – no more than a set of repeatedly tested hypotheses which we have so far been unable to reject.

Criminal investigation and the collection and evaluation of criminal evidence may be conceived of as processes that are undertaken to reduce uncertainty. The view that these processes are similar to those applied in science is rapidly gaining ground. This is largely a result of the advent of DNA evidence, whose interpretation follows the model outlined below. The unprecedented impact of DNA evidence makes it hard for lawyers not to take notice of this model. Or, as the German psychologist Gigerenzer, director of the Berlin Max-Planck-Institut für Bildungsforschung (human development), puts it: 'DNA fingerprinting has ... put new demands on the legal profession. These include overcoming the illusion of certainty and learning how to understand and communicate uncertainties.'[12]

For forensic evidence and for expert evidence in general, this model means that certain plausible hypotheses or scenarios may be excluded categorically after testing, and certain persons or objects may be eliminated as sources of a particular

11 Popper 1959. Or, as Champod and Evett (2001, 105) put it: 'If we wish to address an open population then probabilistic statements are unavoidable. Indeed, this is the notion of the entire discipline of statistics.' De Groot (1994) also points out that so-called single deterministic hypotheses of the type 'all A's are B', 'all ravens are black' or 'all finger prints/ears/handwriting styles/voices differ' may be refuted by a single counter example but cannot strictly be proved: '*Only by examining the entire universe of all instances of A, can we establish with certainty that every A is B.* (translation: APAB)' In practice this is only possible for small closed populations or, in the forensic context, for small potential source/suspect populations.

12 Gigerenzer 2002, 183.

trace or as perpetrators.[13] Elimination is based on deductive reasoning, which leads to a logically correct and necessary conclusion, which, if the premises are true, guarantees the truth of the conclusion. Elimination is based on deductive reasoning, namely, on the scheme 'If A is true then B is true and if B is not true, then A is not true'. A deductive reasoning scheme guarantees the truth of its conclusion if its premises are true. In the case of elimination this means that the conclusion 'A is not true' can be accepted as correct on the assumption that the conditional premise 'If A is true then B is true' is correct and the test 'B is not true' has yielded a truly negative result and not a false-negative result. On the other hand, a truly positive result 'B is true' cannot lead to a categorically positive conclusion, since the scheme 'If A is true then B is true, and B is true, therefore A is true' is deductively invalid.

On the other hand, failure to reject a hypothesis should not lead us to infer that the hypothesis has been proved to be true. Positive evidence, including a positive identification, is not the result of a deductive but of an inductive process. And induction does not lead to an inevitable and categorical conclusion but to a probabilistic one. Just as we cannot conclude that all ravens are black unless we have seen all ravens, we can only conclude with certainty that a trace originates from a particular source when we have compared the trace with all potential sources.[14] And that, in the real forensic world, is not in the vast majority of cases either a practicable or a possible option.

In spite of this, we are happy for our triers of fact to make categorical decisions about the facts of a case on the basis of the available, inevitably probabilistic evidence. We accept that in doing so the trier of fact makes a decision which – on strictly logical grounds – is not defensible. In arriving at their conviction that the facts of a case are proven, the trier of fact ultimately ignores the induction problem. They allow their conviction to be converted to certainty, thereby – to all intents and purposes – reducing the existing uncertainty to zero.

5. Decision-making in the Traditional Forensic Identification Disciplines

Source attribution statements are not only problematical when they are categorical but also when they are probabilistic. Despite widespread, nay virtually universal practice to the contrary, even if a comparative examination of a physical trace like a bullet with a set of reference bullets fired with a particular pistol shows a very high degree of similarity between the striation marks on the questioned bullet and those on the reference bullets and there are no inexplicable differences, this does

13 As long as we are dealing with categorical, discrete or nominal variables (Broeders 2003, 223). For continuous variables rejection of a hypothesis, by means of a significance test, also has a probabilistic basis.

14 However, even then it will not always be possible to state with certainty what the source of the trace is.

not provide a basis for a statement to the effect that the bullet was (very) probably fired with the reference pistol. As long as it is conceivable that there is even a single pistol in the potential pistol population that might leave striation marks that would produce a comparable let alone a higher degree of similarity with the questioned bullet, we are in no position to make a probability statement on the basis of the comparative firearms examination alone. Nevertheless, practitioners of traditional forensic identification disciplines have tended to do just that. In response to questions whether a particular suspect fired a pistol, left a finger mark, wrote a ransom letter, or made a telephone call, they have tended to address precisely that issue and have generally formulated their answers in terms of a verbal probability scale, more or less along the lines of the following model:

The comparative examination leads to the conclusion that the questioned trace material
with a probability bordering on certainty
highly probably
probably
possibly
(does/does not) originate from the suspect.
Format 1: Flawed conclusion format

What discussion there was about the way the findings of forensic examinations should be reported tended to concentrate on the use of words versus numbers or percentages. Because in most forensic identification disciplines quantitative data about the frequency of the characteristics used in the comparison process are a rare commodity, the question did not really give rise to a great deal of meaningful discussion but generally resolved itself in favour of the only remaining option. It is the estimated 'rarity value' (or frequency) of the (combined) characteristics that the trace material and the potential source share that is used to determine which of a range of varying probability judgements is used. If the characteristics are estimated to be (very) rare and if any differences are explicable,[15] this will lead to the conviction on the part of the expert that the degree of similarity between questioned material and reference material is such as to preclude the possibility or probability of their simultaneous occurrence by chance. As Huber (1959–1960) put it:

> When any two items have characteristics in common of such number and significance as to preclude their simultaneous occurrence by chance, and there are no inexplicable differences, then it may be concluded that they are the same, or from the same source.

15 In other words, if the differences are compatible with the common source hypothesis.

What practitioners of traditional forensic identification sciences really do is perhaps best described by Stoney, who used the image of the 'leap of faith' as the mechanism whereby the forensic scientist actually establishes individualization:

> When more and more corresponding features are found between the two patterns scientist and lay person alike become subjectively certain that the patterns could not possibly be duplicated by chance. What has happened here is somewhat analogous to a leap of faith. It is a jump, an extrapolation, based on the observation of highly variable traits among a few characteristics, and then considering the case of many characteristics ... In fingerprint work, we become subjectively convinced of identity; we do not prove it (Stoney 1991, 198).

Although forensic practitioners of the traditional identification disciplines are often aware of the importance of data on the relative frequency of the characteristics in terms of which crime scene material and reference material correspond, very few figures are actually available and estimates used rarely transcend the 'ball park' standard. Figures based on systematic empirical research tend to be lacking, with the marked exception of autosomal DNA profiling.[16]

Summing up, we can say that source attribution, i.e., the attribution of a trace to a unique source, cannot rationally be based on scientific evidence alone but inevitably requires the assumption of an implicit or explicit prior probability of the probability that the trace originates from the source in question. No matter how closely a questioned handwriting specimen resembles the reference handwriting of a particular potential writer, if this potential source was dead at the time the questioned text was written, it clearly cannot make sense to say – on the basis of the observed similarity only – that the questioned text was (very) probably written by this person.[17] Any statement of the probability of a particular source attribution hypothesis necessarily involves two elements: the probability of the evidence under two competing hypotheses *and* an estimate of the prior probability of the hypothesis, i.e., the probability of the source attribution hypothesis before the scientific evidence became available.

---

16 Autosomal, nuclear, chromosomal or genomic DNA is located in the 22 chromosome pairs in the human cell nucleus whose structures are identical. The 23rd chromosome pair is the sex chromosome, which in women consists of an identically structured (and therefore also autosomal) XX-chromosome but in men is composed of a combination XY. In the forensic context, two other types of DNA profiling are frequently undertaken if insufficient cell material is available, i.e., mitochondrial DNA (mtDNA), which is situated in the cytoplasm outside the cell nucleus, and Y-chromosomal DNA. The first, mtDNA, is passed on unchanged in the maternal line, the second in the paternal line. Both types of DNA profiling have a considerably lower discriminatory power than autosomal DNA.

17 After Champod and Evett (2000).

6. Alternatives to the Probability Scales

Attempts to find alternatives to the probability scales do not always lead to greater uniformity in terminology, let alone greater precision. A favourite with many forensic practitioners is the term 'consistent with'. The findings, say, of a comparative paint or fibre examination are then reported as 'consistent with' the hypothesis that trace and reference material have a common source. What remains singularly unclear here is how many other traces – in concrete terms: how many other fibre fragments – would lead to the same conclusion. The phrasing could therefore rightly be dismissed as highly suggestive, precisely because the last consideration is not made explicit. As a better alternative the phrase 'not inconsistent with' has been suggested, because this conveys the central notion that identity of source 'cannot be excluded'. Phrases like 'could have come from', 'possibly comes from' seem to suffer from a similar imperfection in that they also leave unsaid that there are alternative sources which might show at least a comparable degree of similarity and what their number might be. What is lacking in all these cases is an adequate specification of the significance of the similarities and differences observed, preferably one with a quantitative basis.

7. DNA Profiling

It is again forensic DNA analysis that, through the implicit example it sets as a forensic identification procedure with a solid scientific basis, is increasingly being referred to as a standard for other forensic identification procedures. In forensic DNA profiling, the conclusion typically consists of two parts. The first part specifies the result of the comparison, the second specifies its meaning. If the profile obtained from a crime scene sample is compared with a reference sample from a known person, say the suspect in a criminal investigation (and we ignore situations where either sample or both yield no profile), there are two possible results:

1. the profiles do not match (completely);[18]
2. the profiles match.

---

18 Since genetics tells us that close relatives will have similar profiles, an incomplete but close match may be taken to imply that the suspect might have a close relative with the same profile as the crime scene sample. However, the similarity might be purely adventitious, i.e., accidental. Nevertheless, in recent years so-called 'familial searches' of the national DNA database of England and Wales have produced near matches which in some cases eventually led police to the perpetrators, as in the case of 20-year-old Craig Harman, who threw a brick from a traffic bridge killing a lorry driver <www.forensic.gov.uk/forensic_t/inside/news/list_press_release.php?case=23&y=2004>. The first cases in

The statement of the result of the comparative examination needs to be complemented with a statement of its meaning. Assuming that no mistakes were made at any stage of the process between the crime scene and the laboratory, finding (1) implies that the suspect can be eliminated as the source (or donor) of the crime scene material, while finding (2) implies that the suspect *may* be the donor of the sample. Interestingly, in the latter case, the question both the investigator and the trier of fact would most like to be answered by the expert, i.e., is the suspect the donor of the crime scene material, is not directly addressed. What the expert reports in the case of a match is not that the crime scene material probably or almost certainly originates from the matching suspect but the probability that a random member of the relevant suspect population has the same profile, the so-called random match probability. For a full SGMPlus profile[19] this random match probability is typically considerably smaller than 1 in 1 billion. However, partial profiles, which are not uncommon in forensic practice, may be reported with random match probabilities that may be as (relatively) high as 1 in 1,000.

Essentially, what this approach illustrates is that the expert can make statements about the probability of his findings under a particular hypothesis but that he is apparently not prepared to make statements about the probability of a hypothesis, e.g. the crime scene material originates from the suspect, on the basis of his findings, i.e., a match. Such 'transpositions of the conditional' are logically incorrect: if A implies B it does not follow that B implies A. Strictly speaking then, the latter type of statement, a so-called source attribution statement, is impossible for an expert to make. In other words, there is a crucial difference between the probability (P) of the evidence (E), i.e. an observed DNA match, under the hypothesis (H) that the matching suspect is the donor of the crime scene cell material, i.e., P(E|H), and the probability of the same hypothesis given the evidence, i.e., P(H|E). In the same way, the – often vanishingly small – probability of E, finding a match, under −H, the hypothesis that the suspect is *not* the donor of the cell material at the crime scene, i.e. P(E|−H), should not be confused with the probability that the suspect is not the donor if he matches, i.e., P(−H|E). To do so would amount to 'transposing the conditional', i.e., converting a conditional such as 'if A is true, then B is not true' into 'if B is not true, then A is true'. In the context of criminal law, this flawed reasoning has come to be known as the prosecutor's fallacy. It derives its name from the example given by Thompson and Schumann (1987) of a prosecutor who appeared to believe that if a suspect shares a particular characteristic with the perpetrator, i.e., a certain blood type with a relative frequency of 10 per cent in the population to which the perpetrator is believed to belong, the chance that this

---

which this type of low stringency search was used were old cases: the murder of Lynette White in 1988, which was solved in 2003, and the murders committed by the 'Saturday Night Strangler' in 1973, whose identity was established posthumously in 2001 (Broeders 2003, 346–7).

19 SGM in SGMPlus stands for Second Generation Multiplex, a technique involving the simultaneous typing of ten so-called DNA *loci* or markers.

suspect is in fact this perpetrator is 90 per cent (i.e. 100% – 10% = 90%). While the chance of the suspect having the blood type may correctly be said to be 10 per cent if he is innocent, this is erroneously taken to imply that the chance that he is innocent is 10 per cent if he has that blood type.

8. The Bayesian Approach[20]

A simple example may illustrate the problem. Suppose we look out of the window and find that the street is wet. This observation may lead us to assume that it has been raining. However, the single finding that the street is wet, in and of itself, provides insufficient basis for the conclusion that it has been raining or even for the conclusion that it has probably been raining. In countries where rain is rare, the so-called prior probability of rainfall is small and another explanation may therefore be more plausible. There may have been a demonstration, which may have necessitated the use of the water cannon. In countries where rain is an everyday event, the chance of rain is high and so is the prior probability that the streets are indeed wet from the rain. The actual probability that it has been raining if the streets are wet cannot therefore merely be based on the finding that the street is wet. In the same way, the probability that the crime scene material was left by the suspect cannot merely be based on the finding that his DNA profile matches with that of the crime scene material. In general terms, the expert can make statements about the probability of the findings under a particular hypothesis but he cannot do what the trier of fact frequently asks him to do, i.e., to make a statement about the probability of the hypothesis given the evidence.

In a logical model of evidence interpretation the expert's role is limited to making statements about the probability of his findings. An assessment of the prior probability that a particular suspect left the crime scene material, fired the pistol, wrote the ransom letter, or made the telephone call is clearly beyond him. That requires information to which the expert typically has or should have no access. In a logical model, it is the decision-maker or trier of fact who updates his prior probability with the evidence provided by the expert, to arrive at a posterior probability that the prosecution hypothesis is correct. It is this model, developed by Robertson and Vignaux (1995) and Evett et al. (2000), which is currently strongly advocated by many leading forensic scientists, even though it may not in fact be applied very frequently outside DNA profiling.

20 The approach described is named after the Rev. Thomas Bayes, whose 'An Essay towards Solving a Problem in the Doctrine of Chances' appeared posthumously in 1763. In the context of evidence interpretation, instead of the term 'Bayesian', the word 'logical' is fairly widely used to distinguish the type of approach which concentrates on statements of the probability of the evidence from the traditional approach which reports its findings in terms of statements of the probability of the hypothesis, in apparent disregard of the flawed reasoning this implies.

The fact that data about the frequency statistics of relevant characteristics are not available for most other types of identification evidence may explain why the DNA model is not often used outside DNA typing. However, it would be wrong to conclude that a dearth of background statistics makes the model irrelevant. On the contrary, the model serves as a powerful conceptual framework, which makes explicit what data are required to arrive at a source attribution statement and clarifies the distinct roles of the expert, who can testify about the probability and weight of the scientific evidence, and the trier of fact, who combines the weight of the scientific evidence with that of the non-scientific evidence to arrive at an overall, necessarily subjective, but categorical decision.

An elementary quantitative example may clarify the approach. Suppose a partial DNA profile is obtained from cell material recovered from the crime scene. Suppose the profile is the same as that of the suspect, who was arrested in connection with the crime. Let us assume the random match probability, i.e., the probability that a (unrelated) random member of the population could not be excluded as donor of the crime scene sample, is 1 in 1,000. The weight of the evidence can then be calculated in the form of the *likelihood ratio* of the evidence occurring under two hypotheses:

1. Hs: the suspect is the donor
2. Hr: a random member of the population is the donor

Thus, we have:

$$\frac{P(E|Hs)}{P(E|Hr)} = \frac{1}{1/1{,}000} = 1{,}000.$$

We can use this so-called likelihood ratio as input for the so-called odds format of Bayes' Theorem. This says that the probability ratio of two competing hypotheses is the product of the ratio of the two competing hypotheses before the evidence came in, multiplied by the likelihood ratio of the evidence under the two competing hypotheses. Or:

$$\frac{P(Hs|E)}{P(Hr|E)} = \frac{P(Hs)}{P(Hr)} \text{ x } \frac{P(E|Hs)}{P(E|Hr)}$$

Or:

Suppose that, in addition to the suspect, there are 500 men who – in terms of the DNA evidence alone – are equally likely to be the donors of the crime scene material but whose DNA profile we do not know. In this case, the prior probability of the suspect's being the donor of the crime scene material is 1 to 500. The likelihood ratio is 1,000. If we enter these numbers in the formula, this yields:

$$\frac{P(Hs|E)}{P(Hr|E)} = (1 \text{ to } 500) \times 1.000 = 1.000 \text{ to } 500 = 1.000/1.500 = 66.7\%$$

To put this in words: while the probability of the suspect's being the donor of the cell material was believed to be 1 to 500 against, or 0.2 per cent, the posterior probability has risen to 66.7 per cent after the DNA evidence has become available. If only 50 other men were equally qualified to be potential donors, the posterior probability of the suspect's being the true donor would be: (1 to 50) x 1,000 = 1,000 to 50 = 1,000/1,050 = 95.2%. If only five other men qualified as potential donors, the probability of the suspect's being the donor would be: 1,000 to 5 = 1,000/1,005 = 99.5%.

So, it is clear that the posterior probability depends not only on the strength of the evidence, as expressed in the likelihood ratio, but also on the strength of the prior probability. The latter was here defined in terms of the estimate of the number of alternative donors but it may also be determined on the basis of the subjective estimate that the suspect is the donor, based on all the evidence that is available so far, i.e., before the DNA evidence comes in.

Lucia de B.

In the case of the Dutch nurse Lucia de B., a statistician calculated the probability of the nurse's shifts coinciding with a large number of deaths and resuscitation attempts in three hospitals at 1 in 342,000,000. His conclusion was that this could not be a coincidence. Unfortunately, he failed to point out to the court that the figure, whatever its value, represented his calculation of the probability of the coincidence *if* it had arisen due to chance. Worse than that, he suggested that it amounted to the probability *that* the coincidence was due to chance. This error is an example of the prosecutor's fallacy (see above). In a Bayesian approach, we would first calculate the likelihood ratio of the evidence under two hypotheses, not just one. These would be the probability of the evidence, the 'suspicious' deaths and near deaths in the three hospitals, given that the nurse was a killer (let's say we put this at 1, or 100 per cent) and the probability of the evidence, given that she was innocent. Let's say that the latter would equal the probability of the suspicious events, given chance. If we accept the statistician's figure for the evidence, given chance, as 1 in 342,000,000, the likelihood ratio would be 1 divided by 1 in 342,000,000 = 342,000,000. This is a huge figure. However, in order to calculate the prediction value of the evidence, i.e., the posterior or actual probability of the murder hypothesis, we need to consider the prior probability of the murder scenario: how likely do we consider a nurse is to kill her patients? Whatever figure we put on this probability will tend to be extremely small. While there are cases like those of Harold Shipman, not a nurse but a doctor, who was thought to have killed 215 people before he killed himself in 2004, and Charles Cullen, who killed 45 patients between 1988 and 2003, these are extremely rare, and, interestingly, not conspicuous from a statistical point of view. If, for the sake of the argument, we put the prior probability of murder at 1 in 1 million, the posterior probability of murder shrinks to 1 in 342. If we revise the probability of chance, as some statisticians have proposed, we might end up with a posterior probability in the region of 1 in 48 or even 1 in 5, which would not come anywhere near the criterion of beyond reasonable doubt.[21]

9. A New Verbal Format

Initially, attempts to avoid unwarranted posterior probability conclusions in verbal terms led to the use of the phrase '(limited) evidence to support the hypothesis that', as follows:

The comparative examination provides
no evidence
limited evidence
moderate evidence
moderately strong evidence
strong evidence
very strong evidence
to support the hypothesis (Hs) that the suspect (S) is/is not the source of the trace material (T).
Format 2: Improved conclusion format, after Evett et al. (2000)

There are two problems. The first is that no alternative hypothesis is specified, as a result of which the evidence may easily be either under- or overestimated. The second problem is that the phrase tends to be equated with '(limited ... very strong) evidence for the hypothesis', which, even if not tantamount to saying that the hypothesis is (very) probable, is in serious danger of being interpreted as such. A correct if rather cumbersome phrase would be to say that the findings constitute 'a (....) increase in support of the hypothesis'.

The comparative examination provides
a slight increase
an increase
a great increase
a very great increase
in support of the hypothesis (Hs) that S is/is not the source of the trace material T.
Format 3: (Hyper)correct conclusion format, after Aitken (2000, 722)

Apart from the absence of any reference to an alternative hypothesis, this type of phrase has the virtue of being correct: the danger that a very strong increase

21 Buchanan 2007.

in support for a particular hypothesis is equated with very strong support for that hypothesis in absolute terms seems less acute if at all realistic. However, the very precision of the phrase may raise unnecessary questions.

The Netherlands Forensic Institute (NFI) is currently considering a reporting format which seeks to avoid both problems: it refers explicitly to an alternative hypothesis and it is not as easily understood as posterior probability. The format is to be used primarily in the various forensic identification disciplines and looks as follows:

The findings of the comparative examination are
equally likely
more likely
much more likely
very much more likely
under Hp that S is the source of T than under the defence hypothesis Hd that a random member of the population is the source of the trace material.
Format 4: Proposed conclusion format

10. Distinctiveness

On 2 February 2007, a group of predominantly UK based forensic speech examiners and phoneticians published a position statement introducing a new conceptual framework for expressing conclusions in forensic casework. Like Format 4 above, the proposed framework has a sound basis in Bayesian probability theory and seeks to avoid the use of transposed conditionals. Briefly, the new framework consists of two steps. The first step involves a (categorical) decision as to whether the known and questioned samples are compatible, i.e., whether they are deemed to be consistent with having been produced by the same speaker. There are three possible outcomes at this stage: consistent, not consistent and no decision. If the outcome is that the samples are judged to be consistent, this does not necessarily imply that they were produced by the same speaker. The second step in the decision process involves an evaluation of the distinctiveness of the features common to both sets of samples. Distinctive features are – implicitly – defined as 'unusual', or 'not shared by a substantial number of other people in the population'. To assign a rating to the distinctiveness of the features involved, they are located on a five-point scale:

5. Exceptionally distinctive – the possibility of this combination of features being shared by other speakers is considered to be remote
4. Highly distinctive
3. Distinctive
2. Moderately distinctive
1. Not distinctive

Format 5: Conclusion format proposed by UK based phoneticians*

Note: * Although the authors claim that they only recently became aware of the logical flaw in the traditional reporting format set out as Format 1 above, a detailed discussion of the logical approach was published in Forensic Linguistics, in Broeders (1999) and Sjerps and Biesheuvel (1999).

While this framework succeeds in avoiding transposed conditionals, the explanation of the highest point of the scale is flawed. To define the highest point of the scale in terms of 'the possibility of the combination of features being used by *other* [emphasis added] speakers' is to commit the double coincidence fallacy (Stoney 1991). The same error is often made with respect to DNA profiles. What is relevant is not the probability of a *second* person's having the same profile as the crime scene sample and the matching suspect, but the probability of the profile occurring *once* (on average) in the population. Compare throwing dice: the probability of throwing the same number in the second throw as in the first is 1 in 6, not 1 in 36. The correct criterion in the context of speaker identification would be the probability of this combination of features occurring in the speech system of a random person, not of it occurring in the speech system of two people. Put differently, and in parallel with the evaluation of a DNA profile match, it is the estimated frequency of the combination of features in question in the speech of speakers in the population. Besides, the phrasing of the highest point of the scale is such that it seems doubtful whether it will stop the reader from reading it as a traditional posterior probability statement.

11. Expectation Bias and Cognitive Contamination

There are two further threats to traditional forensic identification science which remain largely unaddressed. The first of these is expectation bias. Experts are typically asked to compare questioned material with reference material which the police have reason to believe originates from the same source. In addition, they are frequently exposed to domain-irrelevant information which may bias their findings. The examiner may be told that the suspect has already confessed, or that the result of another forensic examination was positive.[22] In order to avoid any effects of such forms of cognitive contamination, which may be quite strong,

22 For an interesting study of this effect see Dror and Charlton 2006 and Dror et al. 2006.

a strict separation should be maintained between analysts and reporting officers. At the same time, domain-*relevant* information may be of vital importance for an effective approach of the investigation, as is demonstrated by an illustration of the model for case assessment and interpretation advocated by Cook et al. (1998).

The problem of expectation bias may be overcome by the use of an evidence line-up, where the examiner is not just presented with questioned material and reference material but rather with a selection of material comprising the latter but also a number of items that originate from sources comparable to the alleged source. The examination should be blind in the sense that the analyst is ideally not aware of (1) which is the questioned material, (2) which is the reference material and (3) how many different sources are represented in the line-up. For example, in a cartridge casing examination, a line-up of trace material would be prepared for the analyst, comprising not just the casings found at the crime scene and the reference casings produced by firing the suspected source pistol, as is standard practice, but also containing a number of casings fired with pistols of a similar calibre. The analyst would then be asked to group the material, purely on the basis of the information contained in the material, combined of course with his knowledge and experience as an expert. A similar format is recommended for the visual domain, where eyewitnesses are not presented with a possible perpetrator in a 'line-up' of one, but are shown a number of people, including the suspect, who all meet the general description of the person seen at the crime scene.[23]

12. Conclusion

Expert reports may play an essential and sometimes decisive role in settling legal issues both in the criminal and the civil context. They may be used by judges and juries to help them determine the facts of a case or to find for one party rather than another but they may also be used to bolster or to legitimize a preconceived conviction based on non-scientific evidence. There is a danger that forensic expertise, because of its perceived scientific status, may serve to lend an aura of scientific respectability to the legal decision-making process which is not only frequently unjustified but at all times undesirable. The legal decision-making process is essentially that: a legal process. Forensic scientists should not be allowed or take it upon themselves to usurp the role of the judge but should always be aware that the role of the expert is to pronounce upon the weight of the forensic evidence, not to address the ultimate issue. Unlike traditional reporting formats, the model used in the interpretation of DNA evidence is ideally suited to do just that: it forces the expert to report on the probability of the findings under a particular set of hypotheses and leaves the determination of the probability of the (prosecution) hypothesis to the trier of fact.

23 Wells et al. 1998.

References

Aitken, C.G.G. (2000), 'Statistical Interpretation of Evidence/Bayesian Analysis', in Siegel et al. (eds).

Bayes, T. (1763), 'An essay towards a problem in the doctrine of chances', *Philosophical Transactions of the Royal Society* 53, 370–418; reprinted in *Biometrika* 45, 293–315 (1958).

Broeders, A.P.A. (1999), 'Foreword' and 'Some observations on the use of probability scales in forensic identification', *Forensic Linguistics* 6:2, 211–13 and 228–41.

—— (2003), *Op zoek naar de bron: Over de grondslagen van de criminalistiek en de waardering van het forensisch bewijs* (Deventer: Kluwer) (with summaries in English ('In Search of the Source') and French ('A la recherche de la source')).

—— (2006), 'Of earprints, fingerprints, scent dogs, cot deaths and cognitive contamination – A brief look at the present state of play in the forensic arena', *Forensic Science International* 159, 148–57.

Buchanan, M. (2007), 'Conviction by numbers', *Nature* 445, 254–5.

Champod, C. and Evett, I.W. (2000), 'Commentary on A.P.A. Broeders (1999): "Some observations on the use of probability scales in forensic identification", *Forensic Linguistics*, 6:2: 228–41', *Forensic Linguistics* 7:2, 238–43.

—— (2001), 'A probabilistic approach to fingerprint evidence', *Journal of Forensic Identification* 51:2, 101–22.

Cook, R., Evett, I.W., Jackson, G., Jones, P.J. and Lambert, J.A. (1998), 'A model of case assessment and interpretation', *Science & Justice* 38:3, 151–6.

De Groot, A.D. (1994), *Methodologie*, 12th Edition (Assen: Van Gorcum).

Dror, I. and Charlton, D. (2006), 'Why experts make errors', *Journal of Forensic Identification* 56:4, 600–616.

Dror, I., Charlton, D. and Péron, A. (2006), 'Contextual information renders experts vulnerable to making erroneous identifications', *Forensic Science International* 156:1, 74–8.

Evett, I.W. and Williams, R.L. (1996), 'A review of the sixteen point fingerprint standard in England and Wales', *Journal of Forensic Identification* 46:1, 49–73.

Evett, I.W., Williams, R.L., Jackson, G., Lambert, J.A. and McCrossan, S. (2000), 'The impact of the principles of evidence interpretation on the structure and content of statements', *Science & Justice* 40, 233–9.

Fine, G.E. (2006), A Review of the FBI's Handling of the Brandon Mayfield Case – Unclassified Executive Summary, Office of the Inspector General, US Department of Justice, Washington, DC.

Gigerenzer, G. (2002), *Calculated Risks: How to Know When Numbers Deceive You* (New York: Simon & Schuster).

Huber, R.A. (1959–1960), 'Expert witnesses', *Criminal Law Quarterly* 2, 276–96.

Inman, K. and Rudin, R. (2002), 'The origin of evidence', *Forensic Science International* 126, 11–16.

Kirk, P.L. (1963), 'The ontogeny of criminalistics', *Journal of Criminal Law, Criminology and Police Science* 54.

Kwan, Q.Y. (1977), 'Inference of Identity of Source', PhD Thesis, University of California, Berkeley, CA.

Loftus, E.F. and Cole, S.A. (2004), 'Contaminated evidence', *Science* 304:5673, 959.

McRoberts, A.L. (2002), 'Scientific working group on friction ridge analysis, study and technology', *Journal of Forensic Identification* 52, 263–348.

Popper, K.R. (1959), *The Logic of Scientific Discovery* (London: Hutchinson).

Risinger, D.M., Saks, M.J., Thompson, W.C. and Rosenthal, R. (2002), 'The Daubert/Kumho implications of observer effects in forensic science: Hidden problems of expectation and suggestion', *California Law Review* 90, 1–56.

Robertson, B. and Vignaux, G.A. (1995), *Investigating Evidence: Evaluating Forensic Science in the Courtroom* (Chichester: John Wiley & Sons).

Rudin, N. and Inman, K. (2004), 'Fingerprints in print – the apparent misidentification of a latent print in the Madrid bombing case', *CACNews* 4, 14–21.

Saks, M.J. and Koehler, J.J. (2005), 'The coming paradigm shift in forensic identification science', *Science* 309, 892–5.

Saks, M.J., Risinger, D.M., Rosenthal, R. and Thompson, W.C. (2003), 'Context effects in forensic science: A review and application of the science of science to crime laboratory practice in the United States', *Science & Justice* 43, 77–90.

Siegel, J.A., Saukko, P.J. and Knupfer, G.C. (eds) (2000), *Encyclopedia of Forensic Sciences* (San Diego: Academic Press).

Sjerps, M. and Biesheuvel, D.B. (1999), 'The interpretation of conventional and "Bayesian" verbal scales for expressing expert opinion: A small experiment among jurists', *Forensic Linguistics* 6:2, 214–27.

Stacey, R.B. (2004), 'Report on the erroneous fingerprint individualization in the Madrid train bombing case', *Journal of Forensic Identification* 54:6, 706–18.

Stoney, D.A. (1991), 'What made us ever think we could individualize using statistics?', *Journal of the Forensic Science Society* 31:2, 197–9.

Thompson, W.C. and Schumann, E.L. (1987), 'Interpretation of statistical evidence in criminal trials: The prosecutor's fallacy and the defence attorney's fallacy', *Law and Human Behavior* 11, 167–87.

Wax, S.T. and Schatz C.J. (2004), 'A multitude of errors', *The Champion*, September/October, 6.

Wells, G.L., Small, M., Penrod, S., Malpass, R.S., Fulero, S.M. and Brimacombe, C.A.E. (1998), 'Eyewitness identification procedures: Recommendations for lineups and photospreads', *Law and Human Behavior* 23, 603–47.

Chapter 4

Analysing Stories Using Schemes

Floris Bex

1. Introduction

Since the early 1980s stories, or sequences of states and events, have played an important part in theories on how judges, jurors or police investigators reason with the evidence in criminal cases. Authors such as Bennett and Feldman (1981) and Pennington and Hastie (1986; 1993) argue that decision-making in criminal cases is done by constructing stories about 'what happened' using the evidence in the case and then comparing these stories, thus trying to find the best story, that is, the story which is accepted as most probable. A good story should not only be supported by evidential data (e.g. testimonies, forensic data) but it should also be well structured and plausible; a well-structured story is built in such a way that it is easily understandable and a plausible story correctly describes a general pattern of states and events that one expects to come across in the world. Crombag et al. (1994) also argued that a well-structured and plausible story is important in judicial decision-making. However, they also found that in many cases a good or plausible story which is insufficiently supported by evidence wins over a bad or implausible story which is supported by evidence. To overcome this problem, Crombag et al. proposed their anchored narratives theory (ANT), according to which a story should be sufficiently anchored in reality using safe generalizations.[1] This anchoring of stories in reality also plays an important part in the investigative phase of a case (de Poot et al. 2004), where stories serve as guidelines in the search for new evidence. Twining (1999) and Anderson, Schum and Twining (2005) maintain that stories are psychologically necessary in the determination of the facts of a case, in that a story is used to organize and present the evidence in such a way that it is easily understandable. Like Crombag et al., they point to the dangers of stories and develop a simple protocol for analysing the plausibility and evidential support of stories.

1 Generalizations are general 'rules' about how we think the world around us works (Anderson et al. 2005). They can be based on empirical research but they can also be drawn from everyday experience. Not all of these generalizations are safe as they can be based on prejudices and dubious ideas about the world. Examples of generalizations are 'coroners can usually determine for how long someone has been dead', 'witnesses under oath usually speak the truth' and 'people from Suriname are more prone to becoming involved in crime than Dutch people'.

In sum, the main idea in the research of the last decades seems to be that while stories play an important part in evidential reasoning, one should be wary of the dangers involved in reasoning with stories: in Twining's (1999) words, stories are 'necessary but dangerous'. In order to overcome the danger of a good story pushing out a true story, stories have to be critically analysed – both the plausibility (whether or not the story conforms to trustworthy general knowledge about the world around us) and the evidential support (whether or not the story conforms to the specific evidential data in the case at hand) are important to consider.

Pennington and Hastie as well as Anderson et al. agree that these two aspects of stories, plausibility and evidential support, can be tested and analysed separately. Crombag et al. make a less clear distinction between these two aspects but they mention two types of generalizations in which stories can be anchored. Of the first type are generalizations which point to the plausibility of the story irrespective of the evidential data in the case; these generalizations can be causal generalizations, which are about the chain of events in the main story itself, or other generalizations which cover the point of the story or a specific event in the story. Of the second type are evidential generalizations, which link a story to the available evidence. Bex et al. (2006; 2007) have clarified this distinction between the two types of generalizations and argued that a story's plausibility can be analysed by looking at the causal generalizations in the story itself while the evidential support can be analysed by looking at the evidential generalizations linking the sources of evidence to the story. However, the causal links between the events in a story are not always explicit so it is not always possible to immediately analyse the causal generalizations in the story. In its most basic form a story is a sequence of events which are ordered in time and thus the only relations between the events are temporal. In such a case, where the causal relations between the events are not explicitly mentioned, these generalizations will have to be made explicit and/or other ways will have to be found to analyse the story's plausibility.

Pennington and Hastie argue that a story's plausibility also depends on the extent to which it conforms to what they call an *episode scheme*. This idea of an episode scheme is based on the idea of a script or explanation pattern. Schank and Abelson (1977; Schank 1986) argue that knowledge about the world can be expressed as a script or explanation pattern, which specifies the elements a typical story has. A scheme can be abstract or more specific; for example, a scheme for 'intentional actions' specifies a pattern of event types that a typical story about some intentional action contains and a 'restaurant' scheme describes a pattern of events that a typical story about a visit to a restaurant contains (e.g. ordering, eating, paying). The relations between the events in a story scheme can be causal but a very basic story scheme does not contain causal information so it can be used to assess stories which do not contain causal information. Furthermore, a story scheme can also help to make the implicit causal relations in a story clearer; if a simple, temporally ordered story fits the sequence of a story scheme then the causal relations between the events in the story are also based on the causal generalizations in the scheme.

The aim of this chapter is to investigate the notion of *story schemes*, a pattern of events or event types similar to the episode scheme or explanation patterns. Story schemes, their structure and features, will be modelled in a semi-formal way and I will examine how these schemes can be useful in the analysis of stories. The similarities and differences between the notion of story schemes and my previous work (Bex et al. 2006; 2007) will be discussed, and I will also add two simple but not trivial operations to the framework from Bex et al. (2007).

While this chapter does not concentrate on the specific roles which story schemes and analysis using these schemes can play in reasoning about evidence, some ideas about the possible roles of story schemes in different contexts will also be briefly discussed.

Because of the important role the plausibility of stories plays in reasoning with evidence, this chapter is devoted to analysing and assessing this plausibility. The plausibility of a story can be determined irrespective of the evidence in a case; as was argued before, plausibility and evidential support are different aspects of a story. However, this does not mean that I consider the evidential support of a story and the analysis of this evidential support unimportant; when reasoning with evidence in a criminal case, the evidential support of a story is the most important part, as we do not want good stories that have little or no evidential support to win over bad stories that have more evidential support. In our previous work (Bex et al. 2006; 2007), which will be briefly summarized in section 2, we have already discussed extensively how evidence can support a story through evidential generalizations, how these generalizations can be tested and how the evidence can influence the choice between different stories.

The rest of this chapter is organized as follows: section 2 discusses the existing research on the use of stories in legal reasoning, including the previous more formal research on stories and evidence (Bex et al. 2006; 2007); at the end of section 2 I will give examples of two operations on causal generalizations that can aid in the analysis of such generalizations. The first part of section 3 briefly summarizes existing work on story grammars, scripts and explanation patterns; the second part of section 3 discusses the features of story schemes, which are derived from the earlier work on explanation patterns. In section 4 an example will be given of how the analysis of stories using schemes can take place and I will discuss how the plausibility of a story scheme can be tested. Section 5 discusses some of the possible roles which story schemes and an analysis using story schemes could play in different kinds of evidential reasoning and section 6 concludes with a discussion and some ideas for future research.

2. Stories: Necessary but Dangerous

In this section existing research on the use of stories in legal decision-making and crime investigation will be summarized, showing the different ways in which stories can be used in reasoning with evidence. In this summary, the focus will be on how in the existing research the plausibility of stories is defined and assessed. This section is divided into two subsections: first, the research from legal psychology and legal theory on stories and story plausibility will be discussed and in section 2.2 my previous work on developing a logical model of this research will be summarized.

2.1. Stories in Legal Evidential Reasoning

By analysing the way all kinds of different decision-makers in criminal trials (judges, jurors, attorneys) reason and make decisions about the case at hand, Bennett and Feldman (1981) found that judicial decision-making depends on the construction of different stories around the available evidence. According to Bennett and Feldman, a story is organized around a central action or central event, which is essential to the plot of the story, and the rest of the story should act as the context for this central action. Background knowledge about the world allows us to establish connections between the central action and the other elements of the story. A plausible story is a story in which all the necessary connections between the elements of the story are present and these connections are based on unambiguous general knowledge; thus a plausible story is, in Bennett and Feldman's words, 'structurally unambiguous'.

An interesting observation by Bennett and Feldman is that the most plausible story is the story that is often taken to be true. Bennett and Feldman show this with an experiment: they asked 85 students to assess the truth of a number of stories that were told by the other students. Some of these stories were really true (that is, the events recounted had really happened) and other stories were made up. Some of the stories (both true stories and made-up stories) were complete and unambiguous but other stories were incomplete and ambiguous. It turned out that there is a significant relation between the structural ambiguity of a story and its credibility. That is, the more plausible a story, the higher the probability that the story is judged to be true, irrespective of the *actual* truth of the story.

Pennington and Hastie (1986; 1993) further developed the idea of a story in a criminal context. They proposed a model of judicial decision-making based on stories and tested it on human subjects. The model proposed consists of three stages which represent the stages a legal decision maker goes through when evaluating evidence. First, the decision-makers construct stories using the available evidence, knowledge about story schemes and knowledge about similar events. These stories are then evaluated using certainty principles and the best story is then matched to a verdict.

In Pennington and Hastie's work, a story has a standard structure: the basic form of a story is a simple sequence of events and a scheme can be imposed upon such a sequence. This scheme divides the different events in the story into different categories, where each category stands for a different role that an event or a sequence of events can fulfil. Such a scheme is called an episode, and is a basic model about intentional actions (Figure 4.1). This scheme is a simplified version of the scheme Pennington and Hastie proposed in their earlier work (Pennington and Hastie 1986). The links in this model are causal links and thus the model imposes a simple causal structure upon the basic story in accordance with the meaning of and relations between the separate states and events.

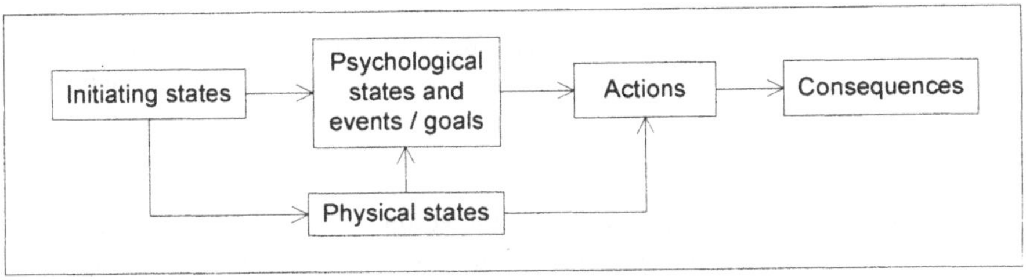

Figure 4.1 Pennington and Hastie's episode scheme

After a number of stories have been constructed around the evidence, the decision-maker should decide which story to accept. Pennington and Hastie proposed two certainty principles for determining 'what the best story is': coverage and coherence. The story's *coverage* stands for the extent to which the story conforms to the evidence presented at trial. The idea here is that the more evidence covered by the story, the more confidence a decision maker will have in that particular story. A story's *coherence*, which is similar to the notion of plausibility mentioned before, depends on three factors: consistency, plausibility[2] and completeness. A story should be consistent in that it does not contain internal contradictions between different parts of the story. A story is plausible if it conforms to the decision-maker's general knowledge of the world[3] and a story is complete when all of the elements from Figure 4.1 are part of the story.

The final stage in Pennington and Hastie's model involves matching the chosen story to a verdict category. For example, if there is a story of one man killing another, the decision-maker can choose between the verdict categories of first-degree murder, second-degree murder, manslaughter and self-defence (not guilty). In the table below an example of one of their verdict categories is given.

2 Pennington and Hastie see plausibility as a 'sub-criterion' of coherence; my definition of plausibility in this chapter is similar to Pennington and Hastie's coherence.

3 In Pennington and Hastie's definition, a story's plausibility is relative to the person assessing the story. An objective definition of a story's plausibility is more problematic, see the end of this section.

Table 4.1 Matching the verdict category of first-degree murder

Verdict Category	Identity	Mental State	Circumstances	Actions
First-degree murder	Right person	– Intent to kill – Purpose formed – Resolution to kill	– Insufficient provocation – Interval between resolution and killing	– Unlawful killing – Killing in pursuance of resolution

Notice how the different attributes of the verdict category correspond to the elements of the episode scheme from Figure 4.1: the mental state corresponds to the psychological states and goals, the circumstances correspond to the initial states and physical states and the actions correspond to the actions in the episode scheme.

Pennington and Hastie tested their model on 26 jurors whom they asked to look at a re-enactment of a murder trial. From the tests it followed that almost all subjects organized the evidence as a story of 'what happened' before deciding on a verdict and that most stories followed the episode structure as shown in Figure 4.1. An interesting observation was that the subjects filled in certain elements of the episode scheme to make complete stories. On average, a story constructed by a test subject consisted of about 55 per cent of elements which were directly inferred from evidence and about 45 per cent of the elements of a story – mainly psychological states and goals – were not inferred from evidence but added by the subjects to make a more complete story.

From Bennett and Feldman's as well as Pennington and Hastie's tests it follows that stories play an important part in reasoning with evidence, in that they help people organize the evidence and make sense of a case. Constructing stories also helps people to fill gaps in a case, as Pennington and Hastie's experiment shows. For example, it is often hard to directly infer from evidence that the suspect had bad intentions. In most cases, these intentions must be inferred from the actions that the suspect performed; in other words, these intentions can be inferred from the story. However, this research also shows that there are dangers inherent to stories, as Bennett and Feldman found that a good story can push out a true story.

Bennett and Feldman argue that a story's plausibility can be tested by looking for ambiguous connections in the story. This is, in my opinion, too vague, especially because the notion 'ambiguous connections', or unsafe background knowledge, is not defined. Rather, in Bennett and Feldman's theory, classifying a connection as such is done intuitively, as if decision-makers are naturally adept at analysing general knowledge about the world around us. Furthermore, Bennett and Feldman's work does not discuss the evidential support of stories.

Pennington and Hastie give clearer criteria for assessing stories: the criteria of completeness and consistency are clearly defined and ensure that the story is structurally sound and conforms to a general scheme of human intentional action we expect to find in the world. It is still unclear, however, how a story should conform to general knowledge of the world and thus when a story can be considered plausible.

Crombag et al. (1994) further investigated how we can make sure that a story is plausible in that it corresponds to general knowledge of the world. They argued that a story should fit and conform to the general episode scheme proposed by Pennington and Hastie. However, a story also has to be anchored using general knowledge of the world around us, and accepting a story is done by accepting a number of generalizations which act as anchors to the story. This is best explained by an example. Consider the case about Haaknat, adapted from Crombag et al. (1994, 138):

> John Haaknat is a drug addict who is desperately in need of money. He knows that the owner of the local supermarket takes his earnings to the bank every Friday, so he decides to rob the owner when he leaves the supermarket. Together with a friend who owns a car, they wait outside the supermarket. When the owner leaves the supermarket with the money to go to the bank, Haaknat gets out of the car and points a gun at the owner, shouting 'Give me the money.' The owner fears for his life so he hands Haaknat the money. Haaknat then gets into the car and drives off in the direction of a nearby park. The police start searching for Haaknat in the park and they find him hiding in a moat.

If we decide to believe the story about Haaknat, we also believe the generalization 'eyewitnesses can reliably identify people', as Haaknat was identified by the owner and other witnesses. Crombag et al. consider only one type of generalization, namely that which links the evidence, in this case a testimony, to the story.

Crombag et al. argue that the generalizations which act as anchors have to be safe for the ultimate decision to be rationally better motivated and not based on dubious generalizations. Say, for example, that there is evidence that at the time of the robbery it was dark outside. The generalization 'eyewitnesses can reliably identify people' can be made more specific: 'eyewitnesses can reliably identify people they saw in the dark'. Clearly, this generalization cannot be regarded as trustworthy general knowledge.

Crombag et al. discuss in detail how generalizations can be analysed in this way and decision-makers are urged to make the general knowledge they use to come to their decision explicit, so that the ultimate decision is better motivated and not based on dubious generalizations. However, exactly when a generalization is safe is not made clear and the details of what part the generalizations play in a story are left unspecified.

Twining (1999) and Anderson, Schum and Twining (2005) argue that a story is 'widely regarded as appealing to intuition or emotion and as a vehicle for irrational means of persuasion'. However, they recognize that stories are psychologically necessary in that they help people make sense of the world and of the events that happened in a particular case.

Anderson et al. give a simple protocol for analysing the plausibility, coherence and evidential support of stories. This protocol consists of a list of questions; some questions point to the evidential support for the story, for example 'To what extent does the evidence support the story?' and 'Is there evidence that conflicts with the story?' Other questions are meant to analyse the plausibility of the story, for example 'Is the story supported by plausible background generalizations?' or 'Does the story fit a familiar story such as Cinderella and what is the relevance of this?' So in Anderson et al.'s work, story plausibility is tested by looking at the background generalizations; here, a story's plausibility is not tested by looking at whether it fits a plausible episode scheme, but it is tested by analysing the generalizations which act as reasons to accept the story. For example, if we decide to believe the story about Haaknat, we also believe the generalizations 'people fear for their lives when they have a gun pointed at them' and 'people value their life higher than money' – this explains the owner's behaviour. These kinds of generalizations can also be made more specific. Say, for example, that there is evidence that Haaknat used a pink toy gun to threaten the owner of the supermarket. The generalization 'people fear for their lives when they have a gun pointed at them' can be made more specific: 'people fear for their lives when they have a pink toy gun pointed at them'. Again, the more specific generalization cannot be regarded as trustworthy general knowledge.

Furthermore, Anderson et al. argue that well-known stories, such as Cinderella, also affect our judgement of a story's plausibility. However, like the other authors mentioned here, they do not give a thorough, analytic account of how exactly these background generalizations and general stories serve as a tool in the analysis of stories.

The research discussed in this section seems to agree on the fact that the plausibility of a story can be analysed by looking at to what extent the story conforms to plausible background knowledge of the world. However, the notion of 'plausible general knowledge' is somewhat problematic. According to Cohen (1977), the plausibility of our general knowledge depends on our 'stock of knowledge', which is accepted through a cognitive consensus within a given group of people (for example, a society): if a generalization or episode scheme conforms to this stock of knowledge, it can be judged as plausible. Anderson et al. (2005) argued that this cognitive consensus about the stock of knowledge is a problematic notion: in any given group of people there will always be disagreements about which knowledge to accept as plausible and the idea of a general consensus is almost impossible in a dynamic, multicultural and multi-class society. However, it is possible and necessary to accept that there is a certain consensus about general knowledge; otherwise we would not be able to draw any conclusions. To meet any dangers posed by differences or arguments regarding generalizations or episode schemes, these generalizations should be as explicit and elaborate as possible. So while the ultimate conclusion about the plausibility of a generalization or episode scheme depends on the person(s) making this decision and their stock of knowledge, this conclusion about the plausibility is stronger to the extent that it is based on explicit and detailed generalizations.

2.2. Formal Argumentative Story-based Analysis of Evidence

In Bex et al. (2006; 2007), we aimed to construct a theory that combines causal stories[4] and evidential arguments. The main reason for developing this combined theory was to give sources of evidence, or evidential data, a more prominent place in a theory for reasoning about evidence with stories. This combined theory, which will be briefly summarized below, also allows for the critical analysis of the causal links within in the story.

The basic idea of the combined approach is as follows. A logical model of abductive *inference to the best explanation* (IBE)[5] takes as input a causal theory (a set of causal rules or generalizations) and a set of observations that have to be explained, the explananda, and produces as output a set of hypotheses that explain the explananda in terms of the causal theory. The combination of hypotheses and causal theory can be seen as a story about what might have happened. These hypothetical stories or *explanations* can then be compared according to the plausibility of their causal generalizations and the extent to which they conform to the sources of evidence in a case. These *sources of evidence* (e.g. witness testimonies, forensics reports) are connected to the stories by defeasible arguments, that is, arguments which can be attacked and defeated. For example, an argument with the premise 'the owner testified it was Haaknat who robbed him' and the generalization 'eyewitnesses can reliably identify people' has as its conclusion 'Haaknat robbed the owner of the supermarket'. This conclusion is an event in the story given earlier. Note that evidential generalizations can also be attacked by arguments. For example, if we have evidence that the robber wore a mask during the robbery, the generalization that eyewitnesses can reliably identify people can be attacked.

Defeasible arguments are also used to attack explanations: the causal rules of the theory are not just given but their applicability can become the subject of an argumentation process. For example, the causal generalization 'people fear for their lives when they have a gun pointed at them' can be attacked by arguing that in this case the generalization is not applicable because the gun was a pink toy gun.

Figure 4.2 shows an abstract graphical notation of stories as causal networks and arguments. In the figure, events that are not supported by evidence are in a dotted box and events that are supported by evidence are in a box with a solid line.

4 It should be noted that we use a naive interpretation of causality; sometimes a causal link does not represent a much stronger relation than temporal precedence.

5 See Lucas 1997 for an overview of abductive reasoning and Thagard 2004 for a slightly different take on IBE.

This is a semi-formal way of representing them, but translating them into well-known formalisms is straightforward (see Bex et al. 2007).

If there is more than one explanation for the explananda, they must be compared according to their plausibility and their conformity to the evidence in a case. The plausibility of an explanation is judged by looking at the plausibility of the causal generalizations in the causal theory. If a causal generalization is deemed implausible, it can be attacked with an argument: the more the causal generalizations are attacked by arguments, the less plausible is the story.

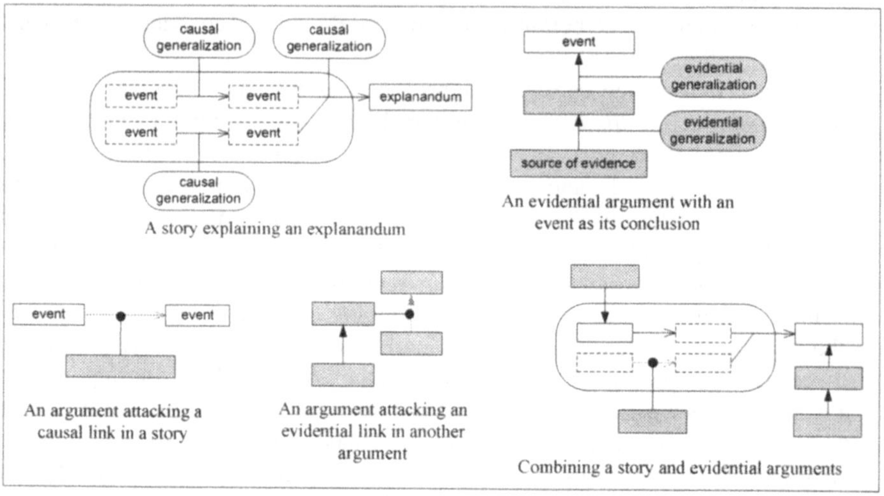

Figure 4.2 Stories, arguments and generalizations

An explanation's conformity to the evidence in a case, or its evidential support, can be measured by looking at how many events in the explanation are supported by an argument that is not attacked: the more events in the story that follow from evidential arguments, the better the story is.

In the model of Bex et al. (2007), the causal generalizations in a story cannot be changed; they can only be attacked. Bex and Prakken (2004) defined two ways of refining generalizations in an argumentation context; these same operations can be defined for causal generalizations. First, a causal generalization can be made more specific by explicitly adding the 'hidden conditions'. For example, say that we have a generalization 'if someone wants to rob another person, this may cause him to threaten that person with a gun'. One of the preconditions for this causal inference to be made is that the person who threatens with a gun actually has a gun, viz.:

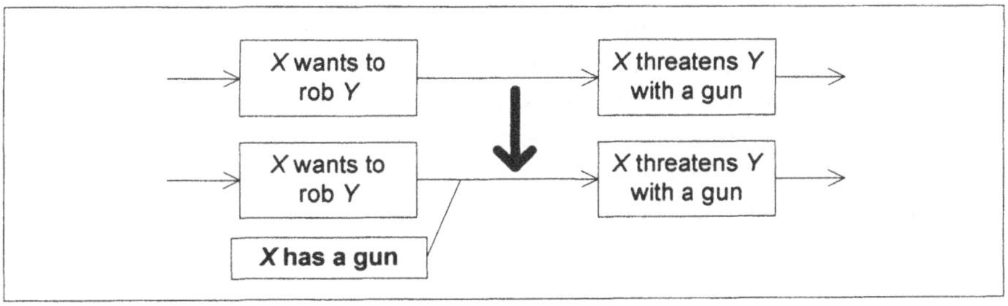

Figure 4.3 Adding hidden conditions to a generalization

Thus the generalization is changed into 'if someone wants to rob another person *and he has a gun*, this may cause him to threaten that person with the gun'.

Second, a causal generalization can be changed into a more specific generalization by 'unpacking' it, changing one causal link into a causal chain:

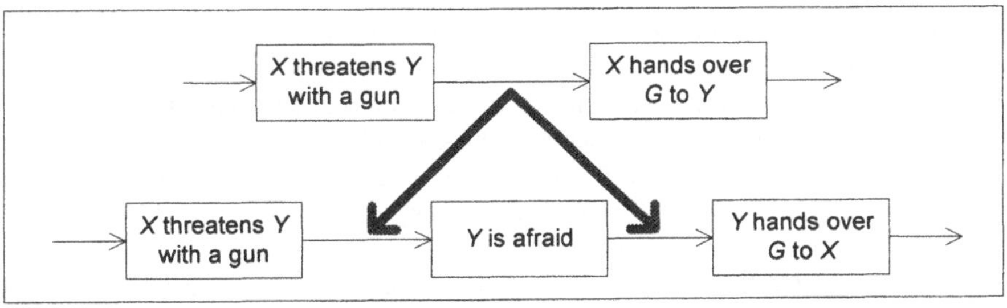

Figure 4.4 Unpacking a causal generalization

Here the causal generalization 'if someone (*X*) threatens another person (*Y*) with a gun, this person will hand over his belongings (*G*)' is changed into two generalizations, namely 'if someone threatens another person with a gun, this person will be afraid' and 'if a person is afraid, he will hand over his belongings'.

To summarize, evidential arguments require one to make explicit the evidential generalizations used and exceptions to these generalizations can be given, thus allowing for a critical analysis of the connections between the evidence and the story. Explicitly modelling the causal generalizations in the causal theory allows for a thorough examination of these generalizations: they can either be changed by exposing hidden conditions or by unpacking, and they can be questioned by attacking the generalizations with arguments. However, as was mentioned in section 1, a story's causal generalizations are not always explicit, so either ways will have to be found to make these generalizations explicit or other ways will have to be found to analyse a story's plausibility. Furthermore, the current formal theory does not allow us to measure the extent to which a story conforms to the intentional episode in the way that Pennington and Hastie proposed. To allow these other ways of analysing stories, the formal theory must be expanded by introducing story schemes. This will be discussed in the next section and in section 4 it will be shown how stories based on schemes can be analysed in more ways than stories based on causal theories.

3. Story Schemes

In the 1970s, the fields of cognitive science and artificial intelligence also took an active interest in stories. This research initially focused mainly on developing formal grammars for describing the structure of a typical story. Pennington and Hastie's episode schemes borrow heavily from the story grammars proposed by Mandler and Johnson (1977) and Rumelhart (1975). These story grammars also divide stories into episodes, which consist of a beginning, development (containing mental responses, goals and actions) and consequences. The episodes consist of either other episodes or individual events. The events are linked by causal as well as temporal links, as both sentences of the form 'event A THEN event B' as well as 'event A CAUSES event B' can be constructed in the grammars.

In later research the attention shifted towards story understanding by using a set of 'general action sequences' or scripts (Schank and Abelson 1977; Schank 1986). While Schank and Abelson (1977) also use a basic episode scheme, they also argue that story understanding is also achieved by using more specific and detailed information about standard patterns of actions when reading and understanding stories. These standard patterns or sequences are modelled as scripts; the much quoted 'restaurant script', for example, contains information about the standard sequence of events that take place when somebody goes to dine in a restaurant. Scripts help us to understand stories by filling in missing information. As an example, take the following (very short) story:

> Nicolas went to a restaurant. He asked the waitress for a plate of spaghetti. He paid the bill and left.

This story is understandable because it references to the restaurant script. Not all of the details (Nicolas taking off his coat, Nicolas reading the menu, etc.) have to be mentioned because they are assumed to happen when somebody goes to eat in a restaurant.

In his later work, Schank (1986) talks about *explanation patterns* (XPs), which contain information to understand the different events in the story and why they happen as they do. These XPs are similar to scripts in that they contain a standard sequence of events. An important difference is that Schank explicitly mentions that XPs are used to explain an event: they connect the event with general knowledge, namely an explanation that has been used in the past to explain the event. As an example, take the XP for 'robbery' (in the broadest sense of the word):

Robbery explanation pattern:

1. Event that the pattern explains: person *Y* loses (physical) ownership of goods *G*.
2. Events which are necessary for the pattern to be a valid explanation: *Y* loses ownership of *G*, person *X* robs person *Y*.
3. Events under which the pattern is likely to be relevant: *X* wants *G*.
4. Pattern of actions: *Y* owns *G* – *X* wants *G* – *X* wants to rob *Y* of *G* – *X* has an opportunity to rob *Y* – *X* robs *Y* – *Y* loses *G*.
5. Other relevant information: the time of the robbery, the place of the robbery, the type of force employed, the nature of the goods *G*.
6. More specific kinds of robbery: armed robbery, mugging, carjacking.

This XP is slightly different from Schank's version of an XP but the main idea is the same. Element 1 is the event that the pattern explains. Note that a pattern can explain more than one event; for example, the robbery XP can also be used to explain the fact that '*X* has *G*'. Elements 2, 3, 5 and 6 speak for themselves. Element 4 is perhaps the most important part of the XP; as Schank puts it, the pattern of actions, or *scenario*, is 'essentially a little story that is a carefully constructed causal chain of states and events [that explains the event to be explained]'. While the examples of patterns of actions Schank gives all seem to be causally or at least temporally ordered, the exact causal relations between the events is often left implicit.

Both the episode schemes proposed by Pennington and Hastie and the explanation patterns proposed by Schank can be seen as instances of something which I will call *story schemes*. These schemes divide the different events in the story into different categories ranging from abstract (Pennington and Hastie's episode scheme) to more specific schemes (explanation pattern schemes). In this chapter, story schemes will be modelled as an ordered list of events or types of events together with the possible relations between these events.[6] These relations will usually be causal relations, but they can also be temporal relations. Like the causal theories from section 2.2, which can abductively explain events, story schemes can also be used to explain certain events; an explanation pattern includes an explicit element 'event to be explained'. In this way, story schemes can explain events without the use of explicit causal information.

Story schemes can be abstract or specific; for example, the robbery scheme contains general instances of quite specific events (e.g. '*X* robs *Y*'), while Pennington and Hastie's scheme for intentional action (Figure 4.1) contains more

6 In this chapter, story schemes are represented through figures, where elements of a scheme are represented by boxes and (causal) relations are represented by arrows. This is a semi-formal way of representing them, but a formal translation along the lines of Bex et al. (2007) is straightforward.

general event types (e.g. 'actions'). The more specific schemes can sometimes be seen as instances of the more abstract schemes; for example, a robbery is an instance of an intentional action. In this way, different story schemes can be said to *match* each other: a story scheme S_1 matches a story scheme S_2 to the extent that the elements in S_1 correspond to the elements in S_2. The relationships between the elements of the intentional action and the robbery scheme are shown in Figure 4.5:

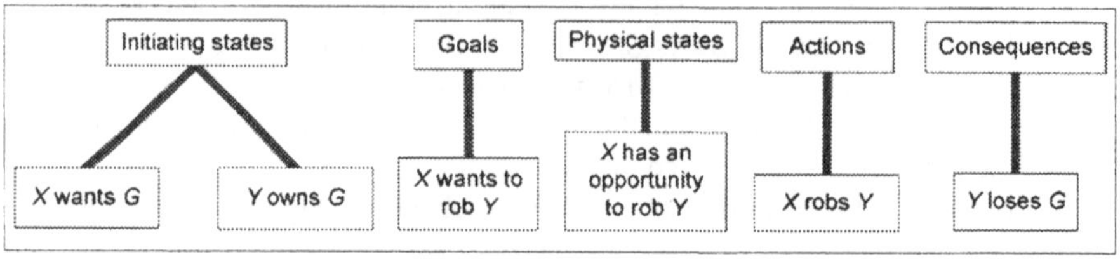

Figure 4.5 The relationships between the intentional action and the robbery scheme

These relationships between the elements of the different schemes can be expressed as generalizations, for example, '*X robs Y* expresses an action'. These generalizations have to be plausible: when such a generalization is implausible, the two schemes do not match. For example, the correspondence generalization '*Y owns G* expresses a goal' is not plausible so there is no relationship between these elements. Note that relationships and generalizations can be attacked by arguments in the same way that evidential and causal generalizations can be attacked (see section 2.2).

Sometimes two matching schemes only differ in one or two elements. For example, the element '*X* robs *Y*' in the robbery scheme can also be modelled as two separate elements, '*X* threatens to use force against *Y*' and '*Y* hands over *G* to *X*', thus making the concept of 'robbery' more specific.

Another aspect of story schemes that has to do with the correspondence between different elements of schemes was already noted by Pennington and Hastie: the so-called hierarchy of episodes. Story schemes are hierarchical, in that each component of an episode may correspond to an episode itself. In Figure 4.6, this recursiveness of the intentional action scheme can be seen. For simplicity's sake, some elements of the episode have been left out.

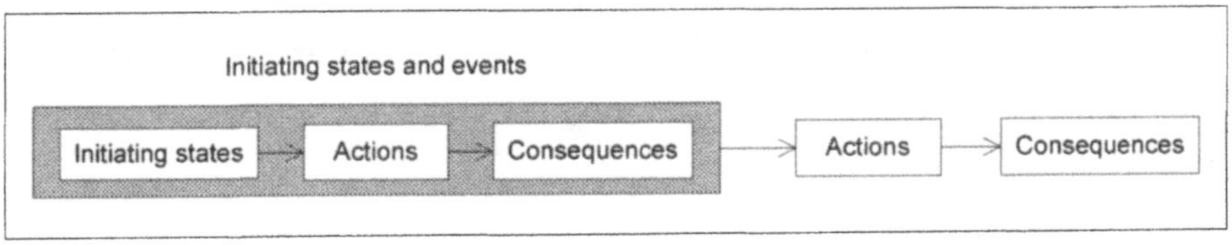

Figure 4.6 Recursive story schemes

Here, the initiating states and events correspond to a separate sub-episode.

If two story schemes match, there is usually also a correspondence between the causal relations in the different schemes. For example, the causal relations of the intentional action scheme (Figure 4.1) can be inserted in the robbery scheme because the elements of the intentional action and the robbery scheme correspond:

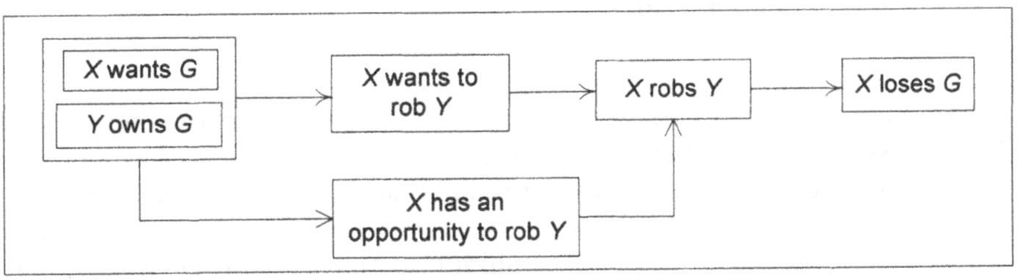

Figure 4.7 The robbery scheme with a more detailed causal structure

In this way, more abstract schemes which causal relations are generally agreed upon can be used as a tool for making the causal generalizations in a specific story scheme more explicit. Note that Figure 4.7 also contains an example of a hierarchical episode: 'A wants G' and 'B owns G' are separate sub-episodes of the robbery scheme. In the figure, the causal relations in this sub-episode have been left implicit.

In this section the basic structure and features of story schemes have been discussed as well as ways to specify story schemes. Story schemes are similar to causal theories as discussed in section 2.2 in that they can be used to explain events. However, explaining events with story schemes is perhaps somewhat simpler: whereas, in a causal theory, all the causal generalizations have to be made explicit, story schemes allow us to explain events by providing only the general pattern of events. This carries a risk, as implicit causal generalizations can be of dubious quality. Using more abstract schemes as a tool for making the causal generalizations in a specific story scheme more explicit allows us to analyse and assess the more specific causal generalizations and thus part of this risk is overcome. In the next section it will be shown how the plausibility of simple story schemes can be analysed and assessed.

4. Analysing Stories

A story is essentially a particular version of a story scheme, where the variables have been replaced by constants. Recall that in section 3 a story scheme for robbery was given; the Haaknat story is a particular instance of this scheme, viz.:

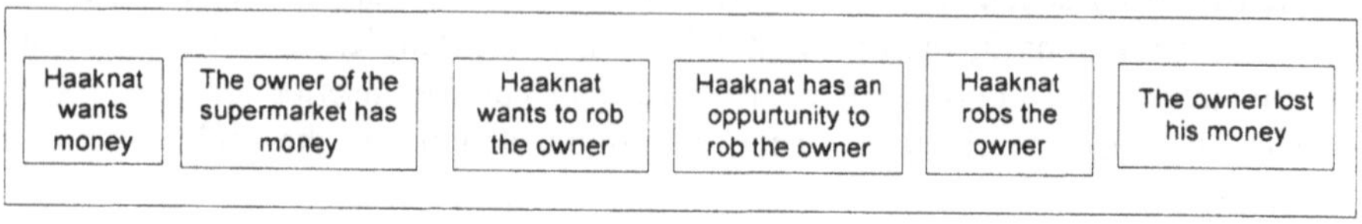

Figure 4.8 The Haaknat story

Here *X* in the scheme has been represented by 'Haaknat', *Y* has been represented by 'the owner' and *G* has been represented by 'money'. In this way, each story has an associated story scheme of which it is an instance. Here, the parallel between a story scheme and a causal theory as defined in section 2.2 can be seen. A causal theory is a collection of causal generalizations which, when the variables are instantiated, forms a story. A story scheme is similar to a causal theory, but in a story scheme the different events are not always linked and if there is a relation between events this relation is not necessarily causal but sometimes temporal. In this way, a story scheme is a less specific version of a causal theory that also allows for stories that do not contain explicit causal information.

In section 2.2 it was argued that the plausibility of a story can be analysed by looking at the plausibility of the underlying causal theory; in the same way, it can be argued that analysing the plausibility of a story that is based on a scheme can be carried out by looking at the plausibility of the underlying story scheme. Schank (1986) also argues that a plausible explanation pattern provides the natural context for the event it explains in the belief–goal–plan–action chain. If this condition for the plausibility of story schemes is added to the earlier condition that the individual causal generalizations in the scheme or theory should be plausible and sufficiently detailed, there are two criteria for determining whether or not a story scheme (and thus a story based on the scheme) is plausible. First, a story scheme should match the intentional action scheme; this ensures that the scheme adheres to the general goal–action chain as proposed by Schank and it also ensures that the scheme conforms to Pennington and Hastie's intentional episode scheme. Second, the causal structure and the causal generalizations of the scheme should be plausible and sufficiently detailed. So a story is plausible and sufficiently detailed if its associated story scheme matches the intentional action scheme and if the causal generalizations in the associated story scheme are plausible and sufficiently detailed. In the rest of this section, a story is said to *fit* a story scheme S to the extent that its associated story scheme matches S and vice versa. For example, Haaknat's story as detailed above completely fits the intentional action scheme because the story scheme associated with Haaknat's story, the robbery scheme, completely corresponds to the intentional action scheme and vice versa (see Figure 4.5).

The causal structure of the Haaknat story as shown above is not very detailed. However, it can be matched to the robbery scheme from section 3; often, a story does not contain explicit causal information but a story scheme does and matching the story to the scheme can give the story an explicit causal structure. As long as the story itself contains no explicit causal relations that contradict the causal relations in the story scheme, the causal relations from the scheme can be used in the story. In this way, the Haaknat story can be updated with the more detailed causal structure from Figure 4.7, providing us with the following story:

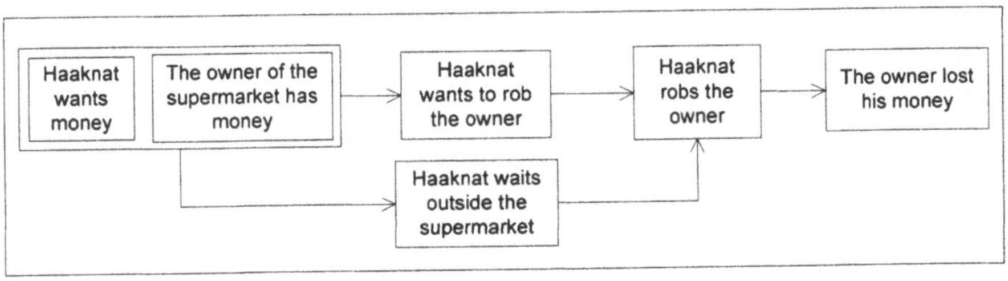

Figure 4.9 The Haaknat story with a clear causal structure

Note that in Figure 4.9, 'Haaknat has the opportunity to rob the owner' has been replaced with 'Haaknat waits outside the supermarket'. This story still fits the robbery scheme because waiting outside the supermarket can be seen as having an opportunity to rob the owner of that supermarket.

To give an example of a less plausible story, consider Haaknat's version of the events that explains why he was found in the moat. Haaknat testified that an hour before he was found, he had an appointment with Bennie, who owed him some money. Bennie did not want to pay back the money and Haaknat and Bennie got into an argument, during which Bennie drew a knife. Haaknat felt threatened by Bennie and he ran away. After a while, Haaknat sees the police officers looking for someone in the park, and he jumps into the moat to hide. Some time later, the police find Haaknat in the moat. The story scheme associated with this story can be written down as follows:

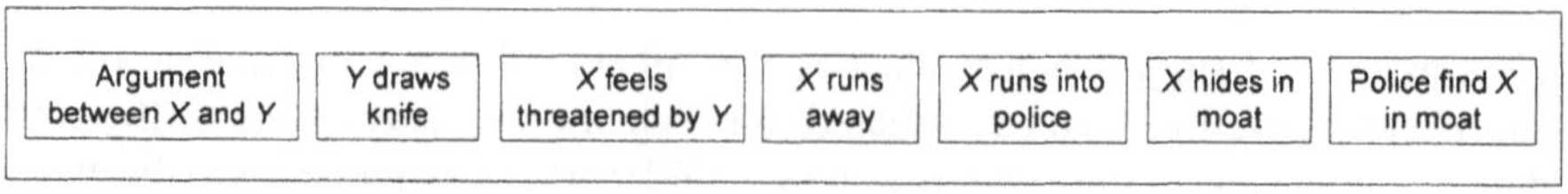

Figure 4.10 The 'hide after threatened' story scheme

The story can be represented in the same way by instantiating X with Haaknat and Y with Bennie. This story can be modelled as two episodes, where the first episode is 'Argument between X and Y – Y draws knife – X feels threatened by Y – X runs away' and the second episode is 'X runs into police – X hides in moat – police find X in moat'. However, when we model the story in this way, it does not fit the intentional action scheme, because the psychological states/goals element does not correspond to events in the story:

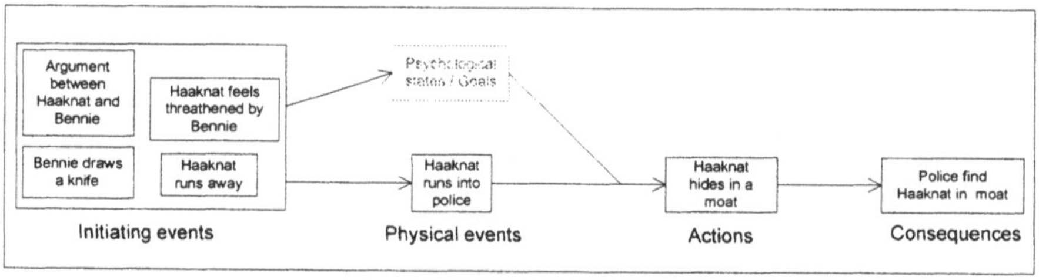

Figure 4.11 Haaknat's version of the story matched to the intentional action scheme

Alternatively, one could argue that 'Haaknat feels threatened by Bennie' is the psychological state in the above story scheme; then the story is modelled as a single episode:

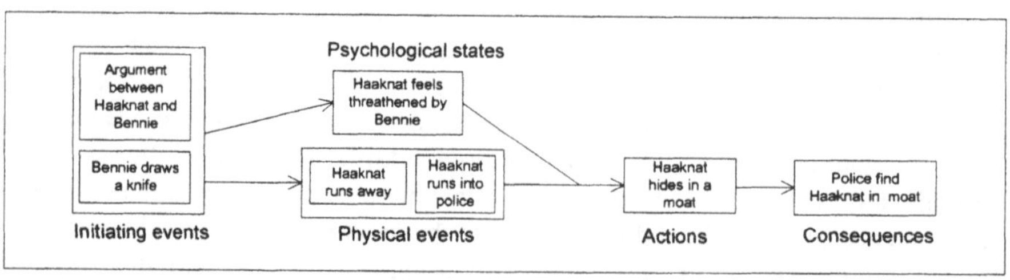

Figure 4.12 The story matched differently to the intentional action scheme

If the story is modelled in this way it does fit the intentional action scheme. However, recall that another requirement for a story to be plausible is that the individual causal generalizations on which the causal relations are based must be plausible. If we look at Figure 4.12, it seems that there is a causal relation 'X feels threatened by Y & X runs into police → X hides in a moat'. Expressed as a generalization, this would read 'someone who feels threatened by another person and encounters the police will hide'. This seems a strange generalization, because one would expect the person who was threatened to seek help from the police. So the story is less plausible because one of its internal causal generalizations is implausible.

During the case Haaknat said that the reason for the fact that he hid in the moat was that he thought the police were looking for him because of the argument with Bennie and that he did not want to be arrested. The story from Figure 4.11 can be updated with this event, filling in 'Haaknat does not want to be arrested' as a psychological state.

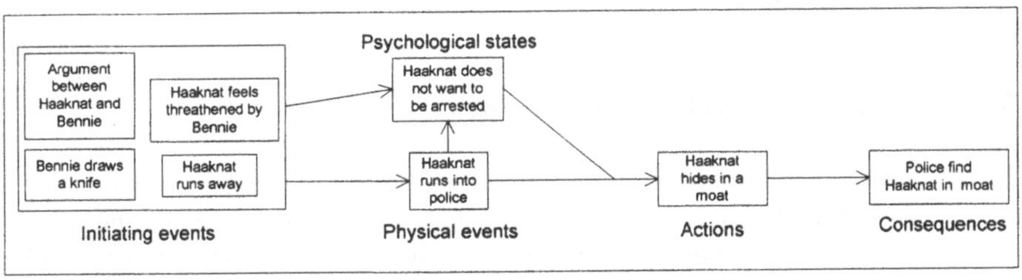

Figure 4.13 The updated Haaknat story

However, this explanation still is not completely plausible: the fact that it was Bennie who drew the knife and Haaknat who felt threatened makes it less plausible that Haaknat was afraid to be arrested. People who are threatened with a knife usually want the police's help, even if they were in a fight themselves. Here, the initiating events are a separate episode with its own causal structure.

In the above example it can be seen that trying to match the story to the intentional action scheme requires a careful analysis of the story and even if a story fits the scheme, it is still important to carefully analyse the causal relations in the story. Matching a story's associated scheme to the intentional action scheme requires one to make the causal relations between the events explicit so that they can be carefully assessed. This approach to analysing the plausibility of a story is perhaps closest to the method Crombag et al. and Anderson et al. propose: make explicit and analyse the generalizations that serve as the basis for the story.

In this section some general features of story schemes and some of the ways in which story schemes can be changed have been discussed. The story scheme approach proposed in this section makes the analysis easier. As was shown in the example in Figure 4.12, the plausibility of causal relations is often dependent on events earlier in the story. So it seems that often it is not just an individual generalization that is implausible but rather a pattern of successive events which are connected by generalizations. Instead of taking one causal generalization and updating by adding further (hidden) conditions, schemes, or chains of generalizations, are added to the model. Take the example in Figure 4.13, where all the events in the 'initiating events' box together with 'Haaknat runs into police' can be taken as conditions of a single generalization: 'if there is an argument between person *X* and person *Y* and *Y* draws a knife and *X* feels threatened by *Y* and *X* runs away and *X* runs into the police then *X* will hide'. However, if these initiating events are modelled as a pattern of events: 'argument between person *X* and person *Y* – *Y* draws a knife – *X* feels threatened by *Y* – *X* runs away – *X* runs into the police – *X* will hide', it is easier to insert and assess the causal relations between the different events. If it is modelled as a single causal generalization with five conditions, the temporal and causal information contained in the 'initiating events' sub-episode is lost and it is impossible to insert and assess any causal relations between the different conditions.

5. Story Schemes in Evidential Reasoning

Story schemes can be used in different ways in evidential decision-making and crime investigation. Their use often depends on the particular goals the person using the story schemes has; a judge or juror can use schemes to analyse a particular story, a lawyer can use schemes to build a persuasive story and an investigator can use schemes as possible hypotheses of what happened in a particular case. It is not my intention to provide a full overview of the different ways in which story schemes can be used for decision-making, persuasion and investigation. The main aim of this section is to briefly discuss some of the uses of the different ways of analysing stories and to provide ideas for future work.

In the decision-making phase, stories put forward by the parties can be critically analysed using schemes, as was illustrated in the previous section. Furthermore, it is also the decision-maker's task to see if the prosecutor's story fits a story scheme that contains the charge in the case at hand. In many jurisdictions, an act or a series of acts which are punishable are defined, often with the required psychological states. Pennington and Hastie argued that these possible verdicts are much like a story scheme, and that the story should be matched to the verdict category in the same way that a story fits other story schemes. Story schemes can also be used by the different parties in court to explain 'what happened' in the case: a sequence or pattern of events can be given as the cause for an event that is to be explained. At the end of the previous section it was made clear that giving a pattern or chain of events as an explanation is more natural and provides more possibilities than modelling the causal relation as a single generalization, giving a conjunction of causes for why a certain event happened as it did.

In an investigation context, story schemes are important in that they serve as possible hypotheses for what happened. According to de Poot et al. (2004), a criminal case which has to be investigated is often interpreted through different scenarios, or reconstructions of 'what happened'. When the investigators are faced with a case, different hypothetical scenarios have to be constructed, which can be done by using story schemes. The fact that story schemes can be used to explain events can also be used in the analysis of stories. For example, in Haaknat's version of the story, the event 'argument between Haaknat and Bennie' is not explained. However, we know that the argument was because of money that Haaknat lent Bennie, so the argument between Haaknat and Bennie can be explained using the following scheme:

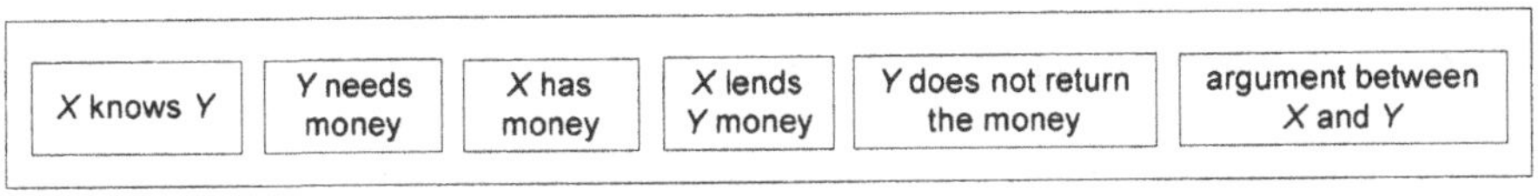

Figure 4.14 The 'argument about money' story scheme

In this way, the story can be expanded and further analysed and in this way also, the search for evidence is guided. For example, if the scheme from Figure 4.14 is used to explain the fact that Haaknat and Bennie had an argument, there must also be evidence for the fact that 'Haaknat knows Bennie'. Note that this was also possible in the formalism discussed in section 2.2 but story schemes allow us to explain events without using abductive inference and thus schemes allow us to build stories without explicit causal information.

6. Conclusion and Future Research

From the research on stories in legal reasoning it follows that stories are clearly 'necessary but dangerous'. Relatively simple patterns of events are easier to handle than complex argument trees. As Anderson et al. (2005) noted, our stock of knowledge contains not just generalizations but also other models of the world and Schank argues that our memories of past events are often organized as stories. So stories serve as a useful addition to, for example, argument trees such as the ones proposed by Anderson et al. (2005) and Wigmore (1931). In the investigation phase, stories play more than just a psychological role, because they serve as scenarios that guide the search for evidence. Whichever role stories are used for, it is imperative that their plausibility and evidential support is constantly tested and analysed.

In my previous work, the analysis and assessment of the plausibility of stories was done by attacking generalizations in a causal theory; at the end of section 2 I have shown another way of analysing these causal generalizations by exposing hidden conditions or unpacking the generalizations. However, this way of modelling stories and background knowledge can be complicated as we are dealing with complex causal networks containing elaborate generalizations with many conditions. Furthermore, stories do not often contain explicit causal relations between states and events which can be modelled in a causal theory.

In this chapter, I have proposed another way of modelling background knowledge, namely as story schemes. This has led to a list of features of story schemes and of the analysis of stories using these schemes:

- Story schemes can be modelled as ordered lists of elements, which are events or types of events, together with the possible (causal or temporal) relations between these elements.
- Story schemes can be used to explain events in the same way as causal theories.
- Story schemes range from *abstract* to *specific*. In more abstract schemes, the elements of the scheme are *general types of states and events* (e.g. actions or goals). In more specific schemes, the elements of the scheme are *specific states and events* (e.g. *X* threatens *Y* with a gun).
- Specific story schemes *match* more abstract story schemes and vice versa to the extent that there are relationships between the elements of the different schemes. These relationships, which can be expressed as generalizations, have to be plausible for the schemes to match.
- If two story schemes match, there is usually also a correspondence between the causal relations in the different schemes.
- Each story has an associated story scheme of which it is an instance (cf. Figures 4.5 and 4.8).
- A story *fits* a story scheme S if its associated story scheme matches S and vice versa.
- A story is plausible if it fits the intentional action scheme and if its internal causal generalizations are plausible.
- A story is sufficiently detailed if its causal structure is sufficiently detailed.

It must be said that explaining events with simple, less causally connected schemes is somewhat of a blessing in disguise: not having to give a detailed causal theory allows for the quick construction of different scenarios about what happened but care must be taken that the scenario or the story based on it is sufficiently detailed; i.e. the causal structure and the causal generalizations of the scheme should be sufficiently detailed.[7]

---

7 Note that exposing hidden premises and unpacking generalizations does exactly this: it makes the causal structure more detailed.

An important parallel can be drawn between story schemes and argumentation schemes (Walton 1996), which are schemes that represent stereotypical patterns of human reasoning through generalizations. Stories and story schemes can be likened to arguments and argumentation schemes, respectively; an argumentation scheme is a general scheme for arguments of a particular kind just as a story scheme is a general scheme for stories of a particular kind. In Walton (1996) a number of argumentation schemes drawn from real world examples are given. In future research it will also be important to define more types of story schemes. Furthermore, argumentation schemes also have critical questions which can be used to test the inference and it would be interesting to see if similar questions that can be used to test a story scheme can be defined.

Another subject that has not been discussed in this chapter is that it is also possible to construct and discuss defeasible arguments about the plausibility of stories. The criteria that a story should fit a plausible story scheme and that a story should be supported by evidence through plausible evidential generalizations are meant to be guidelines for the analysis of stories. For each individual case, the person performing the analysis has to determine which story and what evidence he or she trusts. This decision is also dependent on the task for which the stories are used; maybe an incomplete story will not convince a judge or juror but in a police investigation such a story can be a reason to look for other evidence to make the story complete. While it is impossible to give hard-and-fast rules as to which story is the better one, it is possible to argue about the 'value' of the different stories, using the above criteria as guidelines. These arguments would be on a separate level. For example, arguments could be constructed for or against a single story (e.g. 'your story is not complete' or 'your story is implausible') or stories could be compared (e.g. 'even though my story is not complete, it covers the evidence much better so my story is the best'). In Chapter 7, Verheij and Bex discuss how these kinds of arguments about the plausibility and evidential support can be formulated using argument schemes.

References

Anderson, T.J., Schum, D.A. and Twining, W.L. (2005), *Analysis of Evidence*, 2nd Edition (Cambridge: Cambridge University Press).

Bennett, W.L. and Feldman, M.S. (1981), *Reconstructing Reality in the Courtroom: Justice and Judgment in American Culture* (London: Methuen-Tavistock).

Bex, F.J. and Prakken, H. (2004), 'Reinterpreting Arguments in Dialogue: An Application to Evidential Reasoning', in *JURIX 2004: The Seventeenth Annual Conference* (Amsterdam: IOS Press), pp. 119–29.

Bex, F.J., Prakken, H. and Verheij, B. (2006), 'Anchored Narratives in Reasoning about Evidence', in Van Engers (ed.).

—— (2007), 'Formalising Argumentative Story-based Analysis of Evidence', *Proceedings of the Eleventh International Conference on Artificial Intelligence and Law* (New York: ACM Press), pp. 1–10.

Bobrow, D.G. and Collins, A. (eds) (1975), *Representation and Understanding: Studies in Cognitive Science* (New York: Academic Press).

Cohen, L.J. (1977), *The Probable and The Provable* (Oxford: Oxford University Press).

Crombag, H.F.M., Wagenaar, W.A. and Koppen, P.J. van (1994), *Dubieuze Zaken: de psychologie van strafrechtelijk bewijs*, 2nd Edition (Amsterdam: Contact).

Engers, T.M. van (ed.) (2006), *Legal Knowledge and Information Systems. JURIX 2006: The Nineteenth Annual Conference* (Amsterdam: IOS Press), pp. 11–20.

Hastie, R. (ed.) (1993), *Inside the Juror, the Psychology of Juror Decision Making* (Cambridge: Cambridge University Press).

Lucas, P. (1997), 'Symbolic diagnosis and its formalisation', *The Knowledge Engineering Review* 12, 109–46.

Mandler, J.M. and Johnson, N.S. (1977), 'Remembrance of things parsed: Story structure and recall', *Cognitive Psychology* 9, 111–51.

Nijboer, J.F. and Malsch, M. (eds) (1999), *Complex Cases: Perspectives on the Netherlands Criminal Justice System* (Amsterdam: Thela Thesis).

Pennington, N. and Hastie, R. (1986), 'Evidence evaluation in complex decision making', *Journal of Personality and Social Psychology* 51, 242–58.

—— (1993), 'The Story Model for Juror Decision Making', in Hastie (ed.).

Poot, C.J. de, Bokhorst, R.J., Koppen, P.J. van and Muller, E.R. (2004), *Rechercheportret – Over dilemma's in de opsporing* (Alphen a.d. Rijn: Kluwer).

Rumelhart, D.E. (1975), 'Notes on a Schema for Stories', in Bobrow and Collins (eds).

Schank, R.C. (1986), *Explanations Patterns: Understanding Mechanically and Creatively* (Hillsdale: Lawrence Erlbaum).

Schank, R.C. and Abelson, R.P. (1977), *Scripts, Plans, Goals and Understanding: An Inquiry into Human Knowledge Structures* (Hillsdale: Lawrence Erlbaum).

Thagard, P. (2004), 'Causal inference in legal decision making: Explanatory coherence vs. Bayesian networks', *Applied Artificial Intelligence*, 18, 231–49.

Twining, W.L. (1999), 'Necessary but Dangerous? Generalizations and Narrative in Argumentation about 'Facts' in Criminal Process', in Nijboer and Malsch (eds).

Walton, D.N. (1996), *Argumentation Schemes for Presumptive Reasoning* (Mahwah, NJ: Lawrence Erlbaum Associates).

Wigmore, J.H. (1931), *The Principles of Judicial Proof or the Process of Proof as Given by Logic, Psychology, and General Experience, and Illustrated in Judicial Trials*, 2nd Edition (Boston: Little, Brown & Company).

Chapter 5
The Evaluation of Evidence: Differences between Legal Systems

Marijke Malsch and Ian Freckelton

1. Introduction

Courts make use of evidence for reaching decisions regarding the disputes they have to solve. Varying types of evidence are presented to the trier of fact: witness statements, expert evidence from various disciplines, documentary evidence, and other types of evidence. Decision makers use several ways of tackling the problems they are faced with when confronted with conflicting pieces of evidence. An extensive literature exists about the complexities of evidence and the methods used to clarify them.

Two broad types of evaluating evidence within criminal cases can be identified. One of them concerns a 'holistic' way of looking at the various items of evidence and coming to conclusions about how convincing they are in terms of their probative value. The use of stories, comparing different accounts of what happened, and looking at events as a whole, is central to this model (Pennington and Hastie 1993; Wagenaar et al. 1993; Malsch and Nijboer 1999; Twining 1999; Anderson et al. 2005). The other way in which evidence is evaluated is atomistic, whereby each item of evidence is weighed and scrutinized independently from the other evidence. It represents, in principle, a bottom-up way of coming to conclusions regarding what happened in a case (Anderson 1999; Dingley 1999; Anderson et al. 2005).

This paper sketches the two approaches of testing and evaluating evidence utilized by courts and assesses the advantages and disadvantages of each. An answer is sought to the question, which type of legal system would prefer to use one of the modes of evidence evaluation over the other? Some legal systems may be more inclined to a holistic approach than others, and vice versa.

The first part of the chapter describes the two types of evidence testing and gives examples of each. In the second part, attention is paid to two archetypes of legal systems: the adversarial and the inquisitorial. Taking The Netherlands and Australia as examples of the two types of legal systems, the paper examines those characteristics that can be expected to contribute to a preference for either a holistic way or an atomistic way of evaluating evidence. The paper ends with conclusions and recommendations.

2. A Holistic Approach to Evidence Testing

When confronted with various items of evidence, decision makers can choose a 'holistic' approach, which implies that they do not predominantly distinguish between the various elements of evidence and they do not primarily focus on the contradictions between the constituent parts. Instead they take a story or narrative as a starting point and investigate how far the available evidence supports or contradicts this story. Building a story from the various elements on the basis of a quick and apparent observation of the evidence is one of the first things that is done by such decision makers. This story becomes the leading element that guides the decision maker in the further processing of the case. An attempt is made to reconcile newly emerging evidence to this story. When this does not work, the contradicting evidence may be rejected.[1]

The story model of approaching evidence has certain advantages. Stories play a highly important role in presenting a case to the decision maker. Stories can be highly convincing, even seductive. They attract attention and they give meaning to the facts that are established by the police and by other law enforcement officials (Wagenaar et al. 1993; Twining 1999). Building a story is a creative activity that, in itself, probably is less demanding than testing evidence in other ways (Anderson 1999; Twining 1999). For legal representatives who are arguing in favour of a certain state of affairs, the use of stories can be more attractive and advantageous than a scientific analysis of evidence that may not resonate with or be comprehensible to their audience.

Various functions are fulfilled by the use of stories in an argument. Stories can fill gaps in the evidence. An example may serve as an illustration of this function. A person travelling from a country in Latin America is stopped and searched at Schiphol Airport, Amsterdam, The Netherlands. In his luggage, no drugs are found, but the police do not want to let him go. They start to question him. His ticket appears to have been bought by someone else. Inquiries reveal that the person intends to stay for only two days in The Netherlands and then fly back to where he came from. When asked where he intends to stay, he gives an unclear answer. He has a small piece of paper with him with a telephone number which he says he was requested to ring. From the person answering the phone he expects to hear where he has to go. This is still not sufficient for arresting him as a suspect of drug crime. But the image starts to form. The last element relates to whether the police conclude that they are dealing with a man who has swallowed drugs (drug trafficker). This last element is the man having red eyes and smelling of faeces from his mouth. Although there is still no direct evidence of drugs, the story is

1 The theory of the 'story model' (Pennington and Hastie 1981) claims that the story which a juror constructs determines his or her decision (Pennington and Hastie 1993). Four certainty principles: coverage, coherence, uniqueness and quality-of-fit govern which story will be accepted, which decisions will be selected and the confidence or level of certainty with which a particular decision will be made.

almost complete now, and the man can be arrested. He is taken into custody and placed in a room with a toilet specifically designed for this type of situation. In the days to come, it will become evident whether the police have been correct. The red eyes and the smell coming from his mouth have been the gaps that still had to be filled in the story that has guided the police in their work. The same story has been told already many times in this airport, leading the police to start with a hypothesis and proceeding to search for evidence to prove that story. It can be expected that the same happens in other airports around the world.

Another function that stories may perform is that of giving sense to certain situations (Twining 1999). The killing by a young man of an older man without apparent reason might be explained by a story about what happened during the offender's childhood. His having been sexually abused at a young age by an elderly man may provide an explanation of why, as a grown-up, he has, on an impulse and almost without a direct, obvious cause, killed an elderly man. Such a motive can fill the gap that remains when merely the facts of the killing are there, and a story may be the frame of reference for this motive.

In a recent high profile case in The Netherlands, the so-called Schiedam Park murder, a man was convicted of the murder of a young girl. Later, it appeared that he was innocent. Another man confessed to the murder after his DNA had been detected and investigated.[2] What contributed in a major way to the court's findings about the innocent man's guilt was that he had confessed to the murder. On top of that, he was a known paedophile who had often been in the park where the little girl was murdered (Van Koppen 2003). It was easy and logical to construct a story and to reach a conclusion on basis of these scant data: the story that this man killed the girl. Nevertheless, it later became apparent that he was innocent of the murder. This case illustrates that stories, in their various functions, may play a dangerous role in at least some cases. Fundamentally, this is because an incomplete set of facts has the potential to generate more than one story, one of which wrongly appears the most convincing.

This brings us to a provisional evaluation of the holistic way of using evidence when making decisions, but also when presenting a case in court. Stories make the decision process easier and more speedy. On top of that, the evaluation of a case may become more exciting and interesting than the thorough presentation of evidence is. You generally do not need higher education for understanding a story, whereas higher levels of education may be required for comprehending and weighing complicated evidence. The use of stories is based on recognizing patterns, the use of generalizations and the use of intuition. In the construction of stories, continuous use is made of everyday generalizations and common knowledge, but also of guesses, rumours and untested facts (Twining 1999). The boundaries with gossip, untested facts or opinions, and with prejudices, are easily

2 The offender's DNA was included in the database because he was prosecuted for another offence. It was then established that there was a match between this DNA and the DNA found on the murdered little girl in the Schiedam Park murder.

transgressed, without the storyteller or the decision maker in all situations being aware of it. In legal systems like the one in The Netherlands, in which there are high levels of confidence in the work of the police, there is a great reliance on the stories presented by them as evidence.

The use of stories can be dangerous. It can make an argument more persuasive while, at the same time, the person using it can be completely wrong. Generalizations can remain implicit in the sense that the person presenting an argument uses them without explicitly paying attention to them or indicating the boundaries to the generalizations (Twining 1999). In that situation, such generalizations may play a decisive role without being tested for their reliability. That may, for example, be the case in situations where a suspect of a sexual crime has been convicted before for the same or similar types of crime.

The 'story' of the drugs trafficker described above may still be wrong. All elements that suggested that he transported drugs in his body may be attributable to other causes. Therefore, the Dutch criminal justice system, in most cases, requires direct evidence of the drugs: the drugs, in the case of a trafficker who swallowed them, have to actually leave the suspect's body and they have to be tested by a laboratory specializing in these types of examinations.

In general, the holistic approach that makes use of stories can be characterized as predominantly 'top-down', because it starts with a story holding a (provisional) conclusion as to the facts (the 'top') and continues the reasoning process with that story as a starting point. During the process, elements are sought that support this initial story. The question can be posed whether, in this model, alternative explanations of a state of affairs are always well investigated. Data that are inconsistent with the story that has been accepted can induce a state of cognitive and/or affective dissonance in which the hearers are loath to surrender and discard the initial hypothesis which had resonated with them. The use in actual practice, and the effects that may be obtained with presenting a story, risk becoming more relevant than a thorough examination of all arguments and items of evidence.

Typical questions that a user of the story model may reflect on are:

- How well is this story structured?
- Do all items of evidence fit within this story?
- If not, might those items of evidence have occurred by accident, or through witnesses who lie, or through experts who mispresent their findings?
- Can any alternative version of the story be constructed which is also consistent with the known facts?
- How can the story be best presented to convince the audience?[3]

---

3 This last question may seem somewhat misplaced here. The first questions test the quality of the story while this one concerns the issue of how to present it. Stories can be more attractively presented than atomistic analyses, and they are more easily understood, particularly by a less educated public. For these reasons, we are of the opinion that this question is in place here.

3. Atomistic Approaches of Evidence Testing

An atomistic approach includes a step by step analysis of all items of evidence available. Wigmorean analysis (Wigmore 1937; Anderson et al. 2005) and argumentative analysis (Feteris 1999) are examples of such atomistic approaches. There are more atomistic approaches than the ones presented here, however (Anderson et al. 2005). One of them is the 'outline' method, which is easier to use than Wigmorean chart analysis, but for which it is harder to maintain the rigour that the chart method requires (Anderson et al. 2005, 145). This chapter limits itself to a discussion of Wigmorean analysis and argumentative analysis.

3.1. Wigmorean Analysis

Wigmorean analysis clarifies the relationship between the available evidence in a case and the propositions needed for argumentation making use of that evidence (Wigmore 1937; Palmer 2003; Anderson et al. 2005). A Wigmorean analysis can result in a chart that organizes all arguments used in a dispute with the help of the use of symbols and signs for indicating the types of relations between the arguments, propositions, generalizations and assertions. Performing such an exercise creates awareness of the (subconscious) steps taken when preparing an argument and it shows how many generalizations it is based on (Dingley 1999, 188). It also makes clear how weak some inferences may be, and how far-fetched some of the generalizations are that are necessary to be able to make the argument work. Such an approach often portrays arguments as links in a chain – if one link is shown to be weak or misconceived, the chain leading logically to an inference of guilt is broken.

There are a number of limits to the usefulness of such a Wigmorean analysis. Although it is helpful to order a mass of evidence, such an exercise does not address all issues. For instance, it does not deal with many questions of law, such as whether certain evidence would be admissible at trial, and the way evidence can best be presented in court.[4] Wigmorean analysis, however, is very important in bringing to the surface all the 'hidden' steps lawyers take when trying to make an argument. This is all the more so in cases with complex evidentiary problems (Dingley 1999, 188). In uncontested cases, in which there is no discussion of the proof of the alleged facts, a holistic approach may be considered, by some analysts, to be sufficient. There is a risk, however, that cases are too readily considered to be simple, leading to a too quick adoption of the story model. Anderson et al. (2005) hold the view that narrative complements analysis but cannot be an alternative to analysis. 'Skipping' the more rigorous and demanding methods of analysis in

4 The story model does not address issues like the admissibility of evidence at trial either, but it does use presentation in court as a means for making arguments more persuasive.

favour of just constructing stories would present too serious a risk of inaccurate decision making.

Typical questions that are asked in a Wigmorean analysis of a case are:

- Was the witness able to see what he contends to have seen?
- Did he have any motive for lying?
- Did he himself believe what he said?
- How well does the witness's memory work in general?
- Did witnesses have any contact after they had been summoned but before they were heard?
- How has the expert's investigation been conducted?
- Had the expert sufficient information at their disposal?
- Has the expert given reasons for their opinion?
- What is the expert witness's domain of expertise?
- What is the expert's experience?
- Is this a recognized field of expertise?
- How 'hard' and uncontested is this field of expertise?
- Have experts had any contact before reporting, have they discussed their opinions and have they collaborated in their views (Anderson 1999; Dingley 1999; Malsch and Hielkema 1999; Anderson et al. 2005)?

These questions illustrate how, ideally, each item of evidence is first looked at by itself, after which relations with other pieces of evidence are established. Forming a total picture of the whole case would be postponed until all items of evidence have been assessed and weighed. It has, however, been asserted that atomistic analyses start from a certain standpoint in the case (Dingley 1999; Anderson et al. 2005). The standpoint reflects, among other things, the point in time at which the analysis is made. A historian can look at post-trial evidence: this means that important facts that came up after the trial can be taken into consideration, an advantage that lawyers presenting the sides in a conflict during the hearing of a case do not have (Twining 1994, 270–71; Dingley 1999). On top of that, a theory of the case may be selected in order to be able to understand how arguments are structured and choices are made (Anderson et al. 2005). Since that would imply that the person who performs the analysis has already formed a presumption about how the course of events leading to the case has developed, forming a theory seems contrary to typical characteristics of an atomic analysis. The view that this analysis starts from a certain standpoint or theory, which suggests that the outcome of the analysis might be different depending on which one is chosen, suggests that the analysis does not seem to aim at reaching an absolute truth, but at reaching a relative one.

We hold the view that it is not strictly necessary to first select a theory of the case before analysing it in a Wigmorean sense. This does not do away with the fact that this type of analysis can be very well employed starting from a certain theory about the case. In fact, public prosecution officers and/or lawyers for each side in a conflict always adopt a certain theory of the case when applying an atomistic analysis, namely a theory that best reflects the interests of their office and/or of their clients. In most cases, uncertainties exist, especially with respect to the use of generalizations, personal motives of those involved, witnesses' memories and expert opinions. Thus different views on a state of affairs remain possible, leaving room for different theories on a case when starting to analyse it, even when atomistic methods are rigorously employed.

3.2. A Pragma-Dialectical Perspective

A second example of an atomistic way of reviewing evidence is a pragma-dialectical approach of critical argumentative discussions. This method of reviewing an argumentation scrutinizes the elements which play a role in the resolution of a difference of opinion (Van Eemeren and Grootendorst 1992; Feteris 1999). This approach forms a heuristic tool in finding the elements which have a function in the process of resolving conflicting views. The model is also a tool for determining whether a discussion has been conducive to a resolution, and which factors in the discussion process offer a positive and which a negative contribution (Feteris 1999, 161). The pragmatic part of this approach formulates communicative and interactive rules for the use of argumentative language in various discussion situations. The core of the pragma-dialectical theory consists of an ideal model for critical discussions and a code of conduct for rational discussants. The rules that are thus developed acknowledge the right to put forward a standpoint and to cast doubt on a standpoint (Feteris 1999). The focus of this approach, therefore, differs from a Wigmorean analysis in that it is more concerned with the rules of a debate that may guarantee a 'correct' outcome. Wigmorean chart method, by contrast, takes the items of evidence as they are and tries to identify relations between them.

The aim of pragma-dialectical approach is to reconstruct both the argumentation and the structure of a discussion. With the help of this approach, it should be possible to determine whether a standpoint can be successfully defended against the critical reactions against it. This approach is a useful tool for studying judicial decisions. The various arguments used in a case can be presented in so-called 'diagrams' which reflect all arguments put forward in a case and the explicit and unexpressed premises upon which they are based (Feteris 1999). Such an analysis may show that reasons given for a judicial decision are deficient or incorrect, or that certain generalizations are used that may not be applicable to that specific situation. The analysis may also clarify that certain relevant arguments are neglected by the court.

The focus of these two atomistic methods of analysing evidence, the Wigmorean and the pragma-dialectical analysis, is comparable to a large degree: they start with the individual elements of a case which are, initially, considered independently from the other elements. The strengths and weaknesses of the elements are established. Subsequently, the relationships with the other elements in a case are scrutinized. The question is asked whether each individual element is corroborated by other elements, or, by contrast, whether other elements are inconsistent with it. Background generalizations and premises are revealed and assessed. As such, a diagram or chart can be made that includes all elements and all relations between them. The final standpoint in a case can then be presented. This approach can be characterized as 'bottom-up': starting with the items of evidence or the arguments, investigating them and finally reaching an overall decision. However, this bottom-up nature may be obscured if the analyst departs from a theory or standpoint in a case which, then, dominates or even distorts an objective analysis of the facts.

4. Adversarial and Inquisitorial Legal Systems

Adversarial systems, of the kind that can be found in most common law countries, have a number of characteristics that distinguish them from inquisitorial legal systems. The latter systems are to be found mainly in administration of criminal justice on the continent of Europe. In this section, a rough sketch is made of both types of systems; they have been analysed and portrayed in greater depth elsewhere (Damaška 1997; Van Kampen 1998; Van Koppen and Penrod 2003; Nijboer 2008).

The most conspicuous difference is that in adversarial systems the two parties play the most important role in the collection and presentation of the evidence. The judge chairs the hearing of the case but stays, for the most part, in the background, ensuring that the rules of evidence and procedure are adhered to and that the parties do not behave oppressively or unfairly. Adversarial systems are based on two features: party autonomy and party incentive. The responsibility for conducting a factual investigation lies with the parties. The judge does not perform any investigative tasks (Van Kampen 1998; Malsch and Freckelton 2005).

In inquisitorial systems, by contrast, judges play a comparatively more active role in reviewing evidence and interrogating defendants, witnesses and experts. As such, inquisitorial legal systems have been designated as 'court-centred' systems. Law enforcement officials in inquisitorial systems are expected to fulfil many functions that are generally fulfilled by the parties in an adversarial system. They are expected to adduce evidence both favourable to and against the defendant. Witnesses and experts are generally called to the stand by law enforcement officials and not primarily by the defence. Inquisitorial officials are expected to review all actions and decisions that have been made by other officials who were previously involved in the case (Malsch and Freckelton 2005). The formal equality of the parties is an element that is, as a consequence, stressed more strongly in an adversarial system than in an inquisitorial system (Van Koppen and Penrod 2003). The debate between the parties about which 'truth' ought to prevail is central to adversarial legal systems. Under the inquisitorial model, a legal procedure is considered more as an inquest, an official and thorough inquiry directed at establishing the true facts (Damaška 1997; Freckelton and Ranson 2006).

The differences between the two types of systems have various corollaries. An oral presentation of all evidence to the trier of fact generally plays a larger role in adversarial systems, whereas it is less important in inquisitorial systems. Although oral presentation of evidence would be quite consistent with the inquisitorial model, it is an historical fact that the inquisitorial systems tend principally to rely on documentary presentation of evidence (Van Koppen and Penrod 2003). Still there are important exceptions to this rule. Jury trials in Belgium and France are oral to a very large extent, but procedures without lay involvement in these jurisdictions are not.

Another consequence of these fundamental differences is that trial in open court in adversarial systems is far more relevant than in inquisitorial systems. Adversarial systems stress the importance of questioning witnesses in open court, whereas inquisitorial systems, as in The Netherlands, regularly satisfy themselves with the reports of the interrogations and investigation by officials that have taken place before the hearing of the case.

There probably is no country in the world that unites all aspects described here of both the two types of systems (Honoré 1981; McEwan 1998). And no two national legal systems are totally equivalent. Many differences exist between the legal systems all over the world, and the two types of systems described here are archetypal only.[5] Many systems mix elements of the adversarial and the inquisitorial. However, this brief sketch may well serve as a starting point for our assessment of the influence of the type of system on the way evidence is reviewed. Our analysis continues by narrowing our focus on the administration of criminal justice in The Netherlands, which can be characterized as one of the most 'inquisitorial' systems in the world (Van Koppen and Penrod 2003, 4). We pose the question: what aspects of this system induce a specific way of dealing with evidence (holistic or atomistic)? Next, the characteristics of an adversarial system that lead to a special way of reviewing evidence are explored.

5. An Audit Model of Decision-making: History and Operation

The Dutch criminal justice system has been characterized as an 'audit model' in which the police, under the prosecutor's direction, investigate and review the facts of a case to see if the results establish that the accused committed a crime (Anderson 1999, 50). The prosecutor reviews and audits the work of the police in deciding whether and how the case should proceed. If criminal charges are

---

5 An example in this regard is the reality that even in adversarial systems juries are not presented with a scientifically organized collection of facts to each of which they can attach statistical links to variables and possibilities leading to a verdict. Rather, what occurs is that jurors are expected to organize a mass of data into a story which they can understand and which comports with a verdict either of guilty or not guilty (see Bennett and Feldman 1981).

preferred, a single judge or a three-judge panel in the district court, with the aid of suggestions and comments by the lawyer for the defendant, audits and tests the reliability of the records compiled by the police and submitted by the prosecutor, to decide whether they conform to generally accepted standards and demonstrate that the facts alleged should be accepted as satisfactorily proven. And, finally, a three-judge Court of Appeal panel may conduct a comprehensive de novo audit of the record in light of such further points and tests as the public prosecution officers and the lawyers suggest should be considered or conducted. To the extent that the decisions turn upon points of substantive or procedural law, The Netherlands Court of Cassation stands as the final arbiter (Anderson 1999, 50).

The auditing and reviewing of evidence by a hierarchical higher authority within the legal system is central to the audit model described here. This audit takes place principally on the basis of written reports. As was explained before, inquisitorial systems (like that in The Netherlands), often rely on documentary evidence, in which officials give an account of the actions they have performed, or the decisions they have made. Oral provision of explanations or description of the actions that have been undertaken is largely absent in the Dutch criminal justice system. The hierarchical structure of auditing steps taken by law enforcement officials reveals the roots of the Dutch criminal justice system in the influence of the French occupation (1810–1813). In 1810, the French made The Netherlands a part of their territorial divisions and centralized the government during the years which followed. The French aimed at a unified national state as well as national legislation in codes which would express the idea of legislative power as the highest power in the nation. The laws had to be applied by a hierarchical administration and a hierarchical judiciary. The major task of the courts, especially the higher ones, was to check whether the lower officials had followed the regulations of the procedural code accurately (Nijboer and Sennef 1999).

The legislation that was in use in France, and that was introduced into The Netherlands during this era, stipulated that serial checks should be performed in relation to all steps, actions and decisions made by 'lower' law enforcement officials involved in a case (Nijboer and Sennef 1999). Authorities focused primarily on verification of what had happened in the case before they became involved. The procedural code contained rules which prescribed that the performance of all individual actions had to be recorded in the case file. Non-compliance with these rules was sanctioned by the potential for a higher authority to annul or overturn the initial decisions. This top-down type of control, which still largely exists in today's Dutch criminal procedure, encourages officials to phrase accounts of their actions in the formal terms of the law. As a consequence, police records largely contain phraseology that employs legal terminology. What has happened in actual practice remains unclear, and often invisible, because of this way in which legal actions that have been undertaken are accounted for (Nijboer and Sennef 1999, 14).

The inquisitorial system in The Netherlands leaves only a relatively secondary role for defence lawyers. Most of the investigation in a case is done by the officials of the system: the police, the prosecution and the (investigative) judge. The relatively restricted role of the defence in the Dutch system has its corollary in a tendency to attempt to reach consensus at trial. Although procedures are changing under the influence of verdicts by the European Court of Human Rights (ECHR) in this respect, the Dutch criminal justice system is considerably more compromise-oriented with respect to how a case should be dealt with than are adversarial systems (De Groot-van Leeuwen 2006). In most cases involving expert evidence, only one expert reports, and this expert is generally called to the stand by 'the system'. By contrast with the procedure in adversarial systems, defence lawyers do not often present their own experts (Hielkema 1999). As a consequence of this tendency, Dutch court sessions in criminal cases are generally not characterized by a fierce debate between the two sides. They can be more effectively portrayed as a discussion of the case file by the participants, in which the independent court plays a dominant role.[6]

Thus, in most cases, experts are appointed by the law enforcement officials, and not by the defence lawyers. Not primarily being hired to play a role in the battle between parties has certain obvious merits. The first aim of involving experts in a system such as that in The Netherlands seems to be the finding of the truth and not the winning of the case. The general, underlying presumption in the Dutch system is that such a truth exists independently of the party presenting it, and that it would not make a difference which expert reports in a case. According to this presumption, any expert would be expected to come to the same conclusions when investigating a case. As a consequence of being appointed by 'the system', the inclination of the expert to align with the interests of one of the sides in a conflict seems lower in the Dutch system than in systems where the parties select the experts (Malsch and Freckelton 2005). Experts appointed in the Dutch criminal justice system can be considered as more impartial than those working in adversarial systems. They are less tightly and directly affiliated to one of the parties and they are not primarily expected to play a role in the actual battle between the parties.

Summarizing, The Netherlands 'audit model' of dealing with criminal cases has the following characteristics that bear a relationship to how evidence is evaluated:

- a comparatively considerable independence of the experts who do report;
- a focus on finding 'the' truth;
- a hierarchical audit of the work of law enforcement officials;
- an account of actions in written reports;
- use of the terminology of the law in written reports;
- a tendency to seek consensus;
- indirect testing of evidence in court with the help of written reports; and
- reviewing of evidence primarily carried out by law enforcement officials.

6 This does not hold good for complex, very serious and highly publicized cases, however, which are more strongly characterized by a battle between the parties.

The relationship between these characteristics of the Dutch criminal justice system and a preference for a specific method for reviewing evidence will be explored later in this chapter. Before that, we will address the characteristics of an adversarial system against the background of the question of how this system deals with evidence.

6. The Adversarial Way of Reviewing Evidence

Particular reference is made hereunder to literature on the Australian legal system but its characteristics are broadly representative of adversarial systems more generally. The prosecuting authorities, such as Offices of Public Prosecutions, have the responsibility for presenting evidence in court. The principal mode of evidence presentation is oral and only modest numbers of documents are 'tendered', thereby formally becoming evidence that can be taken into account by the trier of fact, usually a jury. It is the parties, namely the prosecution and the defence, that have principal responsibility for determining what evidence goes before the triers of fact. The judge asks questions to clarify matters but only plays a modest role in how the evidence is placed before the decision-making body, the jury. Where technical questions of evidentiary admissibility are raised, the trial judge, as the trier of law, takes such decisions (Freckelton 1987). The judge generally does not call any witnesses in criminal trials but, rather, plays a role in assisting the triers of fact to understand and contextualize the admitted evidence. On occasions, too, important evidence may not be presented to courts because neither party is prepared to call it – by reason of the potential detriment to the arguments which they are propounding. Even so there are very restricted circumstances indeed in criminal trials in which judges can call witnesses of their own motion to remedy such deficiencies. The judge's passivity in this respect is exemplified by the judgment of Sir Daryl Dawson of the Australian High Court, in *Whitehorn* v. *The Queen* (1983) 152 CLR 657, who at 682 observed:

> A trial does not involve the pursuit of truth by any means. The adversary system is the means adopted, and the judge's role in that system is to hold the balance between the contending parties without himself taking part in their disputations. It is not an inquisitorial role in which he seeks himself to remedy the deficiencies in the case on either side. When a party's case is deficient, the ordinary consequence is that it does not succeed. If the prosecution does succeed at trial when it ought not to and there is a miscarriage of justice as a result, that is a matter to be corrected on appeal.

Typically, the focus of adversary procedure is not on the truth of material facts but upon the truth of the facts put in issue by the accused (Jackson 1988). A consequence of this is that pleas of guilty are rarely scrutinized by judges. The judge restricts himself or herself to making rulings on the admissibility of proposed evidence by reference to exclusionary rules that have evolved as judge-made law ('the common law') or as enactments of Parliament – Evidence Acts. It is common for expert witnesses to be called by both the prosecution and the defence. 'Battles of experts' take place and it is the responsibility of cross-examining counsel to assist the triers of fact to sift the base metal of the expert evidence from the gold, or, put another way, to separate the wheat from the chaff (see Freckelton 1997).

Expert evidence may be excluded on the basis that a witness is not sufficiently possessed of specialized knowledge, the evidence is not about a sufficiently acknowledged field of expertise but is about a matter of common knowledge, or its bases are not proved, or it trespasses upon the ultimate issues to be determined by the triers of fact (Freckelton and Selby 2009). In addition, if expert evidence is more probative than prejudicial in the sense, for instance, of being unduly misleading, confusing or consumptive of time, it may also be excluded by the exercise of the overriding discretion of the trial judge.

The dynamic by which experts are sought out because of their known ideological inclinations on a particular issue, paid by one party, prepared and nurtured for litigation, and then treated supportively by one party and hostilely by the other can lead to problematic affiliations between the commissioning party and the views expressed by the expert. This has brought about significant levels of mistrust and concern on the part of many judges (see Freckelton et al. 1999) and magistrates (see Freckelton et al. 2001) in relation to experts' bias (see Jones 1994; Meintjes-van der Walt 2001; Golan 2004; Caudill and LaRue 2006;).

Under adversarial systems there is generally no presumption that there is 'truth' which is available to be found. Rather, the focus is upon different perspectives and upon available admitted evidence: principally, in the case of criminal proceedings, whether the case is proved beyond reasonable doubt on the evidence that is adduced before the court. As the Australian Law Reform Commission put it in 1987 (p. 160):

> The 'search for the truth' proposition is not valid. Our trial system falls well short of that objective and deliberately so. The parties place the material before the judge. Its extent and quality depends on the energy and resources of the parties and their desire for victory. Generally, both law and tradition prevent the judge from doing more than seeking clarification through his or her own questioning. Often one or both parties may not wish to establish 'the whole truth'. It is also possible for cases to be decided on the basis of assumed facts. Time and cost constraints also limit the 'search'. In reality, what happens is that 'a new kind of truth is established'. The facts as found by the court are taken to be true.

During the last 20 years there has been an escalating view, at least in adversarial contexts, that there is not such a thing as identifiable, objective reality – rather there are relativistic and variable perspectives on what occurred. The question for the courts is not an existential one as to whether truth has been found but, in the criminal context, whether the evidence in sum is sufficient to justify the conclusion that there is proof of guilt to the requisite standard.

7. The Evaluation of Evidence: The Holistic and Atomistic Approaches Revisited

Having addressed two ways of evaluating evidence and two types of legal systems, we now attempt to assess whether certain properties of the two types of legal systems may lead to a preference to use either atomistic or holistic approaches when assessing a mass of evidence.

Direct, immediate ways of testing evidence, such as are more often used in adversarial legal systems, can be expected to be specifically connected to an atomistic approach, in which every element in the evidence is investigated thoroughly before triers of fact reach an overall conclusion. When they have the possibility of directly reviewing evidence, triers of fact do not have to draw their conclusions exclusively on the basis of stories that have been constructed by other participants who have been involved in the case. This is the only characteristic of a legal system (the adversarial system) that is almost exclusively related to an atomistic approach. All other characteristics can be related to a holistic approach as well, or bear no specific relation to one of the approaches.

Helpful for a holistic approach is, most of all, a tendency to compromise, which is characteristic of the Dutch legal culture. Early acceptance of a story that represents the facts in a case may result in a failure to assemble inconsistent information or evidence that emerges at a later point in time. Early acceptance can be accelerated where there is reliance on written reports that contain predominantly formulaic statements in the wording of the law, or that contain suggestions of stories that may cover the facts of a case. Such types of reports do not render further atomistic examinations attractive. Lack of time or other resources can further lead to participants too readily accepting the initial story and not re-evaluating their position.

The use of written materials as evidence can discourage atomistic investigation of cases. In such a situation, it is easier to fall back on what already has been examined before and has been described in reports. There are, however, substantial differences in the ways Dutch law enforcement officials draw up reports of their findings. Some reports provide a summing-up or advance a hypothesis as to what has happened; others have the characteristics of a story. Some reports present both the questions that have been asked during an interrogation and the answers that are given, whereas again others give summaries of what has been said. These different methods of making up reports may lead to different degrees of verifiability for the triers of fact and, thus, to different incentives for using atomist methods for analysing and verifying them.

Summarizing our findings so far, it can be concluded that only a few characteristics of legal systems seem to lead directly to either atomistic or holistic ways of scrutinizing evidence. The strongest relationship seems to exist between a compromise-oriented system (or, culture, see Malsch and Nijboer 1999; De Groot-van Leeuwen 2006) in combination with a customary use of written materials as evidence, with a preference for a holistic, story-based approach. A tentative conclusion may thus be drawn that inquisitorial systems, and especially that of The Netherlands, strengthen the inclination to disregard alternatives. And adversarial systems may have a relationship with a direct, immediate way of testing evidence.

An essential difference between adversarial and inquisitorial systems exists where the first type of system seems to deny the existence of an 'absolute truth', whereas inquisitorial systems take the presumption of an 'absolute truth' as a starting point when engaging expert evidence (Gutwirth and De Hert 2001). The overwhelming trust that the Dutch legal system invests in reports of both the police and of experts, as compared to distrust in many adversarial jurisdictions, seems pertinent to this difference (Nijboer 2008).

8. Conclusions

Stories should not be considered as an alternative to analytical approaches, but rather they complement them (Anderson et al. 2005). Narratives can be used to construct plausible stories which have the potential to be supported by evidence. Stories can complement, but cannot substitute for, a detailed analysis. Stories are constructed to order the evidence so that it logically supports a theory of a case (Anderson et al. 2005). At the commencement of a case and at its end, stories and narratives may help to identify gaps that must be filled. Hypotheses may be constructed with the help of stories that have then to be explored with help of atomistic methods. Switching from one approach to the other, therefore, happens in most cases. Ultimately, the objective of the user of a narrative is to create a story that the fact-finder will accept as the most plausible – as the most consistent with either guilt or innocence.

As such, both detailed atomistic analysis and the use of stories can be helpful in analysing cases. Of both, it has been contended that they are necessary or even indispensable (Wagenaar et al. 1993; Anderson et al. 2005). The conclusions of our analysis so far are that, by reason of their specific characteristics, certain inquisitorial systems may have an inclination to rely on a story model. In The Netherlands' criminal justice system, participants in a trial start from the presumption that there is only one truth, and that one of the most important aims of a trial is to disclose this truth (Gutwirth and De Hert 2001). One expert reporting in a case may, thus, be considered sufficient. When this expert has proffered his or her opinion, other experts are no longer needed, because this one expert is expected to have told the one and only truth. This complacent attitude encourages early acceptance of and adherence to stories as they are presented by this one expert. There is a serious risk that the Dutch justice system too easily adopts a story model and refrains from conducting more atomic analyses, leading to incorrect decisions as to the facts in complex cases.

The critical attitude of lawyers in adversarial systems towards 'the' truth as presented by experts, seems to lead more readily to a detailed analysis of the facts. The sides to a conflict are not easily convinced by the standpoint of the other side. As a result, an ongoing examination takes place of the views brought forward by the parties, although there can still be a problematic element of deference to experts (see Caudill and La Rue 2006). However, the more mistrustful approach to evidence, especially expert evidence, not only leads to more atomistic analyses, it may also have as a consequence that more convincing stories are sought which better cover the evidence that is found. The sides in a conflict in adversarial systems are simply more active on different levels than the participants in criminal trials in The Netherlands. In various respects, the Dutch criminal justice system is too complacent and lacks a sufficiently critical attitude towards police investigation and expert evidence. The risks of partial experts, commissioned and paid by the parties, remains a serious problem in adversarial systems. A better acknowledgement of the existence of, and search for 'the' truth would be advisable in these countries.

References

Anderson, T.J. (1999), 'The Netherlands Criminal Justice System: An Audit Model of Decision-Making', in Malsch and Nijboer (eds).

Anderson, T.J., Schum, D. and Twining, W. (2005), *Analysis of Evidence*, 2nd Edition (Cambridge: Cambridge University Press).

Australian Law Reform Commission (1987), Evidence, ALRC 38 (Canberra: AGPS).

Bennett, W.L. and Feldman, M. (1981), *Reconstructing Reality in the Courtroom* (London: Tavistock).

Caudill, D.S. and LaRue, L.H. (2006), *No Magic Wand: The Idealization of Science in Law* (Lanham, MD: Rowman & Littlefield).

Damaška, M.R. (1997), *Evidence Law Adrift* (New Haven, CT: Yale University Press).

De Groot-van Leeuwen, L.E. (2006), 'Merit Selection and Diversity in the Dutch Judiciary', in Malleson and Russell (eds).

Dingley, A.M. (1999), 'The Ballpoint Case: A Wigmorean Analysis,' in Malsch and Nijboer (eds).

Eemeren, F.H. van and Grootendorst, R. (1992), *Argumentation, Communication, And Fallacies: A Pragma-Dialectical Perspective* (Hillsdale, NJ: Lawrence Erlbaum Associates).

Feteris, E.T. (1999), 'What Went Wrong in the Ballpoint Case? An Argumentative Analysis and Evaluation of the Discussion in the Ballpoint Case', in Malsch and Nijboer (eds).

Freckelton, I. (1987), *The Trial of the Expert* (Melbourne: Oxford University Press).

—— (1997), 'Wizards in the Crucible: Making the Boffins Accountable', in Nijboer and Reijntjes (eds).

Freckelton, I. and Ranson, D. (2006), *Death Investigation and the Coroner's Inquest* (Melbourne: Oxford University Press).

Freckelton, I. and Selby, H. (2009 forthcoming), *Expert Evidence: Law, Practice, Procedure and Advocacy*, 4th Edition (Sydney: Thomson).

Freckelton, I., Reddy, P. and Selby, H. (1999), *Australian Judicial Perspectives on Expert Evidence: An Empirical Study* (Melbourne: AIJA).

—— (2001), *Australian Magistrates' Perspectives on Expert Evidence: A Comparative Analysis* (Melbourne: AIJA).

Golan, T. (2004), *Laws Of Men and Laws of Nature* (Boston, MA: Harvard University Press).

Gutwirth, S. and De Hert, P. (2001), 'Een Theoretische Onderbouw voor een Legitiem Strafproces', *Delikt & Delinkwent* 10, 1049–63.

Hastie, R. (ed.) (1993), *Inside the Juror: The Psychology of Juror Decision Making* (Cambridge: Cambridge University Press).

Hielkema, J. (1999), 'Experts in Dutch Criminal Procedure', in M. Malsch and J.F Nijboer (eds).

Honoré, A.M. (1981), 'The Primacy of Oral Evidence', in Tapper (ed.).

Jackson, J. (1988), 'Two methods of proof in criminal procedure', *Modern Law Review* 51, 249.

Jones, C.A.G. (1994), *Expert Witnesses: Science, Medicine and the Practice of the Law* (Oxford: Clarendon Press).

Kampen, P. van (1998), *Expert Evidence Compared: Rules and Practices in the Dutch and American Criminal Justice System* (Antwerpen: Intersentia).

Koppen, P. van (2003), *De Schiedammer Parkmoord: Een Rechtspsychologische Reconstructie* (Nijmegen: Ars Aequi Libri).

Koppen, P. van and Penrod, S.D. (eds) (2003), *Adversarial Versus Inquisitorial Justice: Psychological Perspectives on Criminal Justice Systems* (New York: Kluwer Academic).

Malleson, K. and Russell, P.H. (eds) (2006), *Appointing Judges in an Age of Judicial Power: Critical Perspectives from around the World* (Toronto: University of Toronto Press).

Malsch, M. and Freckelton I. (2005), 'Expert bias and partisanship: A comparison between Australia and The Netherlands', *Psychology, Public Policy and Law* 1, 42–61.

Malsch, M. and Hielkema, J. (1999), 'Forensic Assessment in Dutch Criminal Insanity Cases: Participants' Perspectives', in Malsch and Nijboer (eds).

Malsch, M. and Nijboer, J.F. (eds) (1999), *Complex Cases: Perspectives on The Netherlands Criminal Justice System* (Amsterdam: Thela Thesis).

McEwan, J. (1998), *Evidence and the Adversarial Process – The Modern Law* (Oxford: Hart Publishing).

Meintjes-van der Walt, L. (2001), *Expert Evidence in the Criminal Justice Process: A Comparative Perspective* (Amsterdam: Rozenberg Publishers).

Nijboer, J.F. (2008), *Strafrechtelijk Bewijsrecht* (Deventer: Kluwer).

Nijboer, J.F. and Reijntjes, J.M. (eds) (1997), *Proceedings of the First World Conference on New Trends in Criminal Investigation and Evidence* (Lelystad: Koninklijke Vermande).

Nijboer, J.F. and Sennef, A. (1999), 'Justification', in Malsch and Nijboer (eds).

Palmer, A. (2003), *Proof and the Preparation of Trials* (Sydney: Thomson).

Pennington, N. and Hastie, R. (1981), 'Juror decision-making models: The generalization gap', *Psychological Bulletin* 89, 246–87.

—— (1993), 'The Story Model for Juror Decision Making', in Hastie (ed.).

Tapper, C. (ed.) (1981), *Crime, Proof and Punishment: Essays in Memory of Sir Rupert Cross* (London: Butterworths).

Twining, W.L. (1994), *Rethinking Evidence: Exploratory Essays* (Evanston, IL: Northwestern University Press).

—— (1999), 'Generalizations and Narrative in Argumentation about "Facts" in Criminal Process', in Malsch and Nijboer (eds).

Wagenaar, W.A., Koppen, P.J. van and Crombag, H.F.M. (1993), *Anchored Narratives: The Psychology of Criminal Evidence* (London: Harvester Wheatsheaf).

Wigmore, J.H. (1937), *The Science Of Judicial Proof as Given by Logic, Psychology, and General Experience* (Boston, MA: Little, Brown & Company).

Chapter 6
Inference to the Best Legal Explanation

Amalia Amaya

1. Introduction

How do legal decision-makers reason about facts in law? A popular response appeals to probability theory, more specifically, to Bayesian theory. In the Bayesian approach, fact-finders' inferential task consists of updating the probability of the hypothesis entailing guilt in light of the evidence at trial in the way dictated by Bayes' theorem. If, by the end of the trial, this probability is sufficiently high to meet the reasonable doubt standard, the verdict 'guilty' is appropriate (Tillers and Green 1988). Bayesianism provides an elegant framework for analysing evidentiary reasoning in law. Nonetheless, in the last decades, the Bayesian theory of legal proof has been subjected to severe criticism, which has shed serious doubts upon the possibility of explaining legal reasoning about evidence in Bayesian terms.[1] In this chapter, I shall explore the feasibility of an approach to legal evidence and proof alternative to the probabilistic one, to wit, an explanationist approach. According to this approach, many instances of factual reasoning in law are best understood as 'inferences to the best explanation,' i.e., a pattern of reasoning whereby explanatory hypotheses are formed and evaluated. More specifically, I shall argue for a coherentist approach to inference to the best explanation for law according to which factual inference in law involves first the generation of a number of plausible alternative explanations of the events being litigated at trial and then the selection, among them, of the one that is best according to a test of explanatory coherence.

The defence of an explanationist model of legal proof will proceed as follows. I start by giving a brief description of inference to the best explanation. I then proceed to articulate a model of inference to the best explanation for law. I shall restrict my analysis to criminal trials, even though the model is also potentially applicable to civil trials. Next, I illustrate this model by means of a well-known case, the O.J. Simpson case. I will then consider a major objection that may be raised against a model of inference to the best explanation for law, namely, the so-called 'problem of underconsideration.' I conclude by examining this problem in detail and suggesting some ways in which it may be overcome.

1 See Amaya 2007a, for a summary of these criticisms.

2. Inference to the Best Explanation: Unfolding the Model

Talk about inference to the best explanation has been very popular in the last decades in philosophy of science and A.I. (Harman 1965; Thagard 1978; Lycan 1988; Ben-Menahem 1990; Day and Kincaid 1994; Josephson and Josephson 1994; Psillos 1999; Flach and Kakas 2000; Lipton 2004; Aliseda 2006). Contemporary discussions about inference to the best explanation take Peirce's writings on abduction as their starting point. Peirce's views on abduction changed significantly in the course of his writings, and they have been subjected to a number of different and often conflicting interpretations (Frankfurt 1958; Anderson 1986; Kapitan 1992; 1997; Hintikka 1998). In his earlier work, Peirce distinguished between deductive reasoning, inductive reasoning, and a kind of reasoning that he called 'hypothesis'. He defined hypothesis as follows: 'Hypothesis is where we find some very curious circumstance which would be explained by the supposition that it was the case of a certain general rule and thereupon adopt that supposition' (1960, 624). Later, Peirce called hypothesis 'abduction'. In this new classification abduction 'furnishes the reasoner with the problematic theory which induction verifies' (1960, 776). That is, Peirce characterized abduction as the coming up with a hypothesis, which is then tested by induction. In this new schema, abduction is a form of hypothesis-generation, rather than a pattern of reasoning that gives us reasons for accepting a hypothesis.

The ambiguities concerning the concept of abduction as characterized by Peirce carry over to the current research on abduction. We may distinguish, following Niiniluoto, between two different conceptions of abduction, a weak conception and a strong one (1999). According to the 'weak' conception, abduction is the process by which explanatory hypotheses are generated. In this view, abduction gives reasons for pursuing a hypothesis, as opposed to reasons for accepting a hypothesis. Thus, in this view, abduction operates in the context of discovery, rather than in the context of justification. In contrast, according to the 'strong' conception of abduction, abduction is not only a method of discovery, but also a method of evaluation. In this view, abduction is best characterized as 'inference to the best explanation' (IBE, hereinafter), that is, as a pattern of reasoning whereby explanatory hypotheses are both formed and justified. Lycan (1988, 129; 2002, 413) defines IBE as follows:

> $F_1 \ldots F_n$ are facts in need of explanation.
> Hypothesis H explains $F_1 \ldots F_n$.
> No available competing hypothesis explains F_i as well as H does.
> Therefore, probably H is true.

That is, an inference to the best explanation proceeds from a set of data to a hypothesis that explains the data better than any available competing hypothesis would. As described above, this pattern of reasoning indeed looks familiar. Many inferences in a vast array of contexts are naturally described in terms of inference to the best explanation.[2] For example, Darwin inferred the hypothesis of natural selection because, although it was not entailed by his biological evidence, natural selection would provide the best explanation of that evidence (Lipton 2000, 184). A doctor infers that a patient has measles because it best explains the patient's symptoms (Magnani 2001). Natural language understanding (Hobbs et al. 1993) and fault diagnosis (Peng and Reggia 1990) have also been characterized as IBE. In law, we may recognize many instances of reasoning about evidence as cases of IBE as well. A prosecutor infers that one of the suspects committed the crime because this hypothesis best explains the fingerprints, bloodstains, and other forensic evidence. When we infer – claims Harman – that a witness is telling the truth, our confidence in the testimony is based on our conclusion about the most plausible explanation for that testimony (1965, 89). A juror infers a plausible narrative about how a crime was committed because it best explains the evidence at trial (Josephson 2002, 290–91). Inference to the best explanation is ubiquitous in the context of reasoning about evidence in law (see Thagard 1989; 2003; 2006; Abimbola 2002; Josephson 2002; Walton 2002; Allen and Pardo 2008). I turn now to the issue of how a model of IBE for law may be developed.

3. Inference to the Best Explanation in Law: A Coherentist Interpretation

A good starting point for developing a model of IBE for law is Lipton's model of IBE, which is, to date, the most elaborate account of how explanatory inference works in scientific contexts (Lipton 2004). It is a basic tenet of Lipton's model that IBE includes a two-filter procedure: one that generates plausible candidates, and a second one that selects from among them. This two-stage procedure seems initially a plausible description of the way in which legal decision-makers reason about evidence. They first generate a number of plausible explanations of the facts under dispute, and then select from among them the one that best explains the evidence at trial. Under this view, factual inference in law works by exclusion, i.e., from a handful of plausible alternatives legal decision-makers eliminate all but one as the best explanation of the disputed facts. That is, it follows from an explanationist account of legal inference that factual inference in law is first and foremost an eliminative kind of inference. An explanatory view of reasoning about evidence in law also brings to light the extent to which factual inference in law is of a defeasible kind: for there is, of course, always the possibility that a better explanation will be discovered which defeats the hypothesis that has been chosen as the best.

While attractive, this picture of factual inference in law is, to be sure, far too sketchy. A model of inference to the best explanation in law needs to rest on a

2 In some of these contexts the *explanandum* is a generic event (as in science) while in others it is a unique event (as in law or medical diagnosis), yet the structure of explanatory inference remains the same across contexts.

detailed account of the different stages in which factual inference proceeds. The suggestion that I would like to put forward is that we may provide such an account by placing a model of inference to the best explanation within a coherence theory of legal justification. In a nutshell, my claim is that IBE in law is best understood as an 'inference to the most coherent theory of the case.' That is, the claim is that the 'best' of the 'inference to the best explanation' slogan is the best on a test of coherence (see, in the context of philosophy of science, Harman 1980; 1986; Thagard 1989; 1992; 2000; Lycan 2002; Psillos 2002).[3] Such a theory of the case is – on a coherence theory of justification – the one that enjoys a higher degree of justification. Thus, the coherence-enhancing role of IBE is ultimately its justification-conferring element (Psillos 2002, 616–20). From this point of view, IBE in law is a process of coherence-maximization, which consists of two stages, the generation of a number of candidate theories of the case and the selection from among them of the one that coheres best. There is, I would suggest, an intermediate stage that is extraordinarily important, to wit, a context of pursuit, in which working hypotheses are subjected to preliminary assessment and developed in further detail (Sintonen and Kikeri 2004, 214–18). Let us now see, from a coherentist perspective, how the structure of inference to the best explanation in law may be described.

3.1. Discovering Explanations

How do legal decision-makers come up with a pool of plausible alternatives? How are hypotheses generated in the forensic context? The mechanisms whereby new hypotheses emerge in the course of legal decision-making are poorly understood. This is hardly surprising, given the relative neglect, until very recently, of discovery-related issues in the legal literature (Schum 2001, 450–505; 2002; Anderson et al. 2005). I do not intend here (neither can I) give a full account of the process of discovery in the forensic context. I shall focus exclusively on the role that coherence plays in this process.

Coherence enters into the process of generation in different ways. First, coherence enters implicitly in the process of generation via background knowledge (Lipton 2004, 150–51). The judgement of plausibility upon which the generation of a restricted number of candidates hinges depends heavily on background knowledge. Our background beliefs – we take it – indicate which hypotheses one ought to seriously consider. Thus, coherence with background beliefs helps narrow down the range of plausible candidates to a manageable size. Explanations of the facts under dispute which fail to cohere with background beliefs, e.g., beliefs about how crimes are usually committed, beliefs about human motivations, causal principles, etc., are not merely discarded, but rather are never considered.

3 A thorough explanation of what such a test of coherence involves is given in section 3.3.

Of course, this tendency to generate hypotheses that cohere with our background beliefs is quite risky. The role that coherence plays – via background knowledge – in the generation stage is a double-edged sword. On the one hand, it focuses inquiry, by avoiding waste of time and effort in formulating and discarding crazy hypotheses that nobody would seriously consider. To state the obvious, no serious lawyer would say that the crime was committed by an unnatural force because we most firmly believe that crimes are 'usually' committed by humans – as one of the Grimm Brothers said.[4] Besides, if we take it (and with good reason, I believe) that most of our beliefs are approximately true or, at the very least, justified, then it is but reasonable that we should disfavour hypotheses that would lead us to reject much of the background. But, on the other hand, the role that coherence with background knowledge plays in the process of generation has also a negative side. Favouring hypotheses that cohere with our background of empirical beliefs might prevent us from considering hypotheses which, rare as they might be, are best supported by the evidence we have in the particular case. Here, we face the recalcitrant problem of conservatism which seems to undermine coherence methods.

Second, coherence also enters into the process of generation through a number of marshalling mechanisms. As Schum and Tillers have argued, the success that we enjoy in generating important new hypotheses and discovering new evidence depends to a great extent upon how well we have marshalled or organized the evidence we have (Schum and Tillers 1991; Schum 1999). Successful inquiry is first and foremost an exercise of interrogation (Sintonen and Kikeri 2004, 227–33). Marshalling methods stimulate asking the right questions without which we stand little chance of generating fruitful possibilities. Some important marshalling strategies such as 'scenarios', 'schemata', and 'theories of the case' are coherence-oriented. Thus, coherence pushes us towards productive investigative paths by contributing to the effective marshalling of the ideas and evidence that we have.

Third, the generation of new elements is sometimes driven by an effort after coherence. The search for coherence motivates the formulation of questions which importantly aid the aim of inquiry. Asking what evidence would cohere with a particular hypothesis, or what hypothesis could make sense of some evidence we have is an effective way of identifying relevant evidence as well as coming up with innovative hypotheses. It is important to notice here that formulating promising hypotheses and discovering relevant evidence go hand-in-hand in the process of inquiry. On the one hand, by supposing that one factual hypothesis is true, we can work out what further evidence might be relevant. On the other hand, we may come up with a new hypothesis by supposing what would, if true, explain a particular piece of evidence we have. There is thus a feedback between hypothesis formation and evidence acquisition in actual legal inquiry, and coherence seems to significantly contribute to this feedback.

Last, *in*coherence is also a driving force in inquiry (Thagard 2000, 67). Emotional reactions, such as surprise or anxiety, that signal incoherence may

4 In the film *The Brothers Grimm* (2005).

trigger hypothesis formation. That is, sometimes the generation of new elements is prompted by failure to achieve an interpretation that adequately satisfies the coherence standards. In the context of law, one may say that the anxiety produced by the fact that a guilt hypothesis fails to make full sense of the available evidence may motivate the search for an alternative hypothesis (which might, in turn, suggest the relevance of additional evidence) that is compatible with a story of innocence. And incongruity of the best solution available to a problem of proof in law with one's firm convictions about the main values which adjudication is meant to protect may be accompanied by a lively sense of non-conformity, which might trigger the search for an alternative explanation (and for evidence which might support the new explanatory hypothesis).

Thus, coherence plays an important role in the process of generation. By the end of this process, fact-finders should have constructed, from an original 'base' of coherence,[5] which includes the evidence at trial and the competing explanatory hypothesis, a 'contrast set',[6] that is, a set of plausible alternative theories of the case to be further considered.

3.2. The Context of Pursuit

In a second stage, initially plausible alternatives are developed and refined into full-blown theories of the case. How may the alternative theories of the case be rendered as coherent as they can be? There are three main coherence-making strategies whereby legal fact-finders may enhance the coherence of the alternatives: subtractive, additive, and reinterpretative.[7] The 'subtractive strategy' constructs coherence by subtracting one (or more) elements from an incoherent set. For instance, a fact-finder may eliminate the belief that a piece of circumstantial evidence is reliable on the grounds that it detracts from the coherence of a hypothesis that is well supported by the independent and credible testimony of several witnesses. The 'additive strategy' consists of adding one (or more) elements to a set in order to render it coherent (or in order to increase its degree of coherence) (Klein and Warfield 1994, 129–30). For example, suppose that a legal fact-finder believes that the evidence at trial strongly supports the guilt hypothesis. However, suppose that she also believes a witness claiming that he saw the accused miles away from the scene of the crime. Upon further investigation it is discovered that, as it turns out, the witness is visually impaired. The legal fact-finder may increase the coherence of the theory of the case entailing the guilt of the defendant by adding the belief that, given the deficient sight of the witness, he would not have been able to identify the defendant, despite his claim to. Last, the 'reinterpretative strategy' amounts to

5 The term is Raz's (1992).

6 The term is borrowed from Josephson 2002.

7 This taxonomy of coherence-making strategies is broadly inspired by the kinds of belief change operations distinguished in the belief revision literature (see Gärdenfors 1988; see Amaya 2007b, for the legal applications of belief revision formalisms).

removing the incoherences in one's theory of the case by revising the interpretation of one (or more) of its elements.[8] For instance, incriminating evidence found in the house of the accused can be reinterpreted, in light of evidence of irregular police conduct, as decreasing rather than enhancing the coherence of the theory of the case entailing guilt. Reinterpretation may be viewed as a composition of subtraction (of the rejected interpretation) and addition (of the accepted interpretation). In the course of deliberation, legal decision-makers may (and indeed should) maximize the coherence of the alternatives under consideration by manipulating them in the ways indicated above.

Again, there are some 'dangers' involved in employing these coherence-making mechanisms. While it seems necessary, in order to ensure a fair evaluation of the different alternatives, that each of the alternatives be shown as coherent as it can be, there is always the possibility that the process whereby the coherence of each of these alternatives is maximized is performed in such a way as to ensure that one of the alternative theories of the case ends up being later selected. That is, there is always the risk that one uses these mechanisms for inflating the degree of coherence of one's preferred alternative and deflating the degree of coherence of the competing alternatives. In fact, this is what happens, according to Simon, in the course of legal decision-making (Simon 2004). One might then make it the case that while rendering each of the alternative explanatory hypotheses the most coherent they can be, one's preferred alternative is shown to be more coherent that it actually is and competing alternatives are rendered in fact less coherent that they could have been shown to be. This, of course, would result then in a biased, rather than a fair, evaluation of the alternatives. We might be so wired – as Simon and collaborators' psychological research shows – that such manipulations of the decision alternatives are an essential part of what is involved, as a matter of fact, in effective decision-making. But while to some extent these manipulations might be indispensable for reaching a decision at all, it still seems possible – and indeed, desirable – to keep these psychological tendencies from running riot. Complementing – in the way that I shall suggest later – a theory of coherence-based reasoning with a theory of epistemic responsibility might be a way of exploiting the drive towards coherence which – as empirical studies show – guides our decision processes, while avoiding the dangers inherent in coherence-based reasoning.

3.3. Selecting the Best Explanation

Faced with a number of plausible explanations, IBE has us select the candidate that is best. The 'best' explanation, I have argued, is the most coherent explanation. To be sure, coherence is hardly a transparent notion. In fact, one of the main objections against coherence theories is that they fail to give a precise account of the nature of coherence. Thus, it might be argued, identifying the 'best' with the 'most coherent'

8 I borrow the term 'reinterpretation' from Conte 1999, 88.

does not seem to clarify what are the standards of evaluation against which we may determine which, among a number of alternative explanations, is best. However, the prospects of elaborating a reasonably clear notion of the kind of coherence that is relevant to factual reasoning in law are not as bleak as they might appear. Thagard has developed a conception of coherence as constraint satisfaction on the basis of which, I would argue, we may work out a precise enough notion of coherence for evidential reasoning in law, which I shall refer to as 'factual coherence'.[9]

According to Thagard, coherence is a matter of satisfying a number of positive and negative constraints. To achieve coherence, he says, we divide up a set of elements into two disjointed subsets, A – which contains accepted elements – and R – which contains rejected elements – by taking into account the coherence and incoherence relations that hold between pairs of elements of the given set. For example, if a hypothesis h_1 explains a piece of evidence e_1, then we want to ensure that if h_1 is accepted, so is e_1. And if h_1 contradicts h_2, then we want to make sure that if h_1 is accepted, then h_2 is rejected. According to the theory of coherence as constraint satisfaction, coherence results from dividing a set of elements into A and R in a way that best satisfies the positive (coherence relations) and negative (incoherence relations) constraints (Thagard and Verbegeurt 1998; Thagard 2000, 15–40).

It is a virtue of this approach that it is applicable to a wide variety of problems. In order to apply the general approach of coherence as constraint satisfaction to a particular problem, says Thagard, we need to specify the elements and the constraints that are relevant in a particular domain as well as the kinds of coherence involved. He distinguishes six kinds of coherence: explanatory, analogical, deductive, perceptual, conceptual, and deliberative. For instance, in Thagard's view, we may view epistemic justification as a coherence problem the solution of which requires the integrated assessment of explanatory, analogical, deductive, perceptual, and conceptual coherence. Thagard has proposed a set of principles for all these kinds of coherence, which specify the relevant elements and constraints.

The justification of factual conclusions in law may also be viewed – I would argue – as a coherence problem.[10] 'Factual coherence' requires the interaction of the same kinds of coherence which, according to Thagard, are relevant to epistemic justification with one major addition, that is, deliberative coherence. Deliberative coherence needs to be added because reasoning about facts in law, unlike other kinds of evidential reasoning, is ultimately a piece of a practical deliberation about whether one should acquit or convict. For the purposes of this chapter, it may suffice to focus on what is, arguably, the most important contributor to factual coherence, to wit, explanatory coherence. In explanatory coherence, the

9 Other prominent conceptual analyses of coherence include BonJour 1985 and Lehrer 1990.

10 The justification of normative, rather than factual, conclusions in law may also be viewed as a coherence problem (see Amaya 2006, for a discussion of the literature).

elements are evidence and hypotheses. According to Thagard's principles of explanatory coherence, positive constraints arise from relations of explanation and analogy and negative constraints result from contradiction and competition (see Thagard 1989; 1992; 2000). Some modifications need to be introduced in order to make Thagard's theory of explanatory coherence suitable to the legal realm. Specifically, it is necessary to add further principles so as to account for the fact that the explanatory evaluation of hypotheses at trial takes place within an institutional context. This context gives rise to additional constraints, more importantly, the presumption of innocence and the standard of reasonable doubt. The presumption of innocence may be treated as a constraint that requires that hypotheses compatible with innocence be given priority in being accepted. In other words, not all hypotheses about the events at trial may be treated equally in determinations of coherence, but hypotheses compatible with innocence should be assigned an initial degree of acceptability. The reasonable doubt standard imposes a further constraint on the acceptance of a guilt hypothesis: this may be accepted only if its degree of justification is sufficiently high to meet the standard. From an explanationist perspective, there are two conditions that a guilt explanation should meet for belief in such an explanation to be beyond a reasonable doubt: it has to be highly coherent with both background beliefs and the evidence at trial and it has to be much more coherent than competing explanations that are compatible with innocence. Together these two constraints ensure that the guilt explanation will be accepted only if coherence overwhelmingly requires it.

The principles of factual coherence, which result from adding the institutional constraints (in italics) to Thagard's principles of explanatory coherence, may be stated as follows:

> Principle E1: Symmetry. Explanatory coherence is a symmetrical relation, unlike, say, conditional probability.
>
> Principle E2: Explanation. (a) A hypothesis coheres with what it explains which can either be the evidence or another hypothesis; (b) hypotheses that together explain some other proposition cohere with each other; and (c) the more hypotheses it takes to explain something, the lower the degree of coherence.
>
> Principle E3: Analogy. Similar hypotheses that explain similar pieces of evidence cohere.
>
> Principle E4: Priority. (a) Propositions that describe the results of observation have a degree of acceptability on their own; (b) *hypotheses that are compatible with innocence have a degree of acceptability on their own.*

Principle E5: Contradiction. Contradictory propositions are incoherent with each other.

Principle E6: Competition. If *P* and *Q* both explain a proposition and if *P* and *Q* are not explanatorily connected, then *P* and *Q* are incoherent with each other.

Principle E7: Acceptance. (a) The acceptability of a proposition in a system of propositions depends on its coherence with them; (b) *the guilt hypothesis may be accepted only if it is justified to a degree sufficient to satisfy the reasonable doubt standard.*

Principle 1, symmetry, establishes that explanatory coherence is a symmetric relation. For example, if the guilt hypothesis coheres with the DNA evidence, then the DNA evidence and the guilt hypothesis also cohere. As principle 2(a) says, a hypothesis coheres with what it explains. For instance, the hypothesis that the perpetrator of the crime was not an outsider (to take a well-known example by Conan Doyle) coheres with the evidence that the dog did not bark. This principle also allows the possibility of hypotheses explaining each other, as when the hypothesis that a family member was the murderer is explained by the motive that he was to inherit from the victim. Principle 2(b) says that hypotheses that together explain some other proposition cohere with each other. For example, the hypothesis that the maid's testimony (saying that no outsider was seen around the house the night of the crime) is true and the hypothesis that the perpetrator of the crime was from within the family, together explain the evidence that the dog did not bark, and thus cohere with each other. The last part of principle 2 says that the more hypotheses it takes to explain something, the lower the degree of coherence. Simplicity is, in law as much as everywhere else, a cognitive virtue. Principle 3 states that similar hypotheses that explain similar pieces of evidence cohere. For example, the hypothesis that a family member was the murderer coheres with well-known stories of domestic violence that explained similarly motivated crimes. The first part of principle 4 says that propositions that describe the results of observations have a degree of acceptability on their own, that is, that they have priority in being accepted. In law, all the evidence at trial will enjoy this kind of priority. The second part encodes the principle of innocence by requiring that hypotheses that are compatible with innocence should also be assigned an initial weight. Contradictory propositions, states principle 5, are incoherent with each other. For example, the hypothesis that the maid's testimony is trustworthy is incoherent with the hypothesis that she was lying, insofar as both hypotheses contradict each other. Incoherence relations might also be established between two hypotheses if they are in competition – as principle 6 says. Two hypotheses compete with each other if they both explain a proposition but are not explanatorily connected. For instance, the hypothesis that the victim was killed and the hypothesis that she committed suicide both explain the evidence of the body, but since neither one explains the other nor do they together explain any evidence, they compete with each other, and they are thus incoherent with each other. Lastly, the first part of principle 7 says that the acceptability of any proposition depends on its coherence with the rest of elements to which it belongs. So, according to this principle, the guilt hypothesis and the innocence hypothesis are to be accepted if they best cohere with the hypotheses put forward at trial and the evidence available. In law, however, the evaluation of the explanatory coherence of the alternatives is subjected to institutional constraints such as the standard of proof, which is encoded in the second part of principle 7.

Thus, under the proposed coherentist framework, the coherence of a particular factual hypothesis in law is computed through the satisfaction of a number of constraints as established by the foregoing principles. IBE in law has us select the explanation of the facts disputed at trial that best satisfies these coherence constraints. An important advantage of using a modified version of Thagard's theory of explanatory coherence, to determine which is best among a set of alternative theories of the case, is that it allows us to compute coherence in a precise way. Thagard's theory of explanatory coherence has been implemented in a computational model, ECHO, which shows how coherence can be calculated. In ECHO, hypotheses and evidence are represented by units that are linked through excitatory and inhibitory links. When two propositions cohere, there is an excitatory link between the two units representing them. When two propositions are incoherent with each other, there is an inhibitory link between them. Activation is spread among the units until they reach a stable state in which some units have positive activation, representing the acceptance of the propositions they represent, and some units have negative activation, representing the rejection of the propositions they represent. Thus, ECHO offers a respectable way for evaluating the coherence of the alternative hypotheses about the events at trial.

Let me recapitulate. On the coherentist interpretation of IBE proposed, legal decision-makers settle on which explanation to infer by a process of coherence maximization that has the following stages:

1. The *specification of a base of coherence*, that is, the set of hypotheses and evidence over which the coherence calculation proceeds.
2. The *construction of a contrast set*, which contains a number of alternative theories of the case.
3. The *pursuit* of the alternative theories of the case by means of a number of coherence-making mechanisms, which results in a revised contrast set.
4. The *evaluation* of the coherence of the alternative theories of the case.
5. The *selection*, as justified, of the theory of the case that best satisfies the criteria of factual coherence.

Some commentary is required. First, this account of factual inference does not assume that the base of coherence remains fixed during the process of coherence-maximization. Rather, the base of coherence is transitory and may be modified in the course of legal decision-making. The pursuit of the alternative theories of the case leads to modifying the base of coherence in several ways, by adding new elements, eliminating some of the elements, or changing their interpretation. This squares well with the dynamics of legal inquiry, for typically evidence and hypotheses become available sequentially in the course of the trial.

Second, the theories of the case are treated as a crucial component of coherence-based reasoning in law. In this model, coherence is not computed at once among all the evidence and hypotheses, but is constructed incrementally, by focusing on subsets of elements (i.e., the theories of the case) at one time. On this view, fact-finders work with a 'traveling focus of attention' (Hoadley et al. 1994), concentrating on some alternatives and then on others. This local approach to coherence-building seems psychologically more realistic than global approaches, for limitations of memory and attention make it unlikely that we are able to consider at once all the coherence relations that hold among the whole set of elements.[11]

Lastly, the different stages of coherence-based inference are distinguished here for the sake of clarity, but in real instances of reasoning, fact-finders would move back and forth between stages. If they are not satisfied with any of alternatives being evaluated, they may strive to find out additional evidence or they may seek out alternative hypotheses in the course of deliberation. New evidence may also prompt the reconsideration of a hypothesis that was discarded before in the process of coherence-construction. Thus, the proposed account of factual reasoning brings to light the extent to which discovery and justification go hand-in-hand in the course of legal decision-making. Let us now illustrate this explanationist approach to evidential reasoning in law by means of an example.

4. An Example: The O.J. Simpson Case

In this section I shall exemplify the explanationist account of legal reasoning about evidence articulated above to one well-known case, the *People of the State of California* v. *Orenthal James Simpson*. This case has generated an enormous amount of literature and discussion not only among legal scholars but also in the media and public at large. There are several reasons why this trial has been perceived by many to be 'the trial of the century'. It is an interesting drama of love and rage, whose main character was the famous football player O.J. Simpson. It raises issues about race and the criminal justice system, about police misconduct, about domestic violence, about social perceptions of black men/white women intimate relationships, about the reliability of DNA evidence, and about the impact of class in justice. It also raised questions about the competence of juries, as the

11 In the context of legal decision-making, Simon's empirical research has shown that judges' attention oscillates between the decision alternatives during the process of decision-making over which coherence is constructed (see Simon 1998, 80–81).

jury reached a verdict which a large part of the population thought wrong. Here, I shall not attempt to give a psychological explanation of the jurors' reasoning in this case. Rather, my purpose is to illustrate how deliberating about the facts of this case involves the generation and pursuit of alternative theories of the case and the selection among them of the theory that is best according to a test of explanatory coherence. But before I proceed to explain how the proposed model of inference to the best explanation would work in a concrete case, let me give a brief overview of the facts of the O.J. Simpson trial.

O.J. Simpson was tried for the murder of his ex-wife, Nicole Brown Simpson, and her friend Ron Goldman. The prosecution relied mainly on three kinds of proof. First, there was proof of Simpson's motive, appearance, mood, and behaviour. O.J. Simpson and Nicole Brown Simpson had a difficult relationship, with episodes of domestic violence both during and after their marriage. The day of the murders, O.J. Simpson was in a rage because of a series of incidents with his ex-wife and his then current girlfriend. He had dinner with a friend, Kato Kaelin; O.J. and Kato parted company at 9.30pm; and O.J. took a plane at midnight to Chicago. The murders occurred between 10.15pm and 10.30pm. When the police arrested him, he had a fresh cut on his hand, which Kato had not seen when they went for dinner. Second, there were physical proofs. In Simpson's back yard the police found a bloody glove that made a pair with one found at the crime scene. They also found a bloody sock in Simpson's bedroom as well as blood drops in the hallway of Simpson's house and in his car. Thirdly, there was DNA evidence. The DNA test revealed that the blood discovered inside O.J.'s car matched that of O.J., Nicole, and Ron. The blood on the sock produced a DNA match for Nicole. The blood drops on the hallway at Simpson's house as well as drops of blood found at the crime scene matched O.J.'s blood.

The defence developed several lines of argument. First, based on Nicole's known use of drugs, they contended that Nicole and Ron were killed by drug dealers. Second, the defence attacked the interpretation of the circumstantial evidence. The defence argued that the evidence incriminating O.J. was planted by the L.A. police department officers who were determined to frame Simpson for the crime. They found evidence that Furhman, the detective who had claimed to discover the glove in Simpson's backyard, was a racist who had said that police planted evidence against black suspects. Moreover, the glove which O.J. supposedly used to commit the murders did not fit when he tried to put it on in court. The defence identified irregularities in the police investigation and in the forensic specialists' work. Detective Vannater had carried a sample of O.J. Simpson's blood for hours and some of that blood went missing; O.J. Simpson's blood was discovered at the crime scene only in July, weeks after the murder, and what is more, some of O.J.'s blood that was allegedly found at the crime scene was absent from a police photo taken in June; this blood as well as the blood on the sock showed traces of EDTA, a preservative used in collection vials. Furhman and Vannater, argued the defence, had ample opportunity to plant the evidence that implicated Simpson and were racially motivated to do so.

How should a fact-finder reason about the evidence in this case? The *first* stage is to specify the evidentiary problem. On the coherentist approach proposed, this involves specifying *the base of coherence*, that is, the set of hypotheses and evidence over which the coherence calculation is performed, as shown in Figure 6.1.

Hypotheses
H1 O.J. Simpson was framed
H2 O.J. Simpson killed Nicole
H3 Nicole was killed by drug dealers
H4 O.J. Simpson is innocent
H5 Furhman is a racist
H6 O.J. Simpson was abusive of his wife
H7 O.J. Simpson was in an emotional turmoil the night of the crime

Evidence
E1 O.J.'s blood at crime scene
E2 O.J.'s blood in his hallway and car
E3 Bloody sock in O.J.'s bedroom
E4 Bloody glove in O.J.'s backyard
E5 EDTA in the traces of Nicole's blood on the sock
E6 EDTA in the traces of O.J.'s blood on the crime scene
E7 Glove did not fit O.J.'s hands
E8 Some of O.J.'s blood at the crime scene was absent in pictures taken in June
E9 Some of O.J. Simpson's blood was unaccounted for

Figure 6.1 Hypotheses and evidence in the O.J. Simpson case

At the *second* stage, the trier of fact tries to specify the *contrast set*, that is, the set of theories of the case (which I will label C in Figure 6.2). This involves determining the coherence and incoherence relations that hold among the different elements, i.e., hypotheses and evidence. In order to do so, the fact-finder needs to consider which evidence is explained by which hypothesis, which hypotheses are explanatorily related, whether there are any significant analogies at work, whether the different hypotheses compete with each other, and whether there are any propositions describing either evidence or hypotheses that are contradictory. For example, the hypothesis that O.J. Simpson was framed coheres with the evidence that there was EDTA on the bloody sock, as this hypothesis explains the evidence of the traces of EDTA. Or, for another example, the hypothesis that Nicole and Ron were killed by drug dealers is incoherent with the hypothesis that they were killed by O.J. Simpson, since they compete with each other. By the end of this process, the fact-finder would have constructed a number of theories of the case, each of which contains several hypotheses and evidence that cohere with each other. Three main theories may be advanced in this case: (i) the O.J.Simpson-did-it theory; (ii) the frame theory; (iii) the drug dealers theory. Letting G stand for the first theory, F for the frame theory, and D for the drug dealers theory, the theories are coherent subsets of propositions describing evidence and hypotheses as shown in Figure 6.2.

explain (H2, E1) explain (H2, E2) explain (H2, E3) explain (H2, E4) explain (H2, H6) explain (H2, H7) explain (H1, H5) explain (H1, E5) explain (H1, E6) explain (H1, E7) explain (H1, E8) explain (H1, E9) explain (H3, H8)	compete (H1, H2) compete (H2, H3) compete (H1, H3) C = {G, F, D} G = {H2, H6, H7, E1, E2, E3, E4} F = {H1, H5, E5, E6, E7, E8, E9} D = {H3, H4}

Figure 6.2 Theories of the case in the O.J. Simpson case

It is important to notice that even though these three theories of the case were put forward by the parties, the triers of fact are not limited to considering those, but they may (and indeed should, as I would argue below) seek out alternative explanations of the facts being litigated in the course of deliberation.

At the *third* stage the fact-finder revises and refines the different theories of the case being considered so as to make them the best – i.e., the most coherent – that they can be. As argued earlier, there are three main strategies whereby coherence may be enhanced: additive, subtractive, and reinterpretative. For example, the fact that the glove was found in O.J. Simpson's backyard may be reinterpreted, in light of evidence of police misconduct, as evidence that lends support to the hypothesis that O.J. was framed, rather than as evidence of guilt. As a result of this reinterpretation, the degree of coherence of the frame theory is augmented. Or adding the belief that Furhman lied in court (which I label H8 in the figure below) makes the frame hypothesis more coherent. The point of this exercise is to give a fair chance to each of the competing theories of the case by seriously considering the possibility that each of them might obtain. By the end of the third stage, the coherence of each of the theories of the case is maximized. Figure 6.3 shows one of the theories of the case – the frame theory – which results from revising it with a view to enhancing its degree of coherence.

F' = {H1, H5, E5, E6, E7, E8, E9, E4, H8}

Figure 6.3 The 'frame theory' revised

At the *fourth* stage, the fact-finder assesses the coherence of the different theories of the case by examining the extent to which they satisfy the coherence constraints. He will ask whether the guilt theory explains most of the evidence at trial or whether, to the contrary, the frame theory does a better job at explaining the evidence. He will consider which of the theories being considered is simpler and which fits better with background knowledge about analogous cases. He will watch out for sources of incoherence and identify inconsistencies in the theories which persist even after each of the theories of the case has been refined. In the explanatory evaluation of these theories of the case it is crucial that he give priority both to the evidence at trial as well as to the theories of the case that are compatible with innocence. A preference ought to be assigned to these theories in the coherence calculation for the presumption of innocence to be duly respected. The aim of this stage is to arrive at a ranking of the theories of the case in terms of their degree of coherence. In this case, the drug dealer theory clearly ranks far below the O.J. Simpson-did-it theory and the frame theory, both of which enjoy a high degree of coherence. As shown in Figure 6.2, while the O.J. Simpson-did-it theory and the frame theory explain a substantial part of the evidence available (E1–E4, and E5–E9, respectively), the drug dealer theory lacks evidential support.

Finally, at the *fifth* stage, the most coherent theory of the case is selected, provided that its degree of justification (on this account, its degree of coherence) is high enough to satisfy the reasonable doubt standard. Which candidate, among the remaining theories of the case, ought to be selected? Thagard has simulated the reasoning in the O.J. Simpson case in ECHO and the program found O.J. Simpson guilty (2003). Although Thagard's simulation of the O.J. Simpson case took into account a large part of the evidence and hypotheses presented at trial, legal institutional constraints, such as the presumption of innocence and the standards of proof, were not given, I would argue, due consideration. The presumption of innocence was not implemented in Thagard's computer simulation and reasonable doubt was implemented by allowing the guilt hypothesis to be rejected if the inhibition of the unit representing it is over 0.065, which is stronger than the default 0.05 excitation value for data, but still not demanding enough to capture the standard of reasonable doubt.

As argued above, there is an important institutional dimension to the explanatory evaluation of hypotheses at trial. In order to give an account of the highly institutional nature of the evaluation of legal evidence, Thagard's principles of explanatory coherence need to be slightly modified. More specifically, I suggested modifying principles 4 (data priority) and 7 (acceptance) by adding two institutional constraints: the presumption of innocence and the reasonable doubt standard. A version of ECHO (let us call it L-ECHO) could be then developed in which these institutional constraints were implemented. The presumption of innocence could be implemented in L-ECHO by treating the innocence hypothesis as a weak form of data. A promising way of implementing reasonable doubt could be by manipulating the decay rate, which is a parameter such that the higher it is the more excitation from the data is necessary to activate a hypothesis. To model reasonable doubt, the decay rate could be set higher for the guilt hypothesis so as to capture the sceptical stance that jurors ought to have towards the theory of the case that entails guilt.[12]

My hypothesis is that the outcome of applying the modified principles of explanatory coherence and L-ECHO to the O.J. Simpson case would be different from the one reached by ECHO. In L-ECHO, hypotheses compatible with O.J. Simpson's innocence will be assigned an initial weight in the coherence calculation so that the guilt hypothesis would only be accepted if it is indeed much better than alternative hypotheses. In addition, the unit representing the hypothesis that O.J. Simpson did it will have a higher decay rate with the result that it will not get very active unless it is highly coherent with the evidence at trial. Although both the O.J. Simpson-did-it theory and the frame theory are reasonably good explanations of subsets of the evidence at trial, I would suggest that (i) the existence of a coherent theory compatible with innocence (i.e., the frame theory) and (ii) the fact that one subset of the evidence (that is, E5–E9, as shown in Figure 6.2 above) is unexplained by the O.J. Simpson-did-it theory raises reasonable doubts over the guilt of O.J, and would lead L-ECHO to reject the guilt hypothesis as unjustified. The institutional constraints on the maximization of coherence – the importance of which is not fully recognized in Thagard's simulation – played, I would argue, a prevalent role in the case being analysed. That reasonable doubt considerations were determinant of the decision of the jury (who found O.J. innocent) has, in fact, been argued by some analysts of this case (see Dershowitz 1996; Hastie and Pennington 1996). Computational experiments in respect of this and other legal cases would need to be done to further understanding of how the institutional aspects of the explanatory evaluation of hypotheses in law may be best implemented and which role they play in the process of coherence-maximization that leads to accepting one theory of the case, from among a number of plausible theories, as justified.

To review, in the previous sections I have argued that IBE provides a useful description of factual inference in law. More specifically, I have argued for a coherentist interpretation of explanatory inference in law according to which IBE involves the generation and pursuit of a number of alternative explanations of the facts under dispute and the selection, among them, of the one that coheres best.

12 I thank Paul Thagard for his suggestions and extended discussion about to how the presumption of innocence and reasonable doubt could be implemented.

In what follows, I shall consider a main objection that may be directed against an explanationist model of legal proof, to wit, the problem of underconsideration.[13]

5. The Problem of Underconsideration

The problem of underconsideration (also called 'the argument from the bad lot') has been formulated by Van Fraassen against IBE as a model of scientific inference. He states the problem as follows:

> [IBE] is a rule that only selects the best among the historically given hypotheses. We can watch no contest of the theories we have so painfully struggled to formulate, with those no one has proposed. So our selection may well be the best of a bad lot. To believe is at least to consider more likely to be true, than not. So to believe the best explanation requires more than an evaluation of the given hypothesis. It requires a step beyond the comparative judgment that the hypothesis is better than its actual rivals. While the comparative judgment is indeed a 'weighing (in the light of) the evidence,' the extra step – let us call it the ampliative step – is not. For me to take it that the best of set X be more likely than not, requires a prior belief that the truth is already more likely to be found in X, than not (Van Fraassen 1989, 143).

Thus, Van Fraassen casts doubts about whether we have any reason to believe that the outcome of an application of inference to the best explanation is likely to be true. Unless we know that it is more likely than not that the true explanation is included among those we have discovered, we have no reason to accept the best explanation as (probably) true. For all we know, he says, the best explanation may just be the best of a 'bad lot'. The true explanation, that is, may well lie among those explanations that we have so far failed to consider.

The problem of underconsideration poses a real challenge to the project of articulating a model of inference to the best explanation in law. After carefully examining the evidence at trial and comparing the relative coherence of the different alternatives available, the jury decides that the guilt hypothesis is the most coherent one, and thus the best candidate for the basis of their decision. However, had the jurors considered the hypothesis that the police had framed the accused they would have realized the relevance of some evidence – so far unnoticed – and concluded that the innocence hypothesis was, all things considered, explanatorily best. I think that it is plain what the problem of underconsideration, which this example illustrates, is. The set of 'available' hypotheses depends on the evidence legal decision-makers have and on their capacities to bring relevant evidence to

13 This problem is, to my mind, the most serious problem that a model of IBE for law has to face. For a discussion of other objections that may be raised against an IBE model for law, see Laudan 2007 and Allen and Pardo 2008.

bear on existing hypotheses or to come up with good hypotheses. Unless we have some reason to think that the set from which legal decision-makers infer to the best is 'good enough', we seem to lack any reason to believe that the best of such a set is likely to be true.

Now, what are the prospects of meeting this, admittedly serious, objection? In the context of philosophy of science, one popular response appeals to the role that background knowledge plays in theory evaluation. Theory choice operates in a network of background beliefs which is approximately true, and this makes it plausible to believe – contrary to what the argument from the bad lot states – that the correct account of the phenomena does lie within the spectrum of theories that scientists have devised (Lipton 1993; Psillos 1996; Iranzo 2001). In the context of legal – rather than scientific – reasoning a similar response can be articulated. The evaluation of theories of the case does not operate in a 'conceptual vacuum',[14] but is rather guided and constrained by background knowledge. This makes it plausible that the true explanation of the facts under dispute lies within the set of theories which legal decision-makers consider in the course of their deliberations.

Appealing to background knowledge may undermine Van Fraassen's argument by showing that, as it turns out, it is plausible that the truth is already more likely than not to be found within the lot of theories available. However, this still does not dissipate the sceptical worries raised by the bad lot argument for even if – contrary to Van Fraassen – it is more likely than not that the truth lies within the theories under consideration, it remains possible that, in a particular application of inference to the best explanation, the truth *does* lie outside the spectrum of the theories that have been generated. The argument from underconsideration might therefore be restated as follows: let us assume (for the sake of the argument) that it is plausible that the truth is more likely than not to be found within the set of theories that we generate, one still never has reason to believe that the best explanatory hypothesis is likely to be true, for, even if the 'bad lot' possibility is not in fact normally realized, we never have, in a particular application of an inference to the best explanation, any reason to believe that the set of hypotheses we consider contains the truth.

So restated, the argument from underconsideration is not an argument against the reliability of inference to the best explanation, but an argument against the rationality of employing it (Okasha 2000). Even if it is conceded that it is more probable than not that the set under consideration contains the truth, this still says nothing about whether we have any reason to believe that this is so. In any particular application of inference to the best explanation, we never know – the argument says – whether the 'bad lot' possibility obtains or not. As a result, we never have reason to believe that the best explanation is likely to be true.

Now, what are we to say to the sceptic who claims that fact-finders are never justified in inferring the best theory about the facts under dispute, for it might be just the best of a bad lot? The defence of the claim that legal decision-makers

14 The phrase is Ben-Menahem's, 1990, 330.

may be justified in accepting a hypothesis on the grounds that it is the best of those that have been considered is two-pronged. In short, I shall claim that once we appreciate first, that inference to the best explanation is a defeasible form of inference, and, second, that standards of responsibility are relevant to attributions of justified belief, we may come to see how particular applications of inference to the best explanation can yield justified beliefs.

A reply to the objection that inference to the best explanation cannot yield justified beliefs because 'best' can only mean 'best among those that have been generated,' and this might well be a 'bad lot,' starts by examining the kind of warrant which we may reasonably expect inferences to the best explanation to confer on their conclusions. The warrant conferred on the chosen hypothesis is, of course, a defeasible kind of warrant. Thus, it might always be possible that new information – e.g., the discovery of a better explanation – will defeat the justification of the chosen hypothesis. But, inference to the best explanation being defeasible, this is as it should be. Of course, this is not to say that just any lot would do. No warrant – defeasible or otherwise – is conferred upon the hypothesis that is best among those that we just happen to examine. The interesting question is: what is the proper set of explanations that need to be considered for belief in the best of them to be prima facie justified?

An answer to this question requires taking a stance regarding the issue of what is the relevant sense of justification at play. There are different senses in which the notion of justification may be understood. Most importantly, one may distinguish between responsibilist and non-responsibilist views of justification (Pryor 2001). While the former asserts that justification is connected with what an agent has done (or failed to do) to ensure that his beliefs are true, the latter takes justification to be a standard of epistemic appraisal that has to be analysed exclusively in terms of evidential support. The suggestion is that it is the former view of justification, rather than the latter, that is relevant for analysing the sense in which judgements of best explanation in law can be warranted. That is, if one has done all that one can be expected to do for insuring that one's claim is not defeated by an alternative explanation in the particular case, there is an important sense in which one's claim may be said to be justified. More specifically, provided that one has conducted a thorough search for other potential explanations and there is no reason that justifies a further search, then one is justified (in the sense that matters) in accepting as justified the best explanatory hypothesis of the events at trial.

Now, the problem arises as to how we are to spell out the idea of doing one's best that – I have claimed – is at the core of the notion of justification. The suggestion that I would like to advance is that appealing to the idea of epistemic responsibility can help us here. More specifically, the suggestion is that, for a model of inference to the best explanation for law to provide a workable account of how to arrive at justified beliefs (beliefs which are justified by virtue of their coherence), it should be wedded to a responsibilist view of legal justification. A belief in an explanatory hypothesis about the facts under dispute is not justified merely because it is the best among those that have been considered, but we need to have some reason to believe that the set of hypotheses from which we have inferred to the best is 'good enough'. Insofar as we lack any such reason, we fall short of meeting the argument from underconsideration. A set of hypotheses is 'good enough' – I contend – if it has been constructed in compliance with the standards of epistemic responsibility. Thus, the claim is that as long as one's contrast set (the set of alternative explanations) has been constructed in an epistemically responsible way, inferring to the best explanation is warranted (as warranted as non-demonstrative inference can be, it goes without saying), and, thus, the argument from the bad lot is undermined.

How does a legal decision-maker behave in an epistemically responsible way? I cannot go here into examining in detail what epistemic responsibility requires in the context of fact-reasoning in law (see Amaya 2008). In short, epistemic responsibility is a matter of complying with some epistemic duties and exercising a number of epistemic virtues in the course of inquiry and deliberation about factual problems in law. Seeking further evidence on uncertain propositions or believing as one's evidence dictates are examples of epistemic duties which legal decision-makers are expected to comply with. Epistemic virtues include virtues such as open-mindedness in collecting and appraising evidence, perseverance in following a line of inquiry, or readiness to change one's views in the face of new conflicting evidence. If one has constructed a contrast set in an epistemically responsible way, then one has done all that can be expected to ensure that the selected explanation is not defeated, and thus belief in such an explanation is justified. General doubts about whether there might yet be a better explanation lying somewhere do not have the potential to defeat justification. And concrete doubts about whether a particular defeater obtains may be easily dispelled, provided that one has constructed a contrast set in an epistemically responsible way. The objection from the bad lot is thus ineffectual against a model of inference to the best explanation that gives duties and virtues their due in legal justification.

6. Conclusion

In this chapter, I have argued that most instances of factual reasoning in law are best understood in terms of inference to the best explanation. I have argued for a coherentist interpretation of IBE according to which IBE leads us to accept as justified the conclusion about the facts under dispute that best satisfies the standards of coherence. Such a coherentist interpretation has two main constructive advantages: it allows us to see why conclusions of IBE are justified, and it allows us to spell out in some more detail the structure of IBE. I have considered one major objection that may be addressed against a model of IBE for law, namely, the objection from the bad lot. This objection, I have argued, while important, fails to undermine the proposed model of IBE for law. Wedding explanatory coherentism to a responsibilist conception of legal justification and recognizing the defeasible nature of IBE allows us to put worries about bad lots to rest. IBE, I hope to have shown, is thus a promising alternative to the problematic Bayesian model of legal proof.

References

Abimbola, K. (2002), 'Abductive Reasoning in Law: Taxonomy and Inference to the Best Explanation', in MacCrimmon and Tillers (eds).

Aliseda, A. (2006), *Abductive Reasoning: Logical Investigations into Discovery and Explanation* (Dordrecht: Springer).

Allen, R. and Pardo, M. (2008), 'Juridical proof and the best explanation', *Law and Philosophy* 27:3, 223–68.

Amaya, A. (2006), An Inquiry into the Nature of Coherence and its Role in Legal Argument. PhD Dissertation (Florence: European University Institute).

—— (2007a), Reasoning about Facts in Law: Essays in Coherence, Evidence, and Proof. S.J.D. Dissertation (Cambridge, MA: Harvard University).

—— (2007b), 'Formal models of coherence and legal epistemology', *Artificial Intelligence and Law* 15, 429–47.

—— (2008), 'Justification, coherence and epistemic responsibility in legal fact-finding', *Journal of Social Epistemology* 5:3.

Anderson, D. (1986), 'The evolution of Peirce's concept of abduction', *Transactions of the Charles S. Peirce Society* 22, 145–64.

Anderson, T., Twining, W. and Schum, D.A. (2005), *Analysis of Evidence*, 2nd Edition (Cambridge: Cambridge University Press).

Ben-Menahem, Y. (1990), 'The inference to the best explanation', *Erkenntnis* 33, 319–44.

BonJour, L. (1985), *The Empirical Foundations of Knowledge* (Cambridge, MA: Harvard University Press).

Conte, M.E. (1999), *Condizioni di Coerenza: Ricerche di Linguistica Testuale* (Firenze: La Nuova Italia).

Day, T. and Kincaid, H. (1994), 'Putting inference to the best explanation in its place', *Synthese* 98, 271–95.

Dershowitz, A.M. (1996), *Reasonable Doubts: The O.J. Simpson Case and the Criminal Justice System* (New York: Simon and Schuster).

Flach, P.A. and Kakas, A.C. (eds) (2000), *Abduction and Induction* (Dordrecht: Kluwer).

Fraassen, B. van (1989), *Laws and Symmetry* (Oxford: Clarendon Press).

Frankfurt, H.G. (1958), 'Peirce's notion of abduction', *Journal of Philosophy* 55, 593–97.

Gärdenfors, P. (1988), *Knowledge in Flux* (Cambridge, MA: MIT Press).

Harman, G. (1965), 'Inference to the best explanation', *The Philosophical Review* 74, 88–95.

—— (1980), 'Reasoning and explanatory coherence', *American Philosophical Quarterly* 17:2, 151–7.
—— (1986), *Change in View: Principles of Reasoning* (Cambridge: MIT Press).
Hastie, R. and Pennington, N. (1996), 'The O.J. Simpson stories: Behavioral scientists' reflections on the "People of the State of California v. Orenthal James Simpson"', *University of Colorado Law Review* 67, 957–76.
Hintikka, J. (1998), 'What is abduction? The fundamental problem of contemporary epistemology', *Transactions of the Charles S. Peirce Society* 34:3, 503–33.
Hoadley, C.M., Ranney, M. and Schank, P.K. (1994), 'WanderECHO: A Connectionist Simulation of Limited Coherence', in Ram and Eiselt (eds).
Hobbs, J.R., Stickel, M.E., Appelt, D.E. and Martin, P.A. (1993), 'Interpretation as Abduction', *Artificial Intelligence* 63, 69–142.
Houser, N., Roberts, D. and Van Evra, J. (eds) (1997), *Studies in the Logic of Charles Sanders Peirce* (Bloomington, IN: Indiana University Press).
Iranzo, V. (2001), 'Bad lots, good explanations', *Crítica* 33, 71–96.
Josephson, J.R. (2002), 'On the Proof Dynamics of Inference to the Best Explanation', in MacCrimmon and Tillers (eds).
Josephson, J.R. and Josephson, S.G. (1994), *Abductive Inference: Computation, Philosophy, Technology* (Cambridge: Cambridge University Press).
Kakas, A.C. and Sadri, F. (eds) (2002), *Computational Logic* (Berlin: Springer-Verlag).
Kapitan, T. (1992), 'Peirce and the autonomy of abductive reasoning', *Erkenntnis* 37, 1–26.
—— (1997), 'Peirce and the Structure of Abductive Inference', in Houser et al. (eds).
Klein, P. and Warfield, T.A. (1994), 'What price coherence?', *Analysis* 54, 129–32.
Laudan, L. (2007), 'Strange bedfellows: Inference to the best explanation and the criminal standard of proof', *International Journal of Evidence and Proof* 11:4, 292–307.
Lehrer, K. (1990), *Theory of Knowledge*, 2nd Edition (Boulder, CO: Westview Press).
Lipton, P. (1993), 'Is the best good enough?', *Proceedings of the Aristotelian Society* 43, 89–104.
—— (2000), 'Inference to the Best Explanation', in Newton-Smith (ed.).
—— (2004), *Inference to the Best Explanation*, 2nd Edition (London and New York: Routledge).
Lycan, W.G. (1988), *Judgment and Justification* (New York: Cambridge University Press).
—— (2002), 'Explanation and Epistemology', in Moser (ed.).
MacCrimmon, M. and Tillers, P. (eds) (2002), *The Dynamics of Judicial Proof* (Heidelberg: Physica-Verlag).
Magnani, L. (2001), *Abduction, Reason, Science* (Dordrecht: Kluwer).
Moser, P.K. (ed.) (2002), *The Oxford Handbook of Epistemology* (Oxford: Oxford University Press).

Newton-Smith, W. (ed.) (2000), *A Companion to the Philosophy of Science* (Malden: Blackwell).
Niinuluoto, I. (1999), 'Defending abduction', *Philosophy of Science* 66, 436–51.
Niinuluoto, I., Sintonen, M. and Wolenski, J. (eds) (2004), *Handbook of Epistemology* (Dordrecht: Kluwer).
Okasha, S. (2000), 'Van Fraassen's critique of inference to the best explanation', *Studies in the History and Philosophy of Science* 31:4, 691–710.
Peirce, C.S. (1960), *Collected Papers*, in C. Hartshorne and P. Weiss (eds) (Cambridge, MA: Harvard University Press).
Peng, Y. and Reggia, J. (1990), *Abductive Inference Models for Diagnostic Problem Solving* (New York: Springer-Verlag).
Pryor, J. (2001), 'Highlights of recent epistemology', *The British Journal for the Philosophy of Science* 52, 95–124.
Psillos, S. (1996), 'On Van Fraassen's critique of abductive reasoning,' *The Philosophical Quarterly* 46, 31–47.
—— (1999), *Scientific Realism: How Science Tracks Truth* (New York: Routledge).
—— (2002), 'Simply the Best: A Case for Abduction', in Kakas and Sadri (eds).
Ram, E. and Eiselt, K. (eds) (1994), *Proceedings of the Sixteenth Annual Conference of the Cognitive Science Society* (Hillsdale: Lawrence Erlbaum Associates).
Raz, J. (1992), 'The relevance of coherence', *Boston University Law Review* 72, 273–321.
Schum, D.A. (1999), 'Marshalling thoughts and evidence during fact investigation', *South Texas Law Review* 40, 401–54.
—— (2001), *The Evidential Foundations of Probabilistic Reasoning* (Evanston, IL: Northwestern University Press).
—— (2002), 'Species of Abductive Reasoning in Fact Investigation in Law', in MacCrimmon and Tillers (eds).
Schum, D.A. and Tillers, P. (1991), 'A Theory of Preliminary Fact Investigation', *U.C. Davis Law Review* 24, 932–1012.
Simon, D. (1998), 'A Psychological Model of Judicial Decision-Making', *Rutgers Law Journal* 30, 1–142.
—— (2004), 'A third view of the black box: Cognitive coherence in legal decision-making', *The University of Chicago Law Review* 71, 511–86.
Sintonen, M. and Kikeri, M. (2004), 'Scientific Discovery', in Niinuluoto et al. (eds).
Thagard, P. (1978), 'The best explanation: Criteria for theory choice', *Journal of Philosophy* 75, 76–92.
—— (1989), 'Explanatory coherence', *Behavioral and Brain Sciences* 12, 435–67.
—— (1992), *Conceptual Revolutions* (Princeton, NJ: Princeton University Press).
—— (2000), *Coherence in Thought and Action* (Cambridge, MA: MIT Press).
—— (2003), 'Why wasn't O.J. convicted? Emotional coherence in legal inference', *Cognition and Emotion* 17:3, 361–83.
—— (2006), 'Evaluating explanations in law, science, and everyday life', *Current Directions in Psychological Science* 15, 141–5.

Thagard, P. and Verbeurgt, K. (1998), 'Coherence as constraint satisfaction', *Cognitive Science* 22, 1–24.

Tillers, P. and Green, E.D. (eds) (1988), *Probability and Inference in the Law of Evidence: The Uses and Limits of Bayesianism* (Dordrecht: Kluwer).

Walton, D.N. (2002), *Legal Argumentation and Evidence* (University Park, PA: Pennsylvania State University Press).

Chapter 7
Accepting the Truth of a Story about the Facts of a Criminal Case

Bart Verheij and Floris Bex

1. Introduction

One task in legal decision-making is to decide about the facts of a case on the basis of the available evidence. This task is not always easy;[1] often the evidence in a case points in different directions, for example, when witnesses contradict each other. Determining what exactly can be concluded from the evidence is also not an easy or trivial task. For instance, when an accused's footprints are found on the scene of the crime one is tempted to assume that the accused has committed the crime, while the footprints by themselves only point in the direction of the accused's being present.

Reasoning about the facts of a case has been studied in several disciplines. For example, in the psychology of law Crombag, Van Koppen and Wagenaar have proposed the anchored narratives theory (Crombag et al. 1992; 1994; Wagenaar et al. 1993): legal decisions about the facts of a case are analysed in terms of structured stories anchored in common knowledge.

This research raised a significant amount of discussion, both among legal professionals in The Netherlands and among evidence theorists. The debate in the legal profession was not a surprise, as it was one of the goals of the authors. Their style, described as 'in some respects closer to "higher journalism" than to "scientific" publications' (Twining 1995, 109), was intentionally provocative as Crombag, Van Koppen and Wagenaar aimed at exposing a failure of the legal system: they argue that errors occur too often when deciding about the facts in criminal cases. Their work can be regarded as a form of social criticism in that it aims to reduce the number of miscarriages of justice, or 'dubious cases' as they call them.

Perhaps somewhat more of a surprise was the critical – albeit civilized – reception of the anchored narratives theory among evidence theorists (e.g., Twining 1995, Den Boer 1995). Among the points of criticism raised were: an imprecise use of terminology, especially concerning the central notions of story and argument (Twining 1995, 109); the treatment of pieces of evidence as a story

1 Whether the task of deciding about the facts is well-defined (considering the problematic, but legally relevant, distinction between questions of fact and of law) is a matter that we ignore here.

instead of as a means of argument (Twining 1995, 110); the lack of distinction between descriptive and prescriptive goals (Twining 1995, 108; Den Boer 1995, 328–9), exemplified by the lack of distinction between empirical generalizations and prescriptive rules; the presentation of too simple, overgeneralized universal rules of evidence (Twining 1995, 113); and an unclear role of, on the one hand, commonsense generic beliefs, and on the other, commonsense knowledge of scenarios (Den Boer 1995, 334).[2]

One thread through these points of criticism is the allegedly insufficient precision and detail of the presentation of the theory of anchored narratives that formed the basis of Crombag, Van Koppen and Wagenaar's project. In the present text this overarching point of criticism is used as a starting point; the goal being to give a treatment of the anchored narratives theory that does justice to the original description by Crombag, Van Koppen and Wagenaar while increasing the precision of its description. We do this by using a specific technique: the methodological development of a coherent set of semi-formal argumentation schemes (to be explained below). Although the aim is to stay close to the original description the result of this chapter is necessarily a reconstruction, an interpretation. Certain choices are made, some of them explicitly for reasons that will be explained, others inadvertently by personal predisposition or biased reading. Also, by the choice of method some themes are enlarged upon while others are neglected. For instance, the method abstracts from procedural constraints, which nevertheless are a recurring theme in the discussions by Crombag, Van Koppen and Wagenaar.

The method chosen is that of analysing and developing argumentation schemes as presented by Verheij (2003b). The method takes Walton's work on argumentation schemes (especially his 1996 book) as a starting point and is styled towards formal techniques in the field of artificial intelligence and law (cf. e.g., Prakken 1997; Hage 2005). In the method, argumentation schemes are treated as a semi-formal generalization of the formal rules of inference of logic and argumentation schemes are specified in terms of their conclusion, premises, exceptions and conditions of use.

By choosing this semi-formal method the chapter connects to a suggestion made by Crombag, Van Koppen and Wagenaar; when they contrast their theory with logical inference theories, they allude to the possibility of extended logical systems that are better suited as models of legal decision-making than the subsumption model (Wagenaar et al. 1993, 22). Especially in the field of artificial intelligence and law such extended logical systems have been designed. Among the topics addressed in these legal logics are exceptions, inconsistencies, gaps, contingent validity and rule properties (see Sartor's comprehensive 2005 work for an overview of the possibilities).

2 Twining (1999) has given a useful adapted and extended discussion of the points of agreement and disagreement between the anchored narratives approach and the school that is inspired by Wigmore, with authors such as Anderson, Schum and Twining himself. Cf. also Anderson et al. 2005.

This text is a development of earlier work on reasoning with evidence, anchored narratives and argumentation schemes (Verheij 2000; 2003b; Bex et al. 2003; Bex et al. 2007a) in the context of the project 'Making sense of evidence' (Bex et al. 2007b). Whereas previously we emphasized the formal modelling of defeasible arguments about story elements, we here use the semi-formal approach of argumentation schemes and show how stories as wholes can have an explicit role.

The rest of this text is organized as follows. In section 2, the theory of anchored narratives is summarized. Section 3 is about dialectical argumentation and argumentation schemes. Section 4 is the heart of this chapter: it contains the reconstruction of the theory of anchored narratives in terms of argumentation schemes. The resulting set of argumentation schemes is listed in the Appendix. Section 5 contains some concluding remarks.

2. Anchored Narratives[3]

In their books *Dubieuze Zaken* (Crombag et al. 1992; 1994, 61ff.) and *Anchored Narratives* (Wagenaar et al. 1993, 33ff.), Crombag, Van Koppen and Wagenaar present the theory of anchored narratives as a model of legal decision-making. The starting point of the theory is that proof in a criminal trial comes down to telling a good story. In the following, the theory of anchored narratives is summarized. More information about the theory and many examples illustrating it can be found in the books mentioned.

In the theory of anchored narratives courts make two judgements in criminal cases in order to establish the facts. First, they determine whether the stories of the parties before them (i.e., the prosecution and the defence) are plausible. Here the *quality* (or *goodness*) of the stories is at issue. Second, courts decide whether the available evidence is sufficiently supported by facts. This is where the *anchoring* of stories is examined.

Crombag, Van Koppen and Wagenaar consider their theory to be a natural development of earlier research on stories in legal psychology. In this research, stories provide the context that gives meaning to the individual elements of the story. This can be illustrated by the following mini-story:

> Peter fired a gun. George was hurt.

When one is told this mini-story, one is inclined to assume that George was hurt by Peter's shooting the gun. This is however not an explicit part of the story, and can be false.

Crombag, Van Koppen and Wagenaar base their discussion about the quality of stories on earlier work by Bennett and Feldman, and Pennington and Hastie.

---

3 This section is adapted from Verheij 2000.

According to Bennett and Feldman, a good story has a central action, to which all elements of the story are related. In the above example, the event that Peter fired a gun explains the action that George was hurt. A good story does not have loose ends. That is, in a good story the setting of the action unambiguously explains why the central action occurred as it did. If not, there are elements missing from the story, or there are contradictions.

Pennington and Hastie extended the theory by Bennett and Feldman; they argued that in a good story, the central actions and their consequences can be causally explained by three types of factors: physical conditions, psychological conditions and goals. So a good story must contain the accused's motives and show that the accused had the opportunity to commit the crime.

An experiment by Pennington and Hastie has shown that a set of evidence in a case does not guarantee a unique outcome. It turned out that, in a case where a person was killed, by different selections and evaluations of the evidence, test subjects reached outcomes ranging from first-degree murder, through second-degree murder and manslaughter, to self-defence. In another experiment, Pennington and Hastie showed the influence of story order on verdicts. The parties' positions about the event that was to be explained, in this case that a dead person had been found, were presented to the test people either in chronological story order, or in random order, such as the order in which witnesses gave their testimonies. It turned out that if a party's position was told in the chronological story order the test person more easily followed that party's position in the verdict. If the prosecution's position was given in chronological story order, while the defence's position was told in random order, the accused was convicted in 78 per cent of cases. If, on the other hand, the prosecution's position was given in random order and the defence's in chronological story order, the accused was convicted in 31 per cent of cases. Crombag, Van Koppen and Wagenaar conclude that telling the story well is half the work.

Crombag, Van Koppen and Wagenaar claim that *story anchoring* is needed in order to justify why a story is taken to be true. For instance, the statement of a policeman, that he saw that Peter fired a gun at George, can support that Peter indeed fired a gun at George. By itself, the evidence consisting of the policeman's statement does not prove that Peter fired a gun at George. If the policeman's statement is considered as proof, this is the result of the acceptance of the rule[4] that policemen tell the truth. Rules need not hold universally; there can be exceptions. No one believes that policemen always tell the truth, but many hold the belief that policemen tell the truth most of the time. According to Crombag, Van Koppen and Wagenaar, there are commonsense, generally true rules that underlie the acceptance or rejection of a piece of evidence as proof. They refer to such rules as anchors.

Crombag, Van Koppen and Wagenaar note that different legal systems can not only use different rules as anchors, but even opposites. They give the example of

4 Some would prefer to speak of a generalization because of the normative, even institutional connotation of the term 'rule'.

the assessment of confessions. Under English law, a conviction can be based only on the accused's confession, while in Dutch law, additional evidence is required. This suggests that the English use the anchoring rule that confessions are usually true, and the Dutch the opposite rule that confessions are often untrue.

Since the rules used as anchors can have exceptions, it can be necessary to show that a particular exception does not occur. Crombag, Van Koppen and Wagenaar discuss the example of the truthfulness of witnesses (Wagenaar et al. 1993, 38). Even if one assumes that witnesses normally tell the truth, the rule is not a safe anchor when the witness has a good reason to lie. Additional evidence is required, for instance, the testimony of a second witness. Even if both witnesses are unreliable, since they have good reasons to lie, it can be argued that when their testimonies coincide the combined statements suffice as proof. The anchor would then be that lying witnesses do normally not tell the same lies. There is, however, another exception: if the two testimonies are not independent, for instance since the witnesses have conferred, the anchoring is again not safe.

In the theory of anchored narratives, stories are hierarchically structured. The main story can consist of sub-stories that in their turn contain sub-sub-stories, and so on. The idea is that each sub-story is a further specification of the story or one of its parts. In each sub-story, a rule is used as an anchor to connect one or more pieces of evidence to the decision of the story or to a part of the decision. A difficulty arises from the fact that the rules used as anchors often remain implicit. Making the naively adopted rule explicit can lead us to reject it (Wagenaar et al. 1993, 38).

If one goes to a deeper level in the story hierarchy, the anchors will become more and more specific, and as such, *safer*. For instance, at a high level, the anchoring rule could be that witnesses normally tell the truth, while at a deeper level it could be replaced by the rule that witnesses who have no good reason for lying normally tell the truth.

Figure 7.1 (adapted from Crombag et al. 1992; 1994, 72; Wagenaar et al. 1993, 39) illustrates the theory of anchored narratives.

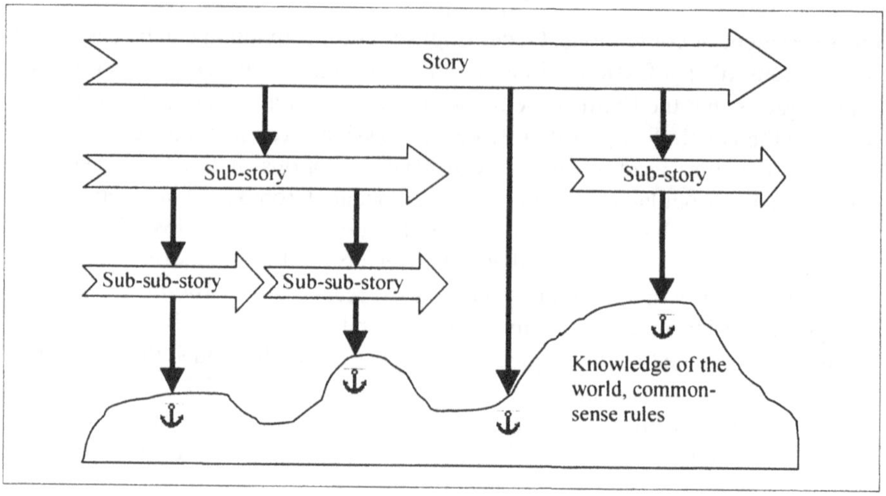

Figure 7.1 The theory of anchored narratives

The use of rules as anchors gives the theory of anchored narratives a deductive element. A decision follows from the evidence on the basis of a general rule. According to Crombag, Van Koppen and Wagenaar, anchoring is not equal to subsuming under a rule, since rules can have exceptions (Wagenaar et al. 1993, 58).

Crombag, Van Koppen and Wagenaar use their theory of anchored narratives in order to explain what they call *dubious cases* (or *dubious convictions*). In their terminology, a criminal conviction is dubious if the district court's verdict was reversed by the Court of Appeal because of a different evaluation of the evidence, or if the defence attorney remained strongly convinced of his client's innocence, even after (repeated) convictions (Wagenaar et al. 1993, 11). Thirty-five of such dubious cases were obtained from criminal lawyers, or were selected from among the cases in which one of the authors served as an expert witness. Crombag, Van Koppen and Wagenaar claim that their set of cases supports the theory of anchored narratives, since the anomalies that occur in the cases can only be explained by their theory.

As a spin-off of their work on dubious cases, Crombag, Van Koppen and Wagenaar present 10 universal rules of evidence (Wagenaar et al. 1993, 231ff.):

1. The prosecution must present at least one well-shaped narrative.
2. The prosecution must present a limited set of well-shaped narratives.
3. Essential components of the narrative must be anchored.
4. Anchors for different components of the charge should be independent of each other.

5. The trier of fact should give reasons for the decision by specifying the narrative and the accompanying anchoring.
6. A fact-finder's decision as to the level of analysis of the evidence should be explained through an articulation of the general beliefs used as anchors.
7. There should be no competing story with equally good or better anchoring.
8. There should be no falsifications of the indictment's narrative and nested sub-narratives.
9. There should be no anchoring onto obviously false beliefs.
10. The indictment and the verdict should contain the same narrative.

Obviously, these universal rules of evidence cannot be applied 'as is'. Wagenaar, Van Koppen and Crombag are fully aware of this. For instance, with respect to rule 8, they explain that it is not necessarily clear what counts as a falsification and what does not (1993, 243–4). For further qualification of these universal rules of evidence, the reader is referred to the original source (1993, 231ff.).

3. Modelling Argumentation

In this section, we will discuss the modelling of argumentation, as relevant for the rest of this chapter. The discussion is informed by interdisciplinary research in the fields of argumentation theory, artificial intelligence and law (cf., e.g., Pollock 1995; Prakken 1997; Hage 2005; Walton 2005; Walker 2007). Here we follow the approach of Verheij (2003a; 2003b).[5] For present purposes, we have skipped formal details. These can be found in the sources mentioned.

3.1. Toulmin's Argument Model

Toulmin (1958) introduced a model for the analysis of arguments that was richer than the traditional logical scheme focusing on premises and conclusions. His model has been and remains influential across a variety of disciplines (cf. Hitchcock and Verheij 2006). The model is shown in Figure 7.2. Datum and claim are analogues of premise and conclusion. Toulmin's original example used 'Harry was born in Bermuda' as the datum and 'Harry is a British subject' as the claim. The warrant is a generic inference licence underlying the step from datum to claim. For example: 'A man born in Bermuda will generally be a British subject'. The backing ('The statutes and other legal provisions so-and-so obtain') provides support for the warrant. The rebuttal is a form of argument attack that allows argumentation against the claim or the support for it (e.g., 'Harry has become a naturalized American'). Toulmin also included a qualifier, in order to make explicit that arguments can lead to a qualified conclusion ('Presumably, Harry is a British subject').

5 This section is adapted from Verheij 2007.

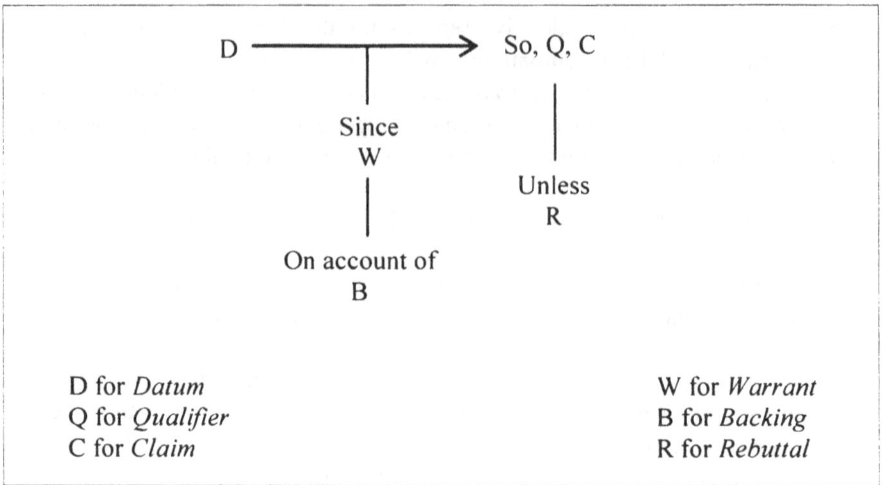

Figure 7.2 Toulmin's argument model

3.2. Datum and Claim

The basic, non-trivial form of argumentation consists of a reason that supports a conclusion. In Toulmin's terminology: a claim is supported by a datum. In the present approach, in order for the claim to follow, two elements are needed: the datum and the connection between the datum and the claim. Figure 7.3 gives a graphical representation of the three basic situations. On top, there is the situation in which the datum and the connection between datum and claim are assumed (indicated by the thick lines). As a result of these assumptions the claim is positively evaluated (indicated by the bold font).

It can occur that the datum is considered a possible reason for the claim, while the datum itself is not assumed (see the middle of Figure 7.3). In other words, the connection between datum and claim is assumed, but not the datum itself. Then the datum and claim are each neither positively nor negatively evaluated, which is indicated by a regular, black font and a dotted border. When the datum is not assumed, argumentation can naturally proceed by providing a reason for the datum (turning the datum into the claim of a second datum/claim pair).

The bottom of Figure 7.3 shows the situation where the datum is assumed, but the connection between datum and claim is not. In that case, the datum is positively evaluated, but the corresponding claim is not.

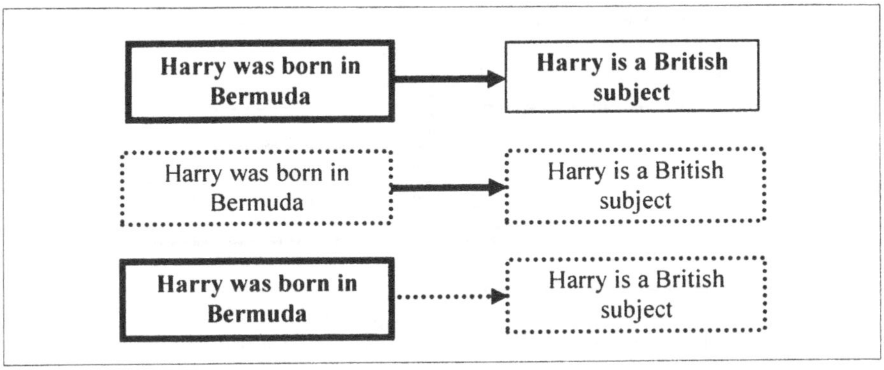

Figure 7.3 A datum and claim

3.3. Warrant and Backing

When the conditional connection between datum and claim is not assumed (as at the bottom of Figure 7.3), a natural argumentative move is to specify the warrant that gives rise to it. A warrant is a generalized inference licence and can as such in ordinary language be phrased as a rule sentence. In this connection, it is important to distinguish between the following three:

A man born in Bermuda will be a British subject.
If *Person* was born in Bermuda, then *Person* is a British subject.
If Harry was born in Bermuda, then he is a British subject.

The first is the warrant, i.e., a generic inference licence phrased as a rule sentence. The second is the scheme of specific inference licences related to it. It is phrased as a conditional sentence with a variable (*Person*). The third is a specific inference licence. It is one of the instances of the scheme preceding it. The first two (the warrant and the associated scheme) are in a specific sense equivalent since either expresses the warrant's core meaning as a generic inference licence. However, obviously only the rule phrase occurs in ordinary language.

Figure 7.4 (top) shows a warrant that is assumed to hold and hence is positively evaluated. As a result of the warrant, the connection between the original datum and claim follows. When the warrant is not assumed (Figure 7.4, bottom), the connection between datum and claim does not follow. Consequently, the claim does not follow either and is not positively evaluated.

In such a case, a backing from which the warrant follows can be given as support for the warrant. The result is that the claim becomes positively evaluated again (Figure 7.5).

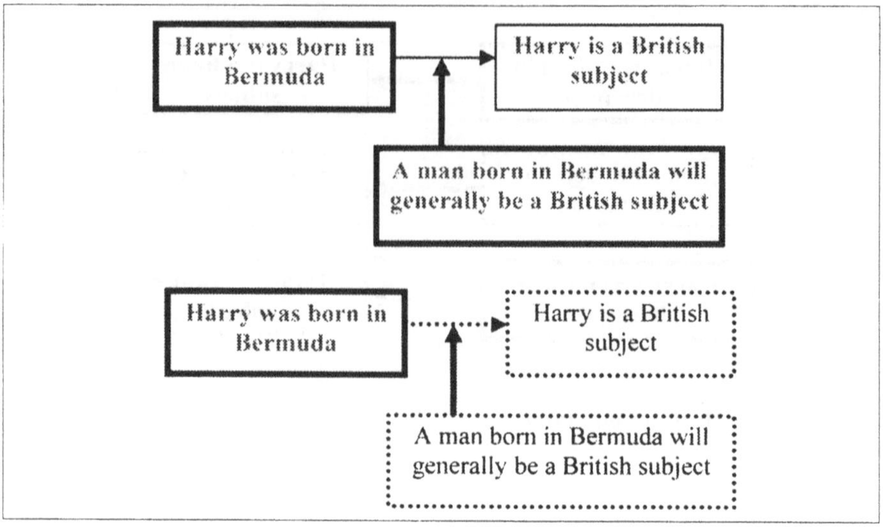

Figure 7.4 Adding a warrant

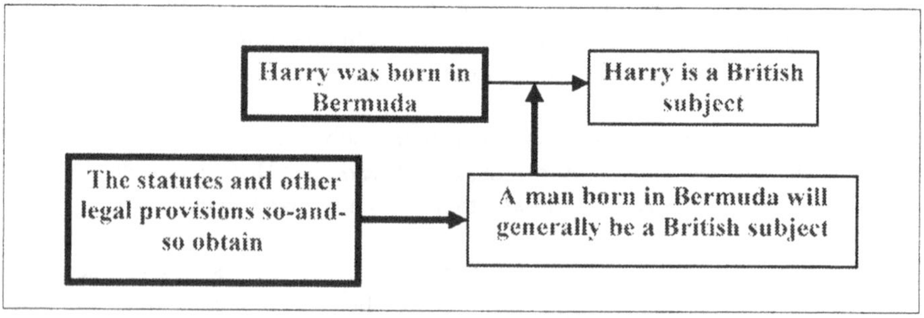

Figure 7.5 The role of a backing

3.4. Attack

The strongest deviation from classical logical analyses of argument in Toulmin's model is the idea of argument attack, in Toulmin's terminology: rebuttal.[6] The possibility of attack involves the defeasibility of arguments: an argument that shows why a conclusion follows can, by new information (counter-reasons, exceptions to a rule, etc.), be overturned. Technically, the

6 Pollock (1995) has distinguished two kinds of argument attack, viz. rebutting and undercutting defeaters. Considering his examples, Toulmin's rebuttals can include both kinds.

effect is non-monotonicity, i.e., it can occur that conclusions that initially follow are retracted, given additional information.

The basic form of attack and its effect on argument evaluation is most easily illustrated in a situation with only a datum and a claim, and no warrant or backing. Figure 7.6 shows the effect of an attack against the connection between datum and claim. At the top, the attacking reason is not assumed (but its undercutting effect is assumed, as is shown by the thick red arrow with a diamond end); hence the claim is still positively evaluated. At the bottom, the attacking reason is assumed, and therefore blocks the connection between datum and claim. As a result, the claim is no longer positively evaluated.

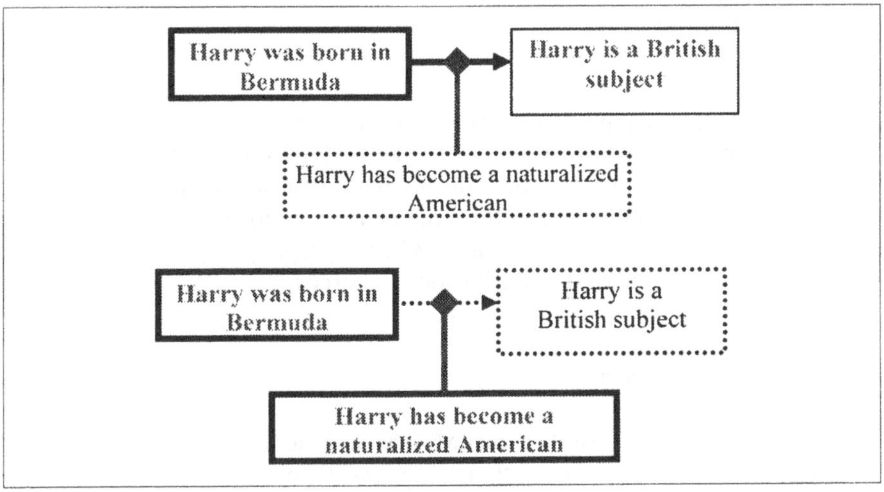

Figure 7.6 An attacking reason (no warrant)

3.5. Reinstatement

An important phenomenon that can occur when argumentation is defeasible is reinstatement. This occurs when a conclusion follows, then by additional information no longer follows, but subsequently – when even more information is added – follows again. For instance, assume an unlawful act case in which someone has broken a window. As a result, it can at first be argued that he has an obligation to pay for the damage caused by breaking the window. That conclusion no longer follows when this argument is attacked by a ground of justification, e.g., because the breaking of the window allowed the saving of a child in the burning house. The obligation to pay can become reinstated again if it turns out that breaking the window was not necessary for saving the child. Figure 7.7 shows the endpoint of this exchange of reasons and counter-reasons.

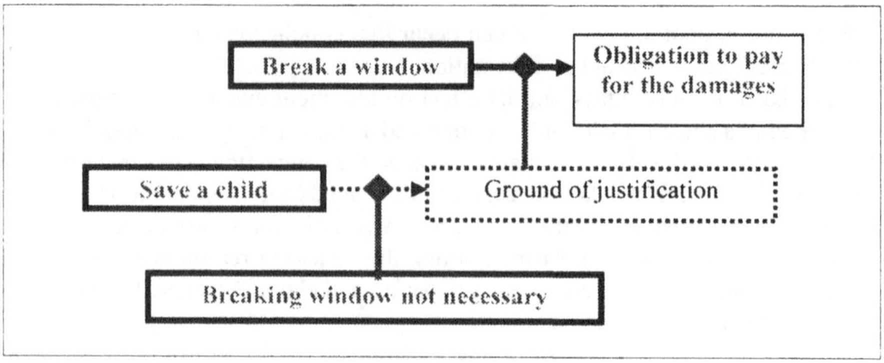

Figure 7.7 Reinstatement

As a side issue, the example can be used to illustrate the need for 'attack warrants'. In the example, it is debatable whether (in an actual legal system) the non-necessity of the property right violation blocks the inference that saving the child gives rise to a ground of justification. It therefore can be relevant to specify the underlying generic attack licence (something like 'When a property right violation is not necessary, there is no ground of justification by force majeure'), and give backing for that.

3.6. Argumentation Schemes

Argumentation schemes can be regarded as a generalization of the rules of inference of formal logic. The notion of argumentation schemes stems from the field of argumentation theory. Walton's (1996) treatment has been influential and provides a useful overview with many examples. There, also, further references to the argumentation theory literature can be found. Here are two informal versions of logical rules of inferences:

(1) *P*. If *P* then *Q*.
Therefore *Q*.

(2) All *P*s are *Q*s. Some *R*s are not *Q*s.
Therefore some *R*s are not *P*s.

The former is a semi-formal version of *modus ponens*, the latter is one of the classically studied syllogisms. These two schemes fit in neat formal systems; the former in many logical proof systems, but in particular in standard propositional logic, the latter in the classification of syllogisms. Both are truth preserving (in the sense that the truth of the schemes' conditions is taken to guarantee the truth of their conclusion) and allow no exceptions. Contrast these with the following two schemes:

(3) Person *E* says *P*. Person *E* is an expert with respect to facts such as *P*. Therefore *P* is true.

(4) Doing act *A* contributes to goal *G*. Person *P* has goal *G*. Therefore person *P* should do act *A*.

The former is a variant of argumentation from expert opinion, the latter a variant of means–end reasoning. Although these schemes are recognizable as patterns that can occur in actual reasoning and are also – to some extent – reasonable, it is immediately clear that the neatness and safeness of the schemes (1) and (2) does not apply to (3) and (4). There is no clean formal system associated with (3) and (4), nor is one to be expected. They are not truth preserving. For (3), it suffices to note that an expert can be wrong and, for (4), it is even unclear how to establish the truth of its conclusion. Furthermore, (3) and (4) allow exceptions. For instance, an exception to scheme (3) occurs when an expert has a personal interest in saying *P*. For scheme (4) it can be the case that there are other, better ways to achieve goal *G*, or it may be impossible to do *A*.

Argumentation schemes are context-dependent, defeasible and concrete instead of universal, strict and abstract. To some, these properties may seem to make argumentation schemes a useless tool of analysis, but it turns out that the properties are in fact what make argumentation schemes useful. At the same time, argumentation schemes require a way of approaching the analysis of reasoning different from one in terms of neat logical systems. And although a full formalistic approach is not feasible given the nature of argumentation schemes, it is not necessary to proceed without any systematicity. As argued by Verheij (2003b), it is possible to approach argumentation schemes in a way that resembles the practice of knowledge engineering, in which knowledge is extracted from domain experts and represented in such a way that a machine can process it. Argumentation schemes can be characterized using a format with four elements: consequent, antecedent, exceptions and conditions of use.

Here is an example of the format for simple arguments based on expert testimony:

Consequent:	*P*.
Antecedent:	Person *E* says *P*. Person *E* is an expert with respect to facts such as *P*.
Exception:	Person *E* is lying.
Condition:	Experts with respect to the facts such as *P* provide reliable information concerning the truth of *P*.

The format seems to abstract completely from the dialogue setting of argumentation. For instance, the format does not have a slot for critical questions, although in the literature on argumentation schemes these play a central role. The reason for this is that in our opinion the critical questions can be determined on the basis of the format. In fact, the format suggests the following four kinds of critical questions:

1. Critical questions concerning the consequent of an argumentation scheme. In the example: are there other reasons, based on other argumentation schemes for or against *P*?
2. Critical questions concerning the elements of the antecedent of an argumentation scheme.
   In the example: Did person *E* say *P*? Is person *E* an expert with respect to facts such as *P*?
3. Critical questions based on the exceptions of an argumentation scheme. In the example: is person *E* lying?
4. Critical questions based on the conditions of use of an argumentation scheme. In the example: do experts with respect to the facts such as *P* provide reliable information concerning the truth of *P*?

This classification of critical questions shows that the proposed argumentation scheme format can provide relevant insights for the dialogue setting of argumentation. In a similar way, the format can be applied to the topic of burden of proof. For instance, the proponent of a claim *P* will have the burden to answer questions by an opponent concerning the elements of the antecedent, whereas an opponent will have to substantiate an exception. With respect to the consequent, it is natural that a proponent of *P* has the burden of giving additional reasons for it, whereas the opponent has the burden of giving reasons against it. Prakken and Sartor (Chapter 9 of this book) and Gordon et al. (2007) provide further discussion of burden of proof in relation to argumentation schemes.

For present purposes, the format is relevant because it provides a natural, systematic approach to develop a set of argumentation schemes with respect to a certain topic. It consists of the following four steps:

1. determine the relevant types of sentences;
2. determine the conditional relations, i.e., the antecedents and consequents of the argumentation schemes;
3. determine the exceptions, i.e, the arguments against the use of the argumentation schemes;
4. determine the conditions of use for the argumentation schemes.

The four steps need not be followed in this order. It even occurs that one often goes back to an earlier step and makes adaptations, until finally a set of argumentation schemes is reached that serves one's purposes. This will be illustrated by the application of the method to the anchored narratives theory in the next section.

4. Argumentation Schemes for the Anchored Narratives Theory

In the following, the theory of anchored narratives (referred to as ANT from now on) will be reconstructed in terms of argumentation schemes. As was said in the introduction, Crombag, Van Koppen and Wagenaar's theory met with some amount of criticism from evidence theorists. We suggested that this criticism could in part be repaired by adding precision and detail to the use of terminology and by further development of a number of key concepts in the theory. For example, Figure 7.1, which plays a central expository role in ANT, suggests that in ANT stories are only anchored in general commonsense knowledge of the world, without a clear role for the pieces of evidence themselves. During our research, we found that over the years the original version of ANT has been subject to changes and interpretations, both by other researchers in the field as well as by its original authors. For our reconstruction of ANT we have drawn from numerous written sources (Crombag et al. 1992; 1994; Wagenaar et al. 1993, De Poot et al. 2004; Wagenaar and Crombag 2006) and from personal discussions with one of the original authors, Peter Van Koppen, in the context of the project 'Making sense of evidence' (Bex et al. 2007b).

For expository reasons, the reconstruction will be performed step by step and contains a number of retracings in the form of adaptations of results attained at earlier steps. For ease of reference, the final set of argumentation schemes that in our view best expresses ANT has therefore been listed in the Appendix.

4.1. Accepting the Truth of a True Story

The first step in the argumentation scheme method is to determine the relevant types of sentences. In ANT, accepting a story as the true account of the facts involves story quality and story anchoring. So here is a first shot at relevant sentence types:

> Story S is true.
> Story S is good.
> Story S is anchored.

The second step of the method is formulating argumentation schemes, i.e., the conditional relations that exist between the sentence types. For these sentences, this is straightforward: the latter two taken together, when accepted as true, can give support for accepting the truth of the former. Hence, an initial formulation of ANT's central argumentation scheme is this:

(1) ANCHORED NARRATIVES: ACCEPTING A STORY AS TRUE
Consequent: Story S is true.
Antecedent: Story S is good.
Story S is anchored.

The scheme makes a fundamental distinction underlying ANT explicit: everything that has to do with the evidential support of a story is dealt with under the heading of anchoring, whereas story quality is related to the overall shape and completeness of the story. In ANT, story quality is a kind of pre-evidential plausibility of a story. It is important and characteristic for ANT that story quality is considered to be independent of the available evidence.

It should be noted that – although the scheme's consequent refers to the truth of story S – the scheme is not intended to guarantee that its consequent obtains when its antecedent does. Clearly, it doesn't, for the truth of a story cannot be ensured by its quality (goodness) and anchoring. This is in line with the nature of argumentation schemes, which point to defeasible reasons and make no claim to truth preservation. The scheme purports to show how, according to ANT, the truth of a story can be reasonably accepted as true. ANT is pragmatic in this respect, and treats reasoning on the basis of evidence as a kind of pragmatic judgement, not as a guarantee of truth. In ANT, quality and anchoring provide a reason for accepting a story as being true. In addition, it is relevant to note that, in ANT, this scheme is the only route to accepting the truth of a story.

How can the acceptance of the truth of a story be undermined in ANT? There are three ways of doing that. First, one can argue that the story is not good, second that it is not anchored, and third that there is an exception to the application of the scheme. Before we continue with the former two in our reconstruction of ANT's treatment of story quality and anchoring (in the following two subsections), we turn to the possibility of exceptions to the application of the scheme (cf. step 3 of the method). When there is an exception, the scheme's conclusion doesn't follow, even though the scheme's antecedent is fulfilled. So the question is: when a story is good and anchored, which exceptional situations can – according to ANT – have the effect that it is nevertheless unreasonable to accept the story's truth?

In ANT, one central exception to the scheme is recognized: the occurrence of another story with equally good or better anchoring. This exception corresponds to number 7 of the universal rules of evidence. Including this exception in the scheme leads to the following adaptation:

(1.1) ANCHORED NARRATIVES: ACCEPTING A STORY AS TRUE
Consequent: Story S about topic T is true.
Antecedent: Story S is good.
Story S is anchored.
Exception: Story S1 about topic T (unequal to S) has equally good or better anchoring.

Looking at this formulation of the scheme leads to a suggestion for refinement: it seems natural to assume that the requirement of goodness should hold both for stories taken to be true and for their competitors. In other words, the suggestion is that alternative stories that are better or equally anchored, but that are not themselves good, are not genuine competitors. Otherwise a rambling, ambiguous story full of contradictions could preclude an otherwise good and anchored story from being taken to be true. Incorporating this idea in the scheme, we get:

(1.2) ANCHORED NARRATIVES: ACCEPTING A STORY AS TRUE
Consequent: Story S about topic T is true.
Antecedent: Story S is good.
Story S is anchored.
Exception: Story S1 about topic T (unequal to S) is good, and
Story S1 (unequal to S) has equally good or better anchoring.

We discuss the adaptation (1.2) here merely as a suggestion. We have modelled scheme 1.2 in such a way that a story need not be better to push out a good story: it suffices that story S1 is good and has equally good anchoring. It is conceivable that version (1.1) is closer to the original intention of Crombag, Van Koppen and Wagenaar (but note the phrasing of universal rule of evidence number 7). One reason for preferring (1.1) could for instance be that even a bad, but better anchored story might give sufficient doubt to reject an otherwise good story. Note, however, that this may depend on the party that presents a story: stories by the prosecutor may need a treatment different from those by the defendant. It is not our goal to settle this issue here. It is noteworthy, however, that the issue has naturally presented itself as a side effect of the argumentation scheme method.

4.2. Story Quality

Let us continue on the issue of story quality: how is story quality established in ANT? A number of themes occur regularly in this respect. Following our method, we express them in terms of sentence types:

Story S has a central action to which all elements are related.
Story S explains how the central action was performed.
Story S explains why the central action was performed.
Story S is unambiguous.
Story S contains the accused's motive.
Story S tells that the accused had the opportunity to commit the crime.
Story S does not contain contradictions.

In general, the central action of a prosecutor's story is the crime itself, though there are examples discussed in ANT's main sources in which the crime is not itself the central action in the story that is the issue of the debate.[7] Hence the accused's motive (the fifth sentence type in the list above) is just one instance of a reason why the central action was performed (the third sentence type). It therefore seems reasonable that, in a generic scheme, the motive is left out. Similarly, opportunity (the sixth type) can be taken as an instance of the general constraint of internal coherence of the story (the seventh type). A first version of an argumentation scheme capturing these points is the following:

> (2) ANCHORED NARRATIVES: STORY QUALITY
> Consequent: Story S is good.
> Antecedent: Story S has a central action to which all elements are related.
> Story S explains how the central action was performed.
> Story S explains why the central action was performed.
> Story S is unambiguous.
> Story S does not contain contradictions.

In section 4.4, we will have more to say about the scheme of story quality (which will lead to refinements), but first we continue with the second central theme of ANT, viz. story anchoring.

4.3. Story Anchoring

It is especially in the part of story anchoring that ANT has occasionally led to misunderstandings: why consider commonsense generalizations as anchors and not the pieces of evidence themselves? Isn't providing good evidence the most important way of justifying one's belief in the truth of a story? Certainly; and presumably Crombag, Van Koppen and Wagenaar don't disagree, or at least not radically. Clearly they have not defended that believing a story is just a matter of the right ('safest') commonsense generalizations, while leaving aside the pieces of evidence. Instead, what they have argued for is that the value of a piece of evidence as proof of the occurrence of an event cannot be estimated independently of the commonsense generalization that connects the piece of evidence to the event. For example, a story can only be reasonably believed on the basis of a confession if *confessions normally contain true stories*. Moreover, ANT emphasizes that the value of a piece of evidence is a function of the safeness of the corresponding

7 For instance, in the Haaknat case (discussed by Crombag et al. 1992; 1994 and Wagenaar et al. 1993) the crime was a robbery, but the point at issue was why Haaknat was found hiding from the police in a moat. Was Haaknat hiding because of his involvement in a fight (as he himself claimed) or was it because of the robbery? From the perspective of the crime, Haaknat's hiding is not a central action, but from the perspective of the decision-making it was. In this way, if the identity of the perpetrator is at issue, the actual crime is always one of the possible stories that explains some kind of (strange) behaviour by the suspect.

anchoring generalization. For instance, if the proof criterion is 'beyond a reasonable doubt' (and not merely 'reasonable'), the generalization '*confessions normally contain true stories*' does not seem to suffice. Then something stronger like '*confessions almost always contain true stories*' should be true. One reason why ANT's authors elaborate at length on the importance of anchoring generalizations is that their safe use can require consultation with experts, for instance on the empirical findings about the safeness of witness testimony.

In a benevolent reading of ANT, there is no serious misconception with respect to the relation between the justification of belief in a story, pieces of evidence and the commonsense generalizations connecting them. ANT's use of the metaphor of anchors is not incoherent. Perhaps the specific version of the metaphor is somewhat infelicitous, given the following observation: when discussing ANT, we have repeatedly encountered that people tend to think of the pieces of evidence as anchors, and that it takes effort to instead think of the generalizations as anchors. A slight change of the use of the metaphor seems in place: perhaps the generalizations should be thought of as the *anchor chains*. This adaptation of the metaphor does justice to the idea that the generalizations connect the piece of evidence (in the metaphor: the anchor) to the story (the 'ship').

Let us continue with determining how the anchoring of a story can be dealt with in our argumentation scheme reconstruction of ANT. A central type of sentence in anchoring is the following. It is phrased in such a way that it avoids the pitfalls of the different interpretations of the anchor metaphor just described:

> (*) Component C of story S is anchored to piece of evidence E by anchoring generalization G.

Different phrasings of the same idea, less tied to ANT's preferred choice of words, are of course possible, e.g.:

> (†) Component C of story S finds support in piece of evidence E on the basis of warranting generalization G.

Here the term 'warranting' is related to Toulmin's (1958) warrants, viz. generic inference licences (discussed in section 3). In certain circumstances, it can be worthwhile to split (†) into two parts, as follows:

> Component C of story S finds support in piece of evidence E.
> The support of component C of story S by piece of evidence E is warranted by generalization G.

As we are reconstructing ANT, we will stay close to its terminology and use (*). It is tempting to propose the following argumentation scheme:

(3) ANCHORED NARRATIVES: ANCHORING
Consequent: Story S is anchored.
Antecedent: There is a piece of evidence E.
Component C of story S is anchored to piece of evidence E by anchoring generalization G.
Anchoring generalization G is safe.

Indeed (3) expresses the core idea underlying ANT that anchoring a story involves that some component of the story S is supported by a piece of evidence E, when a safe generalization connects E and C. However, the present scheme suggests that for a story's anchoring it suffices that *one* component is supported by evidence. This is in general not correct: in a murder case it does not suffice to have evidence for the victim's being killed (although a murder case without a body is in trouble), while there is nothing to support who did the killing. On the other hand, it is also not necessary (nor in general feasible) that *all* components of a story are directly supported by evidence. For instance, sometimes even a murder case without a body can lead to a life sentence for the murderer (Court of Appeal, Leeuwarden, 19 July 2006; the victim had been burnt). ANT takes a middle way: not one, not all, but the *essential* components of a story must be supported by evidence (universal rule of evidence number 3).

One way of capturing these ideas in an argumentation scheme is in terms of the specification of a reason *against* a story's anchoring: a story is *not* well-anchored when there is an essential component that is not safely anchored.[8] A story component is safely anchored when it is anchored to a piece of evidence and a corresponding safe generalization. Scheme 3 is split into two:

(3a) ANCHORED NARRATIVES: ATTACKING THE ANCHORING OF A STORY
Consequent: Story S is not well anchored.
Antecedent: Component C of story S is essential.
Component C of story S is not safely anchored.

(3b) ANCHORED NARRATIVES: COMPONENT ANCHORING
Consequent: Component C of story S is safely anchored.
Antecedent: There is a piece of evidence E.
Component C of story S is anchored to piece of evidence E by anchoring generalization G.
Anchoring generalization G is safe.

Four differences from the original scheme (3) are worth mentioning. First, the scheme's direction of support has flipped: instead of a scheme that expresses how

8 Another way is the use of a universal quantifier: supporting a story's being well anchored requires that *all* essential components are safely anchored.

to support a story's anchoring, it is now replaced by scheme (3a) expressing how to attack a story's anchoring. Second, it is now made explicit that a subset of story elements needs support by evidence, namely the essential components. Third, the choice of words in the consequent is now more normatively loaded: instead of simply speaking of anchoring, we now speak of anchoring well. In this way, it is clearer that story anchoring is a matter of degree and of judgement. This also leads to a slight adaptation of scheme (1.2). The requirement for accepting a story as true now becomes that a story is well anchored, instead of merely being anchored:

(1.3) ANCHORED NARRATIVES: ACCEPTING A STORY AS TRUE
Consequent: Story S about topic T is true.
Antecedent: Story S is good.
Story S is well anchored.
Exception: Story S1 about topic T (unequal to S) is good, and Story S1 (unequal to S) has equally good or better anchoring.

Fourth, we have now two kinds of anchoring: the anchoring of stories (scheme (3a)) and the anchoring of story components (scheme (3b)).

There is no general method for determining the safeness of anchoring generalizations. It is, for instance, always possible to argue that the case under consideration is an exception. ANT gives some advice, though. Specificity is relevant for determining safeness in the sense that it is easier to decide about a rule's correctness when it is more specific, but specificity cannot warrant correctness (Wagenaar et al. 1993, 40). ANT has one general attack against the safety of anchoring generalizations, viz. their obvious falsity (cf. universal rule of evidence number 7):

(4) ANCHORED NARRATIVES: OBVIOUSLY FALSE GENERALIZATIONS
Consequent: Anchoring generalization G is not safe.
Antecedent: Anchoring generalization G is obviously false.

Scheme (3a) is the attack on a story's being well anchored that is most characteristic for ANT: only stories for which the essential components are safely anchored are themselves well anchored. Besides this attack, ANT has two other attacks on a story's being well anchored. One is based on the interdependence of anchoring (scheme (5) below, based on universal rule of evidence number 4), the other on the falsification of a story (scheme (6) below, based on universal rule of evidence number 8):

(5) ANCHORED NARRATIVES: ATTACK BY INTERDEPENDENCE OF ANCHORING
Consequent: Story S is not well anchored.
Antecedent: The anchoring of (unequal) components C and C1 is interdependent.
Component C of story S is essential.
Component C1 of story S is essential.

Interdependent anchoring, for instance, occurs when the case against a suspect (including identity, actus reus and mens rea) is based only on his confession or only on the testimony of the victim.

(6) ANCHORED NARRATIVES: ATTACK BY FALSIFICATION
Consequent: Story S is not well anchored.
Antecedent: Story S is falsified.

There does not seem to be an explicit description of what story falsification amounts to in ANT. The following scheme suggests one approach:

(7) ANCHORED NARRATIVES: FALSIFICATION
Consequent: Story S is falsified.
Antecedent: Component C of story S is essential.
The opposite of component C of story S is anchored to piece of evidence E by anchoring generalization G.
Anchoring generalization G is safe.

It may be worthwhile to emphasize one difference between the antecedents of (7) and (3a): whereas (3a)'s antecedent involves an essential component that *is not* safely anchored, in (7)'s antecedent the *opposite* of an essential component *is* safely anchored.

4.4. Recursiveness of Stories in Reasoning about Evidence

We now turn to an issue related to ANT that we did not learn directly by reading its main sources, but by conversations with one of its authors, Peter Van Koppen. The conversations took place in the context of the already mentioned project 'Making sense of evidence'. Van Koppen emphasized again and again that not only the facts of a crime are stories, but also the pieces of evidence that support or attack the truth of a story themselves.[9] For us, Van Koppen's position was rather surprising as we tended to think of pieces of evidence as giving rise to the reasons that support or attack crime stories. So in our minds there was a dichotomy between reasons

9 This theoretical position nicely fits Van Koppen's conversation style: he is a gifted teller of stories.

and stories, a dichotomy that did not seem to exist (or at least not in the same way) in Van Koppen's conceptualization.

The point is related to the issue of real evidence, in Wigmore's terminology: 'autoptic proference'. With real evidence, no inference is required; the thing itself is its proof. For example, to prove that there is a knife by means of autoptic proference, one only has to show the knife itself. There is, however, a problem with the idea that the thing proves itself: it *only* proves itself. Peter Tillers wrote an interesting piece about this in his web log.[10] Showing a knife and saying 'there is a knife' may prove that there is a knife, but it could just as well be the knife the judge used to cut his steak with the day before. What has to be proved, that the knife was used in a brutal murder, cannot be proved by just the knife itself. We need forensic expertise on fingerprints, police reports about where the knife was found and so on. In other words, it has to be shown why and how the knife is part of the evidence for the event that a person was brutally murdered with the knife.

Van Koppen's position can be regarded as an answer to this problem of real evidence. On one occasion, he argued that finding a hair on the crime scene that matched the accused's DNA did not mean that the accused committed the crime; a good and properly anchored story has to be constructed that tells us that the hair was in fact left on the scene of the crime at the moment that the accused committed the crime.

However, Van Koppen's position that a piece of evidence *is* a story provides a theoretical complication: are pieces of evidence not first and foremost (sources for) reasons that support or attack crime stories? What happens to this idea when pieces of evidence are to be regarded as stories? Are then piece-of-evidence stories supportive for facts-of-the-crime stories? Are pieces-of-evidence stories of 'the same kind' as facts-of-the-crime stories? Are they to be evaluated in the same way? And so on.

In this section, an approach to the resolution of this theoretical complication is proposed. The provided solution leads to the main clarification (or perhaps, adaptation) of ANT resulting from our reconstruction, while retaining ANT's spirit.[11] The approach is based on recursiveness. In argumentation, one version of recursiveness meets the eye immediately. It is the recursiveness of reasons. To defend (or attack) a claim, one gives reasons, but for these reasons in their turn, further reasons can be given, and so on. Recursiveness of reasons occurs in any kind of argumentation, hence also in the context of evidential argumentation (see, e.g., Anderson et al. 2005 and our own previous work, Bex et al. 2007b).

However, in our reconstruction of ANT another kind of recursiveness is used, one that fits Van Koppen's position that pieces of evidence are stories. This

---

10 'The Chain Saw Did Not Speak Clearly', 9 June 2005 <tillerstillers.blogspot.com/2005/06/chain-saw-did-not-speak-clearly.html>. Page accessed on 31 March 2008.

11 It is our hunch that the authors of ANT will not consider what will follow to be a genuine adaptation, but at best a clarification. If so, the reconstruction has succeeded.

recursiveness is the recursiveness of stories in reasoning about evidence:[12] to establish the truth of a facts-of-the crime story, its essential components must be safely anchored (to a piece of evidence by an anchoring generalization; cf. the schemes (3a) and (3b) above). But for this component anchoring, *a story about a piece of evidence must be provided*, and this story must be accepted as true. The recursion arises since accepting the truth of a piece-of-evidence story is analogous to accepting the truth of a facts-of-the-crime story: like a facts-of-the-crime story, a piece-of-evidence story is accepted as true when it is good and well anchored, and there is no competing story (cf. scheme (1.3)). The recursion can continue, since arguing for the truth of a piece-of-evidence story can involve further pieces-of-evidence stories, and so on.

If we apply this idea of the recursiveness of stories in our reconstruction of ANT, scheme (3b) about component anchoring only needs a slight adaptation:

> (3b.1) ANCHORED NARRATIVES: COMPONENT ANCHORING
> Consequent: Component C of story S is safely anchored.
> Antecedent: There is a piece of evidence E.
> Story SE about piece of evidence E is true.
> Component C of story S is anchored to piece of evidence E by anchoring generalization G.
> Anchoring generalization G is safe.

We simply added a conjunct to the scheme's antecedent, viz. 'Story SE about piece of evidence E is true'. Note that the scheme now refers to *two* stories: a story S and a story SE about a piece of evidence used to support a component of story S. The story S can be about the facts of a crime, or, recursively, about a piece of evidence. The effect of this adaptation is that the truth of stories about pieces of evidence is now treated on a par with other stories, viz. by story quality and by story anchoring.

As an illustration, we return to the example of a hair found on the scene of the crime, and use it to establish whether the accused was at the scene of the crime. Initially, there is a very simple story about the hair, so simple that the term 'story' is somewhat unbefitting:

> A hair is found at the scene of the crime and the hair's DNA matches that of the accused.

If this story were to be used to establish that the accused was at the scene of the crime, the following anchoring generalization would be needed:

12 This kind of recursiveness of stories is different from the recursiveness of story schemes mentioned by Bex in Chapter 4 of this book. There, the events of a sub-story are essentially a subset of the main story, while here one story (typically about a piece of evidence) plays a role in accepting another (typically about the facts of the crime).

> If a hair is found at the scene of the crime and the hair's DNA matches that of the accused, then the accused was at the scene of the crime.

The defence could, for instance, argue that this generalization is not sufficiently safe to conclude (using (3b.1)) that the story component 'The accused was at the scene of the crime' is safely anchored.

Let's next consider the more complicated situation of the frustrated investigator. Here is the story:

> A hair is found at the scene of the crime and the hair's DNA matches that of the accused. The hair was planted at the scene of the crime by a frustrated investigator.

If we were to use this story for anchoring, we would need the following anchoring generalization:

> If a hair is found at the scene of the crime and the hair's DNA matches that of the accused *and it is planted there*, then the accused was at the scene of the crime.

This generalization is obviously false, and scheme (4) could be used to attack its use for safe anchoring. As a result, applying scheme (3b.1) to the planted hair does not lead to the safe anchoring of the story component that the accused was at the scene of the crime.

One may wonder whether (3b.1) isn't an unnecessarily involved version of (3b). Why treat pieces of evidence as stories in the first place? Can't they be treated as elementary propositions (as is in a way the case in (3b))? The answer is: that depends on the circumstances, but in this respect the situation for the facts of the crime is analogous to that of pieces of evidence. For *simple* stories, either about the facts of the crime or about pieces of evidence, a story approach as in ANT, in which story quality and story anchoring are established, is indeed often overly involved. Then an approach with propositions and reasons (e.g., styled as in section 3) suffices. As soon as a story gets more complex, or establishing its truth becomes more involved, a story approach as in ANT can come in useful. This can for instance occur when there are several good, and hence plausible, but competing stories, or when discussion is possible about the plausibility of a story or about one of the generalizations used. A defence of a story-based approach against (or in comparison with) a reason-based approach is, however, beyond the goals of the present chapter (see, e.g., Twining's (1999) reflections that are very relevant in this respect).

4.5. Other Story Structures

Looking back at the schemes proposed, after having introduced the recursiveness of stories, it turns out that with hindsight one scheme requires adaptation, namely scheme (2). In fact, the specifics of scheme (2) may be a reason why the recursiveness of stories underlying ANT was not so readily clear: scheme (2) is about stories that involve an intentional crime, and stories about pieces of evidence are not in general about intentional crime. It is noteworthy that scheme (2) is already somewhat more general than the main descriptions of ANT since scheme (2) is in fact a scheme about intentional action in general, and not just about intentional crime.

Our example illustrates the problem: the simple story about the hair does not contain an intentional action, whereas the extended story does. Although the more complex story involves intentional action, this is not in general the case for more complex pieces-of-evidence stories. For instance, there is no intentional action in the situation in which the accused's hair was accidentally dragged to the scene of the crime (e.g., the accused, living in the same street as the scene of the crime, has lost a hair on the street, which subsequently got stuck to the victim's shoe, etc.). In sum, there are stories other than those about intentional action for which it can be relevant to establish truth in terms of story quality (hence plausibility) and anchoring.

The reason why intentional action was so explicitly built into scheme (2) is that intentional action is so explicitly built into ANT. In ANT, story quality is connected to story structures (also called story grammars), and these in turn are connected to intentional action, at least in the main sources of inspiration for ANT (Bennett and Feldman, and Pennington and Hastie). For stories about the facts of intentional crime, this is a wholly natural approach. For other stories that are relevant in reasoning about evidence, such as stories about unintentional crime (e.g., criminally negligent homicide) or about pieces of evidence, this is not so clear.

What is needed is a way to incorporate story structures other than ones for intentional action or crime in ANT's main approach. Here is a proposal to adapt scheme (2) to allow different story structures:

(2.1) ANCHORED NARRATIVES: STORY QUALITY
Consequent: Story S is good.
Antecedent: Story S fits story structure G.
Story S is unambiguous.
Story S does not contain contradictions.

In this scheme, we have deleted all references to intentional crime. Instead, the existence of an appropriate story structure (such as one for intentional crime) has been given an explicit place. We have done this as it seems reasonable that different kinds of stories have different story structures. For instance, it is to be expected that a murder story has a story structure different from a story about a hair on the scene of the crime. One could say that different story structures represent 'factual types'. For instance, a murder story S belongs to the factual type of murders. A hair on the scene of the crime belongs to the factual type of forensic evidence, or perhaps even of hairs on the scene of the crime.

We will not develop a theory of factual types and their story structures here. We will suggest, however, how the story structure for intentional action (the one used in ANT) can be integrated into our argumentation scheme reconstruction. A further scheme is needed that specifies the elements of a story type:

(8) ANCHORED NARRATIVES: FITTING THE STORY STRUCTURE OF INTENTIONAL CRIME

Consequent: Story S fits story structure G.

Antecedent: Story structure G requires a central action to which all elements are related.
Story structure G requires an explanation of how the central action was performed.
Story structure G requires an explanation of why the central action was performed.
Story S has a central action to which all elements are related.
Story S explains how the central action was performed.
Story S explains why the central action was performed.

Bex, in Chapter 4 of this book, describes further work on appropriate story structures.

5. Concluding Remarks

The present reconstruction of ANT relates to our previous work on reasoning with evidence (Bex et al. 2007a, Bex et al. 2007b), as follows. In the previous work, stories are modelled as causal networks that explain the central event. Pieces of evidence are connected to the events in the story using defeasible arguments, thus creating a formal framework for an argumentative story-based analysis of evidence. Several features of ANT also occur in this formal framework. Component anchoring and attacking a story's anchoring, here schemes (3a), (3b.1) and (4), are modelled using defeasible arguments, where an event or component of a story is anchored if it follows from an undefeated argument based on a piece of evidence. Story falsification, schemes (6) and (7), is also modelled, as the opposite of a story component can be the conclusion of an argument based on a piece of evidence. Furthermore, the causal networks that model stories are not allowed to contain contradictions, and implausible or unambiguous causal links can be defeated by arguments, thus ensuring that a story does not contain contradictions and that it is unambiguous (scheme (2.1)). Stories can be compared by looking at how many components of a story are anchored in evidence (cf. the exception of scheme (1.3)).

Anderson et al. (2005) also discuss stories in the context of reasoning with evidence. They give a protocol for analysing the plausibility, coherence and evidential support of stories. This protocol consists of a list of questions. Some point to the evidential support for the story, for example, 'To what extent does the evidence support the story?' and 'Is there evidence that conflicts with the story?' Other questions are meant for analysing the plausibility of the story, for example, 'Is the story supported by plausible background generalizations?' and 'Does the story fit a familiar story such as Cinderella and what is the relevance of this?'

In this text we have developed a reconstruction of the theory of anchored narratives (ANT) in terms of argumentation schemes. The schemes are listed in the Appendix. Our contribution can be summarized as follows.

- ANT's central metaphor of stories anchored by generalizations that connect pieces of evidence with story components can be confusing, especially since many intuitively think of the pieces of evidence as anchors, and not the generalizations. Still, ANT's message that justifying one's belief in a story is a function of the safeness of the generalizations used is sound. Our reconstruction has shown one way to bypass the confusion.
- Our reconstruction in terms of argumentation schemes shows how ANT's story-based approach can be treated in a context of argumentation, while retaining the emphasis on stories as wholes. It provides an integration of argumentation and stories different from the one by Bex et al. (2007a). There we discussed the use of stories in terms of causal networks and abductive reasoning. The emphasis was on formalized defeasible arguments about elements of stories. In contrast, here the focus is on semi-formal argumentation schemes in which the role of stories (as wholes) is made explicit.
- On the basis of the reconstruction we proposed some refinements and clarifications of ANT. A minor one is incorporated in scheme (1.3). We suggested that only good, i.e., plausible, stories with equal or better anchoring can exclude one's acceptance of a story.
- A further clarification is more fundamental: it is the recursive use of stories. Not only the acceptance of stories about the facts of the crime, but also about other factual situations, such as those about a piece of evidence, can be treated in ANT. The clarification is incorporated in scheme (3b.1), in which the safe anchoring of a story component requires a story about a supporting piece of evidence. In section 4.4, it is explained that such extended, recursive use of stories is natural, but may be too complex for simple cases.
- The recursive use of stories led to a further relevant refinement, namely the need for story structures other than a story structure for intentional crime. When stories cannot only be about the facts of a case of intentional crime, but also about the facts of unintentional crime and pieces of evidence, then different story structures are needed in order to establish their plausibility, or, in ANT's preferred terminology: quality. This refinement is specified in scheme (2.1).

In sum, we conclude that an argumentation schemes reconstruction of the theory of anchored narratives is possible, and that the exercise leads to a number of relevant clarifications and refinements.

The result helps to clarify the criticisms against ANT mentioned in the introduction: The notions of stories and arguments have been given a clear and separate role when considering the truth of a story about the facts. There is a definite distinction between reasons based on pieces of evidence and stories about pieces of evidence. The relation between commonsense generalizations and pieces of evidence and the way in which they help (and don't help) in accepting or rejecting facts and stories as true has been clarified. ANT's universal rules of evidence have shown their usefulness for developing the set of argumentation schemes. A place has been found for, on the one hand, commonsense generic beliefs (viz. ANT's anchoring generalizations) and, on the other, commonsense knowledge of scenarios (viz. story structures for different factual types).

As theoretical contribution, we have provided an account of reasoning about the facts in which not only the elements of stories are part of argumentation, but also the stories as wholes. We have argued that accepting the truth of a story can depend on accepting the truth of other stories (cf. the recursiveness of stories: section 4.4) and that story structures different from one for intentional crime are needed (section 4.5).

We conclude that the explicit nature of the set of argumentation schemes (cf. the list in the Appendix) can be the basis for further discussion about the theory of anchored narratives in relation to other approaches towards reasoning about the facts of criminal cases, and for the future development of our knowledge about how such reasoning can and should be done as well as possible. The topic deserves our ongoing attention, since the task of the rational choosing of truth facing our courts is both necessary and dangerous.[13]

---

13 Cf. Twining 1999.

Appendix: The Set of Argumentation Schemes

(1.3) ANCHORED NARRATIVES: ACCEPTING A STORY AS TRUE
Consequent: Story S about topic T is true.
Antecedent: Story S is good.
Story S is well anchored.
Exception: Story S1 about topic T (unequal to S) is good.
Story S1 (unequal to S) has equally good or better anchoring.

(2.1) ANCHORED NARRATIVES: STORY QUALITY
Consequent: Story S is good.
Antecedent: Story S fits story structure G.
Story S is unambiguous.
Story S does not contain contradictions.

(3a) ANCHORED NARRATIVES: ATTACKING THE ANCHORING OF A STORY
Consequent: Story S is not well anchored.
Antecedent: Component C of story S is essential.
Component C of story S is not safely anchored.

(3b.1) ANCHORED NARRATIVES: COMPONENT ANCHORING
Consequent: Component C of story S is safely anchored.
Antecedent: There is a piece of evidence E.
Story SE about piece of evidence E is true.
Component C of story S is anchored to piece of evidence E by anchoring generalization G.
Anchoring generalization G is safe.

(4) ANCHORED NARRATIVES: OBVIOUSLY FALSE GENERALIZATIONS
Consequent: Anchoring generalization G is not safe.
Antecedent: Anchoring generalization G is obviously false.

(5) ANCHORED NARRATIVES: ATTACK BY INTERDEPENDENCE OF ANCHORING
Consequent: Story S is not well anchored.
Antecedent: The anchoring of (unequal) components C and C1 is interdependent.
Component C of story S is essential.
Component C1 of story S is essential.

(6) ANCHORED NARRATIVES: ATTACK BY FALSIFICATION
Consequent: Story S is not well anchored.
Antecedent: Story S is falsified.

(7) ANCHORED NARRATIVES: FALSIFICATION
Consequent: Story S is falsified.
Antecedent: Component C of story S is essential.
The opposite of component C of story S is anchored to piece of evidence E by anchoring generalization G.
Anchoring generalization G is safe.

(8) ANCHORED NARRATIVES: FITTING THE STORY STRUCTURE OF INTENTIONAL CRIME
Consequent: Story S fits story structure G.
Antecedent: Story structure G requires a central action to which all elements are related.
Story structure G requires an explanation of how the central action was performed.
Story structure G requires an explanation of why the central action was performed.
Story S has a central action to which all elements are related.
Story S explains how the central action was performed.
Story S explains why the central action was performed.

References

Anderson, T., Schum, D. and Twining, W. (2005), *Analysis of Evidence*, 2nd Edition (Cambridge: Cambridge University Press).

Bex, F.J., Prakken, H., Reed, C. and Walton, D. (2003), 'Towards a formal account of reasoning about evidence: Argumentation schemes and generalisations', *Artificial Intelligence and Law* 11, 125–65.

Bex, F.J., Prakken, H. and Verheij, B. (2007a), 'Formalising Argumentative Story-Based Analysis of Evidence', in *Proceedings of the Eleventh International Conference on Artificial Intelligence and Law* (New York: ACM), pp. 1–10.

Bex, F.J., Van den Braak, S.W., Van Oostendorp, H., Prakken, H., Verheij, B. and Vreeswijk, G. (2007b), 'Sense-making software for crime investigation: How to combine stories and arguments?', *Law, Probability & Risk* 6, 145–68.

Crombag, H.F.M., Koppen, P.J. van and Wagenaar, W.A. (1992, 1994), *Dubieuze Zaken: De Psychologie van Strafrechtelijk Bewijs* (*Dubious Cases: The Psychology of Criminal Evidence*) (Amsterdam: Contact).

De Poot, C.J., Bokhorst, R.J., Koppen, P.J. van and Muller, E. (2004), *Rechercheportret. Over Dilemma's in de Opsporing* (Alphen aan de Rijn: Kluwer).

Den Boer, M. (1995), 'Anchored narratives: Review', *International Journal for the Semiotics of Law* 8:24, 327–34.

Gordon, T.F., Prakken, H. and Walton, D.N. (2007), 'The Carneades model of argument and burden of proof', *Artificial Intelligence* 171, 875–96.

Hage, J.C. (2005), *Studies in Legal Logic* (Dordrecht: Springer).

Hitchcock, D.L. and Verheij, B. (eds) (2006), *Arguing on the Toulmin Model: New Essays in Argument Analysis and Evaluation* (Argumentation Library, vol. 10) (Dordrecht: Springer-Verlag).

Koppen, P.J. van and Roos, N. (eds) (2000), *Rationality, Information and Progress in Law and Psychology. Liber Amicorum Hans F. Crombag* (Maastricht: Metajuridica Publications).

Malsch, M. and Nijboer, J.F. (eds) (1999), *Complex Cases: Perspectives on the Netherlands Criminal Justice System* (Amsterdam: Thela Thesis).

Pollock, J.L. (1995), *Cognitive Carpentry: A Blueprint for How to Build a Person* (Cambridge, MA: The MIT Press).

Prakken, H. (1997), *Logical Tools for Modelling Legal Argument: A Study of Defeasible Reasoning in Law* (Dordrecht: Kluwer Academic Publishers).

Sartor, G. (2005), *Legal Reasoning. A Cognitive Approach to the Law* (Berlin: Springer-Verlag).

Toulmin, S.E. (1958), *The Uses of Argument* (Cambridge: Cambridge University Press).

Twining, W. (1995), 'Anchored narratives – a comment', *European Journal of Crime, Criminal Law and Criminal Justice*, 106–14.

—— (1999), 'Necessary but Dangerous? Generalisations and Narrative in Argumentation About "Facts" in Criminal Process', in M. Malsch and J.F. Nijboer (eds).

Verheij, B. (2000), 'Dialectical Argumentation as a Heuristic for Courtroom Decision Making', in Van Koppen and Roos (eds).

—— (2003a), 'Artificial argument assistants for defeasible argumentation', *Artificial Intelligence* 150:1–2, 291–324.

—— (2003b), 'Dialectical argumentation with argumentation schemes: An approach to legal logic', *Artificial Intelligence and Law* 11:1–2, 167–95.

—— (2007), 'Argumentation support software: Boxes-and-arrows and beyond', *Law, Probability & Risk* 6, 187–208.

Wagenaar, W.A. and Crombag, H.F.M. (2006), *The Popular Policeman and Other Cases: Psychological Perspectives on Legal Evidence* (Amsterdam: Amsterdam University Press).

Wagenaar, W.A., Koppen, P.J. van and Crombag, H.F.M. (1993), *Anchored Narratives: The Psychology of Criminal Evidence* (London: Harvester Wheatsheaf).

Walker, V.R. (2007), 'Visualizing the dynamics around the rule–evidence interface in legal reasoning', *Law, Probability & Risk* 6, 5–22.

Walton, D.N. (1996), *Argument Schemes for Presumptive Reasoning* (Mahwah, NJ: Lawrence Erlbaum Associates).

—— (2005), *Argumentation Methods for Artificial Intelligence in Law* (Berlin: Springer-Verlag).

Chapter 8
Rigid Anarchic Principles of Evidence and Proof: Anomist Panaceas against Legal Pathologies of Proceduralism

Hendrik Kaptein

1. Introduction

Legal evidence and proof are normally (and loosely) treated as coming down to the following issues. First, there must have been some or other historical (or sometimes future) reality or realities relevant from the point of view of the law (codified law, rules of adjudication, contract and so on). Second, rules of proof are to guide the legally authoritative establishment of such facts. This is the law of evidence. In the very beginning of legal conflict, fact-finding by police or by other bodies has pride of place. Even such fact-finding is limited by legal rules to a certain extent. In court, emphasis is on procedure, offering rights and opportunities to parties and others concerned to 'tell their story of the case'.

This seems unproblematic, apart of course from occasional miscarriages of justice. In fact this standard conception hides from view fundamental differences between what may be called 'anomism' and 'proceduralism' as incompatible conceptions of legal evidence and proof. Anomism may be provisionally defined as follows. In adjudication and in other kinds of application of legal rules to specific facts, what counts is the facts themselves, in as far as they can be reliably established by any means. There ought to be no laws, or as few laws as possible, regulating admissibility of evidence, division of burdens of proof and so on. Or: procedural law is not to stand in the way of knowledge of relevant facts. The one and only role remaining for procedural law is protection of everybody concerned against infringement of interests and rights considered still more important than finding the truth. For example: criminal defendants have the right to remain silent, even if such silence may frustrate the search for the truth of the matter. Thus the concept of anomism is: as few rules as possible, ideally no rules at all.

At least, no legal rules, as opposed to laws of science determining what is to count as knowledge. Indeed, Bentham famously remarked (in 1812, Chapter 1, Part 1):

> The field of evidence is the field of knowledge.

Anomism does not just aim at knowledge. Certainty on given historical (or sometimes future) legally relevant facts is the ideal, however difficult or even impossible to realize in practice. Thus anomism may be summarized in terms of well-nigh unconditional priority of epistemological certainty over legal procedure. The truth and nothing but the whole truth of the matter comes first.

Though anomism as briefly expounded and defended here is one of the core ideas of Bentham's theory of evidence, no attempt will be made to either offer exegesis of Bentham's grand project, or to defend his staunch empiricism. In fact, anomism does not presuppose much more than the possibility of establishing truth (in a basic sense) on facts past, present or (sometimes) future. So no specific epistemology and/or theory of truth is presupposed here, though anomism is not really compatible with radically sceptical views of human knowledge.

Radically opposed to this (and informed by sceptical conceptions of knowledge more than a few times) is 'proceduralism', defined as: the establishment of evidence and proof is a matter of procedural justice. Parties and others concerned are to bring in their standpoints before the court (or any other adjudicating body), according to the rules of the law of evidence. Burdens of proof are duly divided, parties violating such rules by not fulfilling burdens of proof or otherwise lose rights to claim facts, uncontested contentions are taken to state facts and so on. In the end, adjudicators decide who played by the rules, and of those, who made the most convincing impression.

Why are these two conceptions of legal evidence and proof so different? To mention just a few points, to get the picture as clear as possible from the beginning: unlike anomism, proceduralism sees no difficulty at all in statements such as: as soon as courts decide on proof, the facts of the matter are irrelevant. Remember Scalia's terrifying dictum as already quoted in the Introduction: 'Mere factual innocence is no reason not to carry out a death sentence properly reached.' In line with this, proceduralism does not really distinguish between what is proven and what can be proven in principle. Anomism on the other hand does make a principled distinction between what courts accept as proof (maybe mistakenly so) and what really happened (or is still bound to happen). Also, proceduralism proceeds in terms of parties' and others' contributions to the case. They are 'to play the justice game' in order for adjudicators to reach a verdict on the facts (or what are taken to be the facts). This point is also expressed in terms of 'procedural autonomy of parties concerned' and 'parties' responsibilities for guarding their own powers and opportunities to furnish evidence on their behalf'. Proceduralism indeed takes no issue with radically sceptical conceptions of truth and reality. Thus proceduralism is fully compatible with statements such as: every party lives in its own truth of the matter (if there is anything to be called the matter at all), and adjudicator's reality is just one more reality. Some or other kind of connection between these 'realities' is given by no more than the context of procedure, the one and only institutional reality presumably common to all concerned. In this proceduralist conception, adjudicators are no researchers after some or other objective truth, but recipients, weighing contributions of parties and others concerned. Lastly for now, and again in line with this, proceduralism is not even primarily about resolving conflicts about facts, but about conflict resolution per se. Think here of Luhmann-like notions of *Legitimation durch Verfahren* (legitimation by procedure).

Here it will be contended that anomism is the one and only legally and humanly acceptable conception of evidence and proof. Proceduralism will be shown to come down to meta-conflict, instead of conflict resolution. Why is this distinction between anomism and proceduralism so important? Not just because anomism is so superior, but also because more than a few theoretical and practical approaches do not really distinguish between these two conceptions, with sometimes dire results. No analysis of legal evidence and proof may really succeed without taking into account the incompatibility of 'finding out what happened' and 'playing by the rules'. Thus this chapter aims at both confusion resolution and revival of at least an important part of Bentham's project.

A cautionary remark may be in order. Though anomism may seem to be more prominent in continental criminal procedure, just as proceduralism seems prominent in adversarial systems, it is not contended here that these different conceptions of evidence and proof are really linked to different jurisdictions. Different kinds of legal procedures contain elements of both anomism and proceduralism. Or: they do not really exist in their pure forms, though proceduralism is (all too) prominent in at least adversarial trial systems. Again it is important to first clarify distinctions in principle, in order to further analyse and improve the practice of legal procedure (but see also Malsch and Freckelton, in Chapter 5 of this book).

Evidence and proof for anomism against proceduralism will here be further expounded as follows. Anomism is to be briefly explained, and related to monotonic logic in principle (section 2). Section 3 offers an explanation of the problem of the *argumentum ad ignorantiam* (argument from ignorance) in the context of an anomist conception of evidence and proof: decisive counter-evidence, though vitiating a case in principle, may be unavailable in practice. Next, all kinds of human factors and limitations may do the cause of anomism in practice no good (section 4). In line with this it may be questioned whether intentional factors like malice and negligence are to be anomically established at all (section 5). Human –and all too human – factors like malice and negligence seem to lead to subjectivism, relativism and scepticism concerning legally relevant facts, or what is left of them (section 6). Section 7 offers still more practical arguments against anomism, ranging from *lites finiri oportent* (legal conflicts better come to an end) to costs and other interests and even rights of parties and others concerned. This all seems to inexorably reinstate proceduralism and its basic idea of constructed 'reality' Still, such 'pure' proceduralism is shown to come down to giving up the idea of reasonable conflict resolution as such (section 8). What is left to be done, then, is devising rational procedures for unearthing the truth of the matter, or: proceduralism as one important (heuristic) tool in reconstructing reality. Such proceduralism may be effected both in the science of legal evidence and proof and (hopefully) in practice (section 9). Section 10 concludes with a brief agenda: try to respect facts in the first place, and (again) leave them alone when they are not really needed.

2. Anomism: Anarchy of Fact-finding as an Ideal of Evidence and Proof

Once again, no attempt is made here to offer adequate exegesis of Bentham's conceptions of legal evidence and proof. One of its main tenets only is discussed, i.e. the need to base legal evidence and proof on reality, as unhindered by legal procedure as possible. Given the progress of (forensic) science, it is not clear whether Bentham would at once recognize his ideas in this discussion (though he probably would greatly welcome scientific progress, e.g. in the field of DNA identification).

In itself, the anomist ideal of evidence and proof is deceptively simple. Facts to be proven ought to be there, be immediately observable to adjudicators, and repeatedly so, to several adjudicating observers completely concurring in their observations. In such an ideal and thus probably well-nigh unrealistic situation, evidence is equivalent to proof. Nothing needs to be derived or even deduced. The facts are simply there. There are no rules of evidence and proof. Anomism rules. Without intending to annex Bentham's grand project this way, this ideal of direct and indubitable observation may be the core idea of Bentham's identification of evidence and knowledge.

Given that most facts relevant as evidence and proof are past (or sometimes future, think of future damage and so on), literal application of this idea leads to the notion of an ideal observer, unembarrassed by limitations of space and time. Indeed the legal world has been christened 'The New Church'. However accurate, or otherwise, this may be, the anomist (or thus even naive) ideal of evidence and proof seems to equate adequate adjudicators with gods. Only gods would be able to 'contemporize' everything.

For more ordinary human beings, the basic problem of the 'absence' of the facts of the case cannot be solved this way. So language, logic and argumentation are needed, in order to bridge gaps between adjudicators' standpoints and historical realities. Ideally, again, knowledge of 'absent' (past or future) realities is to be based on available knowledge. The scientific paradigm of this is an uninterrupted link of states of affairs connected by deductive-nomological inferences (i.e. inferences applying general laws to descriptions of states of affairs, leading to descriptions of other states of affairs, see Nagel 1979 for the standard explanation of this). Apart from doubtfully deterministic presuppositions, such uninterrupted linking seems as otherworldly with ideal observers being able to do without such 'bridging times'. Still, this ideal implies an important nomic aspect of anomism: reality is to be known with the help of laws of science. Law (legal rules of procedure or even material law) is not to stand in the way of evidence and proof (anomism), which are to be ascertained on the basis of science (nomism in another, positive sense).

To express at least part of this basic idea in terms of Bentham's own words (1812, Chapter 2, Part 2):

> Thus much as to law:—in relation to matter of *fact*, the decision has for its ground the evidence by which term is on every occasion understood some *other* matter of fact, which on that same occasion is presented to the mind or sense of the judge, for the purpose of producing in his mind a persuasion assertive of the existence or non-existence of a matter of fact first mentioned, which is always some *individual* matter of fact supposed to be of that *sort*, which on the occasion in question the legislator is supposed to have had in view.

This may be rather simplistically explained in terms of changing positions of billiard balls within the confines of the cloth. Given a certain initial state (position of the balls) the result of any outside input is to be calculated in principle, given the laws of mechanics. Retrodiction is taken to be symmetric to prediction, then. Plausible as the prediction model may seem in principle, retrodiction at least faces the problem of sufficient conditions for a certain result not necessarily amounting to necessary conditions. Or: observed positions of the balls may be exhaustively explained in terms of causally alternative sets of preceding states.

Generally, such retrodiction is to link presently available evidence with contested facts in the past. Thus – and again ideally of course – there ought to be alibis against any alternative explanation of all available evidence not implying the facts of the case. For example (to refer to a more legally relevant example): traces of DNA on a dead body may be explained in terms of a criminal defendant's conduct in killing that body, but may also be explained in terms of this criminal defendant's handling of the dead body after the killing, and so on. All such alternative explanations are to be excluded if there is to be anomist proof of the facts of the case. Whether this is realistic remains to be seen. Abductive argumentation and its problems are apposite here of course (and will be briefly discussed later).

Still there is no need to know everything. Legal evidence and proof ought to be relevant to the case at hand. This basic rule (see e.g. Tillers 1983) must be acknowledged even by anomism. The rule offers welcome simplification of course (apart from well-known and sometimes rather academic problems of interpretation of facts in terms of the law and vice versa). Thus the ideal adjudicator needs to be an ideal observer of small parts of reality only. (The notion of an ideal adjudicator may lead to Dworkin's well-known ideal of Hercules, knowing all the relevant law of the case, as developed from 1977.)

The rule of relevance also implies that legal instead of strictly scientific realities are apposite in the first place. Legal realities generally conform to commonsense concepts, partly related to institutional facts (apart from more technical fields like fiscal and environmental law). This may lead to problems of 'translation' of (forensic) scientific concepts which are basic for the anomist project into more commonsensical legal concepts of facts.

The same basic rule of relevance also implies that legal evidence and proof are concerned with unique historical (or sometimes future) facts ('individual matter of fact' in Bentham's own words, as just quoted), and not with generic or even general facts (see for example and most interestingly in this connection Von Wright 1963 and 1971 on these distinctions: e.g. this man standing there versus man thinking versus living beings dying). (Sometimes legal evidence and proof are concerned with more or less general facts, e.g. with what counts as reasonable expectations in contract law, in a given setting.)

Even if the field of evidence is taken to be the field of knowledge, this kind of uniqueness means that not all methodological and/or epistemological notions relevant for general knowledge are applicable to legal evidence and proof as well. To mention just a few differences: general knowledge may be corroborated, verified or falsified by repeating specific realities covered by this general knowledge. This is impossible for unique historical facts in principle. Related to this is the idea that counter-evidence against general knowledge may remain a logical possibility, becoming less and less relevant to the extent of ongoing verification and absence of falsification. Related to this again is abductive explanation: there may be some or other better explanation than the 'default' explanation. In issues of general knowledge this may be countered by well-known means such as manipulating as many circumstances as possible in order to determine whether there really are no better explanations in terms of such circumstances, and so on. This does not relate to unique historical (or future) facts relevant in legal adjudication however.

These issues are related to the fallacious appeal to ignorance: 'The Loch Ness Monster exists! Why? Because there is no proof as to its non-existence.' Or: 'The Loch Ness Monster does not exist! Why? Because there is no proof as to its existence.' (Happily enough, there may be other reasons not to take this particular monster's existence for granted!) Issues of legal evidence and proof, however, may well be vitiated by fallacious appeals to ignorance. Thus defendants may be unable to prove their statements, while there still is proof of their innocence in principle (see section 3).

Abduction is also relevant in issues of malice and negligence. Taking specific conduct (like manhandling) for granted, assumption of malice may offer a seemingly acceptable default explanation of the same conduct. But then there may be a better explanation, or explanations, possibly excluding any malice (see section 5).

Worse still, anomism seems to be incompatible with intentional factors like malice and negligence in principle. They seem to be 'pre-scientific', in not clearly referring to observable data fitting in with established scientific theory. Anomist proof in a strict sense amounts to description of orderly sequences of events, inexorably leading to the facts to be proven, given true general laws. But this does not seem far removed from 'hard determinism', implying that everything has a cause, in its turn implying total predictability, excluding free will and thus malice and negligence. Then there are no motivational, rather than causal, laws explaining conduct and no intentional factors possibly having legal consequences in themselves, such as liability. This 'scientific' conception of man and world and its concomitant neuro-physiological determinism seems as impracticable as being completely at odds with supposedly 'pre-scientific' law and legal liability (see Chapter 1 on this).

Such a scientific view of man and world may even imply giving up legally important notions like authorship and causation. What distinguishes 'I' and/or 'other people' from the rest of the endlessly complex world? But authorship must be ascribed to somebody (or to some body in a wider legal sense). Also, legally relevant consequences may have many different and differently related causes. Possibly apart from the criterion of *conditio sine qua non* (certainly not applicable in criminal law as such), determination of 'who caused what' seems to go further than just reconstructing realities 'as they were' (see further Kaptein 1999a).

Still, the basic stance of anomism amounts to the following: ideally there is one and only one true establishment and explanation of legally relevant events, past or future. 'What happened' (or 'what will happen') is given in principle, given closed deductive-nomological links between presently available evidence and proof of events past or future, however difficult it may be to determine this in practice.

An important consequence of this conception of knowledge of legally relevant realities is strict separation of contexts of discovery from contexts of justification. In practice, many different ways and means may be used to establish the truth of the matter. But this truth itself is not determined by such heuristics at all. This is in stark contrast to proceduralism, according to which procedures are constitutive of legal factual truth as such.

Related to this is the irrelevance of non-monotonic logics for anomism in principle. Any possibility of overriding reasons after definitive establishment of the facts of the case would of course vitiate epistemological certainty, or simply the final truth of the matter, which is the very essence of anomism. Also, practically important forms of reasoning on evidence and proof such as analogy, induction, probability theory and abduction are relegated to contexts of discovery (see Kaptein 1999b). Dangers of such forms (or just semblances) of argumentation in contexts of justification need not be repeated here. Analogy may degenerate into stereotyping, telling stock stories, copying popular narrative and so on. (The case of the twelve angry men as depicted by Schafer in Chapter 10 of this book offers ample illustration of this.)

Induction may be fatally used in proof on the basis of 'We assume she did it before, in like circumstances, so she did it again.' (The aforementioned case of the wrongly convicted nurse offers a saddening example of this; see Chapter 2, by Derksen and Meijsing, in this book.) Anomism may even imply that application of any probability theory ideally is of heuristic use only, importantly determining search strategies and so on. (This point is to be considered apart from several other reasons against application of any probability theory to past events, which is not discussed here.)

3. Fallacious Appeals to Ignorance and Attempts to Counter Them in the Context of Adjudication

Appeal to ignorance seems unavoidable in legal proof. As human beings are not ideal observers, there are more than just logical possibilities that important counter-arguments are not taken into consideration. This is at odds with the anomist ideal of indubitable certainty on the facts of the case. Thus parties and others concerned who are completely right in their statements of the facts of the case, without being able to conclusively demonstrate that they are right, may still lose because good reasons seem to be available for opponents' factual contentions.

Or: the fallacious appeal to ignorance (as in the aforementioned case of the Loch Ness Monster) seems to vitiate issues of legal evidence and proof as well; facts may be assumed on the basis of absence of any plausible argumentation against them. But a basic criterion for convincing argumentation is not the unavailability of counter-argument, but the demonstration of unavailability of convincing counter-argument. (See also Van Fraassen's remarks on this, as quoted in Amaya's contribution to this book.) As noted before, fallacious appeals to ignorance are related to problems of abduction. However, appeals to ignorance leave open not just alternative explanations of the same evidence, incompatible with the facts taken to be proven, but also other kinds of defence. Thus a defendant may have a perfect alibi without being able to convincingly demonstrate it, or may be unable to demonstrate the falsity of basic evidence.

Consider the nurse mentioned before, who was charged with killing infants, on the basis of prima facie convincing evidence in terms of the abnormal and extreme coincidence of dead babies and her presence in the ward in which they died. Courts (unable to understand either probability theory or the application of such probability to historical situations) convicted her on these (and equally doubtful toxicological) grounds. The nurse may well know that she did not do it, but then, how to prove this convincingly? Her silence pleaded against her. Drawing any conclusion from this is just as fallacious as arguing for the existence or non-existence of the Loch Ness Monster by merely appealing to availability of proof for or against. To make things worse, the same courts also argued that no other causes of the infant deaths were known, thus further indicting the nurse. No exhaustive inquiries were made into other possible causes however. There may not have been any special coincidence at all (see the contribution to this book by Derksen and Meijsing for more on this case).

Three possible answers to this seemingly unavoidably fallacious appeal to ignorance briefly pass muster here. First, in matters of general scientific and everyday knowledge appeals to ignorance may still furnish good reasons. For example: 'Aspirin may be taken to be a safe drug, as no contraindications have cropped up so far.' The proven fact that normal people have not suffered from taking aspirin so far may be taken to be sufficient guarantee for the safety of aspirin as a drug. But then this is general knowledge indeed, backed by reasonably strong inductive argument (in terms of long-term experience). Legal evidence and proof have to do with unique facts, excluding this kind of alleviation of appeal to ignorance. Or: given such uniqueness, inductive corroboration is impossible in principle. (Still, all kinds of general knowledge backed by non-fallacious appeals to ignorance may be useful in linking evidence with the facts to be proven, of course.)

Second, it is generally accepted that nobody needs to furnish proof of his own innocence, in a wide sense (apart from special cases of reversal of burdens of proof and so on). Everybody is to be treated as if bona fide until there is proof of the contrary. This seems to solve the problem of appeal to ignorance in matters of legal evidence and proof. Though this legal fiction of being bona fide until there is convincing counter-evidence does not fit in very well with anomism (let alone with Bentham's views on evidence and proof), it still seems to solve part of the problem. Legally regarded more than a few facts of any case are taken to be given, or better: parties concerned are to be treated as if there are no facts pleading against them, as long as there is no counter-evidence. Or: in legal terms, the problem of the appeal to ignorance is reduced to facts not covered by the legal fiction backed by presumption of good faith. Also, there may even be convincing evidence on behalf of a defendant's good faith, even without this defendant's needing to state it. It is for plaintiffs (public prosecutors and so on) to offer convincing evidence, in terms of the facts of the case, excluding any possible counter-argument.

This material legal solution of seemingly fallacious appeals to ignorance seems attractive, but it does not solve the problem of seemingly totally convincing evidence against defendants who may wish to offer evidence against it but are unable to do so (as in the nurse's case). One more cautionary note: anomism is not interested in any divisions of burdens of proof as such, only in finding the truth of the matter, without outright violation of rights of parties and others concerned in the process (see also sections 7 and 9).

Also, presumption of innocence may do defendants good, but does not help public prosecution officers and other plaintiffs stating true facts without being able to prove them. Again, their loss is based on an appeal to ignorance.

Third, there is the rather down-to-earth need to put an end to proceedings some time or other. Strict evasion of any appeal to ignorance would exclude well-nigh any proof, as there may always be some or other as well hidden as convincing counter-evidence against any factual contention. This seems to amount to giving up adjudication altogether, which seems too high a price to be paid for anomist ideals in practice (but see Chapter 1). So sometimes Gordian and other knots are to be cut, in the full knowledge that appeals to ignorance are not done away with. Here again differences between general knowledge and specific knowledge of the facts of the case are important. General knowledge may be cautiously taken for granted, given possibilities of counter-evidence which has not yet come to light. The importance of ongoing research may be determined by both the reliability of given knowledge and the scientific and general importance of the issue. But application of specific knowledge of the facts of the matter is definitive and its consequences irreversible in most cases, even if convincing counter-evidence comes to light after all.

4. Problems of *Ad Hominem* and Fallacious Appeal to Witnesses

One more of many problems with anomist ideals in practice is the unavoidable appeal to witnesses, both formally and informally. As total 'presentiation' of legally relevant facts past and future is not really likely in legal practice (or in any practice for that matter), just as strictly nomological relation of facts to be proven with the available evidence is not often feasible (expert) witnesses must play leading roles. Human beings are not ideal observers. God is (once more) replaced by man. Thus man is (again) an obstacle to the facts. Man has not just to investigate historical (and sometimes future) realities, but also other men, witnesses who are more, or sometimes less, telling about such realities. This leads to a shift from *ad rem* (the facts of the case) to *ad hominem* (concerning witnesses' qualities). Thus issues of discovery seem to become relevant in contexts of justification.

The very many ways in which even completely bona fide and competent witnesses may fail the facts need not be repeated here. Witnesses tend to observe what they (unwittingly) think is important, thus possibly completely missing the facts of the case at hand, not the least as a consequence of being ignorant of the legal importance of what is presented to them. Thus most important evidence may be lost for ever just by lack of attention to it.

Indeed, in as far as the objective of legal evidence and proof is nothing else but the establishment of the facts of the case, witnesses are rather imperfect intermediaries between such facts and adjudicators expected to know the same facts and to apply them to the case at hand. Worse, if testimonies could be really tested, they would be superfluous. Such a real test would amount to checking testimonies against the facts testified about. This is why witnesses are heard under oath in the first place. No earthly powers may force them to tell the truth, so God is appealed to after all, in order to guarantee truth. This is not a very safe procedure of course, as practice amply demonstrates. All that can be done, it seems, is marginally checking testimonies in terms of their compatibility or even coherence with established facts of the case, in as far as those are available at all.

Here again the uniqueness of facts to be established in most cases is of negative importance. Doubts about testimonies on generic or general facts may be allayed by appeal to other witnesses and/or repetition of evidence. Expert witnesses are exceptions here sometimes, as their testimonies may indeed be checked against other expert witnesses' statements. (This obvious remedy is not always appealed to in practice.)

But then witnesses themselves may be checked in terms of their general and specific reliability, it may be countered. The law excludes witnesses too closely connected with parties and others involved. In practice this could scarcely be otherwise indeed. Such exclusion is not easily compatible with anomism however.

Anomism would welcome any possible contribution to finding the truth of the matter, just as it would deplore dependence on qualities and circumstances of witnesses themselves, instead of reliably relating proof to reliable evidence, without the doubtful interference of 'who said what'.

Anomism's fundamental distinction between contexts of discovery and contexts of justification is indeed lost on the way as well. In principle, witnesses are to serve heuristic purposes only. Their testimonies are just to facilitate the search for the facts of the case, instead of constituting the facts of the case. In practice, however, their testimonies may be decisive. This necessitates rules of evidence determining who is to testify when and why. Thus procedure in a wide sense, or more or less regulated ways and means to find the facts, become rather imperfect stand-ins for unattainable ideals of justification in terms of proof on the basis of reliable evidence and general laws.

In addition to this, and again at odds with ideals of anomism, is the shift from inquiry into the facts of the case to inquiry into witnesses' qualities and circumstances. Thus fact-finding is inevitably muddled by *argumentum ad hominem*, or: one more prelude to proceduralism (section 8).

5. Intentions Escaping the Seamless Web?

Another human – or all too human – limitation to the anomist ideal is given by the need to furnish evidence and proof for intentional facts like malice and negligence. In a completely scientific conception of man and world such primitive notions would probably be done away with, be it in a deterministic world view or otherwise (see earlier, section 2). Less scientific, and thus regarded probably as 'primitive' law, however, systematically refers to such factors as preconditions for liability.

In civil law and elsewhere, this problem is largely dealt with by 'objectifying' criteria of malice and negligence in terms of wrongfulness of conduct with harmful consequences. Or: standards of subjective malice and negligence are replaced by probably more easily applicable standards in terms of norms. Exoneration presupposes superior force, to be objectified in its turn (apart from strict liability of course). Also, and at least in civil law adjudication, 'malleable' conceptions of malice and negligence are duly manipulated in order to allocate burdens of payment.

In criminal law this will not do however. Absence of mala fide or at least absent-minded motives excludes any punishment. This is a basic principle of criminal law (though not always relevant for minor offences). But how then to determine such subjective factors? In no contemporary conception of varieties of intentionality are such factors interpreted to come down to things or events, to be established in some or other rigorously scientific fashion.

Malice and negligence are more plausibly dealt with in terms of abduction, for example: given the facts of the case, offender's malice seems to furnish the default explanation of his wrongful conduct. In the absence of any special circumstances, such explanations seem reasonably plausible and thus constituting 'proof' of malice or negligence. Not all participants may agree with this. Thus criminal defendants may come up with hitherto not thought of special circumstances, possibly vitiating original abductions of malice or negligence. Also, forensic scientists may step in, explaining why defendants could not help committing the crime after all.

This way, motives may be explained by pre-established conduct, if only abductively. But then such motives may also be appealed to in order to explain conduct in its turn. Think here of the role of motivational laws in anomism. For example: if it is known that the defendant was present at a certain time and place and was confronted with something both valuable and unguarded on the spot, it may be derived from these facts that the defendant had a motive to act and therefore did act. Or recidivist defendants convicted earlier may find it difficult to defend themselves against hidden induction leading to the assumption of repetition of mala fide motives in the present case. This may lead to rather dangerous circularities in argumentation on evidence and proof, of course, as has indeed been seen more than a few times in practice.

Such circularities may be given more hermeneutical slants by noting (again) that notions of malice and negligence are to be determined dialogically. For example: if there is a semblance that somebody did something intentionally, then the absence of acceptable excuses in dialogue between interested parties concerning the offence establishes malice. Only if offenders succeed in convincing victims and others that they really could not help it can malice (and attendant legal consequences) then be excluded (see Hart 1948).

If there is to be reasonable dialogue at all, given competing interests in spheres of legal adjudication, then victims will tend to assume intentionality as long as they are not (made) aware of any visibly superior force against offenders' free will (see Chapter 1 on this). Forensic specialists, on the other hand, may be more like 'anomist ideal observers'. Thus they may have a tendency to 'more scientifically' explain any offenders' serious misconduct in terms of psychopathic forces, fitting in well with tragic life stories, and thus excluding such offenders' liability. This seems part of anomism's scientific slant. But this again tends to a determinist conception of man, excluding any liability.

So as long as legal liability still implies some or other kind of intentionality, at least in terms of malice and negligence, then 'reasoned dialogue between common men' seems to be the only way to discuss such factors. Like the problems with anomism discussed before, this seems to lead the way to proceduralism, relying as it does on legally regimented dialogue instead of on rigorous scientific evidence and proof.

6. So is Anomism Sinking Away in Scepticism Concerning Facts and Reality?

From such sceptical considerations against the epistemological ideal of anomism it is only a small step to scepticism concerning facts to be established by legal proof themselves. If there is no objective or at least intersubjective reality, past, present or future, to be described and explained in objective or at least intersubjective terms, the anomist project must fail completely.

Such scepticism may take many different general and particular forms, which will not, of course, be discussed exhaustively here. General ontological and/or epistemological doubts on the possibility of reality or even realities not completely dependent on specific observers and their special nature and circumstances indeed contradict one of anomism's basic presuppositions. Related to this are more radical doubts as to the existence of anything like 'I', or even as to the sense of any concept of 'I'. This would do away with any notion of personal liability. (Note that this seems to fit in well with contemporary varieties of neuro-physiological determinism, denying any special status of persons in a completely material world; see earlier, Chapter 1.)

Anyway, and without any intention to even try to refute such scepticisms, a probably less welcome consequence of them is complete isolation, 'locking-up' of individuals, groups and cultures (if such concepts still make sense at all) in their own subjective 'realities'. This is one more reason why such scepticisms are deeply incompatible with anomist ideals, directed as such ideals are to rational conflict resolution acceptable to all rational participants. Whatever differences of opinion and attitude there may be between parties and others concerned, they are presumed to refer to the same facts of the case in principle.

More specific doubts relate to historical and future facts as radically different from present facts. Thus paradigm cases of indubitable knowledge may be based on direct observation of a hand stretched out, the sun shining and so on. Memory and prediction are fallible in principle, it is contended, however much general natural and motivational laws may help to (re)construct them. Or it may even be stated that past and future are nothing more than memory and prediction themselves. It does not seem really helpful to put against this that memory and prediction are conceptually related to some or other reality as their objects: something is remembered or predicted. What is the status of such somethings? (But see also section 8, on proceduralism falling foul to Heraclitus' 'flow of everything'.)

Note that such general scepticisms are fundamentally different from doubts on observers' powers to adequately describe legally relevant facts. Witnesses may indeed be under all kinds of undue influence, ranging from short-sightedness to bad faith, preventing them from adequately stating facts. Such doubts about witnesses presuppose some or other denial of general ontological and/or epistemological scepticism, or there would be no criteria for any kind of reliability of testimonies.

Lastly it ought to be noted that anomism does not imply any specific ontology and/or epistemology, apart from denying general scepticisms. All that is needed is the basic presumption that there was, is and will be an objectively or at least intersubjectively ascertainable world, in which legally relevant facts may be determined by proof based on objective or at least intersubjective evidence. Bentham himself, of course, tended toward empiricism, but even denial of the very possibility of epistemology is fully compatible with anomism. Also, more than a few plausible conceptions of ontology and/or epistemology are apologetic in principle, in trying to explain and justify at least paradigm cases of common knowledge such as that there is, or was, or even will be, a cat on the mat.

7. Practical Limitations to Anomist Ideals

Even if all such doubts about anomism may be proven to be unfounded in principle, its practical feasibility still appears less than certain. Given endless resources in terms of time, money and other means, anomist proof may be demonstrated in all cases. But if available at all, then such resources cannot be spent exclusively on realization of Benthamite ideals of evidence and proof. *Lites finiri oportent*, scarce resources need to be spent on other lofty enterprises as well. In any rational administration of justice, criminal or otherwise, the total cost of fact-finding in a specific case is one of several factors determining whether the case is to be adjudicated one way or the other. (No plausible anomist ideal of fact-finding would dictate that there should be one more panopticon, with the task of finding and proving the facts of all legally relevant cases, criminal or otherwise, and not just because such an ideal would be rather expensive.)

In line with this, parties and others concerned may have legally important interests and rights standing in the way of unlimited fact-finding. The need to end legal proceedings in due time also protects everybody concerned against continuing legal insecurity. Criminal and other procedures may be greatly simplified by databases containing DNA fingerprints of the whole population. Apart from its probably rather high financial costs, it seems questionable whether such databases are compatible with privacy rights. Torture may be effective in fact-finding in a few cases, but still seems unacceptable even then. And so on.

Predominant among such rights against unlimited fact-finding is the presumption of innocence and good faith in general, seemingly excluding any burden of proof or even obligation to generally cooperate in finding the facts of the case (see earlier section 3, on the presumption of innocence as an attempt to solve the problem of the appeal to ignorance). This presumption is often interpreted in a factual sense, for example: no one is guilty until a court so decides (see, among others, Walton 1996; Copi and Cohen 2002). This seems one more fallacious appeal to ignorance: innocence is a fact until there is 'proof' (authoritative decision) against it. In this interpretation the presumption of innocence is no solution for fallacious appeals to ignorance, just a variety of it. Also, such a factual interpretation would burden any public prosecution office with an impossible task: how to demonstrate someone's guilt if there is no guilt before a court establishes it?

The presumption of innocence has a rather different meaning: everybody is to be treated as innocent until there is an authoritative decision to the contrary. This is a norm, not any kind of factual contention. Thus interpreted, the presumption of innocence is a special form of the fundamental presumption of good faith. Everybody is to be treated as 'having a clean slate' unless there is authoritative proof to the contrary. This fundamental fiction is not just of legal importance of course. No humanly viable society could do without it.

Still, there seems to be a close connection between the presumption of good faith and the rights not to be forced to demonstrate one's own innocence in any way. The presumption of innocence is even regarded as excluding any burden of proof on criminal defendants in principle. This seems to be a fundamental limitation to any anomist ideal. If important participants need not contribute to establishing the facts of the case, then how to really establish the facts of the case? Against this it may be said that presumptions of innocence and good faith do not strictly imply specific roles in legal fact-finding. Treatment of somebody as if in good faith does not exclude some or other role for that person or body in fact-finding in principle. (In a fallaciously factual interpretation of presumptions of innocence and good faith such burdening would be superfluous nonsense of course, as the really innocent do not even need to demonstrate that they are innocent.) Even the innocent may be expected to cooperate in establishing legal evidence and proof, as long as this does not disproportionally burden them. (Indeed this is one consideration behind the reversal of burdens of proof in civil, administrative and even criminal procedure.)

8. Proceduralism: Panacea for Anomist Troubles and Practical Solution?

Prospects for any anomist approach to problems of legal evidence and proof seem rather dim by now. No ready solutions to more than a few problems with really reconstructing the facts of the case seem available. But then there may be a radical way out. Why take it for granted that legal conflict resolution presupposes evidence and proof in any anomist sense? The semblance of problems may well have been created by confusion of historical, archaeological and generally scientific concepts of evidence and proof with legal evidence and proof.

Thus it is contended that legal evidence and proof are not related to historical or future facts in the first place, but to parties' contributions to the establishment of the facts of the case before court, according to legal rules of evidence and proof. In an anomist approach to the facts of the case, everybody concerned is expected to cooperate in finding the factual truth of the matter. In a 'proceduralist' approach this whole objective, in as far as it possible at all, is taken to be irrelevant in principle. Parties have to convince the court of their standpoints of what happened, according to any divisions of burdens of proof and other procedural rules. Parties are regarded as being autonomous in this respect as well. They are expected to take care of their own ways and means to convince the court of their conception of the facts of the case. If they do not succeed in this, whether 'their facts' conform to historical reality or not, the penalty against them for not sufficiently taking care of any evidence on their behalf is that they lose the case. Adding to the semblance of legitimation of proceduralism is that such and other legal rules of evidence and proof are democratically decided upon and known to be binding for everybody concerned (at least in civilized jurisdictions).

Related to this is a rather more passive adjudicators' role. Anomist courts are expected to actively inquire into the facts of the case, not limiting themselves to parties' contributions in principle. 'Proceduralist' courts seem more like arbiters, seeing over the 'rules of the game' and excluding any party not complying with them. Legal proof, then, is not something like a set of demonstrable relationships of reliable evidence with the facts of the case to be established, but the version of the facts that convinces the court more than the opponent's version does. This fits in well with Wigmore's classical concept of legal proof as already defined by him in 1913 (p. 77):

> Proof is the part concerned with the ratiocinative process of contentious persuasion, – mind to mind, counsel to juror, each partisan seeking to move the mind of the tribunal.

This seems to come down to using the scales of justice in establishment of the legal facts of the case. One party's story has to win in the end (apart from the rare cases of a court's equal division of the real burdens of the case between the parties concerned). For adjudicators, then, nothing much more than a subjectively slightly more convincing version of the facts is needed. For courts and adjudicators in general, this is a humanly feasible task, quite unlike the lofty enterprise of anomism, requiring God-like capabilities of knowledge and reasoning. In addition to this is that courts and other adjudicators are not saddled with collecting evidence themselves, leaving this to parties concerned. This may go together well with (probably subjectivist) probability considerations quite different from anomism's rather uneasy relationship with probability theory in general, relegating it to the realm of heuristics only (see section 2).

Standards of evidence and proof, then, seem to be finally determined by two factors only: degrees of plausibility of parties' contributions in adjudicators' minds and degrees of observance of procedural law. Parties may of course try to win the case by convincing adjudicators of the factual falsity of their opponents' story. But then courts or other proceduralist adjudicators have no legally relevant access to relevant facts apart from parties' contributions. So there can be no appeal to any facts of the case 'as such' (if there are any such facts at all, doubts about which, of course, furnish one of the main arguments in favour of proceduralism).

In proceduralist conceptions there need not be anything like intersubjective, let alone objective realities. It is even contended that legal conflict resolution is related to three different views of the facts of the case, as held by public prosecutors or plaintiffs, by defendants, and by the courts. Thus ontological, epistemological and other problems of subjectivism, relativism and scepticism concerning reality and factual truth cannot plague proceduralism.

So proceduralism offers real shifts of perspective, compared to anomism. Anomism is about anarchic investigation, proceduralism is about legally regulated debate. Anomism is about facts, proceduralism deals with propositions for and against. Or: anomist reality, however intractable in practice, is replaced by proceduralist discourse and rhetoric in principle.

Principles such as client confidentiality and the exclusion of evidence on several different grounds fit in well with proceduralism. Parties and their lawyers may remain silent on facts not welcome to them, as they are not expected to do the job allotted to their opponents. Improperly obtained and other evidence violating the rules in some or other way is not admissible, as being incompatible with fair play and due process. Thus a party putting forward improperly obtained evidence may be 'punished' by exclusion on the basis of the violation of fair trial principles.

In these and other respects, proceduralism is fundamentally different from anomism indeed. Problems plaguing anomism seem to disappear completely in proceduralist lights. To mention just the problems discussed here: the appeal to ignorance as part of legal proof, seemingly fatal for anomism, is no problem for proceduralism at all. Why? Because a party not succeeding in offering convincing counter-evidence, according to the rules of the 'game', is faced with the penalty of losing the case. This may seem strange in the administration of criminal justice, but even then the proceduralist answer may simply be that the defendant did not comply with the rules of the justice game. No wonder then that proceduralist oriented authors like Walton (1996; 2002) do not mention the problem of the appeal to ignorance in adjudication at all.

Again, Malcolm (1999, p. 110) offers a tellingly tragic example of proceduralist consequences of the appeal to ignorance, in her account of a slightly otherworldly, idealist or even naïve, but otherwise clearly innocent, lawyer by the name of Sheila, trapped in the snares of the administration of the law. This lawyer, convinced she would be acquitted, refused to talk because she felt bound by client confidentiality. After she had served her undeserved sentence, Malcolm tried to take a few of her foes to task. Discussion like this ensued (Hulkower being one of Sheila's foes):

> 'I never caught Sheila in any lie,' I said to Hulkower during one of my losing debates with him.
>
> 'I'm not saying she is lying today,' he said. 'I have no notion of where she is and what she is doing.'
>
> 'She wasn't caught in any lies at the trial, either. It was her word against that of other people.'
>
> 'She wasn't caught in any lies because she didn't testify,' Hulkower pointed out. He had me once again, of course. I had no answer.

'Her word against that of other people': silence simply implies that the opponent wins and thus the charge is established. (Note that the same 'logic' governs the consequences of 'I had no answer'.) Proceduralism implies that legal fact-inding is indeed rather different from other kinds of fact-finding. Here are the core elements of proceduralism at their best (or, more accurately, their worst).

In line with proceduralist solutions (or at least the semblance of them) of fallacious appeals to ignorance are factual interpretations of presumptions of innocence and good faith. Such presumptions may be simply interpreted as implying legal innocence and good faith, until legal proof of the contrary is produced. In anomist terms such an interpretation leads to such presumptions being fallacious appeals to ignorance themselves (section 7). Procedural conceptions on the other hand need not bother about the contradiction of such factual interpretation by 'the real facts of the case'.

Witnesses may be less problematic for proceduralism as well. Anomist appeal to witnesses was regarded as deeply doubtful because of their unreliability in reproducing historical and scientific reality in the first place. Proceduralism does not indeed imply any idea of objective historical or future reality. Instead, legal proof is related to parties' stories, one of which best convinces the court some or other way. Witnesses may still be excluded for several reasons, of course. However, while testimonies are anomistically regarded as suspect heuristic or even emergency measures only, such testimonies are the lifeblood of proceduralism. It is parties' and parties' witnesses' statements which are the constituents of what is produced as legal proof in the end.

Concepts of malice and negligence seem to be as intractable in anomism, as they are defined by proceduralism. Remember that these concepts are defined dialogically. The absence of excuses of varying force acceptable to the court thus implies malice or negligence.

One more fundamental difference between these two conceptions of legal evidence and proof is related to differences between contexts of discovery and contexts of justification. In anomism, justification only counts. Methods of discovery are completely anarchic, as long as they do not violate relevant interests and rights. Proceduralism defines the very notion of legal proof in terms of procedure, thus placing its context of justification firmly within the procedural context of discovery.

Proceduralism is related to processes of argumentation in terms of admissible arguments and counter-arguments. This fits in well with defeasible logics, explicitly configured to formalize such argumentation structures. Anomism, on the other hand, seems firmly committed to monotonic logic, modelling validity and proof on the basis of established evidence and relevant general laws.

Pragma-dialectical approaches to legal evidence and proof (see e.g. Feteris 1999) mimic proceduralism. Such conceptions of rational argumentation may be regarded as adaptations and generalizations of proceduralism. Pragma-dialectics indeed consists of rules for rational discussion and argumentation. So it is to be expected that pragma-dialectical analyses of legal fact-finding suffer from the same problems that plague proceduralism.

Also, the relevance of stories for legal evidence and proof seems to fit in well with proceduralism, while its relationship with anomism seems deeply problematic. (Remember that prominent representatives of anchored narrative theory or ANT such as Crombag, Van Koppen and Wagenaar (Wagenaar et al. 1993) originally criticized the psychology of evidence and proof by storytelling because of its all too weak links with the facts. This seems to be left out of account in some interpretations of ANT in attempts to model legal evidence and proof some or other way.) Convincing courts is done by telling stories. Parties with better stories than their opponents can put forward win. Again, problematic relationships of stories with historical realities do not really count in proceduralism, as such historical (or future) realities per se are irrelevant in principle.

Anyway, proceduralism is at best imperfect procedural justice with respect to the facts of the case. Such facts may be established by reasonable procedure, but not in all cases. There is no perfect procedure inexorably leading to the facts of the case to be established independently from any such procedure in principle. But then facts are suspect in proceduralism anyway. From a legal point of view, 'fact' is nothing else but the result of legally authoritative procedure. Proceduralism is not imperfect procedural justice, but pure procedural justice in principle: as long as the rules are followed, any outcome is just and right (see Rawls 1999 for discussion of these varieties of procedural justice). Or (again): the rules of the game rule.

Thus an obvious criticism against proceduralism in the establishment of facts in adjudication is that it may indeed lead to results at odds with reality. But then this does not mean much more than that proceduralism is at odds with anomism. So? Pitting historical (and future) reality against proceduralism may not be outright circular, but still such argument has more than a semblance of *petitio principii*. (Though Scalia's dictum on capital punishment as quoted earlier still suggests an air of absurdity of proceduralism unrelated to any real facts of the case.)

A less welcome consequence of proceduralism, however, is the disappearance of conflict resolution in meta-conflict. Remember that all that counts is the actual effect of parties' arguments on courts' persuasions. Within the rules all and every means, rhetorical and otherwise, may be put to use. Thus conflict resolution indeed disappears into nothing more than processes of persuasion. There is no test of the truth of the matter at all: the outcome of the meta-conflict is to count as 'the facts of the case'. Such conflict resolution by repeating the original conflict is of course heavily influenced by parties' rather different rhetorical and other resources of persuasion. Or: such adjudication is nothing more than repetition of civil and not-so-civil strife. Thus there are no vantage points. Everything disappears in Heraclitean flux, of the wrong kind.

Proceduralism promised ready solutions to problems plaguing anomism. But in the end it falls foul of a kind of disappearing act itself. Proceduralism may have seemed the transposition of ideals of *Herrschaftsfreie Diskussion* (non-authoritative discussion) and *Legitimation durch Verfahren* (legitimation by procedure), or even of the ontological-epistemological idea of 'the constitution of intersubjective realities by the language of dialogue', and so on. Or even more simply: proceduralism may have seemed the expression that establishment of legal evidence and proof is no God-like, solipsist enterprise but the result of human communication and cooperation. But then basic presuppositions of such rational constitutive discussion and cooperation such as the equality and good will of all parties concerned are conspicuously absent in many legal conflicts. The same holds good for pragma-dialectical and other procedural approaches to argumentation in their application to issues of legal evidence and proof. Apart from other problems, such approaches are simply out of place here. So anomism wins, not just on any balance of arguments pro and con proceduralism and anomism (or possibly any other conception of legal evidence and proof). Proceduralism is incompatible with presuppositions of reasonable conflict resolution in principle. If there is no truth of the matter independent of parties' contributions according to the rules, then (again) all that remains is conflict in which the rhetorically (and otherwise) strongest win. But then justice in adjudication ought to be more than just conflict.

9. The Procedural Predicament: Chasing Bentham's Will'-o-the-Wisps Anyway

Doing away with all rules of evidence and proof may be a bit too far-fetched. Complete anarchy will not lead to any reasonable fact-finding. First, heuristic rules are indispensable, however important inexpressible know-how and imagination may be in fact-finding. But then it does not make much sense to even try to summarize all useful investigative rules or even principles to be adhered to in the realization of the anomist ideal. Police investigation is a world of its own, for example, effected by following so many rules of thumb, sudden insights, traditional experience or even science. Final fact-finding by courts in hard cases presupposes lots of theoretical and practical knowledge, not always appealed to even in civilized jurisdictions, it seems.

Second (and not discussed further here), rules of evidence are to determine legally acceptable degrees of justification of factual statements and conclusions. Such rules refer to degrees of verification and falsification, among other things. Thus legal rules of evidence refer to scientific laws or at least generalizations, in order to realize the rigorously scientific anomist ideal (section 2). Difficult and probably not always well-understood issues of probability may crop up, then. (Again, and as already expounded in Chapter 1, the fundamental adagium here is: *in dubio abstine*.)

Third and foremost, any tendency to further 'proceduralize' matters of fact ought to be counteracted as persuasively as possible. Any court's first duty is to find the facts of the case, realizing that this enterprise is fundamentally different from sticking to formal rules of evidence and proof (or even to rules of reasonable discussion as offered by pragma-dialectics). In fact, whatever such rules, they are to be firmly relegated to the endless realm of heuristics, if need rises even *contra legem*. Thus verification is not obtained at all if parties bearing burdens of proof against such verification seem unconvincing or even remain silent. They may still be right and thus ought not to be trapped in the snares of procedure at odds with the facts of the case.

Divisions of burdens of proof as such are uninteresting in anomism. Such issues are to be handled in pragmatic, heuristic fashion only. On the other hand and obviously so, a shift from the facts of the case to witnesses telling courts about them is unavoidable indeed. But this does not imply any proceduralism itself, of course, even if such witnesses' statements are all that the court's verdict can be based on.

Also, presumptions of innocence and good faith in general may still have consequences for burdens of proof. But then such presumptions, however important in other respects (see sections 3 and 7), furnish no more than prima facie reasons not to allocate burdens of proof with defendants (though this may seem to fly in the face of highly esteemed principles of criminal justice).

Other rights and interests of parties and others concerned with the establishment of legal evidence and proof are to be respected as well. Some of these already passed muster in section 7 as well: all relevant costs are to be balanced, legal conflicts are to come to an end some time, privacy is to be respected, confessions, however truthful, are not to be obtained by force.

But such rights and interests concerning burdens of proof and otherwise are not unconditional in anomism. Truth ought to prevail in the first place. Without the truth of the matter there can be no realization of rights. So limiting anarchic fact-finding in favour of rights is a strange kind of balancing: rights against the realization of rights. Thus regarded, adjudicators may not always face easy tasks in realizing anomism in the real world.

Client confidentiality ought to be abolished in principle, as it may stand in the way of the facts of the case and thus of justice and right (as indeed already discussed by Bentham; see also Luban [1988] and Kaptein [2005]). Client confidentiality seems to fit in well with proceduralism, misrepresenting legal conflict resolution as a kind of contest in which parties and others concerned may 'arm' themselves against each other and against the court. But lawyers 'helping' their clients by hiding relevant realities are in fact accomplices in crime. (In civil procedure in The Netherlands, this is now acknowledged by law, as section 21 of the Netherlands Code of Civil Procedure prescribes that all parties concerned ought to inform the court about all relevant facts of the case. This does away with client confidentiality in civil lawsuits, at least on paper. Whether such a rule is really effective remains to be seen of course. Comparable traditions and developments may be seen elsewhere as well.)

Exclusion of improperly obtained evidence is unacceptable too, as improper ways of obtaining evidence do not necessarily touch upon such evidence itself. For example: stolen information may still be completely trustworthy. Exclusion seems to negate such evidence, as if facts on which such evidence is based are illusory after all. Proceduralism tries to justify such irrational exclusion by emphasizing 'fair trial', supposedly covering parties' responsibilities for the facts of the case. Anomism's strict distinction between contexts of discovery and contexts of justification implies that any improper obtainment of evidence cannot thwart such evidence per se. So it may not be excluded on any other grounds than lack of conformity to the facts. Still, parties' and others' improper conduct in obtaining evidence may be sanctioned, for example by making them pay damages to anybody who is injured (see Kaptein 2001).

In line with this, unconditional exclusion of testimonial evidence stated by 'the wrong kind' of witnesses is incompatible with anomism. Next of kin and (other) accomplices may not be the most reliable witnesses, but then they may still helpful in finding the truth. Remember anomism's conception of testimonies as heuristic and/or emergency measures only. In fact, all testimonies are to be suspect in principle, and to be replaced by more trustworthy evidence wherever possible.

The one exclusionary rule to survive and in fact facilitate anomism is the rule of relevance. Not everything needs to be known; only evidence and proof apposite to the case at hand, according to relevant legal rules, are to be considered (see earlier, section 2).

Also, there seem to be no good reasons to differentiate between criminal procedure and other kinds of legal procedure. Interests and rights at stake may be much more important in the administration of criminal justice. The only relevant difference then may be still higher standards of proof in criminal procedure. (The issue of standards of proof is not discussed here. See Chapter 1 and other chapters for more on this.)

It is to be noted that the conception of legal evidence and proof argued for here differs both from Bentham's own detailed views (however extremely interesting after so many years) and from so-called 'Thayerite orthodoxy'. Thus Bentham's utilitarianism is not echoed here. Also, no appeal is made to his (again very interesting) ideas on probability in legal fact-finding. Thayer (1898) treated the rules of evidence as a mixed group of exceptions to a principle of freedom of proof. This is indeed taken to be the reigning orthodoxy. Thayer's rule of evidence however, including exclusionary rules, are rather more strict than the anarchic conception of legal evidence and proof defended here.

Still, one important and often implicit role for this 'mixed group of exceptions' is checking adjudicators' opportunities to reach verdicts at odds with the facts of the case. Thus not locating any burden of proof with criminal defendants may increase the likelihood that the innocent go free. This may still lend importance to rules of evidence, though safeguarding effects may well be overestimated here (but see also Schafer's contribution to this book).

At least one basic principle survives all anomist doubts on rules of evidence and procedure. *Audi et alteram partem* (everybody concerned is to be duly heard) remains important anyway, and this is not just for reasons of fact-finding. Fair trial involves fundamental respect for parties and others concerned, not just in the establishment of evidence and proof (see very interestingly on this, and also concerning normative discourse, Hampshire 2000).

Lastly (for now) and related to this, a seemingly proceduralist element ought to be part of any court's verdict (partially) based on facts. Any court ought to know that, according to anomist standards, indubitable certainty on the facts of the case is really rare. So, generally, any court's establishment of the facts, relying as it does on uncertain evidence and uncertain inference of whatever kind, ought to be clearly qualified as follows: 'Given what reached the courts in terms of reliable evidence in this case, and given standards of proof, the court feels obligated to assume facts x, y, z ... (with legal consequences a, b, c ...)'. This is categorically different from the courts' unqualified statements such as: 'X, y, z happened/were done' (and sometimes attendant moralizing against convicted defendants such as: 'You are a bad person because you did x,' as happened to the above mentioned nurse as well). Thus any unnecessary denials of parties' good faith and lack of respect for parties losing the case may be avoided, as no lies by anybody concerned are implied as long as courts do not state the facts per se. This seems a concession to proceduralist styles of adjudication. In fact it is the opposite, of course. It is acknowledgement that even in the law (almost) nothing may be really certain in anomist terms. Proceduralism, on the other hand, wrongly takes the facts of the case to be settled as soon as one party wins within the bounds of the rule of the game.

10. Conclusions and Recommendations: Stick to the Rigid Anarchic Principle

Logical, argumentative, probabilistic and other approaches to issues of legal evidence and proof may well profit from stricter distinctions between anomism and proceduralism as radically different conceptions of legal evidence and proof in principle. For example: pragma-dialectical approaches may be more or less plausible from proceduralist points of view, but seem to do rather less well in anomism. Issues of probability in anomism may be rather different from 'subjectivist' (Bayesian?) probabilities in proceduralism. ANT seems to fit in with proceduralism better than with anomism, though again it should be kept in mind that ANT was proposed as a critical theory in the first place, trying to clarify shortcomings of legal procedures measured by anomist standards. Non-monotonic logic relates to proceduralist approaches more logically than to anomist ideals. However, given proceduralist aspects of the practical realization of anomism, non-monotonic logic(s) may still be important.

Anyway, too many studies of legal evidence and proof seem to take some or other form of proceduralism for granted. This may be caused by sticking to outward appearances of the practice of legal evidence and proof, or even from scholarly desires to be true to the subject in at least one respect. But such semblances may be false in principle, however important aspects of proceduralism may be in practice.

Anomism ought to have pride of place. This firmly links the study of legal evidence and proof with studies of evidence and proof in history, archeology (in any case concerning circumstantial evidence) and other sciences trying to reconstruct the past (and sometimes to construct the future). Methodologies and epistemologies of forensic sciences are apposite from this perspective as well. There are still too many isolated fields of scholarship and science here. Again: the field of evidence is the field of knowledge. More integration may well lead to (still) better results (see Hampsher-Monk and Twining 2002, among others). And of course: (re)read Bentham himself! (However imperfectly his work on evidence and proof may have been edited up to now.)

Such development of knowledge on legal evidence and proof ought to find its way into practice too. Police and public prosecution officers, lawyers and adjudicators need better training in fact-finding and argumentation concerning facts. They have to unlearn their proceduralist penchant, which implies that knowledge of the law of evidence and proof is sufficient for the establishment of the facts of the case. This could be effective against blatant miscarriages of criminal justice and more misadjudication based on assumptions at odds with reality. In any case, they have to unlearn the well-nigh universal habit of taking the facts of the case for granted beforehand and thus partly or even fatally determining the outcome of the whole process:

> For those who believe, no proof is necessary; for those who don't, none is possible.

(Too often quoted by now to warrant any specific reference.) This, of course, is one of many reasons why the psychology of legal evidence and proof is important, and not just issues of logic, probability and argumentation. Related to this, and no less pressing, is the need for improved methods of police investigation. Advances in forensic science and related improvement of research methods on paper do not always seem to be realized in practice. Remember: *in dubio abstine*, at least in the administration of criminal justice (a principle to be kept in mind in any probability approaches to problems of evidence and proof as well).

One reason for this careful stance, of course, is the human importance of the consequences of adjudication, at least in the administration of criminal justice. In several respects it may be highly interesting and important to acquire knowledge about whichever historical, archaeological or even future facts. In criminal procedure, however, knowledge of the facts is really needed to avoid the utterly repellent injustice of convicting the innocent.

Also (again, see Chapter 1): facts should be left alone if not really needed, in adjudication and otherwise. Again, do not underestimate any facts determining the importance of making a legal or even court issue out of some or other human predicament. At times such facts are at least as interesting and important as all the possible facts determining the conflicts themselves. Do not try to establish such facts, in their turn, in any proceduralist fashion. Try just to find facts which determine the importance of legalizing human issues. Indeed many of these issues are best left alone, and the humanly costly issues of evidence and proof with them.

(No, this is not a *regressus ad infinitum*, just a repetition of the old and sometimes forgotten adage that even in the administration of the law thought ought to precede action.)

In the end, anomism's stance is extremely simple. No conflict resolution, legal or otherwise, or any human conduct in general, can do without facts. Rules, principles, goals and other normative conceptions determine what facts are relevant. But as soon as the facts of any case come to depend on legal (or other) procedure, every foothold in whatever reality is lost. Worse, we are lost, as beautifully expressed by Frankfurt (2006, p. 100, v.):

> … our recognition and our understanding of our own identity arises out of, and depends integrally on, our appreciation of a reality that is definitively independent of ourselves. In other words, it arises out of and depends on our recognition that there are facts and truths over which we cannot hope to exercise direct or immediate control. If there were no such facts or truths, if the world invariably and unresistingly became whatever we might like or wish it to be, we would be unable to distinguish ourselves from what is other than ourselves and we would have no sense of what in particular we ourselves are. It is only through our recognition of a world of stubbornly independent reality, fact, and truth that we come both to recognize ourselves as beings distinct from others and to articulate the specific nature of our own identities.
>
> How, then, can we fail to take the importance of factuality and of reality seriously? How can we fail to care about truth?
>
> We cannot.

This is of self-evident importance for legal conflict resolution as well (if anything needs to be added to this). Facts are the vantage points of conflict resolution. Otherwise we are lost in the wrong kind of Heraclitean flux indeed. So try to determine the facts of the case without too much dependence on the law of evidence in the first place. Try not to be convinced of 'facts' according to whatever seemingly rational procedure, but try to know the facts, however difficult this may be. Stick to rigid anarchic principles of evidence and proof.

References

Bentham, J. (1812), *An Introductory View of the Rationale of Evidence: For the Use of Non-Lawyers as well as Lawyers*, in Bowring and Mill (eds).

Bowring, J. and Mill, J. (eds) (1843), *The Works of Jeremy Bentham*, vol. 6 onwards (Edinburgh: William Tait).

Breur, C.M, Kommer, M.M., Nijboer, J.F. and Reijntjes, J.M. (eds) (2001), *New Trends in Criminal Investigation and Evidence*, vol. 2 (Antwerp, Groningen and Oxford: Intersentia).

Copi, I.M. and Cohen, C. (2002), *Introduction to Logic*, 2nd Edition (Upper Saddle River, NJ: Prentice Hall).

Dahlmann, C. and Krawietz, W. (eds) (2005), 'Values, rights and duties in legal and philosophical discourse', *Rechtstheorie Beiheft* 21.

Dworkin, R.M. (1977), *Taking Rights Seriously* (London: Duckworth).

Eemeren, F.H. van, Grootendorst, R., Blair, J.A. and Willard, C.A. (eds) (1999), *Proceedings of the Fourth International Conference of the International Society for the Study of Argumentation* (Amsterdam: SIC SAT).

Feteris, E.T. (1999), Fundamentals of Legal Argumentation: A Survey of Theories of Justification of Judicial Decisions (Dordrecht: Kluwer).

Flew, A.G.N. (ed.) (1951), *Logic and Language* (Oxford: Basil Blackwell).

Frankfurt, H.G. (2006), *On Truth* (New York: Alfred A. Knopf).

Gray, C.B. (ed.) (1999), *The Philosophy of Law: An Encyclopedia* (New York and London: Garland Publishing).

Hampsher-Monk, I. and Twining, W. (eds) (2002), *Evidence and Inference in History and Law: Interdisciplinary Dialogues* (Evanston, IL: Northwestern University Press).

Hampshire, S. (2000), *Justice is Conflict* (Princeton, NJ: Princeton University Press).

Hart, H.L.A. (1948), 'The ascription of responsibility and rights', *Proceedings of the Aristotelian Society*, 171–94, also in Flew (ed.).

Kaptein, H.J.R. (1999a), 'Causation, Criminal', in Gray (ed.).

—— (1999b), 'Abductive Limits to Artificial Intelligence in Adjudication: Pervasive Problems of Analogy, e Contrario and Circumstantial Evidence', in Van Eemeren et al. (eds).

—— (2001), 'Improperly Obtained Evidence and the End(s) of Punishment', in Breur et al. (eds).

—— (2005), 'Secrets of confidentiality: Adjudication ad ignorantiam against material rights and justice?', in Dahlmann and Krawietz (eds).

Luban, D. (1988), *Lawyers and Justice: An Ethical Study* (Princeton, NJ: Princeton University Press).

Malcolm, J. (1999), *The Crime of Sheila McCough* (New York: Borzoi Books, Alfred A. Knopf, Inc.).

Nagel, E. (1979), *The Structure of Science: Problems in the Logic of Scientific Explanation*, 2nd Edition (Cambridge, MA: Hackett Publishing Company).

Rawls, J. (1999), *A Theory of Justice*, 2nd Edition (Cambridge, MA: Belknap Press of Harvard University Press).

Thayer, J.B. (1898), A Preliminary Treatise on Evidence at the Common Law (Boston: Little, Brown).

Tillers, P. (1983), 'Modern Theories of Relevancy', in Wigmore and Tillers (eds).

Twining, W. and Stein, A. (eds) (1992), *Evidence and Proof* (Aldershot: Dartmouth).

Wagenaar, W.A., Koppen, P.J. van and Crombag, H.F.M. (1993), *Anchored Narratives: The Psychology of Criminal Evidence* (London: Harvester Wheatsheaf and St Martins Press).
Walton, D. (1996), *Arguments from Ignorance* (University Park, Pennsylvania: The Pennsylvania State University Press).
—— (2002), *Legal Argumentation and Evidence* (University Park, Pennsylvania: The Pennsylvania State University Press).
Wigmore, J.H. (1913), 'The problem of proof', *Illinois Law Review* VIII/2: 6–1913, 77–103, also in Twining and Stein (eds).
Wigmore, J.H. and Tillers, P. (eds) (1983), *Evidence in Trials at Common Law* (Boston: Little, Brown).
Wright, G.H. von (1963), *Norm and Action: A Logical Inquiry* (London: Routledge & Kegan Paul Ltd.).
—— (1971), *Explanation and Understanding* (London: Routledge & Kegan Paul Ltd.).

Chapter 9
A Logical Analysis of Burdens of Proof

Henry Prakken and Giovanni Sartor

1. Introduction

The legal concept of burden of proof is notoriously complex and ambiguous. Various kinds of burdens of proof have been distinguished, such as the burden of persuasion, burden of production and tactical burden of proof, and these notions have been described by different scholars in different ways. They have also been linked in various ways with notions like presumptions, standards of proof, and shifts and distributions of burdens of proof. What adds to the complexity is that different legal systems describe and treat the burden of proof in different ways. For instance, in common law jurisdictions the just-mentioned distinction between three kinds of burden of proof is explicitly made while in civil law systems it usually remains implicit.

This chapter aims to clarify matters concerning burden of proof from a logical point of view. We take a logical point of view since, although some differences in notions and treatments might reflect legitimate *legal* differences between jurisdictions, we think that to a large extent the burden of proof is an aspect of *rational* thinking and therefore subject to a logical analysis. In particular, we claim that the burden of proof can be adequately analysed in terms of logical systems for defeasible argumentation, i.e., logics for fallible (but not fallacious!) reasoning. The grounds for this claim are fourfold. First, since legal proof almost always has an element of uncertainty, we cannot impose a deductive form onto real legal evidential reasoning. Second, while this reason still leaves open the use of other approaches, such as story-based or statistical approaches, we think that the notion of argumentation and related notions such as counter-argument, rebuttal and dispute, are very natural to legal thinking. Third (and a special case of the second reason), logics for defeasible argumentation are arguably suitable as a formal underpinning of much work of the influential New Evidence scholars, such as Anderson, Tillers, Twining and Schum (e.g. Anderson et al. 2005, who revived and modernized Wigmore's famous charting method for making sense of legal-evidential problems. (See Prakken 2004 for a defence of the thesis that argument-based logics can be a formal underpinning of this work.) Finally, logics for defeasible argumentation have a firm theoretical basis both in philosophy (especially in argumentation theory) and in logic (especially in its applications in artificial intelligence (AI)). In short, logics for defeasible argumentation are theoretically well-founded and mature analytical tools that fit well with legal thinking in general and with legal-evidential reasoning in particular.

We start in section 2 with an overview of how the various kinds of burden of proof and related notions have been described and related in the jurisprudential literature. Then we describe the logical background of our analysis in section 3, that is, the idea of logics for defeasible argumentation and how they can be embedded in models of legal procedure. We have deliberately made this section of a tutorial nature, since a secondary aim of this chapter is to introduce these logics to the legal-jurisprudential community. Section 4 forms the heart of the chapter: it contains our formal account of the various notions of burden of proof in terms of argumentation logics. In this section we also discuss to what extent shifts and distributions of the three kinds of burden of proof can be logically modelled, and how our logical model accounts for different proof standards. In section 5 we briefly discuss some other notions related to burden of proof that are sometimes distinguished in the law. We conclude in section 6 by discussing to what extent our analysis can be adapted to other approaches, such as statistical ones.

2. Doctrinal Discussions on the Burdens of Proof in Civil Law and Common Law

In this section we briefly discuss accounts of burden of proof in doctrinal analysis, both in civil law and in common law jurisdictions. In common law systems generally a clear distinction is made between the burden of production and the burden of persuasion, although different characterizations and denominations are used for this two kinds of burden (see Williams 2003). What we call the *burden of production* is characterized by Capper and Cross (1999, 113) as 'the obligation to show, if called upon to do so, that there is sufficient evidence to raise an issue as to the existence or non-existence of a fact in issue'. Strong (1992, 425) describes the burden of production as 'the liability to an adverse ruling (generally a finding or directed verdict) if evidence on the issue has not been produced'. This burden is also called the 'evidential burden' (Capper and Cross 1990, 113), or the 'duty to produce evidence' (Wigmore 1940, § 2487), or the duty of passing the judge (Keane 1994, 55), or the burden of adducing evidence (Zuckerman 2006, para. 21.35). What we call the *burden of persuasion* (Zuckerman 2006, para. 21.33) is characterized by Capper and Cross (1990, 113) as the 'obligation of a party to meet the requirement of a rule of law that a fact in issue must be proved or disproved', and by Strong (1992, 426) as meaning that if the party having that burden has failed to satisfy it, the issue is to be decided against that party. This burden is also called the 'legal burden' (Denning 1945, Capper and Cross 1990, 113), the 'risk of non-persuasion' (Wigmore 1940, § 2487) or 'probative burden' (*DPP* v. *Morgan* [1976] AC 182 at 209, Lord Hailsham).

The *proof standards* for these two burdens are quite different. For the burden of persuasion the fact-finder must be convinced that the statement holds 'beyond reasonable doubt' (in criminal cases) or 'on the balance of probabilities' (in civil cases; in such cases the phrase 'more probable than not' is also used). For the burden of production the proof standard is much lower. Sometimes it is said that just a 'scintilla of evidence' is needed, sometimes that the evidence is such that 'reasonable minds can disagree' on the issue, or even that there is evidence 'upon which a jury can properly proceed to find a verdict for the party producing it, upon whom the onus of proof is imposed' (as required in *Improvement Co.* v. *Munson*, 14 Wall. 442, 81 US 448 [1872]).

The distinction between a burden of production and a burden of persuasion is more significant in common law jurisdictions, since in these systems the discharge of the burden of production is a precondition for moving to the trial phase, where the factual issue is decided by the jury according to the burden of persuasion. Accordingly, these burdens are verified at different moments. According to Wigmore (1962, Volume IX at 283, cited in Williams 2003) 'The risk of non-persuasion operates when the case has come into the hands of the jury, while the duty of producing evidence implies a liability to a ruling by the judge disposing of the issue without leaving the question open to the jury's deliberations.' Strong (1992, 426) says:

> The burden of persuasion becomes a crucial factor only if the parties have sustained their burdens of producing evidence and only when all of the evidence has been introduced. It does not shift from party to party during the course of the trial simply because it need not be allocated until it is time for a decision. When the time for a decision comes, the jury, if there is one, must be instructed how to decide the issue if their minds are left in doubt. The jury must be told that if the party having the burden of persuasion has failed to satisfy that burden, the issue is to be decided against that party. If there is no jury and the judge is in doubt, the issue must be decided against the party having the burden of persuasion.

However, the distinction between the two burdens is also recognized in some civil law jurisdictions. For instance, the German legal doctrine distinguishes between a subjective burden of proof (*subjektive Beweislast*, also called burden of providing a proof, *Beweisführungslast*) and objective burden of proof (*objektive Beweislast*). As observed by Hahn and Oaksford (2007), the first corresponds, more or less, to the burden of production and the second to the burden of persuasion (see, for instance, Rosenberg et al. 1993, §§ 112–24).

The relation between the burdens of persuasion and production depends on whether the case is a criminal one or a civil one. For civil cases they usually go together since both are usually determined by the 'operative facts' for a legal claim, i.e., the facts that legally are ordinarily sufficient reasons for the claim. The law often designates the operative facts with rule–exception structures. For example, the operative facts for the existence of a contract generally are that there was an offer which was accepted but this rule can have many exceptions, such as that one party deceived the other party or that the party making or accepting the offer was insane when doing so. Now, in civil cases, the general rule is that the party who makes a legal claim has both the burden of production and the burden of persuasion for the operative facts of the claim, while the other party has the two burdens for any exception.

For instance, if the plaintiff claims that a contract between him and defendant exists then he must produce evidence that he made an offer which the defendant accepted to fulfil his burden of production, and in the final stage the fact-finder must regard it as more probable than not that this offer and acceptance were made, otherwise the plaintiff loses. Suppose the plaintiff succeeds in both tasks and that the defendant claims she was insane when she accepted his offer. Then if the defendant has not produced evidence for her insanity, the plaintiff wins since the judge must rule as a matter of law that she was not insane. However, if she did produce evidence for her insanity, then she only wins if the fact-finder regards it as more probable than not that she was insane, otherwise the plaintiff still wins, even if the evidence on insanity is balanced.[1]

In criminal cases the burdens of production and persuasion on an issue can be on different parties, since the principle according to which one cannot be convicted unless one's guilt is proved also covers the non-existence of exceptions preventing such guilt. More precisely, this principle implies that the accused has to be acquitted when there remains reasonable doubt concerning the existence of such an exception (for instance, self-defence in a murder case), so the prosecution also has the burden of persuasion for the non-existence of such exceptions. In other words, in criminal cases the prosecution has the burden of persuasion not only for the legal operative facts for a claim (say, for murder, that there was a killing and that it was done with intent) but also for the non-existence of exceptions (such as that the killing was not done in self-defence). However, for the burden of production this is different: the prosecution has this burden only for the legal operative facts (in our murder example, 'killing' and 'intent'); for the exceptions the burden of production is on the defence. As Spencer and Spencer (2007, Chapter 2) say, in the British legal system:

> the prosecution cannot be expected to put up evidence to anticipate every specific defence the accused may present; thus in order to plead self-defence the accused will have to provide some evidence to enable the court to consider the matter.

So in our murder case example the defence must produce evidence that he acted in self-defence but once he has produced such evidence, the prosecution has the burden of persuasion that there was no self-defence. Similarly, in the Italian legal

1 It should be noted that our observations in this chapter on allocating the proof burdens only hold as a general rule: legal systems leave some freedom to courts to make exceptions to them in special cases, for instance, on the basis of fairness. The allocation of proof burdens can even be the subject of dispute; see Prakken and Sartor (2007) for examples and a logical formalization of such disputes.

system, the accused has the burden of producing evidence sufficient to create such a doubt in respect of the existence of a cause of justification, while the prosecutor then has the burden of persuading the court that the cause of justification does not exist (see Tonini 2007, 311, who grounds this conclusion on article 530 of the Italian code of criminal procedure, specifying that the judge has to acquit the accused person in a case where there is doubt in respect of the existence of a cause of justification). In sum, in criminal proceedings the two burdens go together only for operative facts; for exceptions they are separated.

As Williams (2003) observes, common law doctrine usually does not clearly distinguish the burden of production from the so-called 'tactical burden', which he characterizes as the situation when, if the party does not produce evidence or further evidence he or she runs the risk of ultimately losing in respect of that issue. The same criticism is raised by other authors, such as Keane (1994), according to whom, by providing evidence a party does not shift the burden of production onto the other party but only shifts a tactical burden, since once the burden of production is fulfilled, the issue is determined regardless of the burden of production. By contrast, the tactical burden of proof is not allocated by law but induced by the defeasible nature of the reasoning and the estimated quality of the evidence and arguments produced so far. In civil law countries, to the best of our knowledge, the distinction between burden of production and tactical burden is not usually explicitly considered. Nevertheless, since this notion is induced by the logic of the reasoning process instead of being assigned by law, it is also relevant for these systems. In the words of Williams (2003), this burden is a matter of tactical evaluation in that a party must assess the risk of losing in respect of an issue if no further evidence concerning that issue is produced.

Suppose in our murder example that the prosecution has provided evidence for 'killing' and 'intent', after which the defence produced evidence for 'self-defence'. The prosecution must now assess the risk of losing if the current stage were the final stage. If this risk is real then the prosecution had better provide counter-evidence on 'self-defence'. In other words, the prosecution now not only has the burden of persuasion but also a tactical burden with respect to self-defence. Clearly, a tactical burden can shift between the parties any number of times during a proceeding, depending on who would be likely to win if no more evidence were provided. In our example, if the prosecution provides counter-evidence against self-defence, then the defence must estimate the likelihood of losing if it does not provide further evidence supporting self-defence. If this likelihood is real, then the tactical burden has shifted to the defence. By contrast, the burden of production never shifts since once fulfilled it is disregarded in the rest of the proceeding. With Williams (2003), we believe that those who argue that this burden can shift confuse it with the tactical burden.

The tactical burden is also relevant in civil cases, for instance, when an exception is not to a legal rule but to a commonsense generalization. Suppose in our contract example that the defendant disputes the plaintiff's claim that the defendant accepted his offer, and that the plaintiff provides two witness testimonies in support of his claim. The commonsense generalization used by the plaintiff here is that if two witnesses say the same, they are usually telling the truth. If the defendant provides no counter-evidence to the witnesses' credibility, then she runs the risk of losing in respect of this issue, since the fact-finder is likely to accept this generalization. However, her burden to provide such counter-evidence is not a burden of persuasion but only a tactical burden: since the plaintiff has the burden of persuasion for his claim that the defendant accepted his offer, the defendant's task is to cast sufficient doubt on whether she accepted the offer; she does not have to persuade the fact-finder that she did not accept the offer. Thus in civil cases the nature of an exception is important: if it is an exception to a legal rule, then it carries the burdens of production and persuasion, while if it is an exception to a commonsense generalization, it only carries a tactical burden, the strength of which depends on whether the generalization is used to fulfil a burden of persuasion or to prevent such fulfilment.

Both the murder and the contract example show that the tactical burden has no single fixed proof standard. A tactical burden can be said to be fulfilled if its intended effect is made likely, and this effect is different depending on whether a party has the burden of persuasion or not. The party that has it must convince the fact-finder (to the relevant degree) that the statement on which it rests holds while the other party only needs to make the fact-finder doubt (to the relevant degree) whether the statement holds.

Summarizing, we distil the following characterizations from the above discussion. The burden of persuasion specifies which party has to prove a statement to a specified degree (its proof standard) with the penalty of losing in respect of the issue. Whether this burden is met is determined in the final stage of a proceeding, after all evidence is provided. That a burden of persuasion for a statement is fulfilled means that a rational fact-finder is, to the required degree, convinced that the statement is true; so if the burden is not met, this means that such a fact-finder is not convinced to that degree that the statement is true; he need not be convinced that it is false. The burden of production specifies which party has to offer evidence on an issue at different points in a proceeding. If such evidence does not meet the (low) proof standard for this burden, the issue is decided as a matter of law against the burdened party, while otherwise the issue is decided in the final stage by the trier of fact according to the burden of persuasion. Both these burdens are assigned as a matter of law. By contrast, the *tactical burden of proof* is a matter of tactical evaluation in that a party must assess the risk of ultimately losing in respect of an issue if no further evidence concerning that issue is produced.

Our task in the remainder of this chapter is to make this characterization more precise. The most important issue is how a rational fact-finder confronted with conflicting evidence and arguments on a claim can decide whether the claim has been proven. Once we know this, we can define how such decisions on various claims affect the overall outcome of a case, which in turn allows us to give a precise characterization of the tactical burden of proof. However, to answer these questions, we first need to find suitable logical tools.

3. Logical Background: Defeasible Argumentation

In this section we sketch the logical background of our analysis, logics for defeasible argumentation as they have been developed in research on artificial intelligence and applied to legal reasoning by ourselves and others.

3.1. Introductory Remarks

Introductory textbooks to logic often portray logically valid inference as 'foolproof' reasoning: an argument is valid if the truth of its premises guarantees the truth of its conclusion. However, we all construct arguments from time to time that are not foolproof in this sense but that merely make their conclusion plausible when their premises are true. For example, if we are told that John and Mary are married and that John lives in Amsterdam, we conclude that Mary will live in Amsterdam as well since we know that usually married people live where their spouses live. Sometimes such arguments are overturned by counter-arguments. For example, if we are told that Mary is living in Rome to work at the foreign offices of her company for two years, we have to retract our previous conclusion that she lives in Amsterdam. However, as long as such counter-arguments are not available, we are happy to live with the conclusions of our fallible arguments. The question is: are we then reasoning fallaciously or is there still logic in our reasoning?

The answer to this question has been given in three decades of research in artificial intelligence on so-called logics for defeasible reasoning (cf. Prakken and Vreeswijk 2002), partly inspired by earlier developments in philosophy (e.g. Toulmin 1958; Rescher 1977) and argumentation theory (e.g. Walton 1996). At first sight it might be thought that patterns of defeasible reasoning are a matter of applying probability theory. However, many such patterns cannot be analysed in a probabilistic way. In the legal domain this is particularly clear: while reasoning about the facts can (at least in principle) still be regarded as probabilistic, reasoning about normative issues is clearly of a different nature. Moreover, even in matters of evidence, reliable numbers are usually not available so that the reasoning has to be qualitative.

In this section we sketch an account of defeasible reasoning that respects that arguments can be defeasible for various reasons. In short, the account is that reasoning consists of constructing arguments, of attacking these arguments with counter-arguments, and of adjudicating between conflicting arguments on grounds that are appropriate to the conflict at hand. Just as in deductive reasoning, arguments must instantiate inference schemes (now called 'argument schemes') but only some of these schemes capture foolproof reasoning: in our account, deductive logic turns out to be the special case of argument schemes that can only be attacked on their premises.

We shall, in this section, deliberately use a tutorial style, since our primary aim is to explain these ideas to legal theorists with an introductory knowledge of logic but with perhaps no knowledge of the modern developments of the last 30 years.

We think it is important that these developments become widely known among legal theorists, since attacks on the usefulness of formal logic for the law often wrongly presuppose that formal logic equates to deductive logic. In this section we present the ideas of a research community rather than just our own ideas, but in order not to overload the text with references we will limit them to a few key and overview publications.

3.2. Logic of Defeasible Argumentation

As stated previously, we assume that any argument instantiates some argument scheme. (More precisely, in general, arguments chain instantiations of argument schemes into trees, since the conclusion of one argument can be a premise of another.) Argument schemes are inference rules: they have a set of premises and a conclusion. What are the 'valid' argument schemes of defeasible reasoning? Much can be said on this and we will do so later on, but at least the deductively valid inference schemes of standard logic will be among them. Let us examine how deductive arguments can be the subject of attack.

According to the Dutch civil code, persons who are not minors have the capacity to perform legal acts (this means, for instance, that they can engage in contracts or sell their property). Suppose also that some person is not a minor. Then these premises instantiate the deductive scheme of *modus ponens*. In formulas of propositional logic:

Argument A:
Person & ¬Minor → Has-Legal-Capacity
Person
¬Minor
Therefore, Has-legal-capacity

(Here '&' stands for 'and', '¬' for 'not' and '→' for 'if ... then'.)

Do we have to accept the conclusion of this foolproof argument? Of course not: any first lesson in logic includes the advice: if you don't like the conclusion of a deductive argument, challenge its premises. (In fact, this is the only way to attack a deductive argument since if we accept its premises then its deductive nature forces us to accept its conclusion.) Suppose someone claims that the person is in fact a minor since he is younger than 18. Then the following deductive argument against the premise '¬Minor' can be constructed, which also instantiates *modus ponens*.

Argument B:
Person & Younger-than-18 → Minor
Person
Younger-than-18
Therefore, Minor.

Now we must choose whether to accept the premise '¬Minor' of argument A or whether to give it up and accept the counter-argument B. Here it is important to note that many cases of premise attack are cases where the premise is assumed in the absence of the contrary. For instance, in our example, being a minor is legally recognized as an exception to the legal rule that persons have the capacity to perform legal acts, so when applying this rule it is reasonable to assume that a person is not a minor as long as there is no evidence to the contrary. Now since argument B provides such evidence to the contrary, we must give up the premise of A and accept the counter-argument.

This leads to a first refinement of deductive logic. It turns out that some arguments have two kinds of premises: ordinary ones and *assumptions*, i.e., premises we are prepared to give up as soon as we have evidence that they are false.

However, not all counter-arguments are attacks on an assumption. Consider again our example. The law of Dutch civil procedure also says that persons younger than 18 who are married are not minors. This gives rise to a deductive argument that attacks the first premise of argument C.

Argument C:
Person & Younger-than-18 and Married → ¬Minor
Person
Younger-than-18
Married
Therefore, ¬Minor

It is important to see that, although superficially argument C attacks argument B's conclusion, C in fact attacks a premise of B, namely its rule premise 'Person & Younger-than-18 → Minor'. This can be seen as follows. If all premises of both arguments are accepted, then a contradiction can be derived, namely, 'Minor & ¬Minor'. To restore consistency, one of these premises has to be false. Since the second and third premise of argument B are also premises of argument C, accepting all premises of C means having to give up the first premise of B. In conclusion, argument C can be extended with:

Argument C continued:
Therefore ¬(Person & Younger-than-18 → Minor)

Moreover, argument B can be continued in a similar way. If all premises of B are accepted, at least one premise of C has to be false. Now the choice is between the rule premise 'Person & Younger-than-18 and Married → ¬Minor' and the factual premise 'Married'. Let us for the sake of illustration assume that the latter is beyond dispute: then argument B can be continued as follows:

Argument B continued:
Moreover, Married
Therefore ¬(Person & Younger-than-18 and Married → ¬Minor)

We now see that the conflict between arguments A and B is not a case of assumption attack, since the conflict is in fact between the two rule premises of these arguments. In such cases some comparative standard has to be applied to see which of these premises has to be preferred. In general, many such standards could be used. When the conflict is caused by conflicting statutory rules (as in our example), we might be able to resolve it on the basis of the hierarchical ordering of the respective regulations (for example, 'federal law precedes state law'), we might prefer the most specific rule on the basis of the principle *lex specialis derogat legi generali* (in our example we could prefer argument C over argument B on this ground) or we might be able to apply some specific statutory conflict rule (for instance, Dutch contract law gives precedence to rules concerning labour contracts over rules concerning other types of contracts). When instead the conflict arises because sources of evidence conflict (such as conflicting witness statements) we might be able to resolve the conflict on the basis of their relative trustworthiness. And when interpretations of a legal concept conflict, we might resort to the underlying purposes or values that are at stake. (Lawyers may even argue about what are the appropriate standards for comparing arguments: this can also be modelled in our account but for simplicity we refer the reader to the literature, e.g. the overview chapter, Prakken and Sartor 2002).

This leads to an important notion of defeasible argumentation, namely a *defeat* relation between conflicting arguments. Whatever conflict resolution method is appropriate, logically speaking we always end up in one of two situations: either the conflict can or cannot be resolved. In the first case we say that both arguments *defeat* each other and in the latter case we say that the preferred argument defeats the other and not vice versa (or that the first argument *strictly* defeats the other). So 'X strictly defeats Y' means 'X and Y are in conflict and we have sufficient reason to prefer X over Y' while 'X and Y defeat each other' means 'X and Y are in conflict and we have no sufficient reason to prefer one over the other'. It should be noted that this 'binary' nature of the outcome of the comparison does not preclude the use of comparative standards which are a matter of degree: even with such standards it must still be decided whether a certain difference in degree is sufficient to accept one argument and reject the other. (As we will explain below in section 4, this is the key to a proper modelling in our approach of differences in proof standards in different legal contexts.)

To summarize, arguments can at least be constructed with deductive argument schemes, their premises are either ordinary ones or assumptions, and arguments can be attacked by arguments that negate one of their premises. If such an attack is on an assumption, the attacker strictly defeats its target, while if the premise attack is on an ordinary premise, some suitable comparative standard has to be used to see whether one of the arguments strictly defeats the other or whether they both defeat each other.

However, this is not all we can say: it turns out that the binary defeat relation between arguments is not enough to determine which arguments we can accept and which ones we must reject. Suppose that in our example argument C is indeed preferred over argument B on the basis of the *lex specialis* principle. Then we have: B strictly defeats A but C in turn strictly defeats B! Clearly in this case we are justified in accepting A and rejecting B even though B strictly defeats A, since A is 'reinstated' by argument C. However, this is not all: while in this simple case the outcome is intuitive, we can easily imagine more complex examples where our intuitions fail. For instance, another argument D could be constructed such that C and D defeat each other, then an argument E could be constructed that defeats D but is defeated by A, and so on: which arguments can now be accepted and which should be rejected? Here we cannot rely on intuitions but need a *calculus*. Its input will be all the arguments that can be constructed on the basis of a given pool of information, while its output will be an assessment of the *dialectical status* of these arguments in terms of three classes (three and not two since some conflicts cannot be resolved). Intuitively, the *justified* arguments are those that (directly or indirectly) survive all conflicts with their attackers and so can be accepted, the *overruled* arguments are those that are attacked by a justified argument and so must be rejected; and the *defensible* arguments are those that are involved in conflicts that cannot be resolved. Furthermore, a statement is justified if it has a justified argument, it is overruled if all arguments for it are overruled, and it is defensible if it has a defensible argument but no justified arguments. In terms more familiar to lawyers, if a claim is justified, then a rational adjudicator is convinced that the claim is true; if it is overruled, such an adjudicator is convinced that the claim is false; while if it is defensible, they are convinced neither that it is true nor that it is false.

This then is a main component of a logic for defeasible argumentation: a calculus for determining the dialectical status of arguments and their conclusions. What does this calculus look like? Currently there is no single universally accepted one and there is an ongoing debate in AI on what is a good calculus. However, we need not go into the details of this debate, since there is a surprisingly simple and intuitive calculus that suffices for most applications. The idea is to regard an attempt to prove that an argument is justified as a *debate* between a proponent and an opponent of the argument. Since the idea of the game is to test whether, on the basis of a *given* set of statements, a justified argument for a statement of interest can be constructed, both players must construct their arguments on the basis of such a given set of statements. (So unlike in actual legal procedures, the players are not allowed to add new statements to those that are available. See further, section 3.3.) The proponent starts with the argument that he wants to prove justified and then the turn shifts to the opponent, who must provide all its defeating counter-arguments. It does not matter whether they strictly defeat their target or not, since the opponent's task is to interfere with the proponent's attempt to prove his argument justified.

For each of these defeating arguments the proponent must then construct one strict defeater (it has to be a strict defeater since the proponent must prove his argument justified). This process is repeated for as long as it takes: at each of her turns, the opponent constructs mutual and strict defeaters of the proponent's previous arguments, while at each of his turns, the proponent constructs a strict defeater for each of the opponent's previous arguments, and so on. The idea is that our initial argument is justified if the proponent can eventually make the opponent run out of moves in every one of the opponent's lines of attack.

This process can be visualized as follows (the difference in colours will be explained below).

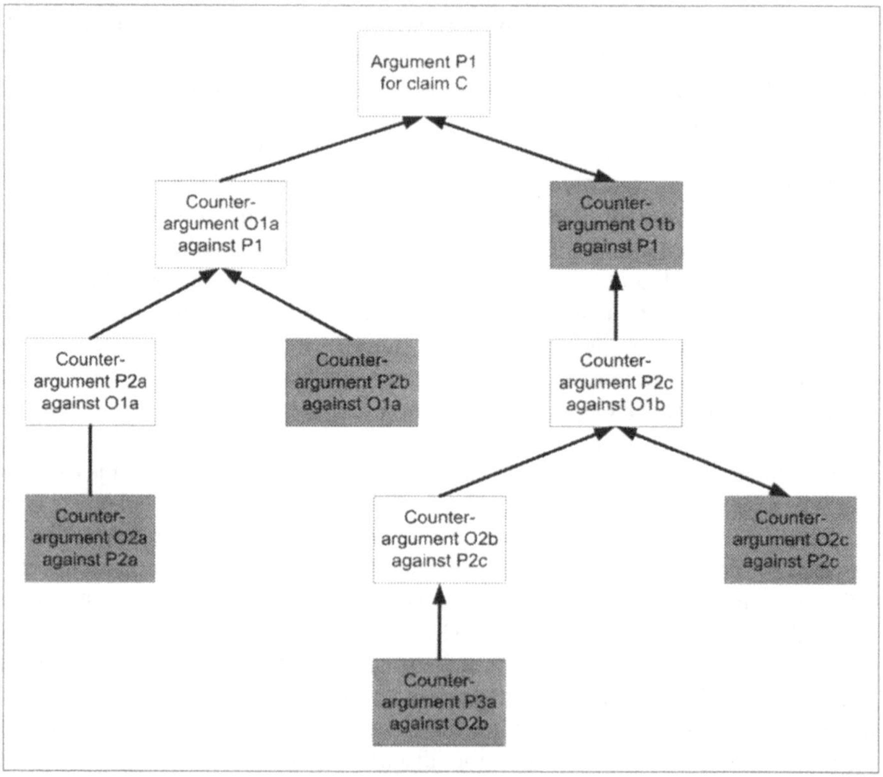

Figure 9.1 A dialectical tree

Note that if an argument is justified this does not mean that the proponent will in fact win the game: he could make the wrong choice at some point. All that it means is that the proponent will win if he plays optimally. In terms of game theory, an argument is justified if the proponent has a winning strategy in a game that starts with the argument. In fact, there is a simple way to verify whether the proponent has a winning strategy. The idea is to label all arguments in the tree as *in* or *out* according to the following definition:

1. An argument is *in* if all its counter-arguments are *out*.
2. An argument is *out* if it has a counter-argument that is *in*.

In the figures *in* is coloured as grey and *out* as white. It is easy to see that because of (1) all leaves of the tree are trivially *in*, since they have no counter-arguments. Then we can work our way upwards to determine the colour of all the other arguments, ultimately arriving at the colour of the initial argument. If it is grey, i.e., *in*, then we know that the proponent has a winning strategy for it, namely by choosing a grey argument at each point where he has to choose. If, on the other hand, the initial argument is white, i.e., *out*, then it is the opponent who has a winning strategy, which can be found in the same way. So in the above figure the opponent has a winning strategy, which she can follow by choosing argument O1b in her first turn.

Suppose now that at the next stage of the dispute the proponent can construct a strictly defeating counter-argument against O2c. Then the situation is as follows:

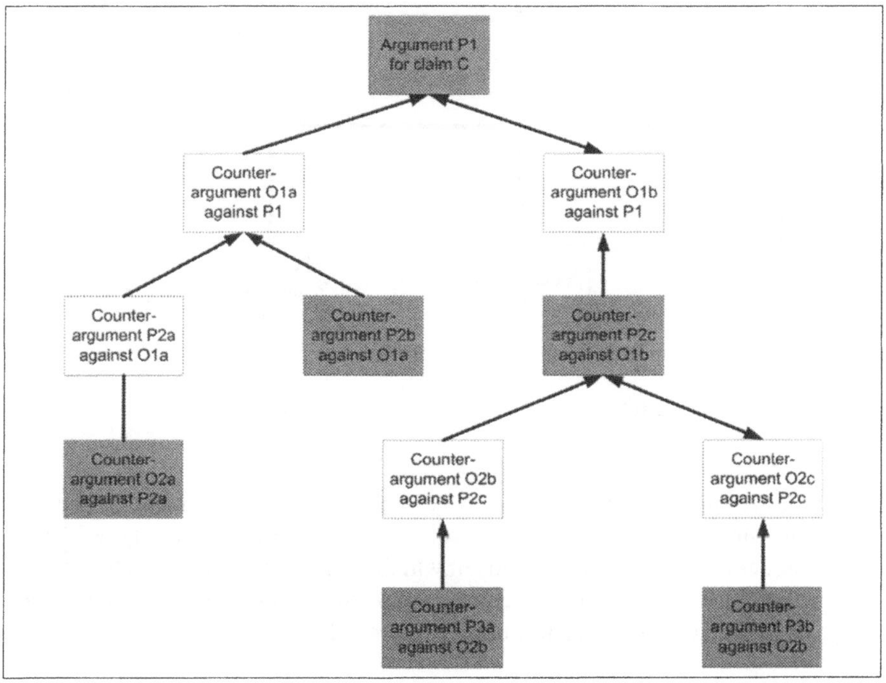

Figure 9.2 An extended dialectical tree

Now argument P1 is *in* on the basis of the new information state so this time it is the proponent who has a winning strategy. He can follow it by choosing P2b instead of P2a when confronted by O1a. This illustrates that when a dispute moves to a new information state, the dialectical status of arguments may change.

Finally, it should be noted that each argument appearing as a box in these trees has an internal structure. In the simplest case it just has a set of premises and a conclusion, but when the argument combines several inferences, it has the structure of an inference tree as is familiar from standard logic. For example, argument B above could be extended with an argument that since the person is a minor, he does not have the capacity to perform legal acts. In tree form, with the conclusion at the top and the premises at the bottom:

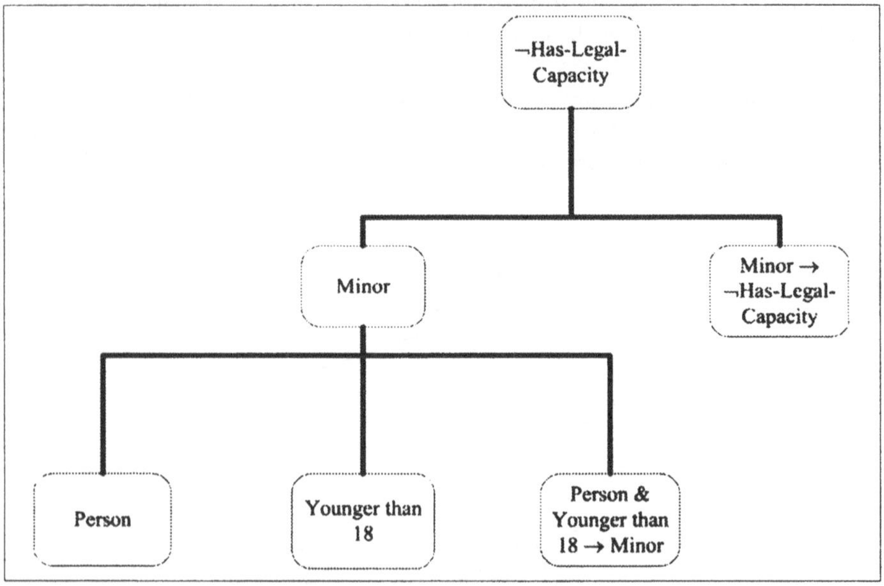

Figure 9.3 An argument

It is important not to confuse these two tree structures. Figure 9.3 displays a single argument: the nodes are statements and the links are inferences. In Figures 9.1 and 9.2 the nodes are complete arguments of which the internal structure is left implicit and the links are defeat relations between arguments. Each node in Figures 9.1 and 9.2 itself implicitly has a tree form as in Figure 9.3.

3.3. Representing Rules and Exceptions

Let us return to the representation of rules and exceptions. The statutory rule used in argument B that persons younger than 18 are minors turned out to have an exception in the case where the person is married. In fact, any statutory rule is subject to exceptions and some of them cannot even be foreseen when drafting the rule. A well-known example is the *Riggs* v. *Palmer* case in American inheritance law (discussed by Dworkin [1977]), in which a grandson had killed his grandfather and then claimed his share of the inheritance. The court made an exception to inheritance law based on the principle that no person shall profit from their own wrongdoing. Moreover, not just statutory rules but also interpretation rules can have exceptions. To use a simplified version of an example of Gardner (1987) on interpretation rules in American contract law, one such rule was 'a statement "I accept" is an acceptance', but an exception was 'a statement "I accept" followed by terms that do not match the terms of the offer is not an acceptance'. Finally, the generalizations often used in evidential reasoning are also subject to exceptions. Consider such generalizations as 'fleeing from the crime scene indicates consciousness of guilt'; an exception would, for example, be that the person may be an illegal immigrant wanting to avoid the police.

Rules that are subject to exceptions are, in AI, often called 'default rules' or in short 'defaults'. Now a convenient way to logically express the default nature of the rules used in legal reasoning is to use general assumptions, which say no more than that there is no exception to the rule. Such general assumptions have their counterpart in legal natural language with expressions such as 'unless there is evidence to the contrary' or 'unless the law provides otherwise'. So, for instance, we could write

R1: Person & ¬Exception-to-R1 → Has-Legal-Capacity
R2: Minor → Exception-to-R1
R3: Declared-insane → Exception-to-R1
R4: ... (and so on)

(Note that we now need to give names to rules, to indicate which rule is to be blocked by an exception.) In the same way, we can give exceptional rules a general assumption, to indicate that they, too, may have exceptions:

R5: Minor & ¬Exception-to-R5 → ¬Has-Legal-Capacity
R6: Married → Exception-to-R5
R7: Representative-consents → Exception-to-R5
R8: ... (and so on)

We could even adopt a further convention to leave the general assumption clauses implicit in the notation, and this is what we will do in the remainder of this chapter.

3.4. Presumptive Argument Schemes

So far we have only considered deductive argument schemes and we have modelled the defeasibility of arguments as the possibility of premise attack, distinguishing two kinds of premises, ordinary ones and assumptions. It has been suggested that this is all we need: if we distinguish ordinary premises and assumptions and adopt a suitable calculus for adjudicating conflicts between arguments, then the only argument schemes we need are those of deductive logic (see e.g. Bayón 2001). However, if we have a closer look at arguments as they are constructed in practice, we see that the assumptions they make often are not just specific statements but conform to certain reasoning patterns. For instance, evidential arguments are often based on stereotypical evidential sources, such as expert or witness testimony, observation or memory. Other evidential arguments apply the scheme of abduction: if we know that A causes B and we observe B, then in the absence of evidence of other possible causes we may presumptively conclude that A is what caused B. Arguments based on such patterns speak about states of affairs in general: unlike specific generalizations like 'summer in Holland is usually cool' or 'fleeing from a crime scene typically indicates consciousness of guilt' they express general ways of inferring conclusions. For these reasons it is natural to regard such patterns not as patterns for premises of an argument but as a new kind of argument scheme, namely, *presumptive*, or *defeasible* argument schemes. (See e.g. Walton (1996) for a general collection of presumptive argument schemes and Prakken (2005) for an overview of schemes for legal reasoning.)

For instance, the scheme for witness statements could be written as follows:

> *Argument scheme from witness testimony:*
> Person W says that P is true
> Person W was in a position to observe P
> Therefore (presumably), P is true

Another common scheme of legal evidential reasoning is that of temporal persistence.

> *Temporal persistence:*
> P holds at time T1
> Time T2 is later than time T1
> Therefore (presumably), P holds at time T2

A backwards variant of this scheme has 'Time *T2* is earlier than time *T1*' as its second premise. Anderson et al. (2005, Chapter 2) discuss an example in which a murder took place in a house at 4.45pm and a man was seen entering the house at 4.30pm and leaving it at 5.00pm. This gives rise to a forward and a backward application of the temporal persistence scheme, both supporting the presumptive conclusion that the man was in the house at the time of the murder. Temporal persistence is also often used for proving the existence of a legal right. For instance, ownership of a good is usually proven by proving that it was bought and delivered; the other party must then prove that later events terminated the right of ownership.

The use of presumptive argument schemes gives rise to two new ways of attacking an argument. This is because even if all premises of a presumptive argument are true, its conclusion may still be false since its premises make its conclusion only plausible. The first new form of attack arises when another scheme with a contradictory conclusion is used. For example, two witnesses may give conflicting testimonies, or a witness testimony may be contradicted by direct observation or an abductive argument. Such a conclusion-to-conclusion attack is usually called a *rebutting* attack. A rebutting counter-argument may attack the final conclusion of its target but it may also attack an intermediate conclusion. For example, argument C above attacks the argument in Figure 9.3 by rebutting its intermediate conclusion 'Minor'.

The second new form of attack is based on the idea that a presumptive argument scheme has typical exceptional circumstances in which it does not apply. For example, a witness testimony is typically criticized on the witness's truthfulness or the functioning of his memory or senses. And an application of the practical syllogism may be criticized by pointing at better ways than *A* to realize the same consequences or at negative consequences brought about by realizing *A*. In general, then, each argument scheme comes with a set of *critical questions* which, when answered negatively, give rise to defeating counter-arguments, called *undercutters*. For example, the witness testimony scheme could be given the following critical questions (based on the work of David Schum; see e.g. Anderson et al. 2005):

> *Critical questions to the argument scheme from witness testimony:*
> CC1: Is the witness truthful?
> CC2: Did the senses of the witness function properly?
> CC3: Does the memory of the witness function properly?

And the main critical question of the temporal persistence scheme is whether there is reason to believe that *P* does not hold at a time *T3* between *T1* and *T2*. Undercutting counter-arguments do not attack a premise or the conclusion of their target but instead deny that the scheme on which it is based can be applied to the case at hand. Obviously, such denial does not make sense for deductive argument schemes, since such schemes *guarantee* that their conclusion is true if their premises are true. In sum then, while deductive arguments can only be attacked on their premises, presumptive arguments can also be attacked on their conclusion and on their inference steps. (We will formalize undercutters as arguments for a conclusion '¬name', where 'name' is a placeholder for the name of the undercut argument scheme.) Note that as with rebutting attack, an undercutting attack can be launched both at the final inference of its target and at an intermediate one.

How many presumptive argument schemes are there? Here the classical logician will be disappointed. One of the main successes of modern formal logic has been that an infinite number of valid deductive inferences can be captured by a finite and even very small number of schemes. However, things are different for defeasible inference: many different classifications of presumptive argument schemes have been proposed, and the debate as to what should count as an argument scheme is still ongoing. Moreover, while some schemes, such as abduction and the practical syllogism, can arguably be used in any domain, other schemes may be domain-dependent. For instance, Anderson (2007) points out that in legal contexts the witness and expert schemes have different critical questions than in ordinary commonsense reasoning. For a detailed discussion of argument schemes relevant for legal evidential reasoning see Bex et al. (2003).

Some readers might wonder whether legal reasoning about evidence is argument-based in the way sketched above at all. In particular, at first sight our approach would not seem to be able to model the ubiquitous phenomenon of accrual, or aggregation of various pieces of evidence pointing in the same direction. For example, if several witness testimonies support the same claim, then the argument scheme from witness testimony gives rise to three different arguments that in no way can be combined, while yet intuitively a party's position seems stronger the more witnesses it can produce who support the same claim. However, in Prakken (2005) it is shown how an argument scheme for argument accrual can be modelled in a logic for defeasible argumentation, and how the resulting formalism can be applied to reasoning about evidence. Because of space limitations, the reader is referred to that publication for the details.

Finally, to return to our question at the beginning of this section, we have seen that there is indeed logic in defeasible argumentation: the form of arguments must fit a recognized argument scheme (of course, still considering the debate on what should be recognized as such), and the dialectical status of an argument can be determined in a systematic dialectical testing procedure. On the other hand, what cannot be provided by such a logic are the standards for comparing conflicting arguments: these are contingent upon input information, just like the information from which arguments can be constructed.

3.5. Embedding of Argumentation in Procedural Settings

The previous subsections assumed that arguments are constructed and their dialectical status is determined on the basis of a given pool of information. However, at least two notions of burden of proof (the burden of production and the tactical burden) assume a dynamic setting in which new information can be introduced at various points in the proceedings. We must therefore explain how our logical account of defeasible argumentation can be embedded in a dynamic procedural setting.

In this chapter we assume that the exchange of arguments in a dispute is regulated by some legal procedure. However, we abstract from the details of such a procedure and simply assume that a dispute consists of a sequence of stages which are characterized by different pools of input information and where the parties (including the adjudicator) can move from one stage to another by formulating new claims and arguments. The information pool of a stage then consists of all claims and the premises of all arguments stated up to that stage. (We also abstract from the fact that many procedures allow the parties to dispute, concede and retract claims and premises.) The outcome of a dispute is determined by applying the calculus for the dialectical status of arguments to the final stage. In fact, when verifying a tactical proof burden we shall also apply the argument game to intermediate stages, to verify what would be the outcome of the dispute if an intermediate stage were the final stage. As for the standards for comparing conflicting arguments, we assume that they are used in the final stage by the adjudicator. This means that if we apply the dialectical calculus to an intermediate stage, we have to guess which standards will be used in the final stage.

In terms of dialectical trees this can be formulated as follows (see also Modgil and Prakken, 2008). At each stage the parties add arguments to the dialectical tree defined above but with one difference: since at intermediate stages the comparative standards are unknown, the parties must move all counter-arguments that they can construct to any argument of the previous turn: at the final stage the adjudicator (after possibly having added her own arguments) applies the comparative standards to the final dialectical tree. In doing so, she may have to prune the tree: if an attacker moved by the proponent does not strictly defeat its target, then the entire sub-tree starting with this argument is pruned from the tree. The same holds for the opponent's arguments that do not defeat their targets. In the resulting pruned dialectical tree some of the opponent's arguments may have more than one strict defeater. It should then be checked whether a unique choice between these strict defeaters can be made in such a way that all branches of the tree end with a move by the proponent: if (and only if) this is possible, the proponent has a winning strategy for his initial argument so that it is justified.

This process is visualized in Figure 9.4.

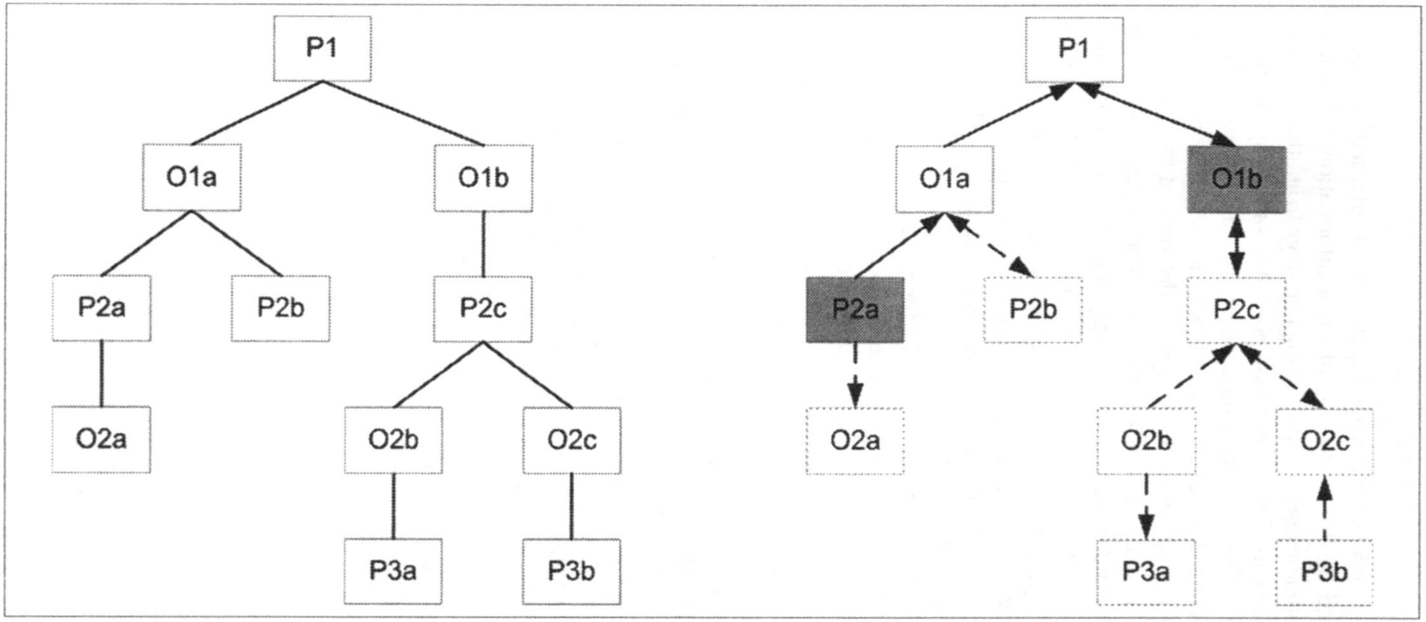

Figure 9.4 Adjudicating conflicts between arguments

In the dialectical tree on the left-hand side the links between arguments have no arrow, to indicate that we only know that they are in conflict with each other. On the right-hand side the adjudicator's decisions are displayed as defeat links. The parts of the tree that have been chopped off are displayed with dashed lines: O2a is chopped off since it is strictly defeated by P2a; then P2b is chopped off since it only weakly defeats O1a, and the entire sub-tree below O1b is chopped off since P2c only weakly defeats O1b. The remaining tree is labelled as above and we find that P1 is not justified.

4. A Logical Account of the Burdens of Proof[2]

We first recall the definitions of section 2. The *burden of persuasion* specifies which party has to prove a statement to a specified degree (the standard of proof) with the penalty of losing in respect of the issue. Whether this burden is met is determined in the final stage of a proceeding, after all the evidence is provided. The *burden of production* specifies which party has to offer evidence on an issue at different points in a proceeding. If the burden of production is not met, the issue will be decided as a matter of law against the burdened party, while if it is met, the issue will be decided in the final stage according to the burden of persuasion. Both these burdens are assigned as a matter of law. By contrast, the *tactical burden of proof* is a matter of tactical evaluation in that a party must assess the risk of ultimately losing in respect of an issue if no further evidence concerning that issue is produced.

How can these notions be analysed against the logical background of section 3? As remarked above, we need two things: a logic of defeasible argumentation and its embedding in a procedure for dispute. We will first formally characterize the three proof burdens and then illustrate them with two legal examples. In the discussion of these examples it will become clear that the procedure given in section 3 for determining the dialectical status of arguments must be refined: in particular since the version in section 3 does not allow for distributions of the burden of persuasion between the sides in a dispute.

4.1. Logical Definition

The *burden of persuasion* for a claim can, in terms of section 3, be defined as the task of making sure that in the final stage of the proceeding there exists a justified argument for the claim. *Proof standards* for the burden of persuasion can be formalized by a careful definition of the defeat relation between arguments, in particular when rebutting counter-arguments are compared: a stronger rebutting argument should strictly defeat a weaker argument only if the degree to which it is

2 The ideas described in this section were earlier expressed in more condensed form in Prakken and Sartor 2006.

stronger satisfies the applicable proof standard; otherwise both arguments defeat each other. For example, if the standard is 'on the balance of probabilities', the fact-finder can already say that A strictly defeats B if A is just a little bit stronger than B, while if the standard is 'beyond reasonable doubt', the fact-finder can say this only if, when faced with only A and B, he would certainly accept A's conclusion. Recall that in section 2 we said that if a burden of persuasion for a statement is fulfilled, a rational fact-finder is (to the required degree) convinced that the statement is true, while if the burden is not met, such a fact-finder is not convinced that the statement is true. Recall also that in section 3 we informally said that if a claim has a justified argument, then a rational adjudicator is convinced that the claim is true, while if it has defensible but no justified arguments they are neither convinced that it is true nor that it is false. We have now seen how the legal notions of section 2 and the logical notions from section 3 are related: having the burden of persuasion for a claim amounts to the task of having a justified argument for it in the final state of the proceeding.

The *burden of production* is harder to define in logical terms. Its logical aspect is that the adjudicator must at the appropriate stage of a proceeding examine whether an evidential argument has been produced for the claim on which the burden of production rests. What goes beyond logic is the demand that this argument must have sufficient internal strength in that 'reasonable minds' can disagree about whether its conclusion would hold if only its premises were known. In section 4.2 we will show how a negative decision on this issue can be expressed as an argument.

Finally, once the burden of persuasion has been assigned by law, the *tactical burden of proof* is automatically induced by the argument game for testing an argument's dialectical status, as applied to any given stage of the proceeding: at a given stage a party has a tactical burden of proof with regard to an issue if the evidence and the arguments thus far provided lead to assessing that issue in a way that goes against that party (and so would likely be concluded by the triers of fact if no new elements were provided to them before the end of the proceedings). In fact, the 'strength' of the tactical burden depends on the allocation of the burden of persuasion: the party who has the burden of persuasion for an initial claim is proponent in the argument game and therefore has to strictly defeat the other parties' arguments, while the other party, being the opponent in the argument game, only has to weakly defeat the proponent's argument. While the dialectical asymmetry of the argument game thus accounts for the fact that for one party the tactical burden is stronger than for the other, its embedding in a dynamic setting accounts for the possibility that the tactical burden shifts between the parties: once a party finds herself in a situation where, according to her assessment, she would likely lose if nothing else is known, this means that the tactical burden has shifted to her.

4.2. A Criminal Case

Consider again our example in section 2 from Dutch law about murder, with a general rule that killing with intent is punishable as being murder, and a separate rule expressing an exception in the case of self-defence. (We now use a double arrow instead of a single one to express that we represent defeasible rules; recall that according to our notational convention each such rule Ri has an implicit assumption ¬Exception-to-Ri.)

R1: Killing and Intent ⇒ Murder
R2: Self-defence ⇒ Exception-to-R1

As said in section 2, the law thus expresses that the prosecution has the burdens of production and persuasion of 'Killing' and 'Intent' while the defence has the burden of production for 'Self-defence' and the prosecution has the burden of persuasion for '¬Self-defence'.

Consider now a murder case and assume that the prosecution can satisfy his burden of persuasion with respect to 'Killing' and 'Intent' with evidential arguments (which we leave implicit for the sake of brevity). Then the tactical burden shifts to the defence, since if she provides no other evidence the adjudicator will likely convict her. The burdens of production then imply that the accused can only escape conviction by providing some minimally credible evidence of an exception to R1, such as that the killing was done in self-defence. For instance, the defence could provide a witness who says that the victim threatened the accused with a knife. (Below we will only list rules and facts; the arguments constructed with them are visualized in Figure 9.5.)

F1: Witness W1 says 'knife'
R3: Knife ⇒ Threat-to-life
R4: Killing and Threat-to-life ⇒ Self-defence

(Note that the argument for 'Self-defence' uses the argument scheme from witness testimony to conclude 'Knife' from fact F1.) Suppose that at this point in trial the judge has to assess whether the defence has satisfied her burden of production with respect to 'Self-defence'. As explained above, this amounts to deciding whether reasonable minds can disagree on whether there was self-defence if only the premises of this argument are known to hold. Let us first assume that the judge rules that this is not the case, so that the defence has not satisfied her burden of production. How can such a ruling be expressed in our logical analysis of section 3? A detailed answer depends on the precise grounds for the ruling but in any case it can be logically expressed as a strictly defeating counter-argument of the defence's argument for self-defence. The proper procedural setting will then disallow counter-arguments to the ruling so that the defence's argument will certainly be overruled in the final stage of the dispute, and the defence loses on the issue of self-defence as a matter of law.

Let us now instead assume that the defence satisfied her burden of production for 'Self-defence'. In Anglo-American systems this means that the issue of self-defence must be addressed by the fact-finder in the final stage of the dispute. Moreover, if the current stage were the final stage, there would be a chance that the defence would win. To avoid the risk of losing, the prosecution should therefore provide additional evidence to take away the reasons for doubt raised by the defence. In other words, the prosecution now at least has a tactical burden to provide evidence against 'Self-defence'. Moreover, the prosecution also has the burden of persuasion against this claim. This is automatically captured by our logical analysis since the prosecution, being the proponent in the argument game, has to strictly defeat the defence's argument for 'Self-defence'.

Let us assume that the prosecution attempts to fulfill his burden of persuasion with a witness who declares that the accused had enough time to run away.

F2: Witness W2 says 'time-to-run-away'
R4: Time-to-run-away $\Rightarrow$ ¬Threat-to-life

Let us also assume that the evidence is of the kind that is usually sufficient to persuade the fact-finder, i.e., it is likely that the fact-finder will say that the argument using R4 for '¬Threat-to-life' strictly defeats the argument using R3 for 'Threat-to-life'. Then the proposition 'murder' is justified again in the new stage of the dispute (again relative to the party's assessment of the likely decisions of the fact-finder). This shifts the tactical burden to the defence to provide counter-evidence that probably makes 'self-defence' at least defensible in the resulting stage. For example, the defence could provide evidence that witness W2 is a friend of the victim, which makes her unreliable.

F3: Witness W2 is-friend-of-victim
R5: Witness W is-friend-of-victim $\Rightarrow$ ¬Witness-Testimony-Scheme

Here Rule R5 expresses an undercutter of the presumptive argument scheme from witness testimony. By undercutting the prosecution's argument for '¬Threat-to-life', the new argument reinstates the defence's argument for 'Threat-to-life' and therefore makes the prosecution's main claim overruled again.

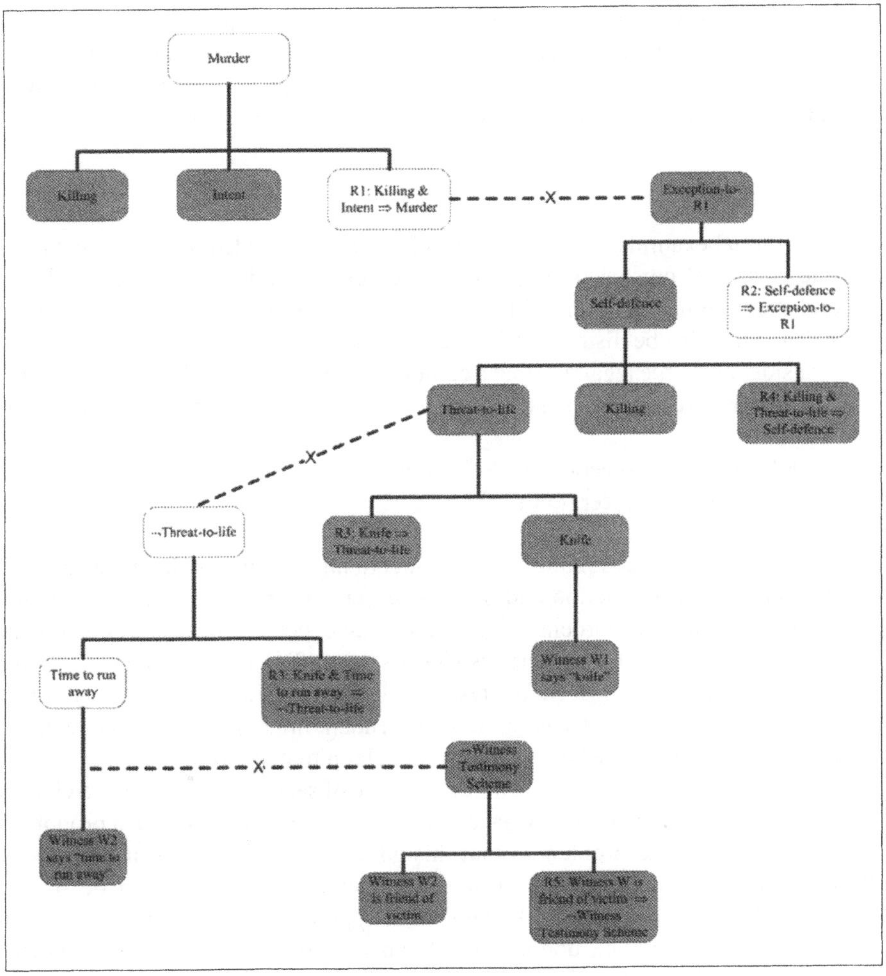

Figure 9.5 The arguments in the criminal case

All arguments constructed so far are visualized in Figure 9.5. The dotted lines with a cross indicate attack relations between arguments. The colouring of the premises and conclusions reflects their dialectical status if all attacks are regarded as successful. A grey statement is justified and a white statement is overruled.

This example has illustrated when and how the three kinds of burden rest on the parties during a dispute. The burdens of production and persuasion are fixed: they cannot shift from one party to the other. The burden of production on an issue is fulfilled as soon as the burdened party provides the required evidence on that issue and after that it is no longer relevant. The burden of persuasion, once created, remains on a party until the end of the discussion of the case, namely, until the point when a party is precluded from giving any further input to the fact-finders. By contrast, the tactical burden on an issue is not fixed; it can shift between the parties any number of times during the discussion of the case, depending on who would probably win on that issue if no more evidence were provided.

4.3. A Civil Case

In our criminal example the burden of production was divided between the parties but the burden of persuasion was on one side only. Is this always the case? Our second example from section 2 illustrates that at least in civil cases the burden of persuasion can also be distributed between the parties.

Consider again the legal rule that a contract is created by an offer and acceptance and a statutory exception in case the offeree was insane when accepting the offer.

R1: Offer and Acceptance ⇒ Contract
R2: Insane ⇒ Exception-to-R1

As we said in section 2, a plaintiff who wants to argue that a contract was created has the burdens of production and persuasion for 'Offer' and 'Acceptance' while the defendant has the burdens of production and persuasion for any statutory exception, in this case, for 'Insane'. So it does not suffice for the defendant to cast doubt in this issue: she must (to the relevant degree) convince the adjudicator that she was insane. In terms of section 3, the defendant must, in the final stage of the proceeding, have a justified argument for the claim that she was insane.

This, however, creates a problem for the logic of section 3. Recall that a claim's dialectical status can be logically tested in an argument game between a proponent and an opponent. The problem is that this game fixes the dialectical asymmetry throughout the game: all of the proponent's counter-arguments must be strictly defeating (i.e., doubt-removing), while the opponent's counter-arguments can be weakly defeating (i.e., doubt-raising). So the opponent's counter-arguments always succeed if they cast doubt. However, our example shows that doubt-raising arguments do not suffice if the opponent has the burden of persuasion: in that case doubt-removing arguments are needed.

To meet this demand, in Prakken (2001) the argument game of section 3 was modified to allow for the two players in a dialogue (plaintiff and defendant) to have different dialectical roles (proponent or opponent) for different propositions. So, for instance, the plaintiff in our example can be the proponent with respect to 'Offer' and 'Acceptance' while he can be the opponent with respect to 'Insane'. Accordingly, the new argument game assumes as input not just a set of arguments ordered by a binary defeat relation but also an allocation of proof burdens for statements to the plaintiff and the defendant, expressing who has the burden of persuasion for each proposition. In fact, an interesting observation can be made here about the relation between logic and law. Usually, an existing logic is simply applied to legal reasoning, but here we have a case where an essential feature of legal reasoning requires a change of an existing logic to make it suitable for modelling that feature.

5. Other Relevant Notions

We now briefly present three additional kinds of burden that are sometimes distinguished, namely, the burden of contesting, the burden of claiming and the burden of argument. In our formal approach they can be accounted for by the embedding of the logic in a procedure for dispute.

A *burden of contesting* exists when a statement unfavourable to a party will be assumed to hold if that party does not contest that proposition. This burden is usually conditional on the fact that the other party has claimed the statement at issue. In other words, not contesting a proposition claimed by the other party implicitly counts as conceding it. For instance, in both Dutch and Italian law of civil procedure, a factual proposition claimed by one party and not contested by the other party must be accepted by the judge even if no evidence for it was provided by the claiming party.

In our formal account this can be modelled by assuming that in the final stage of a proceeding such non-contested statements belong to the available pool of information as a special kind of premise that cannot be attacked by counter-arguments. Thus we have three kinds of premises: ordinary premises, assumptions and 'certain' premises.

The opposite of the burden of contesting is the *burden of claiming*. Such a burden exists for a statement if it cannot be accepted by the fact-finder because it was not claimed by the party for which it is favourable. For instance, in Dutch civil procedure (where this burden is called *stelplicht*) the plaintiff has the burden of claiming (at the first possible stage) all operative facts of his main claim while the defendant has the burden of claiming (at the first possible stage) any exception she wishes to argue for. Note that this is not the same as a burden of production; neither of these burdens entails the other: first, the burden of production, unlike the burden of claiming, implies the burden to give an argument; and second, it is conceivable that a party satisfies a burden of production for an exception by producing evidence for it without explicitly claiming that the exception holds (in our murder case example the judge might be able to infer the possibility of self-defence from the suspect's statements even if he has not explicitly claimed that he acted in self-defence).

In our formal account this burden can be modelled by disregarding, in the final stage of a proceeding, any argument for a conclusion on which a burden of claiming rests if the conclusion was not claimed by the interested party at the required stage of the proceeding.

Finally, the burden of production can be generalized to a *burden of argument*, which, unlike the burden of production, can also apply to non-factual statements. Such a burden exists for a statement if it cannot be accepted by the adjudicator because no argument for it is provided. For example, Dutch civil procedure has such a burden for the plaintiff's main claims and the defendant's main counterclaims, and calls it *substantiëringsplicht*.

In our approach this can be modelled by making sure that statements on which a burden of argument rests cannot be in the pool of information from which arguments are constructed in the final stage of a proceeding. If they are needed to establish some conclusion, they must first themselves be derived as an intermediate conclusion from the available pool of information.

6. Conclusion

In this chapter we have given a logical analysis of several notions concerning the burden of proof. It has turned out that logics for defeasible argumentation, when embedded in a dynamical setting, provide the means to logically characterize the difference between several kinds of proof burdens. Our main contributions have been a precise distinction between two burdens that are sometimes confused, namely the burden of production and the tactical burden, and the insight that the burden of persuasion can be verified by applying an argumentation logic to the body of information available at the final stage of a proceeding.

It remains to be discussed to what extent our analysis applies to other approaches than argument-based ones. As long as any reasoning formalism is used that allows for a fallible notion of proof, much of our analysis still applies. All that is needed is that the formalism accepts as input a description of an evidential problem and produces as output a fallible assessment whether a certain claim has been proven. These assumptions are clearly satisfied by non-monotonic logics that are not argument-based, but the same holds for formalisms such as probability theory or Thagard's connectionist theory of explanatory coherence (Thagard 2004), at least if their output (a posterior probability or a numerical measure of coherence) is combined with a numerical proof standard for proof of the relevant statement. The key is the embedding of such formalisms in a dynamic setting as described in section 3.5, which allows the burden of persuasion to be defined as the burden of making sure that in the final stage of the proceedings the numerical value of the statement exceeds the proof standard. Clearly, such a notion of proof is fallible in that a statement provable in this way may no longer be provable on the basis of extended input information. In consequence, the notion of tactical burden also applies to these formalisms: at each stage in a proceeding a party should assess the likely outcome if that stage were the final stage, and if this outcome is unfavourable to that party, it should introduce new information that changes it.

On the other hand, what cannot be easily modelled in non-logical approaches are the logical relations that sometimes hold between different statements to be proven. See, for instance, our example in section 4.3, where the burdens on the plaintiff to prove offer and acceptance and on the defendant to prove that she was insane were assigned because of the (defeasible) logic governing the legal rules R1 and R2, of which these facts, respectively, are the conditions. So if probabilistic or connectionist methods are used to prove conditions of legal rules, there is still the theoretical issue of combining these methods with the logic governing these rules. This problem does not arise if the evidential part of the reasoning is modelled as argumentation (at least not if the set of argument schemes is sufficiently rich to combine evidential and non-evidential forms of reasoning). The same can be said about the relation with presumptions, since they can have non-statistical justifications. For example, some presumptions are based on considerations of fairness, such as having better access to information. For these reasons it is not immediately clear how they can be modelled in a purely probabilistic or connectionist approach; an argument-based logic, by contrast, can naturally model reasoning with presumptions, since presumptions usually have a rule-like structure, saying that if certain facts are proven, certain other facts may be taken to hold in the absence of counter-evidence (cf. Prakken and Sartor 2006).

Having said this, a full account of the relationship between presumptions and the three kinds of burden of proof is by no means trivial. However, such an account goes beyond the scope of the present chapter and must await another occasion.

Concluding our investigations, we have, of course, not proven that our argument-based account of burdens of proof and presumptions is fully adequate, but at least we hope that we have put a tactical burden of proof on those who want to argue otherwise.

References

Anderson, T. (2007), 'Visualization tools and argument schemes: A question of standpoint', *Law, Probability and Risk* 6, 97–107.

Anderson, T., Schum, D. and Twining, W. (2005), *Analysis of Evidence*, 2nd Edition (Cambridge: Cambridge University Press).

Bayón, J.C. (2001), 'Why is Legal Reasoning Defeasible?', in Soeteman (ed.).

Besnard, Ph., Doutre, S. and Hunter, A. (eds) (2008), *Computational Models of Argument: Proceedings of COMMA 2008* (Amsterdam: IOS Press).

Bex, F.J., Prakken, H., Reed, C. and Walton, D.N. (2003), 'Towards a formal account of reasoning about evidence: Argumentation schemes and generalisations', *Artificial Intelligence and Law* 11, 125–65.

Capper, C. and Cross, R. (1990), *Cross on Evidence* (London: Butterworths).

Denning, A. (1945), 'Presumptions and burdens', *The Law Quarterly Review* 61, 379–83.

Dworkin, R.M. (1977), *Taking Rights Seriously* (Cambridge, MA: Harvard University Press).

Engers, T.M. van (ed.) (2006), *Legal Knowledge and Information Systems. JURIX 2006: The Nineteenth Annual Conference* (Amsterdam: IOS Press).

Gabbay, D. and Guenthner, F. (eds) (2002), *Handbook of Philosophical Logic*, 2nd Edition, vol. 4 (Dordrecht, Boston and London: Kluwer Academic Publishers).
Gardner, A. von der Lieth (1987), *An Artificial Intelligence Approach to Legal Reasoning* (Cambridge, MA: MIT Press).
Hahn, U. and Oaksford, M. (2007), 'The burden of proof and its role in argumentation', *Argumentation* 21, 36–61.
Kakas, A. and Sadri, F. (eds) (2002), *Computational Logic: Logic Programming and Beyond. Essays In Honour of Robert A. Kowalski*, Part II. Lecture Notes in Computer Science 2048 (Berlin: Springer Verlag).
Keane, A. (1994), *The Modern Law of Evidence* (London: Butterworths).
Modgil, S. and Prakken, H. (2008), 'Applying Preferences to Dialogue Graphs', in Besnard et al. (eds).
Prakken, H. (2001), 'Modelling defeasibility in law: Logic or procedure?', *Fundamenta Informaticae* 48, 253–71.
—— (2004), 'Analysing reasoning about evidence with formal models of argumentation', *Law, Probability and Risk* 3:1, 33–50.
—— (2005), 'AI and law, logic and argument schemes', *Argumentation* 19:3, 303–20.
Prakken, H. and Sartor, G. (2002), 'The Role of Logic in Computational Models of Legal Argument: A Critical Survey', in Kakas and Sadri (eds).
Prakken, H. and Sartor, G. (2006), 'Presumptions and Burdens of Proof', in Van Engers (ed.).
Prakken, H. and Sartor, G. (2007), 'Formalising arguments about the burden of persuasion', in *Proceedings of the Eleventh International Conference on Artificial Intelligence and Law* (New York: ACM Press) pp. 97–106.
Prakken, H. and Vreeswijk, G.A.W. (2002), 'Logics for Defeasible Argumentation', in Gabbay and Guenther (eds).
Rescher, N. (1977), Dialectic: A Controversy-Oriented Approach to the Theory of Knowledge (Albany: State University of New York Press).
Rosenberg, L., Schwab, H. and Peter, G. (1993), *Zivilprocessrecht* (Munich: Beck).
Soeteman, A. (ed.) (2001), Pluralism and Law (Dordrecht: Kluwer Academic Publishers).
Spencer, M. and Spencer, J. (2007), *Q and A: Evidence 2007–2008* (Oxford: Oxford University Press).
Strong, J.W. (1992), *McCormick on Evidence*, 4th Edition (St. Paul, MN: West Publishing Company).
Thagard, P. (2004), 'Causal inference in legal decision making: Explanatory coherence vs. Bayesian networks', *Applied Artificial Intelligence* 18, 231–249.
Tonini, P. (2007), 'Onere della prova nel processo penale', in *Enciclopedia Giuridica del Sole 24 Ore* (Milan: Il Sole 24 Ore), pp. 306–12.
Toulmin, S.E. (1958), *The Uses of Argument* (Cambridge: Cambridge University Press).

Walton, D.N. (1996), *Argumentation Schemes for Presumptive Reasoning* (Mahwah, NJ: Erlbaum).

Wigmore, J.H. (1940), *A Treatise on the Anglo-American System of Evidence in Trials at Common Law*, 3rd Edition (Boston, MA: Little, Brown & Company).

—— (1962), *Evidence in Trials at Common Law*, vol. IX (New York: Little, Brown & Company).

Williams, C.R. (2003), 'Burdens and standards in civil litigation', *Sydney Law Review* 25, 165–88.

Zuckerman, A. (2006), *Zuckerman on Civil Procedure* (London: Sweet & Maxwell).

Chapter 10
Twelve Angry Men or One Good Woman? Asymmetric Relations in Evidentiary Reasoning[1]

Burkhard Schafer

1. Introduction and Methodological Preliminaries

Over the past couple of years, analysis of evidentiary reasoning has taken centre stage in the artificial intelligence (AI) and law community, after decades of almost exclusive preoccupation with formalizing and modelling legal interpretation and reasoning with rules.[2] For many reasons, this shift in emphasis is highly welcome. In legal practice, the overwhelming majority of cases that reach the courts are decided on questions of fact. Academic 'highcourtitis', the obsession with a statistically small number of appeal court cases as basis for theories of legal reasoning, distorted the design philosophy of legal expert systems in similar ways as the sometimes distorted picture such renowned sociologists as Max Weber drew of the law. From this perspective, the past preoccupation of legal AI to develop realistic models of legal interpretation was trying to solve an overly complex problem with little practical utility.

What this chapter shares with the above-mentioned approaches is the belief that formal models of legal argumentation can offer us valuable insights into the inner working of the process of adjudication, its strengths and weaknesses. However, in some respects what is outlined here differs in emphasis from existing approaches to computational theories of evidentiary reasoning (henceforth CTE). What they

---

1 Research for this chapter was generously supported by the ESRC grant RES-000-23-0729 'Evidence, its nature and evaluation'. I'm grateful to Colin Aitken, David Lucy, Natalia Bochkina and Dimitrios Mavridis for helpful comments and suggestions on earlier drafts of this chapter. While using the word 'we', the chapter does, of course, not absolve me from responsibility for any mistakes, which are entirely my own, but it accurately reflects the quality and quantity of their input

2 Prakken, Reed and Walton (2003) was arguably the first major contribution to this new field, and defined much of the ensuing research. Walton (2005) gives an up-to-date overview of the field. Other important contributions that together define what we will call the 'mainstream' in modelling reasoning about evidence include Bex and Prakken (2004), Prakken and Sartor (2006), Gordon et al. (2007), Verheij (2007) and Walton (2008).

have in common, despite their considerable differences in detail, is an interest in *rational* theories of legal argumentation. That is, they take as their starting point a general theory of rational deliberation that is justified by insights from logic, argumentation theory or epistemology, and apply them to law. Where legal procedure is at odds with the preferred theory of rational discourse, so much the worse for the law. Put differently, all these approaches are inherently normative, not descriptive, and where law and theory of rational argumentation diverge, it is the law that is in need of reform, not the theory (e.g. Prakken and Sartor 2007, 97).

By contrast, what this chapter wants very tentatively to explore is a *legal* theory of rational argumentation, that is, a theory that takes the rules of legal procedure as a starting point and aims to describe the way in which they function in a legal argument. It employs formal modelling not primarily with the aim of building software tools that eventually may help lawyers to reason more efficiently, but rather as a methodological tool to better understand the precise nature of the rules of evidence and procedure, in particular the rules of criminal procedure.

In particular, we will try to show how formal approaches to evidentiary reasoning allow us to reconsider the role of certain rules of legal procedure. These rules are often cast as inimical to establishing the truth and in conflict with our best theories of rational argumentation. However, we will argue that both the successes and shortcomings of formal models of reasoning with evidence indicate a rather more nuanced picture, where many of these rules turn out to be 'truth enhancing' rather than 'truth hindering', given the unique epistemic constraints under which legal deliberation takes place. This, however, will require the rethinking of some core assumptions about the nature of the trial, and as a consequence also the theoretical framework of modelling trials computationally.

A particularly helpful starting point for our discussion is Kaptein's contribution to this book on the Benthamite distinction between anomic and procedural theories of legal fact-finding (Chapter 8; see also Bentham 1808; Twining 1985). In a nutshell, anomic theories of legal fact-finding are closely aligned to the rationalist tradition, emphasizing truth values and excluding procedural limitations on the attempt to reconstruct a unique historical event through a chain of valid causal reasoning. For Bentham, the central mistake of the laws of procedure was to allow values other than the search for truth to distort proceedings. He rejected, in particular, the idea that procedural technicalities can function as guarantors of liberty (Draper 2004). Liberty, in his view, requires that the guilty and only the guilty are convicted; any procedural constraints of this effort to establish the truth are therefore also detrimental to liberty. At the core of legal fact-finding is the 'rectitude of decision' which requires a pursuit of truth through rational means. This also means that at the core of legal fact-finding is a concept of rationality that is not particular to the law, but rather converges strongly with rational inquiry in the natural sciences. What sets the law apart from scientific discourse is the need to *also* accommodate other 'extrinsic' values, 'subordinate ends' or 'side constraints' (Twining 1990, 185). A typical example used by Bentham that will be relevant later is rules against undue delay. This introduces time constraints on legal adjudication that are alien to scientific discovery. While a scientist can reserve judgement in the light of insufficient evidence, courts need to come to a decision at a given point in time.

Present day evidence scholars in the rationalist tradition, such as Twining and Tillers, also employ this conceptual dichotomy for building their theories. Those laws of evidence that are consistent with universal precepts of rational inquiry are identified as the core of the law of evidence; those that aren't are explained as part of the 'periphery' or side constraints (see, e.g., Tillers 2008). Comparative criminal procedure too is indebted to this approach, with the rationalist core being the reason for convergence between legal systems, and the (often culture-specific) side constraints, a source of divergence (Damaska 2003).

As *rational* theories of legal reasoning, existing approaches to CTE in the field of AI and law can broadly be seen as the newest member in this family of anomic theories of evidence, where procedural restrictions, to the extent that they are represented at all, are modelled as a contingent add-on to the core logic. Indeed, the approaches to CTE cited above can be seen as the formal counterpart of the rationalist tradition of 'new evidence scholarship' (henceforth NES), the formal model of evidence that we would expect if these informal theories were true (see in particular Bex at al. 2003, 128ff). This convergence will later allow us to draw conclusions for a theory of core evidentiary concepts by studying where these computational approaches and legal reality converge, but also where, in our opinion, they diverge.

Most important for our purpose is what we call the 'continuity doctrine' that existing computational approaches and NES share. This continuity doctrine is an inevitable consequence of using, as a yardstick for evidential rules, a universalist notion of rationality rather than developing a sui generis notion of 'legal rationality' (see, in particular, Tillers 2008).

The result is first a continuity between legal and non-legal inquiry into facts. In Twining's words, evidence is best studied as a 'multidisciplinary subject' (Twining 2003), and legal reasoning with evidence shares important features with both natural scientific reasoning with facts (epitomized in the use of science in court) and evidentiary reasoning in the humanities, in particular, in history. With history, it shares its use of evidence to reconstruct unique past events, while the sciences contribute the methodology to evaluate the universal causal laws that back this reconstruction (see, in particular, the contributions in Twining and Hampsher-Monk 2003).

Second, there is also a high degree of continuity in the 'timeline' of a given case, from the initial investigation to the pre-trial and trial stages and ultimately to sentencing and possible appeals. In the field of evidence scholarship, this idea is expressed, for instance, by Tillers and Schum in their analysis of the marshalling processes throughout the life cycle of inferential problems in litigation (1991).

The same continuity thesis seems to inform, if implicitly, much of current research in AI and law. Schafer and Keppens use techniques developed for reasoning about ecological systems and diagnostics in engineering for the analysis of both trial (Keppens and Schafer 2004) and investigation settings (Keppens and Schafer 2006). Bex et al. (2007) propose an approach to model crime investigations that draws on research into scientific methodology (Thagard 2005) and their own previous work on evidentiary reasoning in trials (Bex et al. 2006, with comments on usefulness for the investigative stage) and indeed on reasoning about laws (Verheij 2003).

While we are generally very sympathetic to this approach, there is a concern that using a very specific, law-external model of rationality for the analysis of legal reasoning with evidence may mean relegating prematurely evidentiary concepts to the 'subordinate' or 'extrinsic' category. Rather than studying their logical and epistemic features, they are then explained as supporting values such as fairness and due process, and in doing so juxtapose, in a potentially problematic way, these categories. What is proposed here, then, is an alternative view on the logical structure of reasoning with evidence, an alternative view that could, on the one hand, lead to a rethink of the boundaries between rational core and 'subordinate' values in evidentiary reasoning, and on the other, to a different computational approach that corresponds to this reassessment.[3]

Ultimately, the difference in approach between what is attempted here and the theorists mentioned above will be gradual and nuanced. We do not claim, of course, that every rule or procedure in every legal system makes a contribution to the rationality of the fact-finding process that deserves to be represented as an integral part of a logic of evidentiary reasoning. Rather, we suggest two rebuttable presumptions: the 'presumption of procedural rationality' and the 'presumption of conceptual efficiency'. The presumption of procedural rationality claims that if an evidentiary concept, or a form of procedural argumentation scheme, can be found across several legal systems, then we should prefer, ceteris paribus, that CTE is capable of showing how this rule contributes to rational fact-finding. Similarly, the presumption of conceptual efficiency claims that if we find that across a range of legal systems a conceptual distinction is made, that for instance one type of argument is treated differently from another, we should, ceteris paribus, prefer that CTE also treats the two types of argument differently. In practice, the 'ceteris paribus' clause might have to do quite a lot of work.

Despite this principal difference in approach and objective, what is proposed here is that we can learn important insights for such a legal theory of rational argumentation if we analyse some features of the legal process that existing computational theories do not, or do not quite, capture. Not of course as a criticism of these theories, which, as we argued above, set themselves different tasks from the one undertaken here, but because we believe that we can gain important insights

3 'Computational' is used in this chapter in the recursion-theoretical sense of Boolos et al. (2002), that is, as a meta-logical feature of formal theories. It does not require that a theory is in fact implemented on a computer; instead, it merely rules out certain formal theories, for instance, theories with infinitely long sentences.

when we identify systematic and near universal aspects of legal reasoning that are at odds with well-established theories of rational argumentation.

The chapter is structured around two stories which display very different ideas of what 'reasoning with evidence' in law could mean. Both are taken from popular fiction, not just because of the familiarity this can create for readers from outside the legal field, but because we think that often implicit, but very powerful, cultural assumptions and ideas guide us in our intuition as to which parts of legal discourse are rational and which are not. Popular culture can make these cultural assumptions more explicit than many real life examples.

Both are examples of bona fide rational argumentation with facts in a legal setting. Indeed, both are intentionally devised to promote a specific notion of legal rationality. In the first part, we introduce dialogues from the film *12 Angry Men*. We will argue that these dialogues are convincingly and comprehensively captured by what has become, since 2003, the 'mainstream' of AI approaches to evidentiary reasoning. However, we will also argue that this is at least partly due to the fact that the jury deliberation shares some crucial features with extra-legal reasoning, and that some of the implicit preconditions that enable this type of debate in the jury room are missing in the open trial. Therefore, a one-to-one transition of the model to legal reasoning in trials seems precarious. In the next part, we therefore introduce another story, from Dorothy Sayers' novel *Gaudy Night*. We will argue that the particular features that this story displays are a direct consequence of the lack of certain preconditions of rational argumentation that we identified in *12 Angry Men*. We then discuss what features a CTE would have to have in order to model the reasoning in *Gaudy Night*. In the final part, we compare the two approaches and their underpinning conception of the trial, and indicate how we perceive the relation between the two.

Current research into computational models of evidentiary reasoning has created a whole range of approaches and systems with often significant differences in detail and emphasis. Several of the most prominent writers in this field have in addition adjusted and modified their account over the past decade, quite often considerably. We take as point of departure Walton's work as laid out in Walton (2005), which influenced several other writers in the field and created a certain 'family resemblance', with certain underlying themes and assumptions that they broadly share.

2. The Standard Model: *12 Angry Men*

If current research projects into evidentiary reasoning wanted to adopt a canonical example to illustrate their approach, they could do worse than look at Sidney Lumet's film classic *12 Angry Men*. In this courtroom drama, we see how 11 jurors first convinced of the suspect's guilt are slowly won over to the side of reasonable doubt by Henry Fonda's Juror 8, the only one willing to take the process seriously enough to at least look over the details of the case. What are the main facts?

1. A middle-aged lady asserts that she has seen from her window how the suspect committed the murder.
2. An elderly man states that he heard a quarrel between the victim and the suspect (the victim's son) and also testifies that he saw the accused running down the stairs from the crime scene at the time of the murder.
3. The suspect has bought, on the evening of the murder, an allegedly very rare type of knife. A knife consistent with the description has been used for the murder, and the suspect cannot account for the loss of his knife.
4. The suspect's alibi is weak. He claims to have been in a movie at the time, but cannot remember the name of the film, or the names of the actors.

For 11 of the 12 jurors, these facts are initially enough for them to form a conviction of the guilt of the accused. Juror 8 begs to differ:[4]

> According to the testimony, the boy looks guilty ... maybe he is. I sat there in court for six days listening while the evidence built up. Everybody sounded so positive, you know. I ... I began to get a peculiar feeling about this trial. I mean nothing is that positive. There're a lot of questions I'd have liked to ask.

Fonda's character then proceeds asking just these 'critical questions' that concern him. Some concern the reliability of the evidence. Is it plausible that a visually impaired witness, in the middle of the night and probably without her glasses, was able to identify a person on the other side of the road while a train was passing between them? In a similar vein, he also queries the truthfulness of the witnesses by looking at inconsistencies in their stories: could an elderly man really get from his living room to the stairs in just fifteen seconds? If not, he simply cannot have seen what he claims he saw. Other queries concern the relevance of the evidence. Is the knife really as rare as the prosecution claims? Do the words 'I could kill you' indicate criminal intent, or are they merely a figure of speech?

Juror 8 does not claim that the initial belief of the other jurors is irrational, nor does he claim that his line of reasoning yields an absolute truth. Rather, after having swayed nine more jurors:

> Nine of us now seem to feel that the defendant is innocent, but we're just gambling on probabilities – we may be wrong. We may be trying to let a guilty man go free. I don't know. Nobody really can.

If Fonda's Juror 8 epitomizes how a rational decision *should* be reached, his main adversary, Juror 3, epitomizes the wrong attitude: unshakable resistance to reconsider a position in the light of new arguments and evidence:

---

4 All quotes are from the internet movies database at <http://imdb.com/title/tt0050083/quotes>; see also Asimov 2007.

> Brother, you really are something, you sit here vote guilty like the rest of us, then some golden-voiced preacher starts tearing your poor heart out about some underprivileged kid, just couldn't help becoming a murderer, and you change your vote.

The above quotes introduce three crucial elements frequently found in CTEs.

Interpretation and evaluation of evidence is a *process* that extends over time (Walton 2005, Chapter 3; Verheij 2007). During that process, people will draw conclusions on the basis of the facts as presented at a specific time, but they should be willing to *revise* this conclusion in the light of new evidence. All knowledge is ultimately defeasible and only temporarily accepted (Prakken 2001; Walton 2002, Chapter 5). A particularly good way to revise wrong inferences is through a *dialogical* process (Bex and Prakken 2004), in particular a 'persuasion dialogue' (Walton 2002, 165ff; Prakken et al. 2005; Gordon et al. 2007) where two combatants try to convince each other by asking 'critical questions' that can undercut the prima facie assumptions proposed by the opposing player. In CTEs this is normally modelled by using a non-monotonic, defeasible logic, often with a game theoretical or otherwise dialogue-based semantic. Critical questions can be represented as a series of domain-specific argumentation schemes (Walton 2005).

Let us look at one example from the film that introduces some more specific expressions of this basic idea.

> Juror 8: Look, there was one alleged eye witness to this killing. Someone else claims he heard the killing, saw the boy run out afterwards and there was a lot of circumstantial evidence. But, actually, those two witnesses were the entire case for the prosecution. Supposing they're wrong?
>
> Juror 12: What do you mean, supposing they're wrong? What's the point of having witnesses at all?
>
> Juror 8: Could they be wrong?
>
> Juror 12: What are you trying to say? Those people sat on the stand under oath.
>
> Juror 8: They're only people. People make mistakes. Could they be wrong?
>
> … I'm also guessing that she probably didn't put her glasses on when she turned to look casually out of the window. And she, herself, testified the killing took place just as she looked out. The lights went off a split second later – she couldn't have had time to put them on then. Here's another guess: maybe she honestly thought she saw the boy kill his father – I say she only saw a blur.

One way to analyse this fragment of the discussion so that it displays some of its logical features more prominently would be like this. Juror 12 asserts that he believes the defendant is guilty and cites as warrant for this assumption the witness statement. Juror 8 challenges this, initially by questioning whether just one witness statement is a sufficient warrant for such a conclusion. The response by Juror 12 is two-pronged. First, he asserts that inferences from witness statements to truth are generally valid: 'What [would otherwise be] the point of having witnesses at all?' In doing so, he could be seen as claiming that his arguments instantiate a valid argument scheme, the argument from a 'position to know' (Walton 2002, 45). Second, he gives an additional reason why we can believe in the truthfulness of the statement – the witness was under oath. With that, he has done everything that can be expected of him and more: he has justified his inference by a warrant, has shown that it is the right type of warrant that instantiates a valid argumentation scheme, and has in addition given reasons why the warrant 'witnesses normally tell the truth' is likely to be valid. At this point, we should provisionally accept the guilt of the accused. With that, the onus is on Juror 8 to show why, exceptionally, the inference may be unsound. He is doing this by making a distinction first: witnesses can be mistaken or lying. The oath only ensures (if that) that the witness believes what she says, but does not protect from honest mistakes. He then offers reasons why this specific juror is unreliable: she normally wears glasses, but probably did not when she observed the crime. It was dark, the scene was far away and her view was interrupted. All three statements attack the default inference from a witness statement to the facts that the witness states. If considered valid, then Juror 12 is now no longer able to draw the inference, unless again he has additional reasons why the defeaters of Juror 8 are in this case inapplicable.

Existing approaches to CTE, despite differences in detail, are tailor-made for this type of exchange.

In the film, different jurors change their opinion at different stages of the debate. Some switch to a not guilty verdict after only one prosecution argument was successfully attacked; others hold out longer. What they all, apart from Juror 3, accept, however, is that their overall conviction in the guilt of the accused can be broken down into beliefs in individual arguments. Similarly, the formal models of evidentiary argumentation that we have been discussing so far also take as the 'unit of critical assessment' the individual pieces of evidence, 'evidence atoms', so to speak. This means that the assessment of the credibility of the eyewitness is in principle independent from the question of the evidentiary value of the knife found in the possession of the accused. 'Evidence atomism', the idea that individual pieces or 'atoms' of evidence can be evaluated in isolation, is therefore the third common theme in computational approaches to evidence. This does not mean of course that these approaches assume by logical fiat that individual pieces of evidence are independent, or that theory evaluation can be reduced to a simple addition. Rather, the claim here is only that the strength of the overall case is directly dependent on the strength of its sub-parts or atoms, and not an emergent property on the level of the theory itself. But the relation between atoms and theory can of course be quite complex and may need to account for the possibility of 'double counting' and other forms of interdependency.

In addition, we find other examples of reasoning in *12 Angry Men* that several CTEs have also identified as crucial aspects of the logic of proof, even though they are maybe not quite as commonly used as dialogue semantics and defeasible logic.

In the eyewitnesses example so far, it is unclear which one of the disputants actually won the dialogue. True, Juror 8 prevented the inference proving the suspect's guilt. But he has not presented any independent arguments for the defendant. As it is, the only inference we can draw is that we can draw no inference. One of the unique features of legal debate, and its most important contribution to a general theory of rational argumentation, is, of course, the notion of burden of proof. The failure of the witness inference therefore also entails the 'innocence' of the accused, in the procedural sense that a person is presumed innocent until proven guilty.

While this would be the outcome prescribed by law, the jurors in the film are sufficiently confused about the concept that it too becomes the subject of a 'meta-level' debate between them:

> Juror 2: It's hard to put into words. I just think he's guilty. I thought it was obvious from the word, 'Go'. Nobody proved otherwise.
>
> Juror 8: Nobody has to prove otherwise. The burden of proof is on the prosecution. The defendant doesn't even have to open his mouth. That's in the Constitution.
>
> ... We may be trying to let a guilty man go free, I don't know. Nobody really can. But we have a reasonable doubt, and that's something that's very valuable in our system. No jury can declare a man guilty unless it's SURE. We nine can't understand how you three are still so sure. Maybe you can tell us.

By contrast, Juror 3, unsurprisingly, thinks differently:

> Everything ... every single thing that took place in that courtroom, but I mean everything ... says he's guilty. What d'ya think? I'm an idiot or somethin'? Why don't cha take that stuff about the old man; the old man who lived there and heard every thing? ... The old man SAW him. Right there on the stairs. What's the difference how many seconds it was? ... you can't PROVE he didn't get to the door! Sure, you can take all the time hobblin' around the room, but you can't PROVE it!

If we are charitable to Juror 3, then what he is talking about is not the legal burden of proof, but the 'tactical' burden: Yes, the legal burden of proof is with the prosecution and stays there, but psychologically, there can come the time in a case where the prosecution has given sufficient reasons to convict the accused so that unless he is able to provide some arguments of his own, he will be convicted (see Prakken and Sartor (2007) on how this legal notion has been received by AI and law research). What Juror 3 is saying could be understood as: 'The statement of the witness is a good prima facie reason to infer the guilt of the accused. The tactical burden of proof is now with him; he would lose the argument if it were put to a neutral arbiter now. Mere speculation as to the unreliability of witnesses in general is not sufficient to satisfy this burden. Unless he can prove that the old man did not see him running down the stairs, I'm entitled to believe the witness.'

Prakken and Sartor (2007) in particular have shown how to model all three features of the concept of burden of proof that these quotes express: from the basic idea that the side which has the burden of proof will lose an argument if all its claims have been rebutted to the more sophisticated distinction between legal and tactical burden and finally to the idea that the issue of burden of proof can itself become the subject of legal debate. Burden of proof in general is arguably the one genuinely legal concept that has been widely studied and convincingly modelled in rational, computational theories of evidentiary reasoning.

Finally, two specific strategies employed by Juror 8 to undermine the arguments of the prosecution deserve attention.

> Juror 10: I don't understand you people! I mean all these picky little points you keep bringing up. They don't mean nothing. You saw this kid just like I did. You're not gonna tell me you believe that phony story about losing the knife, and that business about being at the movies. Look, you know how these people lie! It's born in them! I mean what the heck? I don't have to tell you. They don't know what the truth is! And lemme tell you, they don't need any real big reason to kill someone, either! No sir!
>
> Juror 8: I'd like to ask you something: you don't believe the boy's story; how come you believe the woman's? She's one of 'them', too, isn't she?
>
> Juror 10: You're a pretty smart fella, aren't you?

From this quote, we can learn two important things. The first is the importance of consistency. Juror 8 wins this argument by showing that Juror 10 accepts as valid in one context an undercutter that he rejects in another. Consistency is a constraint on acceptable arguments that is one of the most obvious for a computational theory to model.

The second is a recurring theme of the film, the dangerous power of stereotypes, stock stories and popular narratives. On the one hand, they are inevitable, and Juror 8 employs them himself when speculating about whether or not the female witness was wearing her glasses when seeing the crime:

> Juror 8: [*to Juror 4*] Do you wear glasses when you go to bed?
>
> Juror 4: No. I don't. No one wears eyeglasses to bed.

> Juror 8: It's logical to assume that she wasn't wearing them when she was in bed. Tossing and turning, trying to fall asleep.
>
> Juror 3: How do you know?
>
> Juror 8: I don't know – I'm guessing! I'm also guessing that she probably didn't put her glasses on when she turned to look casually out of the window. And she, herself, testified the killing took place just as she looked out.

Strictly speaking, this is just a 'story' based on generalizations. 'People' just don't have their glasses on at night. 'They' toss and turn trying to fall asleep and when they then go to the window they don't put their glasses on. This is what 'we' all know – even though, of course, she may have fallen asleep while reading, with her glasses still on. However, this use of narrative seems reasonable and rational, in contrast with the blatantly racist stereotyping of Juror 10. To him, Juror 8 rightly remarks:

> It's always difficult to keep personal prejudice out of a thing like this. And wherever you run into it, prejudice always obscures the truth.

Storytelling approaches to evidentiary reasoning have been modelled in the 'anchored narrative approach'. 'People do not wear glasses when sleeping' and 'Hispanics lie' would both be modelled as 'anchors' in this approach. More recently, the connection between theories and the storytelling/anchored narrative approach has become a focus of research within this approach (see also Chapters 4 and 7, and Verheij 2000).

Finally, the jurors also use a combination of abductive reasoning and hypothesis testing that is popular in CTEs (Walton 2005, 159). According to the statement of the elderly witness, he first heard the dispute between father and son through the wall, and then saw the boy run down the stairs. Juror 8 points out a problem with this:

> I'd like to find out if an old man who drags one foot when he walks, cause he had a stroke last year, could get from his bedroom to his front door in fifteen seconds.

In other words, if the witness's story is true, something else has to be true too: it must have been possible for him to get from bedroom to stairs in 15 seconds. This implication of his story is in principle open to empirical testing, and within the severe limits of the courtroom, this is what the jurors try, by finding out just how far one of them can get in that time. Once they decided that their findings were inconsistent with the prosecution story, they are looking for an alternative explanation for the evidence in an abductive process of reasoning:

> Juror 3: Why should he lie? What's he got to gain?
>
> Juror 9: Attention, maybe.

The desire to get attention is here used by Juror 9 as an alternative explanation of one piece of evidence, the eyewitness statement. Juror 8 offers a third alternative:

> Here's what I think happened: the old man heard the fight between the boy and his father a few hours earlier. Then, when he's lying in his bed he heard a body hit the floor in the boy's apartment, heard the woman scream from across the street, got to his front door as fast as he could, heard somebody racing down the stairs and assumed it was the boy.

An alternative story is offered that accounts for all the evidence, and is immune from the inconsistencies of the prosecution narrative.

To recap: in the film, we could identify patterns of reasoning that have been successfully tackled by existing CTEs, and the main structure of the plot shares features that are found in all or many of these approaches:

- Evidentiary reasoning is a process of belief revision over time.
- Inferences at any given time are defeasible and open to revision.
- Subject to this revision are individual inferences, based on individual pieces of evidence (atomism).
- It is typically in the form of a persuasion dialogue.
- Elements of this dialogue involve:
    - critical questions
    - consistency checks
    - abductive reasoning
    - hypothesis formation and testing.
- The law allocates different burdens of proof to the parties.
- In addition, the tactical burden of proof can shift over the duration of an argument.

So far, what we have indicated is a success story for CTEs. So why our initial concern? The question is whether this is a *generic* model for legal reasoning. The jury deliberates 'in the shadow of the law', this is certain, and as we have seen, some legal concepts such as the burden of proof feature in their deliberations. Apart from that, however, they are no different from any group of citizens who debate a past event. With one important exception that we will discuss below, their discussion could as well have been between people who learnt of the trial in the newspapers. This raises the question of whether concepts that work well in such a setting are equally appropriate for the modelling of evidentiary reasoning by lawyers in open court. In the next section, we will argue that this transfer is problematic, arguing the case for 'legal exceptionalism': rational models of argumentation that work well in scenarios such as the jury room rely on preconditions that are not present in the trial setting.

3. An Alternative Approach: One Good Woman

In Dorothy Sayer's novel *Gaudy Night*, crime author Harriet Vane revisits her old Oxford College for a student reunion. Just acquitted as a suspect in the murder trial of her former lover, and continuously stalked by the memory of the events and of her rescuer, Lord Peter, it is inevitable that former tutors and fellow students interrogate her about her experience (Sayers 2003, 36–9):

> 'I'm not sure,' said Harriet, 'but you know, it was just as well for me that he did make a hobby of it. The police were wrong in my case – I don't blame them, but they were – so I'm glad it wasn't left to them.'
>
> 'I call that a perfectly noble speech,' said the Dean. 'If anyone had accused me of doing something I hadn't done, I should be foaming at the mouth.'
>
> 'But it is my job to weigh evidence,' said Harriet. 'And I can't help seeing the strength of the police case. It's a matter of a + b, you know. Only there happened to be an unknown factor.'
>
> …
>
> 'Surely,' said Miss de Vine, 'whatever comes of it, and whatever anybody feels about it, the important thing is to get at the facts.'
>
> 'Yes,' said Harriet, 'that's the point. I mean, the fact is that I didn't do the murder, so my feelings are quite irrelevant … The particular trouble I got let in for was as much accident as falling off the roof.'

This discussion shows the crucial difference between the debates between different jurors in the jury room, and the debate between prosecution and defence during open trial. The relation between the jurors is symmetrical: they have all heard the same facts, they are equally ignorant about what really happened, and they all have at their disposal the same methods for scrutinizing the evidence. In the trial context, however, one of the disputants has privileged access to the truth. Apart from highly unusual situations such as sleepwalking or serious mental illness,[5] the

5 These apparent exceptions can be explained as 'deviant' forms of legal procedure: the ultimate purpose of the criminal trial is to attribute responsibility. In situations where the accused honestly did not know what he was doing, this purpose cannot be achieved; the criminal courts are not the right forum for this type of event. However, law is also self-

defendant will know whether or not he committed the actions in question (though, of course, not necessarily their precise legal significance). No argument by the prosecution, regardless how convincing, will persuade him otherwise. Indeed, we would consider it deeply irrational if they did. The converse is, of course, not true: the defendant may well convince the prosecution of his innocence, though as we will see, this is rare for other reasons. Persuasion dialogues between defence and prosecution that assume a symmetrical relation between them cannot capture this asymmetrical access to information.

But as Harriet points out, her personal knowledge of her innocence is also irrelevant, a matter for personal feelings and not the rational assessment of the evidence. She may know the truth, but the trier of fact has good reasons to doubt her assertions. Set up as the epitome of scientific rationality by Sayers, Harriet is able to acknowledge that the proof by the prosecution could not be faulted. This obviously requires a considerable amount of detachment.

While the accused has privileged access to the *truth*, knows what has really happened but may not be able to prove it, the prosecution has privileged access to *the means of proof*. They have command over the resources of the police and, typically, the state-run forensic laboratories. More important, though, than this imbalance in resources are legal and 'temporal' asymmetries between defence on the one hand and prosecution and investigative authorities on the other. With legal asymmetry, we mean that regularly only the state will have the right to collect certain types of proof, for instance by compelling witnesses or searching dwellings. Most important for the purpose of the argument that we are developing here are, however, what we call 'temporal' asymmetries. They are best explained by an example. In the investigation of the murder of Jill Dando, a famous UK TV presenter, a crucial piece of evidence was a minute speck of gunpowder residue.[6] This was collected by the police and analysed by forensic experts. Because of the small size of the sample, the very process of testing destroyed it. This meant that the tests could not possibly be repeated. You only have one go at a crime scene, and often also only one go at the evidence collected there. Because prosecution/police and defendant are involved at different times in the process, they have, of necessity, different epistemic access to the facts.

While rules of procedure can minimize the impact of this, for instance, through requirements to document investigative actions taken, and by threatening sanctions for misbehaviour by the investigator or prosecution, it is inevitable that ultimately an element of trust is required. Once again, this necessary assumption of trust is

reflexive, that is, sometimes we use legal procedure to determine whether or not an issue is a legal question appropriate for the courts in the first place. In these cases, the question shifts away from a debate over the facts to a procedural meta-debate over the correct forum, medical or legal.

6 For more background see <http://news.bbc.co.uk/1/hi/programmes/panorama/7067290.stm>.

asymmetrical: in a criminal trial, we *need* to have greater trust in the assertions of the side that has the *less* reliable, merely indirect, access to the truth.

We can now formulate our 'trial exceptionalism' theory more precisely. For rational theories of legal debate, this asymmetrical access to information is problematic. From the outset trials seem to violate the most basic preconditions of modern scientific rationality. Premodern 'science' was characterized by asymmetric access to the truth. Certain authorities (the Church, Aristotle, the Bible) were deemed to have privileged access to the truth, so appeal to authority therefore was a legitimate argumentation scheme. Modern science, and its philosophical counterparts of enlightenment and empiricism, replaced this asymmetrical, inegalitarian model with a symmetrical, egalitarian model of truth finding: through our senses, we all have equal access to the one shared reality. From this it follows that every idea has to be subjected to the public forum of reason where everybody can be a participant, and everybody has, in principle, equal ability to establish the truth. Since the participants in this scientific discourse are freely interchangeable (i.e. it does not matter who makes an observation) intersubjective agreement over the facts is therefore both possible and desirable at least as a limiting ideal for rational deliberation. Honest disagreement is simply indicative that not all possible observations and tests have yet been carried out. Scientific rationality is premised on an open-ended process of criticism and confirmation; it does not matter who proposes a theory: if it cannot be replicated by everybody else, at least in principle, its truth claim is invalid.

In a trial situation, however, as we have seen, these preconditions are not met, appeal to the authority of the expert and trust in the system is inevitable, and intersubjective agreement that includes the defendant is not always a possibility even in principle. This presents a small paradox: modern trials rely more and more on scientific evidence but the way scientific evidence is presented in court of necessity violates some of the conditions that are normally presupposed in scientific inquiry. It is presented by an expert whose assertions can to some extent be scrutinized, but not replicated or tested by the audience.

This means that reasoning about facts in a criminal trial is different from other modes of rationality, due to the unequal distribution of knowledge and means of proof. An important function of the rules of procedure is to mitigate this inevitable tension between the modern ideal of rational inquiry and the constraints of the trial situation.

We can now see how (some of) the rules of criminal procedure aim towards 'rational decision-making in a hostile environment'. As we have seen, agreement over the facts may be impossible in principle in some situations (due to asymmetric access to the facts and means of proof). But as Harriet Vane's example shows, rational agreement over what has been *legally proven* is always possible in principle. If we therefore understand evidentiary reasoning to be not about the facts at all, but about what has been proven, we are closer to a situation where the preconditions of rational inquiry apply and intersubjective agreement becomes possible. The price to be paid is a proof predicate with an 'odd', legal procedural feature: for Harriet Vane, or any other accused, the following statement can be consistently asserted:

> I know the accused (i.e. I) is innocent, and it has been proven beyond reasonable doubt that she is guilty.

No other stakeholder in the process can consistently assert this statement – indeed, in most legal systems it would be considered in conflict with the duties of the prosecutor as officer of the court if he truthfully asserted it.[7]

We notice that, as a result, the statement is in a way the mirror image of Moore's paradox, the statement that 'p is true and Burkhard does not believe that p is true'. This statement will be true for many facts p and can be asserted by any speaker but me. If I, however, utter the statement, I commit a self-contradiction. Discussions of Moore's paradox in the literature often analyse the statement in an epistemological context and assume that implicitly, 'p is true' is only asserted when there are good reasons to believe that p is true. This reading brings Moore's paradox even closer to our 'Sayers' paradox'.

The converse formulation of the sentence, however, does not display these paradoxical features. 'The accused is guilty and has been legally proven to be innocent' can be uttered without self-contradiction by all the stakeholders in a trial. The reason for this is, of course, that the first part of the assertion refers to 'knowledge gained by any means' whereas the second part refers to 'knowledge established through legally admissible ways and observing the allocation of the burden of proof'. Procedural norms therefore ensure that as far as disproving the guilt of the accused is concerned, prosecution and defence are in this respect back in a symmetrical position.

This lays the groundwork for revisiting the asymmetric assignment of the burden of proof in criminal trials. While having explicit rules on the burden of proof is a feature unique to legal trials, they turn out not to be contingent procedural requirements in pursuit of some extra-scientific notion of justice. Rather, they are the logical consequence of the way in which the cards are dealt at the onset of the trial. As a general rule, the burden of proof will rest with the party that is in the best position to prove an issue in question. For most facts directly pertinent to the alleged acts in question, it will be the prosecution who has command over the greater 'proof resources' (police, laboratories and so on). However, for certain issues, the defendant is the only one who can have initially the relevant information at his disposal. Consequently, we find that while the legal burden of proof rests generally with the prosecution, defences such as self-defence or mental illness typically impose a 'burden of production' on the defendant (for a comparative approach see, e.g., Ogloff 1991). The more difficulties the prosecution has to establish the relevant facts, the more the defendant will be burdened with

7 In his situation, the prosecutor would have positive knowledge of the fact that the accused is innocent, and nonetheless go for a conviction on the basis of his evidence.

producing them – less in self-defence cases where there are external facts that the prosecution can pursue, but more in respect of mental illness issues which are almost totally within the sphere of the defendant (see, in particular, Williams 1977, 127; see also Clermont and Sherwin 2002).

While our focus so far has been on rules about the burden of proof only, we would claim that these are not an isolated phenomenon. Rather, they are but examples of a whole group of procedural norms that all try to transform an initial problematic asymmetrical distribution of epistemological positions into a symmetrical situation that more closely resembles the situation at the onset of a scientific inquiry.

Pre-trial disclosure rules are another expression of the same attempt by the law to address the unequal initial access to information, by imposing duties on the parties to make their respective information accessible to the other side. This is particularly relevant with respect to one other feature of several CTEs, the 'critical' or falsificationist ethos that they sometimes put at the centre of their model (see, in particular, Keppens and Schafer 2006; see also Bex et al. 2006). We described this above as 'hypothesis testing and falsification'. It requires the hypothesizing of what other facts have to be true if the theory under investigation were true. However, unequal access to means of proof and the time limits imposed on a trial mean that the defence will often not be able to subject claims by the prosecution to this particular type of scrutiny, as it requires the introduction of new facts. In *12 Angry Men*, to permit this type of hypothesis testing and to achieve the associated dramatic effect, the producers had to play fast and loose with the rules of criminal procedure. Juror 8 tests the prosecution hypothesis that knives such as that owned by the defendant are rare. If it were true, he, as a good citizen without contact with the criminal underworld, should find it difficult to acquire one. But he succeeds in buying one without any problem, thus falsifying the prosecution claim. However, procedurally introducing this new fact into the jury deliberation, without the ability for the prosecution to cross-examine, would have been impermissible. The role, at least of the modern day jury, is to act as the neutral arbiter of the facts presented by the parties, not as independent investigators. As the court argued in *Krause* v. *State*: 'It may be stated that the record discloses he [the juror] apparently thought he was the county attorney and assumed the role of prosecutor'.[8] Following Bentham again, Twining characterizes this constraint as the principle that 'adjudicative decisions should be based on the issues, the evidence and the arguments presented in open court, rather than … on knowledge of particular matters relating to the case obtained outside the courtroom' (Twining 1990, 184).

While procedurally unproblematic, defence lawyers in open court will frequently struggle to use this type of argument for more practical reasons. It makes considerable demands on investigative resources. As a result, cross-examination will mainly focus on internal inconsistencies to undermine a prosecution claim more than inconsistency with new facts established by the defence.

8 *Krause* v. *State*, 75 Okla. Crim. 381, 386, 132 P.2d 179, 182 (1942).

Pre-trial disclosure rules are the set of rules that address in particular this issue (see Corker 1996; Plotnikoff and Woolfson 2001; Taylor 2001). They impose a burden on the parties to inform the other side in advance of some of the evidence they are going to submit. As a result, these rules make possible the critical theory revision that features prominently in several CTEs. Despite this, they have so far not received any attention by the researchers in the field. In the analysis proposed here, pre-trial disclosure rules are the mirror image of rules on burden of proof allocation. Asymmetric allocation of the burden of proof mitigates the 'synchronic' epistemic asymmetry discussed above. Pre-trial disclosure rules address the 'diachronic' asymmetry, the fact that different agencies have at different times access to the evidence. As is to be expected, pre-trial disclosure rules also tend to be asymmetric, typically imposing a higher burden on the prosecution. Indeed, only recently was a corresponding duty for the defence recognized in many common law countries (Duff 2007). Even now, though, only the prosecution, and not the defence, will have to disclose evidence that can be used directly as an 'undercutter' or 'falsifier': the prosecution has to inform the defence that their investigation has discovered a witness providing an alibi; the defence, by contrast, is regularly prohibited from informing the prosecution if their investigation has discovered an incriminating witness. Burden of proof rules and pre-trial disclosure duties often interact. In those cases where, exceptionally, the defence has an initial burden of production (for instance in the UK in alibi defences) it will also have a pre-trial disclosure duty. This too indicates that a formal account of the burden of proof rules should also incorporate pre-trial disclosure rules. Some of the functions of these rules have a direct computational equivalent: they enforce 'closed world assumptions'. Evidence that was not disclosed, despite a duty to do so, may not be used later in court, and 'does not exist' for the purpose of the trial. The Benthamite principle of publicity of the trial mentioned above plays a similar role: evidence not explicitly introduced has to be discounted. Since these rules are binding, they achieve one of the aims of the trial; a stable conclusion within limited time that is no longer open to revision. We will use this feature below to argue for a more limited scope of defeasibility than current CTEs assume.

One final element for our theory is still missing. Let us return briefly to the case of Harriet Vane. In the above quote, she concedes that the case of the prosecution against her was compelling. She cannot find fault with the arguments offered by the prosecution; rather, additional facts were crucial for her eventual acquittal.

What were the facts of the case as recounted in Sayers' novel *Strong Poison*? The victim is a certain Philip Boyes, erstwhile lover of the accused. Having first persuaded Harriet against her better self that marriage is a bourgeois aberration, he later proposed to her. She, feeling deceived and treated as a 'wife on probation', breaks off the relationship after a public and acrimonious confrontation. Boyes then dies after repeated episodes of illness. Arsenic poisoning is then established as the cause of death. The prosecution can prove that Harriet had bought arsenic secretly under assumed names. The purchases coincided with Boyes' attacks of illness.

He last saw her on the afternoon of his death. Motive, means and opportunity are sufficient for the majority of the jurors.

How would the computational dialogue systems mentioned above analyse the situation? The prosecution has the initial burden of production of evidence, and the overall legal burden of proof. The evidence presented is strong enough to shift the strategic burden of proof to the defendant. At this point, Harriet has only one option: she must show that the defeasible inferences argued by the prosecution can be defeated, or loses the argument and the case. However, none of the facts is under dispute. She personally disagrees that she had a sufficiently strong motive, and also has an explanation for the clandestine purchase of poison. However, this personal belief is insufficient to rebut a prosecution narrative that is based on strong 'anchors', generalizations about normal human behaviour.

What saved, quite literally, her neck is Lord Peter's success in identifying an alternative suspect. He discovers the real culprit is Boyes' cousin Urquhart, who had misappropriated a client's money. Boyes, the heir of the client, stands between Urquhart and the inheritance. With him out of the way, Urquhart becomes the heir. Lord Peter also establishes that Urquhart had in fact laced an omelette with arsenic and shared it with Boyes. Urquhart himself was immune to the arsenic, having regularly consumed small doses beforehand. While possibly not even necessary to undermine the prosecution case – after all, he has shown that for every *type* of prosecution evidence, there is an equally strong piece of evidence incriminating an alternative perpetrator – Lord Peter also tricks the real perpetrator into a confession.

Intuitively, it is clear that this defence argument is at least capable of raising reasonable doubt. However, just like the alibi defence, it does so not by undermining any specific prosecution argument. Rather, a totally separate story is introduced, and the trier of facts asked to judge it on its merits. If the case of the defendant against the alternative perpetrator is at least as strong as that of the prosecution against the original defendant, this should establish reasonable doubt. Indeed, even a weaker case against an alternative perpetrator might often be sufficient. Since different legal systems have created considerable burdens on this type of evidence, often treating it with clear suspicion (McCord 1996), the more conservative assumption is chosen here: to believe simultaneously that the guilt of the accused has been proven, that there is better evidence against an alternative perpetrator and that only one of the two can be guilty should be provably inconsistent for any acceptable legal proof predicate. Assuming that Urquhart is indeed guilty, consistency constraints allow us, of course, to deduce that *something* must have been wrong with the prosecution case. However, it is neither necessary, nor always possible, to decide which of the prosecution arguments was indeed faulty.

Dialogical models of argumentation can to some extent account for this possibility by modelling this type of argument as a 'rebuttal', in the sense of Pollock (1992), a dialectical move that introduces a new argument with a contradictory conclusion, and for their purposes, this may well be sufficient. The 'costs' of this strategy are, however, problematic for the project we described above. Several legal systems make a distinction between 'top level rebuttals' of the type described here, of which alternative perpetrator defences and alibi defences are the two best known examples, and 'lower level' rebuttals that attack only specific statements by the opposition. An example of a lower level rebuttal could be a situation where both prosecution and defence call an expert witness to interpret a certain piece of evidence. In some situations, these experts may reach opposing conclusions without necessarily demonstrating any mistakes in their opponent's reasoning. Instead, it is left to the jury as to which of the two approaches it believes. For situations like these, rebuttals are an appropriate form of representation. But legal regulations in some jurisdictions, and legal practice in others, distinguish this type of rebuttal within a dialogue from the 'top level' arguments discussed here. Scotland labels the alibi and 'alternative perpetrator' defence (incrimination) 'special defences', triggering specific pre-trial disclosure rules (Ferguson 2004). Several US jurisdictions create high procedural burdens for the admissibility of alternative perpetrator evidence (McCord 1996). Discussions with practitioners from continental jurisdictions indicate that similar results can be observed in practice. Our methodological requirement of 'conceptual economy' therefore makes it desirable to account for the different logic that these two strategies display. 'Top level rebuttals' are not so much part of a dialogue as a refusal to participate in the dialogue. In our example, the prosecution maintains: this is the accumulative evidence against Ms Vane, if you judge it on its strength you will see that it proves her guilt beyond reasonable doubt. Lord Peter, by contrast, argues: this is the evidence against Urquhart; it establishes his guilt to a degree sufficient to acquit Ms Vane. Both their theories are self-standing and intelligible without necessary recourse to the arguments of the opposition or the assumption of a dialogical exchange.

This situation should sound familiar to theorists of science. Quine (1951) argued famously that 'theories face the tribunal of experience as a whole'. Lakatos made use of this insight in his response to Popper and Kuhn (Lakatos 1976). We are able, typically, when given an already fully developed competitor theory, to decide that a theory is misaligned with reality and should be rejected in favour of the better alternative. But which part exactly of the original theory was wrong is often impossible in principle to determine. Theory of science rather than theory of argumentation, and the 'moderate holism' rather than an issue-by-issue exchange (Gordon and Walton 2006) seem to capture this idea well. They also explain why, once a verdict is reached, no new evidence will be sufficient cause to reconsider the case, even if this evidence would have been admissible and potentially decisive in the trial stage. This gives this approach an additional advantage over defeasible logics that assume in principle an open-ended process of belief revision.

There is further corroboration in legal procedure for this 'moderate holism'. Legal procedures across a wide range of jurisdictions try to ensure that the trier of facts forms their belief about the respective merits of prosecution and defence arguments only after all the evidence has been heard, and not, as dialogical models of evidence interpretation would predict, as soon as all rebuttals to a specific point have been made. In the US, jurors are barred from discussing the case between them before the closing arguments of the parties, and are, for the same reason, sometimes prohibited from taking notes. Prohibitions on the juror to participate actively in the debate are regularly motivated by the need to keep an open mind until all the evidence is presented. In Scotland, the instruction to prospective jury members reads:

> Listen to all the evidence given. Do not make your mind up after hearing only parts of the evidence, as you may be unable to give proper consideration to evidence which is yet to be heard. Once all the evidence has been given in the case, you should then listen to the speeches from the prosecutor and on behalf of the accused.

This quote indicates that the unit of assessment is not the individual arguments and counter-arguments as they develop over the duration of the trial, but the speeches by the two counsels which present 'instantaneous' and 'whole' stories.

In continental jurisdictions, the 'dossier', the complete collection of evidence and materials submitted to the judge before the trial, fulfils a similar function. Evidence in criminal trials is typically not presented to judge and jury through a direct dialogue between the parties, but through the presentation of complete theories in the opening and closing speeches by the respective solicitors.

4. Analysis and Evaluation

12 Angry Men and *Gaudy Night* give us two very different ideas or 'models' of what reasoning with evidence in a legal setting can mean. In the former, reasoning with evidence is a *dialogue* in which the different sides try to *persuade* each other about the *facts* in a potentially *open-ended process* of criticism. The 'units of assessment' of this criticism are the individual propositions that the parties propose or reject. By contrast, we analysed the reasoning in *Gaudy Night* as two '*co-ordinated monologues*' about what can be *proven* relative to the prosecution and defence theories, reaching a definite conclusion that can be intersubjectively tested by all the parties involved. The theories are now assessed as a whole.

For the first model, we have, in the ideas developed by Walton and others, a fully articulated formal theory that accounts for a broad range of the features of the debate that was conducted by the jurors. The general theory of argumentation provides the backbone for this approach. For the second model, no such theory yet exists. We have, however, indicated that certain theories of science, in particular 'semantic' theories such as those proposed by Lakatos, are good candidates for such a project.

Rational theories of legal argumentation, we argued, take tried and tested models of rational argumentation, often inspired by scientific discourse, and apply them to law. By contrast, we have argued the case for 'legal exceptionalism'.[9] The internal logic of the trial situation forces the protagonists into a discourse where, from the outset, the normal preconditions of rational deliberation are only partially met. In the sciences, and also in history, these preconditions ensure that intersubjectively verifiable results can be achieved, warranted by the application of appropriate methods of inquiry.

For legal contexts too, the overriding objectives are intersubjectively verifiable results as a requirement for the rational acceptability of trial outcomes. It is a basic tenet of justice that the results of a trial should be intelligible to *all* parties involved, hence the rules that excuse those too mentally ill to understand the process from criminal responsibility. Interestingly enough, in debates about legal interpretation, the problems that we identified for evidentiary reasoning do not occur. Despite the use of scientific evidence in the factual part of the trial, and its absence in reasoning about law, legal interpretation is symmetrical: defence and prosecution have, at least in theory, equal access to all the relevant information, the statutes, court cases and academic writing. Prosecution and defence can therefore rationally convince each other of the correctness of their respective interpretations of the law. Unsurprisingly, in the context of law interpretation, we do not find the corresponding asymmetrical allocation of burdens of proof through procedural rules.

However, due to the systematic asymmetries between the parties that we identified, we cannot directly apply common methods of scientific deliberation in trials, but need the rules of procedure to achieve as close an approximation as possible. This, however, does by no means suggest that legal reasoning about facts is irrational. Quite on the contrary, as we argued that only the unmodified adoption of scientific models of rationality to an unsuitable set of circumstances can result in irrational legal deliberation. Instead, we argued for the possibility of a *legal* theory of rational reasoning with evidence. In this theory, the rules of procedure are not, as Bentham argued, inimical to rational or anomic deliberation, but rather try to establish the conditions under which such a discourse is at all possible *despite* the constraints imposed on the participants. Since the 'initial situation' between the participants in legal discourse about facts is asymmetrical, the corresponding rules of procedure too impose asymmetrical conditions on the parties to counteract this effect. Burden of proof is but one prominent example of such an 'adjustment through procedure', and should therefore be modelled as such: not an add-on to be analysed in isolation, but together with other procedural rules as constitutive for legal debates about facts. The juxtaposition of 'truth values' and 'procedural values' is more problematic than often assumed. Often, the rules

9 Just how 'exceptional' legal fact-finding is could be an interesting question for further research. There may well be other examples of deliberation that also display the problematic features of the trial situation. Certain types of moral or theological debates, which may invoke personal, non-repeatable experience as evidence, could be candidates.

of procedure are (also) 'mediating' rules that further the discovery of the truth under difficult circumstances.

The most significant contribution of the rules of procedure, and 'proceduralism' about evidentiary reasoning, is a redefinition of the very subject matter of a trial: contested between the parties are not the facts themselves, but which facts are provable. On this issue, intersubjective agreement is possible.

This compels us to take the notion of proof more seriously than the above-mentioned approaches to CTE. They see the exchange between the parties in the trial as a debate over the facts, and interpret on a meta-level those debates that follow certain rules of rational argumentation as proof of these facts. For a formal legal theory of evidentiary reasoning, we should therefore not (just) try to *interpret* meta-theoretically a dialogue about facts as a proof, but rather introduce explicitly a proof predicate in the object language. Since both parties can and will regularly express their intervention in terms of proof and provability, a more realistic model of legal reasoning about facts should directly represent this feature.

The legal proof predicate, however, has several unusual properties. In particular, since only 'proof beyond reasonable doubt' is required, proof does not entail truth. This is the same intuition that leads most present CTEs to adopt non-monotonic logics as modelling tools. By contrast, what is proposed here is to understand the prosecution and defence claims as claims about the provability of an assertion relative to a theory, a relation which can be modelled as traditional deductive inference. This is to a large extent a methodological choice rather than an ontological statement about the nature of proof. The aim is to capture the idea that once a verdict is delivered, it is no longer possible to extend the set of premises using the same rules of procedure – rather, where possible the debate is reopened, and sometimes started wholly anew, in the appeal stage, with its own rules of evidence and allocation of burdens. One reason that deductive inference is chosen here is to make explicit this 'shift of perspective' that takes place when we look at the trial reasoning 'from the inside' and 'from the outside'. Scientific theories, too, are typically presented by the scientists that develop them as deductively closed. Only when we take an outsider's perspective, say as a historian or theorist of science, do we 'see' that what was held to be a deductive inference was 'in reality' a fallible inference that could, and often was, revised over time. Being able to make this analogy explicit will help us to understand the way in which evidentiary and procedural rules ensure 'closure' of debate in a non-arbitrary way. Seen from the inside, a trial result is the necessary, irrevocable consequence of the facts as established. Seen from the outside, however, from the perspective of the appeal system, we realize that this 'closure' or finality too is contested and can be challenged on appeal. Semi-formally, the prosecution claims that $T_{pro} \models$ provable-in-law (p), where $\models$ stands for '(deductively) provable' and p stands for 'the accused is guilty'. The defence only needs to claim that this provability relation does not hold, expressing thus the different allocation of burden of proof within the framework of classical logic. A special case of the defence argument *can* be to show that $T_{def \vdash}$ not (p), that is, that relative to the facts as established in their opinion, it is positively provable that their client is innocent. We encountered this special case in the alibi and incrimination defence. These semi-formal statements come close to the natural-language counterparts used in court, and also display the relevant procedural asymmetries. In their closing speech, counsel for the defence will routinely refer explicitly to the proof relation between the evidence they have presented and the conclusion they want the jury to draw: I put it to you that the prosecution has failed to prove beyond reasonable doubt the guilt of my client, whom you therefore should acquit.

Following up the argument presented above, the theories that entail the prosecution and defence claims are not best understood as mere sets of sentences in a dialogue, but as structured objects similar to the formal reconstruction of scientific theories proposed by Lakatos in particular. These structures contain not just generalized statements and individual facts, but rather a layered structure of law-like statements, ad hoc assumptions, heuristics, indented applications and methodological precepts (the rules of procedure in our intended legal application). This 'moderate holism', mentioned above, allows us to model formally the idea that, for the defendant at least, certain statements will form part of a 'protective core' that is immune to belief change or falsification.

Finally, some remarks follow about the relation between the 'procedural' approach promoted as an alternative research project in this chapter, which uses ideas from the theory of science, and the established dialogical approach which uses the theory of argumentation. Ultimately, the two approaches should be understood as complementary rather than opposed. In our opinion, the notion of criminal trials as *persuasion* dialogues between prosecution and defence is untenable for logical, epistemological and legal reasons. However, the dialogical approach to CTE seems to have come to a similar conclusion already (see Prakken, forthcoming). The other differences are mainly questions of emphasis, the intended use and the degree to which rational reconstructions are deemed helpful for them. The approach outlined here scores against the targets it set itself in the first part:

- A range of diverse rules of procedure that can be found across jurisdictions can be explained as the expression of the same underlying principle, the need to address the asymmetric access to information at the outset of the trial. Furthermore, these rules can be explained as non-contingent and truth enhancing, given the specific circumstances of the trial. The dialogical model, by contrast, addresses burden of proof in isolation, and does not in itself give reasons why burden of proof should be asymmetrically assigned.
- The 'moderate holism' matches more closely legal practice than the dialogical model that rationally reconstructs the court proceedings. In reality, direct issue-by-issue exchanges between the two parties are rare. Rather, what we typically find (in both common law and continental jurisdictions) are the initial and closing presentations by the parties, where they present their theories in their entirety, uninterrupted by the opposition

and if referring to the opposition case at all, only in the concluding 'wrapping up'. Dialogues *do* take place, although not primarily between the parties directly, but between the parties and their respective witnesses. These dialogues, however, are not as yet directly represented by CTEs. Interestingly enough, some of these dialogues can have an element of persuasion to them. When cross-examining a witness for the opposition, a lawyer may not only want to show problems with the witness's account for the benefit of the listener, he may also try to convince the witness that his initial confidence in his statement was objectively misplaced, and bring the witness to withdraw his statement.

- Moderate holism, together with the idea that the outcome of the trial is a *deductively* valid inference of what has been proven in law (as opposed to an inference from the facts themselves), gives a rational justification for the fact that across many jurisdictions, once a verdict has been reached, considerably more new evidence has to be provided to overturn that verdict than would have been necessary during the trial. For defeasible logics, the 'closure' that the trial reaches in a given time limit, by contrast, is an artificial ad hoc constraint. The result of procedural rules of evidence is a social practice that comes closer than most to the ideal of logical proof – even if this means using the rules of procedure to 'force' a closed world model. The benefits are a concept of trial that seems to reconcile otherwise contradictory demands of justice; an intersubjectively verifiable and hence rational outcome, which is intelligible also for the accused; and as a result a degree of 'closure', even if, like Harriet Vane, the accused knows that the outcome is factually incorrect.
- The use of a proof predicate in the object language allows us to model directly acts of speech that are typical in a trial, such as the shifting in a legal argument of the discourse between factual and legal-evidentiary statements.

By contrast, the dialogical model, as we have seen, gives an accurate account of the type of arguments a jury should develop when testing the case that was presented to them. This opens up the way to integrate the two models. One of the important insights of Lakatos and other post-Kuhnian theorists of science was the inseparability between the 'substantive' aspect of a scientific theory and the theory of measurement that informs the construction of appropriate devices to test that very theory. If Newton's theory were substantially mistaken, then the methodology to construct scales to test it would also be in question. Formal accounts of scientific theories, therefore, also have to account for their own theory of measurement. By analogy, we can see the dialogues that take place in court not so much as constitutive for the defence and prosecution theories themselves, but as part of the adjunct theory of measurement. In the same way in which a scientist will check a suspicious piece of measuring equipment in a methodologically guided process, a lawyer will examine a witness through a dialogical exchange along prescribed 'methodological' (i.e. procedural) lines.

In evidence scholarship, the position most closely related to what is proposed here is, in our opinion, Stein's 'reformulation' of the foundations of evidence law. Unlike the Benthamite tradition that dominates the new evidence scholarship, his account gives a positive, truth enhancing role to the rules of procedure (Stein 1997). We also borrowed from him the concept of rules of procedure as 'mediating rules' (Stein and Biersbach 2007), not, as he does, as rules mediating between substantive and procedural law, but as rules mediating between the conditions of the trial and the ideal conditions of rational scientific inquiry. This, however, echoes another of his insights, that an understanding of evidence in the trial often requires the understanding that the 'second best' option (Stein 2001) is what we have to settle for.

References

Asimov, M. (2007), '*12 Angry Men*: A revisionist view', *Chicago-Kent Law Review* 82, 711–17.

Bentham, J. (1808), *Scotch Reform*, reprinted in J. Bowring (ed.) (1838–1843), *The Works Of Jeremy Bentham*, vol. 5 (Edinburgh: William Tait; Simpkin, Marshall & Company), pp. 1–53.

Bex, F.J. and Prakken, H. (2004), 'Reinterpreting Arguments in Dialogue: An Application to Evidential Reasoning', in Gordon (ed.).

Bex, F.J. and Prakken, H., Reed C. and Walton, D.N. (2003), 'Towards a formal account of reasoning about evidence: Argumentation schemes and generalisations', *Artificial Intelligence and Law* 11, 125–65.

Bex, F.J. and Prakken, H. and Verheij, B. (2006), 'Anchored Narratives in Reasoning about Evidence', in Van Engers (ed.).

Boolos, G.S., Burgess J. P. and Jeffrey, R.C. (2002), *Computability and Logic* (Cambridge: Cambridge University Press).

Boolos, G.S., Burgess J. P. and Jeffrey, R.C. (2007), 'Formalising argumentative story-based analysis of evidence', in *Proceedings of the Eleventh International Conference on Artificial Intelligence and Law*, Stanford (New York: ACM Press), pp. 1–10.

Clermont, K.M. and Sherwin, E.A. (2002), 'Comparative view of standards of proof', *The American Journal of Comparative Law* 50, 243–75.

Corker, D. (1996), *Disclosure in Criminal Proceedings* (London, Sweet & Maxwell).

Damaska, M. (2003), 'Epistemology and legal regulation of proof', *Law, Probability and Risk* 2, 117–30.

Draper, A. (2004), 'Corruptions in the administration of justice: Bentham's critique of civil procedure', *Journal of Bentham Studies* 7.

Duff, P. (2007), 'Disclosure in Scottish criminal procedure: Another step in an inquisitorial direction?', *International Journal of Evidence and Proof* 11, 153–80.

Dunne, P.E. and Bench-Capon, T.J.M. (eds) (2006), *Computational Models of Argument: Proceedings of COMMA 2006* (Amsterdam: IOS Press).

Engers, T.M. van (ed.) (2006), *Legal Knowledge and Information Systems. Jurix 2006: The Nineteenth Annual Conference* (Amsterdam: IOS Press).

Ferguson, W. (2004), 'Reverse burdens of proof', *Scots Law Times* 22, 133.

Gordon, T.F. (ed.) (2004), *Legal Knowledge and Information Systems. Jurix 2004: The Seventeenth Annual Conference* (Amsterdam: IOS Press).

Gordon, T.F. and Walton, D.N. (2006), 'The Carneades Argumentation Framework: Using Presumptions and Exceptions to Model Critical Questions', in Dunne and Bench-Capon (eds).

Gordon, T.F., Prakken, H. and Walton, D.N. (2007), 'The Carneades model of argument and burden of proof', *Artificial Intelligence* 171, 875–96.

Harding, S. (ed.) (1976), *Can Theories Be Refuted?: Essays on the Duhem-Quine Thesis* (Berlin: Springer).

Jackson, J., Langer, M. and Tillers, P. (eds) (2008), *Crime, Procedure, and Evidence in a Comparative and International Context* (London: Hart Publishing).

Keppens, J. and Schafer, B. (2004) 'Murdered by Persons Unknown. Speculative Reasoning in Law and Logic', in Gordon (ed.).

Keppens, J. and Schafer, B. (2006), 'Knowledge based crime scenario modelling', *Expert Systems With Applications* 30, 203–22.

Koppen, P.J. van and Roos, N.H.M. (eds) (2000), *Rationality, Information and Progress in Law and Psychology. Liber Amicorum Hans F. Crombag* (Maastricht: Metajuridica Publications).

Lakatos, I. (1976), 'Falsification and the Methodology of Scientific Research Programmes', in Harding (ed.).

McCord, D. (1996), 'But Perry Mason made it look so easy! The admissibility of evidence offered by a criminal defendant to suggest that someone else is guilty', *Tennessee Law Review* 63, 917.

Ogloff, J.R.P. (1991), 'A comparison of insanity defense standards on juror decision making', *Law and Human Behavior* 15, 509–31.

Orman Quine, W. van (1951), 'Two dogmas of empiricism', *The Philosophical Review* 60, 20–43.

Plotnikoff, J. and Woolfson, R. (2001), '"A fair balance"? Evaluation of the operation of disclosure law', *RDS Occasional Paper No 76* (London: Home Office), available at <http://www.homeoffice.gov.uk/rds/pdfs/occ76-disclosures.pdf>.

Pollock, J. (1992), 'How to reason defeasibly', *Artificial Intelligence* 57, 1–42.

Prakken, H. (2001), 'Modelling defeasibility in law: logic or procedure?', *Fundamenta Informaticae* 48, 253–71 .

—— (forthcoming), 'A Formal Model of Adjudication', in Rahman (ed.).

Prakken, H. and Sartor, G. (2006), 'Presumptions and Burdens of Proof', in Van Engers (ed.).

Prakken, H. and Sartor, G. (2007), 'Formalising Arguments about the Burden of Persuasion', *Proceedings of the Eleventh International Conference on Artificial Intelligence and Law* (New York: ACM Press), pp. 97–106.

Prakken, H., Reed, C. and Walton, D.N. (2003), 'Argumentation Schemes and Generalisations in Reasoning about Evidence', *Proceedings of the Ninth International Conference on Artificial Intelligence and Law* (New York: ACM Press), pp. 32–41.

Prakken, H., Reed, C. and Walton, D.N. (2005), 'Dialogues about the Burden of Proof', *Proceedings of the Tenth International Conference on Artificial Intelligence and Law* (New York: ACM Press), pp. 115–24.

Rahman, S. (ed.) (forthcoming), *Argumentation, Logic and Law* (Dordrecht: Springer Verlag).

Sayers, D. (2003), *Gaudy Night* (London: Hodder and Stoughton).

Stein, A. (1997), 'Against free proof', *Israel Law Review* 31, 573–89.

—— (2001), 'Of two wrongs that make a right: Two paradoxes of the evidence law and their combined economic justification', *Texas Law Review* 79, 1199–234.

Stein, A. and Bierschbach, R.A. (2007), 'Mediating rules in criminal law', *Virginia Law Review* 93, 1197–258.

Taylor, C. (2001), 'Advance disclosure: Reflections on the Criminal Procedure and Investigations Act 1996', *The Howard Journal of Criminal Justice* 40, 114–25.

Thagard, P. (2005), 'Testimony, credibility and explanatory coherence', *Erkenntnis* 63, 295–316.

Tillers, P. (2008), 'Are there Universal Principles or Forms of Evidential Inference?', in Jackson et al. (eds).

Tillers, P. and Schum, D. (1991), 'A theory of preliminary fact investigation', *UC Davis Law Review* 24, 931.

Twining, W. (1985), *Theories of Evidence: Bentham and Wigmore* (London and Stanford: Stanford University Press).

—— (1990), *Rethinking Evidence* (Oxford: Blackwell).

Twining, W. and Hampsher-Monk, I. (eds) (2003), *Evidence and Inference in History and Law* (Evanston, IL: Northwestern University Press).

Verheij, B. (2000), 'Dialectical Argumentation as a Heuristic for Courtroom Decision-making', in Van Koppen and Roos (eds).

—— (2003), 'Artificial argument assistants for defeasible argumentation', *Artificial Intelligence* 150, 291–324.

—— (2007), 'Argumentation support software: Boxes-and-arrows and beyond', *Law, Probability and Risk* 6, 187–208.

Walton, D. (2002), *Legal Argumentation and Evidence* (University Park, PA: Penn State Press).

Walton, D.N. (2005), *Argumentation Methods for Artificial Intelligence in Law* (Berlin: Kluwer).

—— (2008), *Witness Testimony Evidence: Argumentation, Artificial Intelligence and Law* (Cambridge: Cambridge University Press).

Williams, G. (1977), 'Evidential burdens on the defence', *New Law Journal* 127, 182.

Index

For Product Safety Concerns and Information please contact our
EU representative GPSR@taylorandfrancis.com Taylor & Francis
Verlag GmbH, Kaufingerstraße 24, 80331 München, Germany